TALES
FROM THE
OTHER SIDE

TALES FROM THE OTHER SIDE

Growing Up Jewish in Nazi Germany

HANS BENJAMIN MARX

TALES FROM THE OTHER SIDE
GROWING UP JEWISH IN NAZI GERMANY

iUniverse books may be ordered through booksellers or by contacting:

iUniverse
1663 Liberty Drive
Bloomington, IN 47403
www.iuniverse.com
1-800-Authors (1-800-288-4677)

ISBN: 978-1-5320-3374-2 (sc)
ISBN: 978-1-5320-3375-9 (e)

Library of Congress Control Number: 2017914602

Print information available on the last page.

iUniverse rev. date: 01/31/2018

TABLE OF CONTENTS

PROLOGUE ix

INTRODUCTION: Connecting with the Past xiii

I. A Backward Glance xiii
II. A Bit of History xxxi

PART I: The Early Years (1933-1938)

Chapter 1: First Impressions 3
Chapter 2: Growing Up Jewish 20
Chapter 3: School 35
Chapter 4: Prelude to Destruction 50

PART II: The Closing Door (1939-1941)

Chapter 5: The House of Mrs. Levy 81
Chapter 6: Separated 112
Chapter 7: Eighth Grade 137
Chapter 8: A Three Day War 152

PART III: The Destruction (1941 – 1942)

Chapter 9: The Boys of the Anlernwerkstat 169
Chapter 10: Transports 192
Chapter 11: Confrontations 217

PART IV: A Ghetto Without Walls (1943 – 1944)

Chapter 12: Among the Remnants....253
Chapter 13: In Double Jeopardy....277
Chapter 14: Adventures of a Street Sweeper....300

PART V: Survival (1945)

Chapter 15: A Train Ride to Nowhere....323
Chapter 16: Stories from Behind the Wall....341
Chapter 17: Disintegration....365
Chapter 18: Liberation....381
Chapter 19: The Return....396

DEDICATION

To my children and grandchildren:
May they always remain proud Jews

To my wife:
Whose love healed so many wounds

To the memory of my mother
Who never gave up

PROLOGUE

THINGS REMEMBERED

"You Shall Tell Your Children"

More than half a century has elapsed since six million Jews were murdered by Nazi Germany. Yet telling the story of the Holocaust remains topical. This episode in history, the destruction of Jewish life in Europe, is still being talked about, to this very day the subject of numerous debates, controversies, and inquiries. The world has not yet been able to come to terms with the event; perhaps it never will. In this age of science and technology it remains difficult to grasp that a nation believing itself to be at the forefront of this modern age also believed that it had been tasked by destiny to totally exterminate another people.

Those who somehow survived the hell created by Germany, too, had to come to terms with their experiences. Many felt a need, at first perhaps acknowledged only with reluctance, to justify their survival to themselves and to others. By telling what they saw and experienced, they tried to unburden themselves of their terrible memories.

Other survivors tried to forget, to bury the past, to banish the Holocaust from the mind; they felt the past must not be allowed to intrude into the present. Remembering one's humiliation produces embarrassment and shame, and so does the memory of having at times compromised with evil in order to survive. It is so much easier to remember past heroic deeds.

Of the still unanswered questions concerning the Holocaust many will remain unanswered. Was the Holocaust merely an aberration in the history of civilization?

How much did the democratic world's indifference to racism and anti-Semitism contribute to this unspeakable horror?

Soon the last of the survivors will be gone. The six million murdered will be just a number, a statistic taking its place alongside other statistics in history books. Intellectuals will quibble about the exact number of victims; they will argue about this or that detail. Professors will make up questions for examination papers, questions reflecting their interpretations and biases.

Many survivors asked themselves "Why was I permitted to live?" There are as many answers as there are survivors. Each survivor has had a unique story to tell.

Between the world of 1933 to 1945 and the present world lies a chasm that, like the River Styx of mythology, separates the world of the living from the nether world, the world of the condemned. The Kabbalah speaks of the "Sitra Achara," the other side, the side dominated by evil. The world in which I live now seems to have little in common with the world of the other side. They appear to be two different worlds, one real, the other but a bad dream. Yet this other world was not just a bad dream, it was as real as the world of the present.

The few allowed by fate to return from the nether world, the world of evil Nazi Germany had created, and reenter the world of the living, carry with them the burden of remembering those they had to leave behind. It is incumbent upon us to tell their stories so that what was done to us will always be remembered, so that the memory of the millions left behind will never die.

When I left Germany after the war's end, I told myself that this phase of my life was behind me, to be forgotten, and best thrown into the garbage bin of time. But my children's questions made me realize that my memories of those evil days do not belong to me alone; they also belong to the next generation and even to generations yet to come. We are constantly taught: "Remember we were slaves in the Land of Egypt."

Here, then, are stories from the "Sitra Achara," from the realm of the tortured. With the exception of verifying important facts and dates I did no research into the past. I will be telling the stories just as I remember them.

Memory can be elusive and is always selective. Some events, important ones as well as some that appear trivial, are remembered with clarity; others, perhaps of great importance, are all but forgotten, leaving only vague traces behind. At times images spring up, apparently belonging nowhere, and attempts to fit them into a wider picture only make them disappear. Some remembrances are mere shadows, vanishing ghostlike at the slightest attempt to focus a light of clarity upon them.

Rummaging through my memory, what stories, what remembrances, did show up? Of course most of the stories are highly personal. Some tell of events that had a strong impact on me; some are about people whose memory I wish to preserve; others are about people who, though they played an evil role, needed also to be mentioned. Now and again I take a brief look at history, at least at that part of history relevant to the stories.

Some stories were not easy to tell. Recalling my gradual isolation, first from community and friends and finally from my family, brought back that feeling of despair and utter loneliness when, toward the final days of the war, cold and hungry, I had to confront death itself.

A few of the stories recalled here tell of experiences that could have happened to any child anywhere in the process of growing up. However, everything that happened to me during that time happened within the context of discrimination, persecution, and violence, and eventually destruction and death. Thus even the most ordinary occurrences became in some way part of a terrible mosaic. Only a few of my stories have happy endings.

Today Germany is again a respected member of the world community. Her political influence is worldwide; she has a seat on the councils of Europe and in the UN. Germany's economic power spans the globe; the Deutschmark is one the strongest among the world's currencies. And once again Germany has an army.

The Jewish people, however, have not yet been permitted to fully recover from the devastation of the Holocaust. The world's Jewish population has not regained its pre-Holocaust size. Once again, or perhaps still, we are engaged in a struggle for survival: our enemies try to destroy us, using bombs and murder; in the UN Israel's legitimacy is being challenged; and in the democratic West assimilation and intermarriage weaken the coherence of our people.

Squabbles reminiscent of the divisiveness that contributed to the Second

Temple's destruction beset us, turning ever more bitter and emotional. What meaning can these squabbles have in a world that permitted the Holocaust to happen? The ashes of the murdered Six Million, the ashes of the pious and the non-believers, of the orthodox and the liberals, of the traditionalists and the assimilationists, of the proud Jews and the self-haters, they are all mixed together. Can anyone sort them out?

I do not wish to sit in judgment of the German people. There were many good people. But the sin of the great majority was their indifference toward evil and their false patriotism. After the war a German remarked to me that he had been aware that the Nazi regime was evil. Yet, he asked, how could he, a German, hope for Germany's defeat in the war? To him the murder of millions of men and women, the deliberate killing of one and a half million children was the lesser of two evils.

And what about us Jews? There were some among us who failed during these horrifying trials. A few tried to buy favors from their oppressors by betraying fellow Jews; others sought escape in suicide. There were some who struggled with all their strength and with the limited resources remaining to them against a terrible fate. But most were just ordinary people, seldom written about, who did their best trying to cope with the daily miseries. If nothing else, they kept their dignity and integrity, while trying to help others, especially the young, to do likewise. You will meet some of these people in the pages that follow.

Jerusalem, Israel
Pesach 5764
2004 CE

INTRODUCTION

CONNECTING WITH THE PAST

I. A BACKWARD GLANCE

A Brief Period of Peace

My parents met and were married during the troublesome time that beset Germany and much of Europe as World War I came to a close. The defeated country had to come to terms with its new place in a changed and changing world. At the time my parents, a budding salesman and a young and pretty clerk, met, they were both working in the office of a (Jewish) wholesale lace company which had managed to remain afloat even during the years of war.

The nation, beset by revolutions and counter-revolutions, had sunk into economic chaos. Most major cities saw almost daily mass demonstrations, many of them violent. Street warfare endangered life and property. But above all else, the rampant inflation undermined the nation's stability. Salaries and wages were paid at the end of each working day prior to the announcement of the day's devaluation. As soon as they had received their pay, people rushed to the stores to quickly spend the day's earnings before the money lost its value.

What life must have been like during those unsettled days is difficult to imagine. Barter economy took the place of monetary economy; labor strikes multiplied at the same time unemployment soared; savings of ordinary people vanished, driving them into poverty; while many real estate operators and currency speculators, including some of the largest banks and insurance companies, became fabulously rich. Corruption had invaded business and public life. No wonder popular discontent and resentment spread, providing a fertile soil in which extremist political movements, both right and left, could flourish.

Before agreeing to marry my father, my mother converted to Judaism, although my father didn't care whether she became Jewish. (Later he came to appreciate her decision.) At the time he proposed to my mother, he was full of resentment toward the Jewish community. When my paternal grandfather died he left behind a widow with three small boys and very little money. Apparently the community refused to provide assistance to my widowed paternal grandmother. In time his resentment toward the community did ease somewhat. I am convinced he really appreciated my mother's insistence.

A token process of conversion would not satisfy my mother; she insisted on a conversion following orthodox practices. Her children, she argued, should never be in doubt where they belonged; never should they find themselves in the awkward position of trying to find a place between two chairs. If my father refused to agree to an orthodox conversion, she threatened, the marriage would be off; she would live with him without being married.

My father gave in. The idea of living together unmarried was too much for my father's middle-class sensibilities. Although she could not have anticipated the consequences of her resolve, perhaps she did sense that the times required clear, unambiguous positions.

I have never regretted their decision. I felt superior to the children from intermarriages who had not become Jewish and who, as a consequence, felt never sure to which camp they belonged. Not fully accepted by German Christians, yet no longer part of the Jewish community, many of these children took to hating their Jewish parent, putting the blame on them for the situation in which they found themselves.

Upon her conversion my mother took the name of Rachel and that, in part, was the reason my Jewish name is Benjamin. A custom among German Jews was to give a secular first name and a Jewish name, in memory of a deceased grandparent, as a middle name; this my father refused to do.

According to the story of Jacob, as told in the in the Torah, Benjamin was the youngest son of Jacob's favorite wife Rachel, who died in childbirth. My mother came near death when I, her second child, was born. With most of her ovaries removed she could have no more children. And, like the Biblical Benjamin, I remained her youngest child.

Born in 1927, I entered the world during that brief period of relative calm between the post–World War I turmoil and the world economic collapse of the late '20s and early '30s. The period was one of economic prosperity and apparent economic stability. Nations seemed to have put the catastrophe of the First World War behind them, looking to the League of Nations to help resolve still-festering international disputes. Germany's international position, both politically and economically, was steadily improving. Great optimism prevailed. It was a period of innovation and tolerance, of artistic and social experimentation.

I was not yet five years old when, triggered by the New York stock market crash of 1929, the bubble of prosperity burst and the world's economy collapsed, and with it hope, tolerance, and my parents' good fortune.

The company for which my father worked became a victim of the worldwide depression. In 1931 it was forced to declare bankruptcy. Thanks to his reputation, a major competitor hired my father immediately.

About a year before Hitler assumed power, we left the "ancestral" home in Mannheim and moved to the city of Frankfurt Am Main.

The economic desperation of ordinary people, caused by the economic collapse and fueled by the memory of the economic chaos of the post-war inflation, was manipulated by big industry and the banks and aimed at breaking the power of the Socialist labor movement. In this endeavor, the big industrialists were supported by the professional military, especially by high-ranking officers of the General Staff. Many of these officers were eager to regain the prestigious and privileged position in society that they had enjoyed in Imperial Germany. A large segment of the population never accepted the outcome of the War, preferring to believe that only high treason by elements within German society had brought about the victory of the anti-German alliance.

The Nazi Party ruthlessly exploited these popular sentiments. Their vicious and unceasing propaganda, much of it paid for by some of the country's largest corporations, as well as the Party's frequent recourse to violence against competing political parties and other rivals (a strategy also used by the Communists, but more poorly financed), produced a dangerous mood in Germany. This mood favored resolving economic and financial problems by non-democratic means and solving border and population issues that had resulted from the peace accords by threats of military action.

My father, a sales representative for a large wholesale lace company, enjoyed widespread international business relationships. Business took him away from home for long periods of time. Of his comings and goings prior to our move to Frankfurt I remember little. Then his travels had been limited to Europe, mostly to the Balkans. His new position brought with it an increase in travel abroad with the Middle East, including Palestine, becoming the major part of his itinerary.

The frequent absences from home, often for periods of three months several times a year, made my father more like a visitor at our home. At least in my eyes the "regular" family was my mother, my sister, and I. (Perhaps this helped to prepare us for the time after my father had to leave Germany permanently and the three of us had no choice but to cope alone.)

It was always exciting when my father returned from his travels bringing gifts from strange countries and showing us the many photographs he had taken of the places he had visited. After some time at home, however, he would become restless. Feeling confined within the four walls, he developed a mood that would cause increased tension in the household.

Following Hitler's ascent to power my father's restlessness became even more pronounced, as social life became increasingly restricted. My father had been a member of an "Odd Fellows" lodge. (The lodge, a social club somewhat like the Free Mason but far less powerful and well financed, had, again like the Masons, been outlawed by the Nazi regime.) Throughout the year the lodge sponsored many social and charity events of which some were formal affairs: top hats and tails for the men, evening gowns for the ladies. I remember my father's top hat sitting for many years unused on the upper shelf of the wardrobe in my parents' bedroom.

With cinema and the theater controlled by the Minister of Propaganda, my parents lost their interest in these activities. Except for occasional visits with friends, they seldom went out in the evening. Outside Germany, my father said, he felt much freer.

My father had been much stricter with us children than my mother, especially with me. This, when added to his restlessness after he had been home for some weeks, added to my own discomfiture. I often felt a bit relieved when the time had once again come for him to leave on a business trip. His frequent absences, however, placed a heavy burden on my mother. More and more she had to cope by herself with the increasing difficulties that confronted us, including the problems of bringing up her two children in these uncertain times.

With considerable optimism, and despite the growing signs of danger, we settled into our new home. What was to have been the beginning of a good life in a modern suburb was but the beginning of a long nightmare.

Family Affairs

Any knowledge I have concerning the background of my father's family and his upbringing is rather vague and fragmentary. My father spoke only with reluctance of his childhood and of his parents. At least he did not speak about these things in front of us children. Hence, I am not sure that the bits and pieces that I recall are at all accurate, or are merely conglomerations of some facts that I picked up here and there, with some misunderstandings on my part and even a few imaginings.

I never thought of my father's father as "grandfather;" I knew so very little about him. I cannot recall ever having heard stories about him. Neither my father nor his brother, Uncle Hugo, ever spoke about their father. My father was about nine when my grandfather died. I don't know the cause of his death. In my father's study hung two large portraits, now lost, of my father's parents. The portrait of my grandfather showed a bearded stern-looking man. To me he looked very much the Victorian.

The early death of my grandfather apparently resulted in a lot of family feuding, or more likely, it brought feuding to the surface. There were hints that he left behind a great deal of bitterness, and not much else. My grandmother, my father said, had wanted to open a store to supplement the family's income and, after her husband's death, to provide for herself and her three sons. She appealed to her relatives and her husband's for a loan. But the relatives, some of them well off, refused to lend her anything. They considered it improper for a middle-class Jewish woman to have to work for a living. She was supposed to be occupied with the proper upbringing of her children. Thus she was forced into dependency, living on contributions from members of the extended family. The results were not all that happy.

It soon fell upon my father, the middle of three sons, to assume the role of the "Man in the House," a role which, by rights, should have belonged to his older brother Julius.

Little was ever said about Uncle Julius. From a few conversations I surmised that he had been a troublesome boy. Shortly before the outbreak of the First World War, Julius left for America. Apparently he got himself into some serious trouble. The family, at least those members who paid most of the bills and hence made most of the family's decisions, agreed to bail him out. He had to promise to leave the country at once. It was not uncommon during those days for families to rid themselves of their "bad apples" by sending them to America.

For a while his mother received letters from Julius, but apparently the letters contained nothing about his life in America. During the period of hyperinflation in Germany after the war, he helped his mother by occasionally sending her some dollars. (With the German Mark nearly valueless, dollars were most welcome.)

Following my grandmother's death, no further letters arrived from Uncle Julius. After the Nazis came to power and my parents began thinking about leaving Germany, my father made some attempts to find his brother. He even engaged a detective agency. But beyond some vague and unconfirmed stories, he learned very little about the whereabouts of his brother. Apparently Julius had, at one time, worked on railroad construction in the Dakotas and had been married to a widow with many children. My father made the unkind remark that Julius most likely ended up in Sing-Sing, the New York State prison in Ossining, New York for hardened criminals.

The story of my father's younger brother, Uncle Hugo, also had a rather poor beginning, but it had a better ending.

Uncle Hugo never learned a trade. He had wanted to become a schoolteacher, so he said, but his mother did not have the resources to permit him to finish school and enter a teachers' seminary, and once again relatives refused to provide financial assistance. (My father had wanted to study music, but that too had been ruled out as a waste of money.) Whatever the facts may have been, and I can't be sure that Uncle Hugo really wanted to be a teacher (he did not always tell the truth), he was never able to hold down a decent job. He made himself a burden to the family, the community, and especially my father.

Uncle Hugo lived in Worms. The city is well known for the Rashi Chapel, part of a synagogue dating back to the 12th century, and for the oldest Jewish cemetery extant in Europe. The Jewish community of Worms provided him with occasional jobs. Tradition and political prudence demanded that the Jewish community assured that no Jew became a public burden. Assertions made by anti-Semites that Jews were parasites must not be given even the remotest justification.

Uncle Hugo's jobs were all within the Jewish community: filing at the aid office, opening and closing the curtain at the Jewish theater, and the like. During the summer months, he did odd jobs for the Maccabi Sports Club. Local Jewish merchants would occasionally also give Uncle Hugo work, but these jobs never lasted very long.

Uncle Hugo had a reputation for dishonesty. I don't know how true any of these accusations were; these things were never discussed in front of children. What I do know was that on several occasions, my father had to cover shortfalls in the cash register of the store that had hired my uncle, or in those of the theater or the sports club. A scandal may have landed Uncle Hugo in jail, and that had to be avoided. Every time something like this happened, and my father had to pay up, there were terrible fights between the brothers. When these quarrels took place during one of Uncle Hugo's visit to our home, I would run upstairs to my room to hide my head under my bed pillow. I didn't want to hear the shouting and the terrible words that passed between the brothers.

I thought that Uncle Hugo preferred my sister to me, but then I always felt that people favored Claire. After all, I was only the second born; she was a whole year older, and she was so much smarter than I. But there were also some occasions when he preferred me to my sister. I remember one such occasion: The Maccabi soccer team from Worms was playing Maccabi Frankfurt. Uncle Hugo, who had come with the club to Frankfurt, took me to the game. He refused to take Claire, asserting that soccer was not for girls. Uncle Hugo exhibited at times a superior air towards women.

With the increasing restrictions imposed upon the Jews in Germany, it became ever more difficult to find jobs for Uncle Hugo. The community made great efforts to maintain as normal a life as possible. With an increasing number of Jews forced into unemployment while available funds shrank, many of the community's activities had to be curtailed. The limited resources had to be used to assist families who no longer had an adequate income, especially those families with children. There was also an increasing need to assist people in their quest for emigration. To make things even worse, the government periodically imposed collective fines on Jews for this or that misdeed. The Jewish community's shrinking resources became severely strained.

The Jewish leadership of Worms had to decide what to do about Uncle Hugo. Should they permit him to continue to be a burden to the community, or should they help him to get out of Germany? To let him become a public burden was out of the question. It would surely have condemned him to a concentration camp. The community leaders opted to "help" him emigrate.

The Kibbutz Movement, prevented by British restrictions from settling Jews in Palestine, responded to the urgent need to find refuge for the Jews from Germany by proposing to establish Kibbutz-like communities in Argentina. Perhaps they hoped that these could later be transferred to Eretz Israel.

Argentina had expressed interest in developing remote areas in the country and the government was willing to make land available to settlers. In return for the permission to settle in Argentina, Jewish settlers would take on the obligation to develop the allotted land for agriculture. The Argentine Jewish community had to provide guarantees that at no time would the settlers become a burden to the state. In 1936-1937 Jewish groups were organized for settlements in Argentina.

The Jewish community of Worms gave Uncle Hugo no choice: Join a settlement group or get off our back! Uncle Hugo decided to go to Argentina. There was one hitch, however: All members of a settlement group had to be married. Uncle Hugo was not. The community now set about finding a wife for Uncle Hugo. The woman they recruited was another troublesome person. Uncle Hugo married a "lady of the street."

Before the newlyweds departed for their new home, Uncle Hugo brought his bride to our house to introduce her to the family. My father had a fit. It took all the self-control he was able to muster, reinforced by many warning glances from my mother, not to toss the pair out of the house within the first few minutes. Throwing Uncle Hugo out of the house had not been an unusual event. During many of his visits he made my father furious with his haughty air, while insulting everybody, especially my mother.

What happened next we could only surmise from my uncle's occasional letters. Some of what he wrote had to be taken with a grain of salt. The story went something like this: Trouble began soon after the group had boarded the ship. Hugo's wife started to "entertain" members of the crew. Not long after arriving at their destination in Argentina she started up "friendships" (Uncle Hugo's term) with a group of local cowboys. The settlement's leaders demanded an end to her activities. Obviously, she could not pursue her "friendships" and at the same time fulfill her obligations to the community. Uncle Hugo and his wife were given an ultimatum: Do your assigned duties or get out! Her cowboy friends solved the problem their way. One night, according to one of his letters, her friends came galloping into the settlement. Wildly firing their guns they "kidnapped" Uncle Hugo's wife. Uncle Hugo thus was rid of his troublesome wife. But without a wife, according to the settlement rules, he now had to leave. (I don't know if they ever got a divorce. But then, this mattered little.) The settlement turned Uncle Hugo over to the Jewish community of Buenos Aires.

Now the story took a turn for the better. At first Uncle Hugo worked mostly as a dishwasher in Jewish-owned restaurants and clubs and after a while also took on other kitchen duties as well. One day, the restaurant in which he was working at the time found itself short of an assistant cook. According to one of his letters Uncle Hugo was asked to help out. And with that, Uncle Hugo discovered a talent: cooking. Finally, he was able to embark on a real career.

Advancing from assistant cook to chief cook, he succeeded in establishing a good reputation for himself among the local restaurants. Better jobs came his way and he moved up steadily to more prestigious restaurants. One of the people who appreciated his culinary talents was the Chinese ambassador to Argentina. He offered him the position as the embassy's chef. And so the Jewish refugee from Germany deserted by his wife and kicked out of a pioneering settlement became a Chinese cook. Uncle Hugo kept his position at the embassy until his retirement. He eventually died of diabetes.

My father's mother's maiden name was Weil. Before the Holocaust one could find many Weils along the Rhine River in southwest Germany. Branches of the family also existed in the United States and in several of the Western countries. The Marxes on the other hand were coming to the end of the line. Had there been no son to my father, the family line would have ended with him. (Provided Uncle Julius had no male children.) Marx is not an uncommon name, but as far as I know, other Marxes have no connection with our family.

Even though there had been a number of marriages between first and second cousins among the Weils (my grandparents had been second cousins), I have the feeling that the Weils were not a very cohesive clan. During the immediate period before the war, few efforts were made to help family members still in Germany. Just one example: a second cousin of my father's, a doctor somewhere in New York State, would not let his mother come to America. "She would not have liked it there," he said. She died in Auschwitz.

The only members of the extended family I knew well were my father's Aunt Amalia and her husband Gustav Valfer. There were two children: a son, Hugo, and a daughter, Alice. I do remember Hugo but have only a vague memory of Alice. My great-aunt and great-uncle owned a shoe store in the small town of Bruchsal near the French border. In the summer of 1932 (the Nazis were not yet in power, and I was not yet in school) I spent a few weeks at their home. I had a good time making a nuisance of myself in their shoe store. It was there that I heard the word "Nazi" for the first time.

It had been a warm sunny day. The store was closed for the day because a large parade with flags and bands was scheduled to come marching through the street. I wanted to go out on the balcony to watch, but my aunt said no. "These are Nazis!" Of course I didn't understand what that meant, but from the tone of her voice and from the tension I sensed in the room I concluded that "Nazi" was not a good word; to me it sounded more like a curse word.

French Connections

As a child I had rather fanciful ideas about the origin of my parents' ancestry. Most likely my ideas were far more romantic than the facts warranted. As I wanted to have as little to do as possible with the country of my birth, I searched for family connections outside of Germany. Both my parents' families had "French Connections," though on my father's side these were rather uncertain. As had become my habit, I looked to history to provide me with answers. From my father I knew a Marx family tradition that said the family had originally come from Spain but settled in the Rhine Valley many generations ago.

Jews first came to Gaul (France) and the Rhine Valley with the Roman legions. From there they had drifted eastward to the limits of Roman rule. (The move of Jews into Eastern Europe dates from a later period.) The cultural and economic decline of the region, a consequence of the disintegration of the Roman Empire, did not spare the Jews. The Christian successor states to Rome were generally hostile to Jews, and the Jewish communities were destined to remain economic backwaters for many years. And as happens so often in history, political and economic instability hit the Jews especially hard.

While the Jews of Western Europe suffered, Jews in Iberia prospered under Muslim rule. The well-educated, but also more assimilated, Jews of Spain maintained contact with their less fortunate fellow Jews in France and Germany, often hiring Rabbis from there. These were considered to be more observant of the traditions than those from prosperous Spain. (They also asked for less money.)

With the decline of Muslim prosperity, and even before the expulsion of the Jews from Spain following the Christian conquest, Jews had been drifting north, many settling in France, including the eastern region now known as Alsace-Lorraine (formally the two Provinces of Alsace and Lorraine). Prominent among the Jewish communities in which Sephardim settled was the community of Metz. It is from this city that my father's forebears most likely came.

A few bits of evidence, not very conclusive and now lost, suggest that during the latter part of the 15th century, about the time of Columbus and the final expulsion of the Jews from Spain, members of the Marx family moved from Metz to the east bank of the Rhine River (Germany). My father was rather skeptical about this reconstruction of family history. Yet even he brought up the "French Connection" when the discussions turned toward leaving Germany. Our connection with Alsace-Lorraine at least was real.

The region of Alsace-Lorraine had long been in dispute between France and Germany. (The region reverted to France at the conclusion of World War II. Germany renounced all claims to this area forever.) The Jews of Alsace-Lorraine, just like their non-Jewish compatriots, had lived at times under French rule and at other times under that of the Germans. Jewish wealth, unlike the wealth of the non-Jewish population, which was mostly in land, was readily moved. Not bound to the land (they could not own land), Jews were more mobile and tended to move with all their belongings back and forth between Germany and France, depending on which local ruler was the least hostile to the Jews at the moment. My father's aunt told me that many Jewish families had furniture, especially heavy dining room tables, made with hollowed out legs for hiding their movable wealth, gold and jewelry.

My father's mother had been severely diabetic. By the time my parents married, she was already disabled, one leg having been amputated. She refused to have the other leg amputated, opposing the doctor's recommendation. Her refusal most likely hastened her death.

Though dependent on my father's income and facing opposition from her son, my grandmother kept a kosher home. But as her illness worsened, her disabilities increased and her interest in her home waned. She was no longer willing or able to fight with him over kashrut.

When my mother joined the household, she helped her mother-in-law cope. As long as my grandmother was alive and still willing, my mother supported her in keeping the kitchen kosher, although gradually more and more of the rules of kashrut were being violated. But after her death, my mother gave in to her husband's wishes, and kashrut was gradually abandoned. By the time we moved to Frankfurt, all vestiges of a kosher home were gone.

It puzzled me that my father distanced himself from anything religious. He never talked to us about any "Jewish" experiences he may have had as a child. I don't even know whether he had a Bar Mitzvah, although I assumed he had. When in 1930 we moved to Frankfurt, my grandmother's household was dissolved. Many items common in a Jewish household disappeared. Yet there were inconsistencies. My father still had his father's tfillin (phylacteries for prayer) but he did not have any of his own, nor did he have a tallit (prayer shawl). I cannot imagine that my grandmother did not have candlesticks for Shabbat, yet none came with us. Among the few items that did go with us to Frankfurt were things needed for the Passover Seder: A hand-embroidered towel for washing the hands, a matching pillowcase, and a cover for the Matzot, all very old. Yet there was no Haggadah (Passover prayer book). Neither was there a Chanukkia (Hanukkah candelabra), though one must have existed in my grandmother's home.

Among old Hebrew books we had in our home was my grandmother's Machsor (prayer book for Rosh Hashanah). In the back of the book were some handwritten notes, most likely records of births and deaths within the family. Generally it had been the Jewish woman who kept the family records, and Machsorim intended for women frequently included blank pages for this purpose. The handwritten entries in the back of my grandmother's Machsor were written in an old Hebrew script. I doubted that my grandmother had been able to write the script, so I suspected that the Machsor was an old family possession. Since I knew nobody able to decipher the script, we will never find out what the entries said. The book, probably of some historical value, was destroyed during the war. The notes will remain forever a mystery. My father thought the notes were recipes.

When during the war a law prohibited private ownership of Jewish religious articles, the few items that we still had in our possession went into hiding. These included, in addition to what we had from my grandmother's house, my (Bar Mitzvah) Machsorim and my Tanach (Bible). We divided the items into small packages and hid them in various places. Some of these survived, some fell victim to Allied air attacks. Those that were saved went with us to the United States. Some are now in Israel.

Although my father's "French Connections" were rather vague, my mother's French connections are far more definite, dating back to the period of the Reformation.

The year 1572 saw the beginning of the persecution of French Protestants, known as Huguenots. As France moved toward royal absolutism, the King, trying to break the power of the nobles, who had to a significant degree converted to Protestantism, allied himself with the Catholic Church in trying to eradicate the Protestant heresy.

Paris mobs, urged on by the Catholic clergy, massacred the Huguenots living in the city. The massacre, remembered in history as the "Night of St. Bartholomew," signaled the beginning of the violent struggle between the alliance of Church and Crown and the Protestant nobility. In Paris, the alliance succeeded in breaking the power of the Protestants, but was unsuccessful in dislodging the Protestant aristocracy from their fortified castles in the country. The king was forced to compromise.

The agreement, the Edict of Nantes, protected the rights of the nobles and guaranteed the safety of the Protestant villagers. In return, the aristocrats swore allegiance to the king. During the period of peace between the king and the nobles, the Protestants became increasingly involved in what was the beginning of the Industrial Revolution. To all appearances they prospered, and once again the king perceived them as a threat to his absolute rule. By 1653, the royal house felt strong enough to revoke the Edict of Nantes and to resume, again with the aid of the Church, the campaign to suppress Protestantism in France. The Huguenots were forced to flee France. Many settled in Germany, England, South Africa, and the United States.

The fleeing Huguenots took with them their enterprising spirit and industrial know-how. One of these noblemen moved his factory, together with nearly the entire population of his village, to Germany. There, in a small town near the city of Mannheim, he settled his villagers and reestablished his mirror works. And from this town in Western Germany came the family of my mother's mother.

The French Protestant refugees integrated only slowly into German society. For a long time they maintained their French ways and language. My mother's grandfather never learned to speak German. The Protestants had brought with them a strong anti-Catholic bias, which persisted even to the days of my mother's childhood. Not far from the house in which my mother grew up stood a Catholic church. My grandmother forbade her children to pass directly in front of the church. They had to cross over to the other side of the street.

Perhaps it was the experience of persecution that made many Huguenots sympathetic toward Jews. The nineteenth century German-Huguenot poet Adelbert D'Chamisseau became involved in the drive for Jewish emancipation. His story "Peter Schlemiel" tells of a man, tired of having his shadow follow him wherever he went, who sold his shadow to the devil. He learned too late that without a shadow he was invisible to people. It took me a while to understand that without our past, our history, we were like the man without a shadow. The story, likely of Yiddish origin, was given to me by my father to read.

During World War II, when the French Vichy government aided the German occupier in hunting down Jews, a Huguenot village near the Swiss border saved a number of Jews by hiding them in their homes.

In pre-World War I Germany it had been customary for rural families to send their sixteen to eighteen year old daughters to the cities to serve as household help in middle class families. This practice served two purposes: The rural family, often poor, was relieved of taking care of the young woman, while at the same time the young countrywoman was given the opportunity to learn the "proper" way to run a household. (The custom endured, to some extent, even after the social upheaval that followed World War I. At the time we lived in Mannheim we had a young woman with us. She helped my mother with the children and did other chores in the household, such as helping our daily cleaning woman.)

Middle-class Jewish homes were considered very desirable for these young women. Jews had the reputation for being very generous and in Jewish homes there were fewer incidents of sexual abuse of the girls. (Nazi propaganda turned this on its head, claiming that Jews took in these girls for the purpose of sexual abuse.) When she was a young woman, my grandmother was placed in a Jewish home to learn her housekeeping. As a consequence, some of her housekeeping practices reflected the Jewish (kosher) practices she had learned. Thus she used separate dishes for meat and dairy and thought it improper to wash these dishes together. My mother, in turn, learned many of these practices from her mother, making it easier for her to adapt to her mother-in-law's household.

Following the Nazi seizure of power, the first country of which my parents thought as a possible place of refuge was France. My father's cousin, Hugo Valfer, went to France soon after the Nazis took power in

Germany. A bit wild, Hugo had run into a problem, the kind of problem not discussed in front of children. From what I could gather, he had been living with a non-Jewish girlfriend (an actress or dancer). With the Nazis now running the show, she decided to trade Hugo in for a Nazi bigwig. She denounced Hugo for violating one of the new racial segregation laws. Her denunciation would surely have landed him in jail or worse. He did not wait to find out. His sister Alice followed him to France where she married a French Zionist leader by the name of Metzger. My great aunt and uncle joined their children a bit later.

My father's Aunt Amalia and Uncle Gustav were taken to the French internment camp at Gures where Amalia died. Uncle Gustav and his daughter Alice were shipped to Auschwitz. They did not survive. The fates of Hugo and Alice's husband remain unknown.

Growing Apart

My mother's father was the only one of my grandparents I knew. I remember him as a gentle old man. Yet according to my mother, gentleness had not been one of his characteristics, at least not during his younger days.

The spelling of my mother's maiden name, Rihm, hints at possible Dutch ancestry. The Rihms may have been among the itinerant boat people that plied the Rhine River between the seaports of Holland and the industrial cities along the upper Rhine. Eventually some of these river people settled down near the city of Mannheim. I would have liked to hear tales about my grandfather's forbears, about life on riverboats. But I can't recall anyone ever talking about it: not my mother, not my uncles, and not my grandfather. Perhaps there were no tales to tell and no one but me thought the subject interesting.

My grandfather was not a big talker. Once every couple of months, a story tells, my grandfather, then married, got together with his older brother over a few glasses of beer. After sitting in silence for a while sipping their drinks, one of them would start a conversation thus: "Mm. . ." A bit later the other responded with a similar grunt. This "conversation" went on for about two hours or until the allotted amount of beer had been consumed. Returning home my grandfather told his wife: "Had a good talk with my brother."

My grandfather was a carpenter. He had his own business. Though he was a good carpenter, he was not a good businessman. Several times his business went into near bankruptcy. Finally my grandmother took over the business and made their enterprise more successful. Resenting his dependency on his wife, he took to drinking and to beating his wife. Eventually his sons turned against him.

As a young journeyman my grandfather had been politically active. He became a socialist when socialism was not looked upon with favor in Imperial Germany. He was arrested a number of times for brawling in the street or in bars. Once my grandmother, not yet his wife, had to bail him out of jail.

His socialism had made him indifferent to religion, which according to him, was a "woman's thing." As his resentment of his wife's success in business increased, his tolerance for religion decreased. No longer did he permit prayer books, or a Bible, to be kept in the house. To keep my grandmother's family Bible safe, my mother kept it in her room. My grandfather never entered my mother's room without her permission.

My mother was the only person in the household to whom my grandfather would listen. One day, when she caught him beating his wife, she ordered him out of the house. She told him not to return until he was ready to apologize. To her astonishment he obeyed. For several days he slept and had his meals in the shop. After a while he did apologize to his wife. My mother was in her mid-teens.

My grandmother died of cancer when she was in her late fifties. Shortly after her death my grandfather remarried. He had started a relationship with a widow when his wife became bedridden. As his wife was slowly dying, he brought his not yet second wife into the house. My mother threw her out.

My mother, the only girl, was the oldest of five children. (Two children born before her had died in infancy.) As her mother became increasingly involved in the business, it fell upon her to take care of her brothers. As conflicts in the house increased and my grandmother's health worsened, the boys became ever more dependent on their older sister.

Following my grandfather's second marriage, his children left home. My uncles married very quickly, rather too quickly. The youngest, when only eighteen, had made a girl pregnant. He was forced to marry her. Not unexpectedly, the quick marriages created all kinds of problems. Again and again big sister had to step in. In the end the marriages turned out all right, though the wives did somewhat resent their husbands' dependence on their sister. After my mother converted and married a Jew, contact with her brothers became less close.

My grandfather's second wife was a simple woman with strong family feelings. After the wedding she set about to improve relations among the family members. After first curing her husband of his drinking, she worked on reconciling him with his sons and succeeded in making peace between them. Yet her relationship with his children could never be called warm. She remained, together with her own two sons, a family outsider.

Before 1938, my grandfather spent a few weeks with us at our home in Frankfurt and we spent a few summer weeks at his house. While visiting us, every morning he would walk to the local inn for a glass of apple cider. Since it was summer and I was home, he insisted I go with him. At the time, Jews were already prohibited from entering restaurants, bars, inns, etc., and I felt rather uncomfortable going with him. He dismissed this as a load of nonsense. The Rihm family subscribed to the philosophy that it was best for the people to ignore governments as much as possible. Governments were capable only of doing stupid things.

I saw my grandfather briefly when I was in Germany as an American soldier. By then, he had suffered a severe stroke, and I'm not sure he knew who I was. He died shortly after my visit.

Uncle Max was my mother's favorite brother. A professional diver and underwater construction specialist, his expertise was sorely needed for construction of bridges and fortifications along the Rhine River. Even though he refused to join the Nazi Party, he enjoyed protection from the highest government echelons. And he did not mind taking advantage of this when the need arose.

Uncle Max's son, Max Jr., a few years older than Claire, was, like his father, independent minded. He refused to join the Hitler Youth. But that was not enough: Max Jr.'s best school buddy was a Communist. The two boys refused to greet the teacher upon entering the classroom with the obligatory Nazi salute. All this caused my uncle a heap of troubles, yet he fully backed his son. It took all his high connections to protect his family from harassment. (Max Jr.'s friend managed to escape to the USSR.)

Max Jr. was the only member of the Rihm family who did not return from the war. Presumably he was killed at the Russian front, though his death was never confirmed. He had been Uncle Max's only child.

Gradually contact with my mother's family was broken; my mother did not want her brothers to get into trouble and they, of course, had to look out for the welfare of their own families. After the war Uncle Max took the initiative to renew contact. However, after my mother's death all contact lapsed again. The distance between us had just grown too wide.

II. A BIT OF HISTORY

Timeline to Destruction

The political developments in Germany during the 1930s, especially those that affected the Jews, could not be hidden from the children. My parents discussed the situation openly, explaining to Claire and me the restrictions imposed on Jews and the precautionary restrictions they had placed on us for the sake of safety. At the same time they made great efforts to conduct our life as normally as circumstances permitted.

Of course, it did not take long for me to be made brutally aware of what was going on. Even before entering school I had to recognize that the world outside of home could be rather "unfriendly" to me because I was Jewish, though the "why" was far from clear.

In March of 1933 the Nazis seized control of the government. Following the Coup-d'etat known as "Machtergreifung," public and many private organizations became mere parts of the government bureaucracy: Labor Unions, youth groups, sports clubs, etc. Jewish organizations too came under government control, although they did not, of course, receive government financial support.

Although the Nazis did not formulate a coherent policy against the Jews immediately (this had to await the party rally of 1935), a reader of Hitler's blueprint "Mein Kampf" could have deduced the direction in which the Nazis intended to move. But it was so much easier to dismiss Hitler's words, gassing the Jews, as mere rhetoric of a politician seeking power. Reality, the argument went, had always forced politicians to modify their aims.

Few among the Jewish leadership believed that the Nazis would go beyond segregation and expulsion. That the Nazis' true aim was the annihilation of the Jewish people was simply beyond imagination.

Four major milestones mark the progression from restrictive legislation to the attempt to annihilate the Jewish people. The implementation of the "Endloesung" (The Final Solution to the Jewish Question), the killing of all Jews, came to a halt only with Germany's total military defeat.

The First Major Milestone --- Shortly after the seizure of power, the Nazis removed Jews from public life: Government offices, the police, and the judiciary were made "Judenrein" (cleansed of Jews.) Next the news and entertainment industry, in which Jews were strongly represented, was cleansed of Jews; in fact, Jews disappeared from Germany's public and cultural life. Disenfranchisement of the Jews marked the completion of the first phase.

The Second Major Milestone --- The "Nurnberg Laws," announced at the party convention in Nuremberg in 1935, provided the foundation for all anti-Jewish legislation and actions. With "Nurnberg," the Nazi program against the Jews became more coherent and also more sinister.

The law defined various degrees of "Jewishness:" The offspring of a mixed marriage brought up Jewish was designated "Jew By Law" (Geltungsjude), meaning the child was legally equal (or nearly so) to a "Volljude." A "Volljude" was defined as having at least three Jewish grandparents. (In accordance with the laws definitions my sister and I were classified as "Geltungsjuden.")

The laws established the legal structure for segregation. Jews were stripped of civil rights and many impediments were placed on them: Jewish doctors could treat Jews only; Jews could not employ non-Jews; the legal profession was closed to Jews; and many similar restrictions and limitations were imposed. Intermarriage was prohibited, and sexual relations between a Jew and a non-Jew (outside of marriage) was defined as a criminal offense. Jews had no recourse to the legal system.

New rules governing employment and education severely limited the ability of Jews to earn a good living and to educate their children.

What was initially a quota system, adapted from the previous century, was revived: High schools and universities admitted only a limited number of Jewish students. Eventually Jews were barred from all institutions of higher learning, including high schools; Jewish high schools were closed.

Jewish organizations, officially if they could, unofficially if they had to, tried to mitigate the impact of the Nazi policy on the community. Organizations for welfare, education, and even recreation were expanded and strengthened. Financial priority was given to those organizations that benefited children the most. For a time some Nazi officials aided these efforts, or at least they did not stand in the way.

Concerned that international reaction to the persecution could make it difficult for German business to earn the foreign currency required for the purchase of raw materials needed for the rearmament program, the Foreign Office and the Ministry of Trade tried to mitigate the severity of the anti-Jewish regulations. (The German mark was no longer accepted in the international trade.) They need not have worried.

Jews were pressured to emigrate, at least by some officials. Perhaps these officials thought it would be better to push Jews into leaving Germany than to have a suppressed minority in her midst. Rumors claimed that the German government gave support to Zionist organizations preparing Jewish youth for settlement in Eretz Israel. Perhaps the government thought settling Jews in Palestine would stir up trouble between the Arabs and the British Mandatory Government. If true, any good will towards the Zionists that may have existed quickly came to an end. Germany opted for gaining Arab support in their war against the democracies and against the Jews.

Increasingly restricted and isolated in their activities, the Jewish leadership undertook to pull together the various religious and secular factions to create a Jewish community life reminiscent of the pre-emancipation period.

In 1934 the "Reichsvertretung der Juden in Deutschland" (National Representation of the Jews in Germany), known as the "Reichsvertretung" was organized, headed by Rabbi Leo Beck. (Rabbi Beck survived the war and lived out his life in England.) With an ample supply of unemployed artists, musicians, writers, and actors, orchestras and theater groups sprang up. Sports clubs, many Zionist-oriented, were strengthened. Recreational facilities were set up. For a time, the city administration of Frankfurt aided this effort, providing the Jewish community with a concert hall, a soccer field, and swimming facilities along the Main River.

Education was redirected. Emphasis was placed on Jewish values rather than assimilation and on helping children to cope with the hostile environment that surrounded them. Zionist groups and the international organization of ORT expanded the training of young Jews in trades and skills assumed to be needed in Eretz Israel and in those that would be helpful for settling in countries willing to accept Jewish refugees. "New Hebrew" (Ivrit), the language of Eretz Israel, became a regular part of the curricula. With emigration to the United States the goal of many Jews, English was stressed.

The "Reichsvertretung" also tried to calm internal quarrels, even hostilities, which continued to plague the community. The Orthodox, the left and right wing Zionists, the "assimilationists," the German-Jewish veterans' organizations from World War I, and various other groups, each had its own idea of what had to be done. Some tried to arrange deals with the Nazis, or were accused of doing so by rival organizations.

Two weekly newspapers were published: the Zionist-oriented "Judische Rundschau" and the non-partisan "Judische Familianblatt" to which my parents subscribed. The "Familianblatt" had a children's supplement, which in contrast to the "neutrality" of the main paper, leaned toward Zionism. Translations of Hebrew and Yiddish writers into German were regular features in the children's supplement.

The Third Major Milestone --- Kristallnacht marked the next step on the road to destruction. During this government-instigated rampage, most of the country's synagogues were destroyed. Jewish businesses and homes were vandalized, Jews were beaten and many killed. Thousands of Jewish men were sent to concentration camps. The large monetary fine imposed as punishment for "collective misdeeds" placed a heavy financial burden on the Jews of Germany, amounting to a confiscation of much of

Jewish wealth. Insurance companies were instructed not to pay claims for property damage caused by the pogrom, while the Jewish community was held responsible for all repairs to buildings in which they had their businesses or homes. Many small towns expelled their Jews. Jews became concentrated in a few large cities.

Following the outbreak of war, the Reichsvertretung was dissolved and replaced by two organizations: the "Reichsvereinigung der Juden in Deutschland" (Alliance of the Jews in Germany) and the "Judische Kulturbund" (Jewish Cultural Association). The Reichsvereinigung represented the Government. The decrees regulating Jewish life were now issued by Jews and not by the Nazi Government.

Jewish leaders were in a difficult position: Issue the decrees as ordered or risk incarceration and possibly death. But by refusing to issue the decrees, they not only placed their own lives in jeopardy but also the lives of their families. The Nazis had instituted the cruel concept of "Sippen Haftung" (kin responsibility): An offender's immediate family shared in the responsibility and hence had to share in the punishment. Resigning from their positions was not an option available to the appointed leaders. Suicide was not uncommon among them.

The Kulturbund, chartered to coordinate Jewish cultural activities, was short-lived. Whether it was dissolved or just faded away for lack of funds, loss of personnel, or perhaps loss of interest, I don't recall.

The Fourth Major Milestone --- Following the German invasion of the Soviet Union, the "Final Solution to the Jewish Question," the deportation to camps and ghettoes and the systematic murder of millions of Jews planned at the Wannsee Conference in January 1942, was set in motion. Actually, mass killings of Jews had preceded the conference by several months.

The Reichsvereinigung was abolished. The Jewish communities came under the direct supervision of the Reich Sicherheits Hauptamt (Reich Security Head-Office), the Gestapo headquarters. (Adolf Eichmann, one of the major organizers of the Holocaust, was one of its officials.) With the acceleration of mass deportations to the camps, all semblance of Jewish life came to an end in Europe. All that was left to the Jews was to try to survive, refrain from despair, and pray for a speedy victory for the Allies.

The Intrusiveness of History

With persistence, history forced itself into my consciousness. The family background, the threatening political situation, the ideas of Zionism, all were linked to the past. Even the name of the Frankfurt suburb where we lived, Romerstadt, named for an encampment of a Roman legion nearly two thousand years ago, provided a connection with by-gone days. History was not merely a subject to be studied in the classroom, or to be read about in books, but a process in which we were most intimately involved. I began to see history as a relentless reality impacting on each day of my life.

Seeing the events of the time not as mere disconnected aberrations of the moment, but in the context of the unfolding historic process, helped me to look at myself not as a victim of an arbitrary and mindless fate but as a participant in a drama stretching all the way back to Biblical times, or beyond, and which are destined to continue past the visible horizon. Perceiving the present as a link in an unending chain of events made what was happening to me far less personal and hence less of a psychological threat. It permitted me, at least mentally, to briefly step outside the ring and for a moment to see myself not as a helpless victim, but as a critical observer of history in the making. This rather defensive attitude gave me some protection, not physical protection of course, but protection against the constant denigration of my being by the world around me.

Yet there was a price to be paid. Creating a protective zone between the world and myself tended to produce an emotional distance from people. Friendships, like the events of the day, were only passing phenomena. And after losing all my friends I felt the best defense was not to let anyone come too close. Therefore I often felt alone.

Adopting a "historical perspective" also influenced my perception of being Jewish. Not coming from a religiously observant home, yet having belonged to an orthodox congregation and thus gaining an awareness of what religious observance required, I had to develop my own rationale for being Jewish. There were times when I felt that it was important to be more observant. But aside from these brief interludes, I felt a need to find my own conception of what being Jewish implied.

A passive rationale for being Jewish, being born Jewish and therefore having no choice in the matter, was inadequate. Simple acceptance could not provide a sufficiently strong defensive armor against the constant drumbeat of Nazi anti-Semitic propaganda. Nor was it a consolation as hostilities and restrictions increasingly governed my life. I needed something more to be able to deal successfully with the constant mental, emotional, and physical intimidations.

Being Jewish, I concluded, was not being merely a member of a community that follows more or less common religious practices and beliefs, some of which I saw as rather antiquated, but to consciously share in the people's past and present existence and problems. I saw the existence of this People Israel as an endless struggle to preserve the People's uniqueness in the face of ever-present hostilities and the seductions of Hellenism, Christianity, Islam, and modern universalistic secularism; and I could find no reason why we Jews should ever surrender our uniqueness.

And so I came to appreciate that in this search for meaning in this troublesome Jewish existence I was not alone. This search seems to be a never-ending process that had its beginning when the Old Testament patriarch Abraham left his father's house.

* * * *

About a year after we moved into our pleasant home in one of Frankfurt's modern suburbs, the Nazis came to power and I entered first grade. In my mind the new home, the advent of Nazi power, and the start of school will always remain connected. Together these three events form the starting point for the stories told in the following pages.

PART I

THE EARLY YEARS (1933-1938)

CHAPTER I

FIRST IMPRESSIONS

Home

Our home in one of the modern suburbs of Frankfurt am Main was not just home, to me it epitomized the very idea of "home": A house, a garden, a quiet neighborhood, a room of my own; and on a clear day, the outline of mountains visible on the horizon. It was the home to which I wanted to return once the "troubles" were over. Not that I wanted to return to the actual place from which we had been expelled following the pogrom of 1938. After all, what I wanted most was to get out of Germany as quickly as possible, never to return. Yet the home, as I remembered it, remained a dream for many, many years. Much history had to pass before once again there was a place I could call home.

For nearly seven years we made our home in the suburb of Romerstadt, having moved there in early spring 1932. There my sister, and a year later I, first went to school, and there I experienced for the first time some of the more unpleasant consequences of being Jewish.

The suburb, one of the new "Garden Cities" which sprang up around Europe's major cities during the 1920s, was a middle-class community of mostly one-family row homes on pleasant tree-lined streets. Each home was set back from the street and was fronted by a broad lawn. Flowerbeds along the walk leading to the front door provided the first color in spring and the last color in fall. At the back of each home was a terrace leading to a private garden. The Garden City Association was responsible for building maintenance, as well as the front lawns, trees, and flowerbeds. The garden in the back of the house were the renter's responsibility. Here the occupants could do more or less as they pleased: grow vegetables and flowers, have a lawn, and perhaps a sandbox for the children.

Designed for young families, the community had its own modern grade school and a shopping area along its tree-lined main street. Among the shops were a bar and grill, where at times I picked up a pitcher of beer for my father, and a large drug store. I remember the drugstore best. There my father has his travel photos developed. Once this store exhibited enlargements of his photos from Greece and Egypt. We did not do our shopping in the local stores, preferring a Jewish grocery store and butcher. Groceries, kosher meat, and bakery goods were delivered to the house. The bakery wagon came twice a day, bringing fresh rolls early in the morning, and in the afternoon bread and cake. Each day, by the time we got up in the morning, fresh milk was outside our front door.

Suburban Romerstadt owed its existence to the social changes that followed the catastrophe of the First World War. The ordinary people of Europe, who had suffered much during the four years of war, demanded a better quality of life. One response to the people's demands was an extensive development of new housing, both attractive and affordable. Most of these government-sponsored developments were aimed at workers and at members of the middle class, permitting them to move out of the crowded inner city tenements into the more open spaces of suburbia.

The innovative architectural thinking of the post-war housing movement had its beginning in the "International Style" of architecture developed during the 1900s. The dogma of this architectural school was to blend the new building methods and materials that had become available with strict functionality and yet create designs pleasing to the eye. In 1919, after the interruption by the Great War, the leadership of the "Bauhaus" changed the movement's direction to address the urgent housing needs of the big cities. The new building materials and construction methods were now employed to construct mass housing for the common man that was both attractive and affordable. One result of the effort was the development of modern suburbia.

The advent of the Nazi government brought the Bauhaus movement to an end: first in Germany, where it had been very strong, and eventually in all of Europe. Hitler condemned the new architecture as decadent, inspired by "Jewish Bolshevism," and alien to the German spirit. As a consequence, many of the movement's leading proponents left Europe to make their contributions elsewhere in the world. A number of Jewish architects who had played a leading role in the movement went to Palestine, where their influence can still be seen. The architect who had designed Romerstadt was a Jew. He fled Germany in 1933, escaping to the Soviet Union. There, it was said, he took part in building Stalin's city, Stalingrad.

Romerstadt was involved in more than just the architectural history of the day. Its very name, Town of the Romans, was based on the area's connections with the past. As the Empire expanded, Roman legions crossed the Rhine River into the territory of the Germanic tribes. During the suburb's construction a number of archeological finds were unearthed, providing evidence that a Roman legion was once encamped here. My first grade teacher found sufficient fragments of a shattered urn to allow him to completely reconstruct it. He displayed his Roman urn in our classroom. We had great fun looking for "Roman shards." Much of what we found turned out to be construction debris. Yet once I did find a real Roman shard, a jug handle.

The location of Romerstadt is close to the limit of the eastward expansion of the Empire into the territory of the Germanic tribes. The "Limes," a line of moats and earthworks that marked the frontier, passed through the Taunus Mountains not far from our suburb. Along the Limes, at intervals of a day's march by a Roman legion, watchtowers and forts had been constructed. One of the forts, known as the "Saalburg," dated from the reign of Emperor Hadrian (117 to 138 CE). Restored, it functioned as a history museum. Near the fort stood a temple dedicated to Mithras. During the Empire's waning days, the Mithras cult, of Persian origin, had rivaled Christianity as a potential state religion.

It took about an hour's ride on a suburban rail to reach the historic site, passing through small towns and villages, fields and forests. Together with friends, we made many excursions there, sometimes getting off the train at an earlier stop to hike the rest of the way up the mountain to the fort. These walks through the stillness of the forest to finally emerge at a piece of ancient history are among my fondest memories of that time.

The community's street names reflected the area's Roman past. The main street was named after Emperor Hadrian; there was a "Forum" and a "Mithras Strasse." These references to history were indeed stimulating and contributed to my growing interest in the past. Yet the way I looked at history, and especially at the Romans, was influenced by the increasingly anti-Semitic atmosphere. My feelings toward Rome were ambivalent: The Hadrian who fought the Germans was a good emperor; but the Hadrian who had made war on the Jews, defeating one of my heroes, Bar Kochba, and who in 135 CE destroyed Jerusalem, he, of course, I placed among history's most evil tyrants.

Our house had two stories and a full basement. The living/dining room, my father's study, and the kitchen were on the first floor. The kitchen had built-in cabinets and work surfaces, innovative features at the time. The living/dining room was the hub of family activities. It connected with the kitchen, the study, the hallway, and the garden. The large table in the center of the room was not just for taking our meals. Here Claire and I did our homework and my mother used it for cutting patterns and fabric for a dress or a blouse for my sister or herself, or even something for me. In the evening, after dinner, we often gathered around the table to play a family game. Even my father, when home, preferred the living room table to his desk in the study. The radio too was here. There we often listened to operas or concerts, and increasingly to news. We also entertained guests in this room.

Though never off limits to us children, I seldom ventured into my father's study, even when he was not home. The room was part of the adult world, a world serious and real, not a world of games and make-believe. I went into the room only to pick something to read from the large book cabinet.

On the second floor were the bedrooms and the bathroom/toilet. There was a large bedroom for my parents, a smaller room for my sister, and a small narrow chamber, part of which was over the stairway, for me. The part of the floor directly over the stairs was raised by a couple of inches, forming a narrow platform. There stood my bed. A dresser for my clothing and a set of shelves for my toys completed the room's furnishings.

Above the head of my bed, near the ceiling, was a narrow window. Looking up from my bed I could see a small patch of sky. At night I could see the flickering stars, and sometimes the moon, without interference from buildings or trees. I especially liked the morning sky of summer.

Waking up early, just after the sun came up, I could see my window filled with the blueness of the sky. There was barely a sound to be heard, only the early morning chirping of birds and the occasional buzz of a passing bee. I imagined myself alone on a peaceful island.

My room, the garden, they were my world. What was outside was far too often hostile. Here I could read my books of adventure, of world travels, of the heroic past of the Jewish people. In the garden I could observe the busy ants, look for colorful butterflies, and watch lizards at play in the sun. Here I could dream my dreams.

Do Jews Have Horns?

The day, early spring 1933, was gray and cool. The occasional rain had kept us indoors. I had been hanging around the house with nothing to do but to annoy my mother. With the lunch dishes put away, my mother sat down to write a letter to my father who was abroad on business. By the time the letter was completed the rain had stopped. My mother asked my sister Claire and me to take it to the mailbox. At least that would get us out of the house, even if only for a brief moment.

The mailbox was only a couple of blocks away. After depositing the letter, we made our way home, most likely quarreling about something unimportant, as sisters and brothers are wont to do. Suddenly we found ourselves surrounded by a group of boys and girls, children our age, some perhaps a bit older. They taunted us with personal insults and anti-Semitic epithets, most of which I did not understand. We just stood there, baffled and not a little scared. Nothing like that had happened to us before. Eventually they let us pass and we ran home crying.

The incident was a rude initiation into the "New Germany." Of course I knew that there were Christians and that there were Jews; but to me this only meant that we had our holidays and they had theirs; we went to the synagogue on Saturdays, they went to church on Sundays; we believed in God, they believed in Christ. I was also aware that there were many more Christians than Jews and that some Christians didn't like Jews. I had dismissed this as "adult stuff" of no concern to me. Now I realized that being outnumbered could not so easily be ignored; it involved risks.

Another incident that occurred a few months later reinforced this new feeling of vulnerability. Again Claire and I were out on an errand and once again we found ourselves surrounded by a group of children. But these children were not satisfied with just calling us dirty Jews. They became aggressive, pushing and shoving us, and would have beaten us if an elderly lady, just passing by, had not intervened.

"Why are you harassing them?" she demanded to know.

"They are Jews. Jews are dirty."

"Oh no," exclaimed the kindly lady, "They are not Jews. They don't have any horns." Although I thought her remark rather stupid, it worked. The kids left us alone.

Despite the Enlightenment, despite universal education, and despite the post-WWI social revolution proclaiming equality for all, medieval superstitions about the Jews continued to find resonance among the people, especially among the simpler folks. This persistence of anti-Semitic beliefs made the job of the Nazi propagandists that much easier. Of course, at the moment these thoughts were not on my mind as I tried to deal with a different phenomenon: my apparently obvious Jewish looks.

The second incident had raised a problem: How could these children, strangers to us, see that my sister and I were Jewish? Of course in this particular case there is an easy explanation: at least one of them knew who we were. But soon there were many occasions in which that explanation would not hold. Jews, I was sure, didn't look any different than non-Jews. Yet again and again I was readily identified as a Jew, despite the kindly old lady's opinion.

Jews certainly did not look anything like these grotesque cartoons with overly large crooked noses and shifty eyes. True, I did have a crooked nose, but I knew this had nothing to do with being Jewish. When I was very small my nose had been damaged in a fall. My parents had planned to eventually have my nose repaired. Being told on many occasions that I had a Jewish nose, I swore never to have any repairs done to it.

What had I done that I should find myself hated? Or what had my parents done, or the other Jews I knew? It happened from time to time that a kindly passerby came to the aid of a frightened boy with the remark: "It is not his fault that he is Jewish." Why did it have to be anybody's "fault"? Was it such a bad thing to be Jewish?

Name-calling had become almost a daily occurrence, and that I learned to ignore. But soon name-calling turned into beatings, and many times I came home with a bloody nose. My parents urged me to fight back. "Boys always get into fights" my mother commented. How could I fight back when I was always outnumbered and among my attackers there were often a few older than I? A better way was to avoid attacks. To counter these dangers lurking in the streets I adopted a number of strategies. I always looked out for groups of boys. If I spotted a group I quickly changed direction, hoping that I had seen them before they had a chance to see me. Paradoxically, if the boys were in their Hitler Youth uniform, I felt safe. The rules of the Hitler Youth discouraged engaging in street brawls while in uniform. When on an errand I tried to use different routes for going and returning and wherever and whenever possible, I used main streets. Side streets seemed much more dangerous.

Fear of the street remained with me for a long time. It took many years after liberation before once again I felt at ease walking in the streets.

Fire

Early spring days, I recall, were rather dismal: lots of rain and wind, at times even snow. The garden looked uninviting, puddles in the pathways and here and there wet clumps of dead leaves. The grass, matted down from the winter's snow, showed yet no hints of green. Only the trees and a few of the shrubs showed signs of spring: Green buds could be seen along their branches.

Yet not all March days were that dismal. As I woke up in the morning blue sky greeted me, promising a bright sunny day.

Except for the weather, the day started out fairly routine. My father was away on business. By the time I was out of bed and had come downstairs for breakfast, my sister Claire had already left for school. My mother had started her house cleaning, preparing for the weekend.

In the late twenties and the early thirties law and order in Germany deteriorated. Increasingly common crime and political violence, including political murders, overburdened the police and the justice system. The Army, supported by conservative politicians and prominent business leaders, persuaded the President of the German Republic, the aging and politically naive General Von Hindenburg, to appoint Adolph Hitler, leader of the National-Socialist German Workers Party (NSDAP or Nazi Party), to head a new government. The Nazis were at the time the largest party in the Reichstag (Parliament). It was thought that a coalition of right wing parties supported by the Army would end the violence while reviving the collapsed economy. Hitler, they argued, once saddled with the responsibilities of governing, would restrain his goons, who were behind much of the violence. Business leaders in control of the economy would prevent Hitler from implementing his wild economic ideas.

With a conservative member of the government, and not a Nazi, in charge of the police, labor unrest would be brought to an end. Hindenburg, frightened by the disorder in the country, and fearing an election victory by the left, put his trust into his old army buddies. Overcoming his mistrust of the "little corporal" he agreed to the plan. Little did the aging President realize that Hitler had made secret deals with the Generals, and with some conservative bankers and powerful industrialists.

The Nazi Party was already past its zenith. Tired of strikes and violence, voters had begun to desert the extremist parties both on the right and the left, moving toward the center. Recognizing the trend, the Social Democrats wanted to form a left-leaning Parliamentary coalition, strong enough to stop a right wing coalition from coming into power. Convinced a far right government would hasten the coming of the revolution, the Communists refused to join the Socialists. The Christian Center, leaning toward the right, preferred a neutral stance. By the end of January 1933 the President asked Hitler to form the new government.

About a month later, the headquarters of the Reichstag went up in flames. Arson was suspected. A Communist Party leader, Dimitroff, a native of Bulgaria, was accused of the deed and brought to trial. The trial became an embarrassment for the Germans. The accused, a clever man, not only proved that he did not set the fire, but produced evidence suggesting that the Nazis themselves had instigated the crime. Dimitroff was acquitted and later deported to Bulgaria. A mentally challenged Dutch citizen living in Berlin "confessed" to the deed. The world laughed at Germany.

But the world had laughed too soon. The frightened President declared a national state of emergency. To prevent the dissolution of his government, Hitler appealed to the Army. Assuring the generals of non-interference into military matters by the Party, he promised them a large rearmament program. Further, he acceded to their demand to disarm the Storm Trooper Formations (the SA), which the generals feared as a potential rival army. With the Army now behind Hitler, the old President signed the "Enabling Act;" the Reichstag had already passed the legislation, granting Hitler extraordinary powers. In March 1933 democracy came to an end in Germany.

Enough history; now back to my story: Ordinarily I was of no great help to my mother in housecleaning. But there was an exception: I liked polishing the floor using the heavy floor-polisher. The polisher consisted of a thick brush weighed down by two heavy iron blocks. The brush and weights were attached to a long broom handle.

While my mother vacuumed the carpets, I polished away with enthusiasm. Suddenly I saw sparks flying from the vacuum cleaner cord. I tried to attract my mother's attention, but she could not hear me over the noise the vacuum cleaner was making. Then the sparks ignited the drapes hanging over the living room windows. Flames rapidly climbed up the drapes and curtains.

"Fire, fire!" I yelled, now in panic. Burning fabric rained down, igniting a rattan armchair that stood near the window. With fascination I watched the spreading flames while slowly retreating toward the other end of the room.

The fire and smoke, now visible outside, alerted our neighbors. Several came rushing to help. While the doctor next door called the fire department (the doctor had the only telephone on the block), our next-door neighbor unwound a garden hose ready to douse the spreading flames. I was most impressed by the actions of a young man who had come to our aid. I had seen him as he came running (he lived four houses away from us), leaping with his long legs over the hedges that separated the gardens from each other. He reached our house so quickly and went into action with such determination that no one but my mother had yet been able to do anything. The young man took charge. With his bare hands he grabbed the drapes and curtains that my mother had pulled down and tossed them into the garden. The fiercely burning rattan chair followed. Next he took the goatskin rug which had been on the floor in front of the armchair, and beat out the remaining flames. By the time the fire engine arrived, the fire had been put out.

(The young man, from an aristocratic family, later joined the new German Air Force. He was killed fighting in the Spanish civil war. Goering, by then head of the German Air Force, dispatched "volunteers" to Spain to test his new airplanes and pilots.)

I must confess I found the fire exciting and rather enjoyed the ensuing to-do. I felt important. I thought that at least some of the credit for preventing a larger conflagration belonged to me. After all, I had been the first to notice the fire, at the very start, and had raised the alarm. The tall firemen, looking even taller in their firemen's helmets, the neighbors running in and out of the house, Claire rushing home from school to see what was happening, this wasn't just a break from the daily routine, it was a great adventure.

After the firemen and all the neighbors had departed, my mother closed off the living room. She made a belated lunch, which we ate at the round table in my father's study. This made the day even more exciting. Seldom did I enjoy lunch as much as on that day.

A day or so after the fire an arson investigator showed up. Recently, he explained, there had been a rash of suspicious fires in Jewish businesses and homes, and he wanted to make sure that the cause of the fire had been as reported. Sometime later we learned that the investigator had been dismissed from the fire department. Apparently he had been too vigorous in his arson investigations.

The weather soon returned to normal, much rain with an occasional snowflake dancing in the blustering wind. Our home, too, returned to normal, though changes were in the air.

The Judge

The judge and his wife lived across the street from us. A few months after the Nazis came to power, the judge retired from the bench, forced out by the new government. One of the Nazi's earliest actions was to purge "undesirables" from the judiciary. "Undesirables" included judges suspected of left leanings, judges who had at one time convicted a Nazi and, of course, judges who were Jewish. Judges who had served on the bench for a long time and were close to retirement were given their pension early. The others were dismissed.

The judge's wife was not Jewish. As there were no children to worry about, and being liberal and tolerant people, the mixed marriage posed no special problems for them. Both enjoyed living the good life, and with an adequate pension, they were ready to make the best of their situation. They felt sure, as did so many, that the Hitler regime could not last very long.

Darkness descends early in the months of the Christmas season. In the cold gloom of the winter afternoons the brightly lit stores, with their Christmas decorations and their displays of toys and sweets, appeared as beacons of warmth and cheer, seducing both children and adults alike. For the children of our small Jewish community it was not always easy to deal with these enticements. Of course, not one of us would ever admit to this. After all, we were Jewish and all that Christmas stuff in no way tempted us.

Some parents tried to make Hanukkah fit into the season by giving gifts and candy. A few went so far as to give their children chocolate Santa Clauses, calling them "little Hanukkah Men." My parents never took part in this. I felt very contemptuous of this aping of Christmas.

I have to admit that my sister and I had it a bit easier than the other children in our community. My sister's birthday was mid-December while my own birthday is in early January at the end of the Christmas Season. My parents were always very generous, hence there were plenty of birthday gifts: New toys, new books, new clothing. With the lighting of Hanukkah Candles, and the baking of birthday cakes, which incidentally kept the house warm and cozy during the long winter evenings, Christmas had no special allure.

The judge and his wife celebrated all holidays, Christian as well as Jewish, but celebrated them in a style all their own. One Hanukkah/Christmas, probably 1934, my mother, my sister, and I (my father was in the Balkans or perhaps Arabia) had been invited to the judge's home for an evening of cookies and cake. In their living room stood a Christmas tree and next to it on a small table a Hanukkiah. After greeting us, the judge lit candles on both the tree and on the Hanukkia. Placing one arm around his wife, he lifted the Hanukkiah (Hanukkah candelabra) high and danced with his wife around the Christmas tree singing "Maoz Tzur" (the Hanukkah hymn "Rock of Ages"). My sister and I thought this performance ridiculous. Secretly we made fun of the judge and his redheaded wife. I did enjoy the cake and cookies.

When returning home from foreign lands, my father often brought back with him recipes he had picked up in "exotic" places: Algiers, Morocco, Gibraltar. After having been home for a while, and with urgent business taken care of, he turned to the kitchen to try his hand on a few of the newfound dishes, demonstrating his skill as a cook. He was an excellent cook.

An appreciative audience was important. For simple recipes, members of the immediate family were quite adequate as appreciative diners. The more elaborate and difficult recipes, however, required more sophisticated guests. The judge and his wife, appreciating a good and piquant meal, fully met his requirement.

These dinners, rather formal affairs, were late in the evening. The good china came out of the cupboard and there was good wine and excellent coffee. And of course, it was for adults only. After politely greeting the guests, my sister and I were sent to bed. This seemed not very fair to me, but the dinners were past our bedtime. Besides, children were not supposed to participate in adult conversations. I remember lying in bed trying hard to stay awake and listen to the lively talk drifting up from the dining room. Usually I fell asleep quickly.

The viciousness of the Nazi regime became more evident every day. The hate campaign against Jews was gaining momentum. In newspapers and on the radio there was a constant drumbeat about the depravity of the Jewish race. Incitement to violence against Jewish-owned stores and individual Jews had created a threatening atmosphere. Particularly vicious in its propaganda was Der Sturmer, a vile and pornographic Nazi paper. Its specialty was reporting, in great detail, grotesque and sadistic sexual deeds allegedly committed by lecherous old Jews on beautiful and innocent German maidens. These hate fantasies were often illustrated with explicit and utterly revolting cartoons.

Although Der Sturmer was also anti-Christian, it did not hesitate to play to Christian anti-Jewish sentiments. The killing of Christ, the paper asserted, reviving an old libel by the Church, was the most hideous crime ever committed in history, and it was the Jews who had committed it. The article was illustrated with drawings showing ugly Jews torturing a very "Aryan" looking Christ. Despite the disgusting nature of many of the illustrations, copies of Der Sturmer, in form of posters, were on display in many public places: busy street intersections, trolley stops, railroad stations.

The judge had the habit to go into center city just to walk around. Perhaps he was reminiscing about the days when he was one of the City's respected citizens. His walks must have become increasingly depressing. Doubts must have entered his mind: he must have feared Hitler may not pass into history as quickly as many wished to believe.

One day, while taking his customary city walk, the judge came upon one of Der Sturmer's vicious posters. Losing his composure, he spat at it. Two storm troopers had seen his action. After beating him they turned him over to the police. In the early days of the Nazi regime the Gestapo had not yet assumed sole jurisdiction over Jews. This was lucky for our judge. Brought before a regular court, he was sentenced to two weeks in jail. Perhaps the presiding judge knew him from the days he had been on the bench.

On completing his sentence, the judge was released. He went at once to the railroad station and bought two tickets out of Germany. The world was not yet afraid of being flooded with Jews trying to escape the Nazis; hence it was still relatively easy to cross the border into a neighboring country. All that was needed was a ticket and a valid passport.

The judge and his wife departed from Germany so quickly they had barely time to say good-bye to their friends. The judge had seen the warning signs and had taken them seriously. Far too many failed to heed them.

Portrait of a Nazi

It ought to be obvious that no close personal, or even just good neighborly, relationship could possibly have existed between our family and that of a Nazi. And yet, this is not entirely true. There was one family with whom we remained on friendly terms for quite a while, even though the man of the house was a convinced Nazi. However, I assume that they were aware my mother had not been born Jewish.

I don't recall when, nor how, we first met the F's. Most likely it was during the summer of 1934. The family F, husband, wife, one son, lived on the next street. The back gardens of our two streets faced each other, separated only by a pathway that ran between them. Hence, when they visited us, or we went over to their house, it was only a few steps from one garden to the other, avoiding having to walk around the block, from front door to front door. Also, it made visits less noticeable to neighbors, especially after dark. At first this was of no importance, but with the increasing hate propaganda against the Jews I'm sure the F's were not too keen to let the neighborhood know that they remained at friendly terms with us. Most of our neighbors probably didn't care, but it took only one person eager to ingratiate herself or himself with the Party to cause trouble.

Most of the time Mr. F's gaunt face displayed a bitter and angry expression. Surely, life had dealt him some bad cards, yet had also handed him some strong aces. But he had permitted his misfortunes to dominate his outlook on life. During the First World War he had been a soldier. Badly wounded, his left arm, including the shoulder, had to be amputated. The surgeons had been unable to fit him with an artificial limb. All he had was a stiff and useless "arm" ending in a just as useless "hand," a stuffed glove. Mr. F was a determined and stubborn man. He set out to do in his spare time – he had a good job and worked long hours– all the things people with two arms and two hands were able to do, and do them better. Beginning with learning to tie his shoes with one hand, he quickly progressed to the use of all kinds of carpentry and other tools. Being not only skillful but also inventive, he designed various types of clamps and gadgets to assist him with his work when ordinary tools were not suited for one-hand manipulation.

Thus equipped, he used his one hand to build a radio from scratch. Having succeeded with that, he constructed a large and elaborate model railroad: Railroad stations, landscapes, and much more. When this was no longer enough of a challenge, he learned the delicate skill of clock repair. Yet despite of all these accomplishments his anger and bitterness remained. He continued to bemoan his lost arm and all that he could have become had he been whole.

And for what had his arm been sacrificed? For a lost war! Not that the German soldiers hadn't fought well. Mr. F was sure they had, and had fought better than all the other soldiers. But politicians and greedy money interests had betrayed them.

Of course Mr. F did not talk politics with us. But occasionally he did expound on his philosophy: God and nature were identical and nature obviously favored the strong. Life is a continuous struggle for survival. Only those who are physically and mentally vigorous and who have the will to use their superiority are fit to survive. One only had to look at nature to see, as Darwin had shown, that this world was made by and for the strong: The larger tree shades out the smaller, the most ferocious lion gets the biggest portion of the kill, the strongest bull mates with the female, and only the quickest antelope escapes the hunter.

Mr. F considered himself anti-Christian. The teachings of Christianity, and of most other organized religions, were contrary to the laws of nature. The major religions preached, like democracy, equality of all human beings. Nature, on the other hand, clearly showed that there were superior and inferior individuals and races. The mistaken ideas of equality were at the root of the betrayal of the white race, the race superior to all other races. Like England, Germany ought to be among the rulers of the world. But the betrayal at Versailles, at the end of World War I, had deprived the German Nation of her rightful place. Angered by this perceived injustice, Mr. F became a Nazi. Adolph Hitler, Mr. F declared, had the vision that could set right the terrible wrong done to his country. The Fuhrer was the only leader capable of restoring Germany to her rightful place of greatness among the nations, and he had the will to do so.

I was shocked and dismayed by this philosophy; yet it fascinated me. Not counting myself among the strong of this world, I felt challenged. The world's great religions, Judaism, Christianity, and Buddhism (Islam I ignored) had laid down moral laws that were enshrined in the Ten Commandments. These laws provided the basis for civilized society, fostering peaceful coexistence of all kinds of people. Civilization, unlike raw nature, permits the strong and the not so strong to live together in peace. If mankind could find a way to live according to these moral principles it would eventually liberate itself from war and violence. It all had appeared so simple.

Now I needed new answers. I read books on evolution, on animal life, on Buddhism; I even tried to tackle Darwin and Nietzsche. That was hefty stuff for someone ten years old. Obviously, I did not make much sense out of what I read, so I pestered my mother with thousands of questions, expounding to her my theories on morality and the struggle for survival, a new theory every other day. When I am old enough, I promised her, I would write a book correcting many of the misconceptions concerning the notion of the "Survival of the Fittest."

At the end of the First World War, Mr. F married the nurse who had taken care of him in the military hospital. They had one son, and the son was the other reason for Mr. F's bitterness and disappointment in life. Helmuth, the F's son, had been born with an exposed chest cavity. The doctors, convinced the baby could not survive, simply stretched what skin there was, and there wasn't much, over the exposed internal organs. Yet the child survived. However, the botched operation kept the child in constant discomfort, growing worse as the child grew older. The boy's chest, I recall, looked extremely ugly. As a consequence, the boy would not, or could not, participate in sports, avoided youth groups, and even was exempt from joining the Hitler Youth. His mother pampered him. In short, he seemed to be the very opposite of the ideal "Aryan" male.

I did not like Helmuth. Two years my junior, he was to me just a spoiled kid who whined too much. Few of the children in our neighborhood wanted to play with him. Even though we were Jewish Mrs. F liked her son to get together with Claire and me. Perhaps this was because my parents did not subscribe to her husband's philosophy of the rule by the strong. Also we were willing, somewhat prodded by my mother, to play with him. It seemed only natural that the neighborhood's outcasts would get together. However, in time the relationship became ever more difficult. First, there was the difference in age, but more important, there was a steady increase in the divergence of interests and concerns. I do not know what his parents told their son about us and why we too were being shunned by the other children in the neighborhood.

For us there were some benefits in the relationship with the F's. My mother was especially grateful to Mrs. F for her help during my sister's serious illness. I was six or seven years old when my sister required a difficult and risky operation. My mother had to spend much of her time with her at the hospital. My father was away and unable to return home in time. During the critical days and nights when my mother had to stay at the hospital with my sister, Mrs. F took care of me.

Occasionally Mrs. F took Claire and me along on excursions into the country when it was no longer a risk free proposition for Jews. Although I still looked "Jewish," accompanied by Mrs. F (no one would ever mistake her for being Jewish) we could visit places where Jews could no longer go. We took long walks, passing through small picturesque villages, stopping perhaps at a country inn (marked with a sign "Jews and dogs not permitted") for a glass of apple cider or lemonade, or even a piece of cake. Or we would walk along the small river that wound its way between the city and our suburb. I loved walking through the meadows along the river, looking for wildflowers and watching butterflies.

Even after the pogrom of November 1938, when we were kicked out of our home in Romerstadt, our relationship with the F's did not end at once. They visited us a number of times at the city apartment to which we had moved. When Mr. F noticed that our old pendulum clock had been damaged during the move, he came to repair it. Shortly after the outbreak of the war, all contact between us finally came to an end. I think it was my mother who broke off the relationship. She simply did not tell Mrs. F that we had to move again.

Shortly after the war Mrs. F did manage to locate us. The war's end had not been kind to the F's. Romerstadt had been taken over by the United States Army to house soldiers. All residents were evicted. Mr. F lost his job. To complete his humiliation, his wife was now the breadwinner, working for the American occupier. But their misfortune did not end there. Helmuth contracted meningitis. He died at the age of sixteen. The funeral took place at the Romerstadt cemetery. We were invited.

Mrs. F's boss, the American officer in charge of the Red Cross Canteen, was very generous. He opened the facility, located in the Romerstadt grade school, to the funeral party, providing coffee and doughnuts. And so I found myself back in the building where I had first started school many, many years ago. The building held no fond memories for me.

After the funeral Mrs. F did not go home with her husband. Their marriage had come to an end. We never heard from either of the F's again.

CHAPTER 2

GROWING UP JEWISH

Thoughts about Being Jewish

Jews had felt very much at home in the post-World War I German Republic. The country prided itself in its high standard of industry, social legislation, education and culture, and Jews, despite lingering anti-Semitism, had played a major role in these developments. Progress toward a fully egalitarian state was thought inevitable. With the election victory of the Nazi Party and the subsequent Hitler dictatorship, this optimism proved an illusion. Not only did social progress come to a halt, it went into reverse. The Jews in Germany found themselves returned to pre-enlightenment days.

In 1932, when we moved to suburban Romerstadt, the struggle in Germany between democracy and dictatorship was still undecided. Political parades and rallies were daily occurrences. Militant party organizations marched through the streets with bands playing and flags flying. All loved wearing uniforms: There were the brown-shirts of the Nazis, the green-shirts of the socialists, the black shirts of the fascists, and the gray shirts of the right wing veterans' party. Not infrequently, and often deliberately, demonstrations turned violent. Street battles between Nazis and militant left wing organizations at times ended in gun battles. The Nazis and other extreme right wing parties liked to resort to guns, including machine guns, while the Communists preferred mass strikes, street barricades and destructive riots. The police appeared helpless in dealing with the violence.

Walls, advertising columns, display signs, even thoroughfares and sidewalks, were covered with party slogans, party emblems, and political graffiti. On our block the Three Arrows of the Social-Democrats dominated. As children we at times used the symbols painted on streets and sidewalks for games. I remember playing a game of trying to jump across the three parallel arrows of the Socialists without stepping on them.

In February 1933 all this changed. The aging President of the Republic, General Von Hindenburg, granted Hitler, then chancellor of the Reich, extraordinary powers to curb the violence. And with this action, democracy died in Germany. Now only Nazi organizations were parading. Soon anti-Semitic posters and graffiti joined the nationalistic symbols and posters of the party in power.

To "legitimatize" the dictatorship, the new government conducted a public referendum. Only "yes" or "no" votes were permitted. As my mother was leaving the polling station - Jews were still permitted to vote - our block warden proudly told her that our district was voting 98% in favor of the Fuhrer and that our street was doing even better, providing a 100% "yes" vote. Of course, we knew better. Quite a few of the voters in our street were voting "no."

For the first couple of years after moving to Romerstadt, we had no problems with our non-Jewish neighbors. Gradually, however, social contact declined. I suspect most of our neighbors turned their backs on us not out of conviction, but due to pressures from the local Party, from some family members and perhaps even from employers. To avoid troubles for themselves, they avoided us. There were two exceptions: The family F and the couple living next door to us. Both husband and wife were doctors. They looked after Claire and me when we were sick.

From the Jewish community, on the other hand, we received at first a rather cool reception. The congregation was orthodox and we certainly were not. My mother, a convert, was looked upon with suspicion. My parents' insistence that Claire and I attend school on Saturdays further reinforced their skepticism concerning our "Jewishness." And my father's attitude did not help to assuage the community's feelings. Opposed to religious organizations, he would not set foot inside a synagogue and he refused to make an exception even now. A more accommodating attitude on his part would certainly have made it easier for us to be accepted by the congregation.

For my father, inviting people to dinner was important in establishing good social relationships. However, since we did not keep kosher the congregation's leading families would not eat at our home. With this avenue of approach closed, my father simply ignored the community. That was easy for him as he was away from home much of the time. This left my mother to deal with this unhappy situation mostly on her own.

I was of course too young, having turned six at the time Hitler came to power, to understand what was happening. I had been told a number of times to stay away from Nazi parades, but I took these admonitions as one of the many things adults feel obliged to warn their children about. Their worries about the Nazis, I thought, were the result of too much newspaper reading and too much listening to radio news. The increasing hostility toward me from children in the neighborhood, and especially in school, soon convinced me otherwise. No longer could I ignore what was going on.

Being Jewish was being different from most people around us, although I would have been hard pressed to say what these differences were. To me the religious and political differences between some of the Jewish families in the community and us were far more obvious. This was all too confusing, so I tried to ignore the adult world and took refuge in fantasies. My imagined world seemed a much easier world to understand. But increasing hostility toward me by children in the neighborhood and especially in school did not let me escape.

Probably influenced by my father I reacted by turning against everything German. Most of all, I did not want to be German. Yet at the moment my Jewish identity was not adequate to provide me with an alternative. I could see being Jewish only in religious terms. The idea of a Jewish People in a Jewish Land had not yet entered my mind. Everyone needed to identify with a country, of that I was sure. People without a country were like lost souls. Did I have a country?

Most members of the local Jewish community were orthodox, yet they also thought of themselves as patriotic Germans. Their first names and the names they had given to their children, especially to their sons, clearly showed their identification with Germany. One could find among them many names from the Germanic legends, like "Siegfried" and "Manfred." The men who had served in the German Army during the First War took great pride in the service they had rendered their fatherland. They looked upon Jews who had not been at the front as an embarrassment to the Jewish community. These Jews, the ex-soldiers feared, seemed to confirm a common, and false, public perception that Jews had shirked their duty, staying home making money from the tragedy that befell the German nation.

My father had not served on the frontline during the Great War. Early in the war, while in the army, he had contracted a severe kidney infection. One kidney and part of the second had to be removed. Upon release from the hospital he was discharged from the military. I felt rather good that my father had not helped to defend Germany.

Were the Nazis right? Were the Jews a rootless people, a people without a country, the legendary "Wandering Jew?" Yet was it really so bad to be without a country? Some of the world's greatest minds had transcended the narrowness of nationalism. The Socialists branded nationalism the root of all wars. So I took refuge in what I saw as the international background of my parents, the "French Connections." That, and my father's extensive travels abroad, made us world citizens; and that, most importantly, made me less German.

Once the Nazis had taken control, German intellectual life declined rapidly.

Theaters, museums, cinemas, and even the concert hall, all became instruments of propaganda. Now my parents seldom went out, even before places of entertainment were closed to Jews. Shirley Temple movies were an exception. For whatever reason, they had not fallen victim to the Nazi censor. My parents took Claire and me to see several of them.

With public entertainment no longer accessible to us, books, which always had an important place in our home, now took center stage. In the Nazis dictatorship not only had newspapers come under the yoke of Dr. Joseph Goebbels' Propaganda Ministerium, but also book publishing. Luckily, we did not depend on German publishers. My father was able to obtain books that did not conform to Goebbels' criteria for good reading. Frequently on his way home from the Middle East, my father made a brief stop in Basel, Switzerland to buy chocolate and books that were not yet on the Nazis' banned book list, but no longer available in Germany.

What interested my father was Greek and Roman history. He was fascinated by the struggle between autocracy and democracy. He had the habit of reading to my mother passages that struck him as especially relevant to the existing political situation in Germany, often interrupting her from whatever she was doing at the moment, whether reading, sewing, preparing lunch or supper, or even sleeping.

Stimulated by my father's travels and by what my parents read and discussed, mostly over dinner, I began to see in books a way to gain understanding of what was happening. Many of my ideas of what it meant to be Jewish and what it meant to live in a world often hostile to Jews were thus formed by books.

A book that greatly influenced me was a children's version of the Bible written by Rabbi Prinz of Berlin, Germany. (The Rabbi went to New Jersey, escaping the Holocaust.) His two-volume rendition of the Bible stories had a strong Zionist flavor. Included in the Prinz Bible were the apocryphal stories of Judith, the Maccabees, and Bar Kochba. These Jews had not been afraid to fight the enemies of the Jewish people; they had even defied mighty Rome. I was sure they would not have been afraid to fight the Nazis. I imagined that the Jews, let by David and his friend Jonathan, had fought not the Philistines but the Germans. Other books that contributed to shaping my perception of being Jewish were Thomas Mann's Joseph trilogy and Franz Werfel's "Saul," a sympathetic portrayal of the unhappy king.

Influenced by my reading, by my father and by the increasing severity of anti-Semitic propaganda, I turned toward Jewish nationalism. Of course I did not dare to use the word "nationalism;" in our home nationalism was a dirty word.

In 1935, while I struggled to understand what it meant to be Jewish, the Nazis passed the "Nurnberg Laws," giving us their definition of who was a Jew and who was not. The Jewish community, its membership determined by anti-Semites, gradually became segregated from the general population and thus forced to draw closer together.

With school segregation, "Jew classes" did not meet on Shabbat. Claire and I could attend Shabbat services more or less regularly, often accompanied by my mother; and defying her husband, she did all her food shopping at the kosher stores. Under external pressures and due to my to mother's actions, we finally became part of the Jewish community, despite my father's opposition.

A Journey to Palestine

My father's travels were exciting: Cities like Istanbul, Damascus, and Baghdad evoked pictures from the Arabian Nights, while Palestine and Egypt brought to life stories from the Bible.

Of course I was little aware of the heavy burden my father's frequent and long absences from home placed on my mother. She had to deal mostly by herself with the many problems that confronted us: Adjusting to our new community, seeing her children enter first grade, and handling the many financial difficulties that still plagued the family as a result of the economic upheavals of the late twenties and early thirties. And after 1933, the new anti-Jewish actions and laws added another load to her burdens. In some of her letters to him (the letters were found among her things after her death), she complained bitterly about his lack of direct involvement.

Yet being frequently away from home may not have been such a bad thing. He was less exposed to the daily harassments to which Jews in the Third Reich were being increasingly subjected. I'm not sure how he would have handled the many daily annoyances and petty restrictions. His reaction could well have landed him, and us, in trouble. Yet had he been more directly exposed to them, he might have taken action sooner and with more vigor to get us out of Germany.

The move from Mannheim to Frankfurt in 1931, Hitler coming to power in Germany in 1933 and my entering school shortly thereafter were not the only profound changes affecting my life in that short span of time.

As a result of his new job with a wholesale company of lace and fashion articles, my father's absence from home increased. His business territory, previously confined to the Balkans, expanded to include much of the Middle East and countries around the Mediterranean: North Africa, Gibraltar, and until the Spanish civil war, Spain, Spanish Morocco, and the Canary Islands. This meant a lot more traveling, although occasionally he was able to bypass the Balkans, leaving the routine business there to his agents in Zagreb, Croatia, and in Istanbul, Turkey. On those occasions he went by ship from Italy directly to the Middle East, usually to Beirut, Lebanon, reducing his time away from home.

Pesach 1934 found my father on a ship bound for Haifa, then the main port of the British Mandate of Palestine. The journey to Haifa turned out to be one of those occurrences in life, which, though happening by chance, nevertheless produce a profound effect on one's future.

Among the passengers to Haifa were groups of Jews on their way to settle in Eretz Israel. These "Olim" came from many countries: Poland, Romania, Hungary, Germany and possibly others. They represented a wide range of Jewish attitudes, from anti-religious socialists to religious Zionists. The ship's captain was Jewish, and he invited his Jewish passengers to the Captain's Table to celebrate the Seder (home Passover service). Most, if not all, of the Jewish passengers accepted the captain's invitation, and that included the anti-religious left wingers. The Seder, the circumstances in which it took place, and especially the response of the Jewish passengers, all impressed my father.

As once again violent anti-Semitism threatened the Jewish people, a new Exodus was needed, an Exodus from Europe. And here groups of Jews, as diverse as the Jews must have been that crossed the Red Sea from Egypt, were crossing the sea on their way to the Promised Land. Despite the differences in religious and political outlooks they, like their ancestors from long ago, were returning to their true home. With even the anti-religious finding resonance in remembering the Exodus, my father argued, then there must be a broader meaning in the celebration of Seder than merely a traditional religious one. From now on, my father resolved, a Seder would be celebrated in our home, and so too would be the lighting of the Hanukkah candles.

Why observe these two, and only these two, holidays? Not for religious reasons of course, my father would never have admitted to that. Pesach, he explained to my sister and me, celebrated the liberation of the people from oppression, while Hanukkah celebrated the liberation of the land from foreign occupation. By foreign occupation he did not mean the British. To my father they were protectors of the Jewish homeland. But he did mean all the others who at one time or another had laid claim to the Land of Israel, from the Romans to the Arabs.

Among the few "Jewish things" my father had brought with him from his mother's home were items associated with the Seder table: a cover for the special Matzot used during the Seder, a hand embroidered hand towel for the washing of the hands, and a cover for the chair cushion used by the master of the house while leading the Seder; this too had been hand embroidered. All these things were rather old and fragile. But now they were taken from wherever they had been stored, to be available for the holiday. Since no Haggadah was found among the stored items, my father went to Kauffman's, the only Jewish bookstore left in Frankfurt, to purchase one. For Hanukkah my father designed and made a wooden Hanukkiah. Among his many talents, he was skilled with his hands. Lighting the candles and saying the prayers was my duty.

At the first Seder at home that I remember, my father, to my astonishment, read the Brachot in Hebrew. How little did I know about my father! He followed the order of the Haggadah up to the recitation of the Ten Plagues. Breaking away from the traditional reading he told us about his Middle East travels: seeing the Pyramids, the ancient temples, and the great palaces of the Pharaohs, which as legend says, had been built by Jewish slaves. Switching from Egypt to the Land of Israel, he described the new settlements built by Jewish hands for the Jewish People returning to their homeland.

When my father wasn't home my mother, Claire and I were usually guests at the Sterns' or the Schwelms' Seder table. At one Seder at the Schwelms – it was very long – the three boys, Freddy, Manfred, and I, became rather bored. With no one paying attention to us, we kept pouring ourselves cups of wine. When the Seder finally ended, the three of us were rather drunk. I felt rather foolish and thought my father's Seders were much more interesting.

With increasing persecution came a stepped-up search for places of refuge. Whenever Jews came together, sooner or later conversations drifted to the topic of leaving Germany and to the question of where to go. For many the United States was the preferred country of refuge. Some considered the Union of South Africa, which, at least for a while, welcomed Jews, especially those with money. Others looked for refuge in South America.

Many, however, sought only temporary refuge. They believed that once Hitler and his gang had been relegated to the garbage heaps of history, they could return to Germany to resume their normal life once again.

For my father the Middle East was a more logical solution. There he had connections and had gained familiarity with the mode of life of European expatriates, including Jews from Germany, who had settled there. Although Cairo was the center of his activities, it was to Palestine that he looked for our future home. In many of the cities, Haifa, Tel Aviv, Jerusalem and others, he had business connections and friends. He was a frequent guest at a home in Ramot HaShavim, a Moshav (settlement) near the town of Hod Hasharon.

My father's travels had moved the "Land of Israel" out of the realm of the Bible and of storybooks into the present. He always brought back many photos. (Photography was another one of his many interests). I especially enjoyed looking at pictures from Eretz Israel: Modern houses under construction in Tel Aviv, the Technion in Haifa, neat homes on a Moshav. One of his photos showed a mailbox standing on a hillside with nothing around it but a telephone pole. The box was clearly marked in Hebrew: "Doar."

Frequent verbal assaults, and occasionally physical attacks even from adults, made the way to and from school always tense. With Jewish post offices and buses and even Jewish policemen, going to school in Eretz Israel, I felt, would be safe for me.

Gradually, and with some reluctance, my parents concluded that it would be best for us to leave Germany and move to Palestine. But there wasn't yet a sense of urgency.

The Synagogue

Why my parents decided to join the small orthodox congregation in the nearby suburb of Heddernheim, I can only speculate. Joining a liberal synagogue in the city would have been much more appropriate. Going to services by bus and streetcar on the High Holydays, and once in a while on Shabbat, certainly would not have been a problem for them. Perhaps they thought that the times demanded supporting of the local community; or they felt it was important that their children felt at ease among Jews, no matter what the religious orientation. More likely the decision was just another indication of my father's ambivalence: Liberals just weren't Jewish enough.

Following the main road, the walk to "shul" took about an hour. I didn't mind the walk, except on rainy days, of course. Usually Claire and

I took a shortcut which, bypassing a good part of main road, made its way past an archeological dig of the area's Roman past. There I wanted to linger a while to look for "Roman shards," but my sister usually dragged me away telling me not to get my pants dirty. On the way back, however, I never wanted to linger. Then I was eager to get home for the waiting lunch. When my mother came along we never took the shortcut.

During spring and fall, when the weather was fair, the walk on Shabbat morning was rather pleasant. With the schools, except Jewish schools, in sessions, I felt fairly safe from harassment. Yet I did like the walks even during the summer, although with school closed they were riskier. Often we followed a different, somewhat longer route that meandered its way through a park and past private gardens where summer flowers perfumed the air.

Regrettably, I'm not able to tell more about our synagogue: who founded it and what the past community was like. I remain convinced that there must be a fascinating history connected with the old shul. I don't recall anyone in the congregation ever talking about the shul's early days. More likely, I just hadn't paid attention to any of the stories.

Until industry moved into the small towns and villages that surrounded the city of Frankfurt, Heddernheim had been a farming village in the Duchy of Nassau. Even after being incorporated into the big city as an industrial suburb, center town had retained much its rural character. Old half-timbered houses, many a bit off plumb and misshapen by age, lined the cobble-stoned streets. And on one of these streets, somewhat hidden from view, our synagogue once stood.

The synagogue dates from about 1760, at least a hundred years before the village was incorporated into the City of Frankfurt. At that time its Jewish quarter is said to have been the largest in the Duchy. Certainly, the synagogue could seat many more worshippers than attended our shul, even during the High Holidays. Why Jews settled in this small town not far from a city in which congregations had existed since the Middle Ages, I do not know. Where did these Jews come from, what were their trades? Gravestones in the nearby Jewish cemetery may have been able to provide some clues. But the stones, made of local sandstone, were badly weathered and most inscriptions had become unreadable. The still readable stones date from the nineteenth century.

The synagogue stood in a small courtyard shaded by a large oak tree. A single door led into a narrow, poorly lit vestibule, bare but for a small basin. There the men could wash their hands before entering the sanctuary. A narrow stairway wound its way up to the women's section.

The arrangement of the sanctuary hinted at a possible Sephardic background of the original congregation, or at least betrayed Sephardic influence. The bimah (altar), which we called the "Almemar," a Sephardic term, stood in the center. However, unlike in many Sephardic synagogues, the benches faced forward toward the Aron HaKodesh (Holy Ark) on the eastern wall, opposite the entrance. A few wide steps lead up to a broad platform in front of the Aron HaKodesh. The reader's stand, in front of the steps, faced toward the platform. A second reader's stand, on the platform, was turned toward the congregation.

Above the Aron HaKodesh two golden lions held a crown high between them. Below the crown was the Ner Tamid (Eternal Light). I was very much bothered by the two lions. I thought of them as a violation of the second commandment, which prohibits the making of images of living creatures. No one else seemed to mind these animal figures. I was too shy to ask questions about them.

To the right of the Aron HaKodesh, set into a corner about three meters above the floor, was a small wooden structure, a pulpit, accessible only via a curved narrow stairway. From there, looking down on his congregation, a rabbi would have given his sermon. The pulpit may also have been used during special readings, such as the Meggilat Esther on Purim or sections of the Haggadah on Pesach, as it is still the custom in some Sephardic congregations.

The pulpit fascinated me. No one in the congregation could recall when it had been used last or for what purpose. Originally painted blue and gold, it was in need of a fresh coat of paint. I very much wanted to climb up its narrow creaky looking stairs to gaze down at the assembled men.

The Aron HaKodesh held eight Torah scrolls, a considerable wealth for a small and rather poor congregation. Perhaps the number of scrolls too hinted at a more prosperous past. However, only two of the scrolls could be used on a regular basis. The others were in too delicate conditions, and there was not enough money to have them repaired. However, during the Simchat Torah services, all eight scrolls were taken out and joyfully paraded around the sanctuary.

Across the street from the synagogue, behind a high wall, stood some tall horse-chestnut trees. When in leaf, their boughs provided a green canopy high above the narrow lane. In fall, during the period of the High Holidays, we gathered the chestnuts that had fallen into the street. Stringing them together, we made long chains for decorating our sanctuary for the Sukkoth and Simchat Torah festivals. A long time after the war, when I searched for the old synagogue, these tall trees guided me to the place where it once stood.

When we joined the congregation, it had shrunk to more or less a family affair. The Mais, the Sterns, and the Schwelms, related by blood and/or marriages, provided the core of the congregation. Old Mr. Mai, the patriarch of the three families and the local kosher butcher, had one son and three daughters. I don't remember much about the son. He wasn't married and worked in his father's butcher shop. Two of the daughters had married two brothers, the Stern brothers. The third daughter was married to Mr. Schwelm, a local salesman. Although one of the Stern brothers (the "one armed" brother, who had lost an arm in World War I) had moved out of the suburban community into the city, he continued to take an interest in the congregation's affairs. On the High Holidays he and his family always came to shul in Heddernheim.

The congregation had neither a rabbi nor a professional Hazzan. On Friday evenings and Shabbat mornings Mr. Schwelm, who was also the shul's "shames," conducted services. During the High Holy Days he shared his duties with his brother-in-law, the "one armed" Stern. The other Mr. Stern, Siegfried Stern, also a handicapped veteran of WWI, never conducted services. Yet he was considered the most learned of the three men. In arguments over ritual procedures, his opinion was usually accepted as correct.

The congregation had difficulties assuring Shabbat morning Minyans (quorums). Only nine "regulars" could be depended upon to show up every Shabbat. Old Mr. Mai, though active in the community's affairs, did not like to come to shul on Shabbat morning. Attending to his butcher shop six days a week, he wanted to relax on the day of rest. However, once in a while he had to be called upon to be the "tenth man." Sitting in the back of the shul he read his newspaper. Occasionally he fell asleep. Feeling a bit disoriented upon waking up, he would fold up his paper and walk out, bringing the service to an abrupt halt.

The Siegfried Sterns had their home in "Romerstadt," a short walk from us. They had two children, Ruth and Freddy. Ruth was a year older than my sister while Freddy was my age. The Schwelms also had two children, a girl and a boy. The girl was about sixteen or seventeen. She did not want to have anything to do with us children, considering herself an adult. Her brother Manfred was the same age as Freddy and I. The three of us were the only boys in the congregation. Our Bar Mitzvot were eagerly awaited. The addition of three "men" would make it easier to have a Minyan.

During services I always sat with Freddy and his father. Mr. Stern considered it a "mitzvah" to instruct me alongside his son. I used an old Machsor, my grandmother's, of which I was rather proud. Yet the old book gave me lots of troubles and taught me an early lesson in Judaism: I had believed, or I had been taught, that synagogue services were the same throughout the world. Now I learned that there were differences; and to me these differences were rather confusing.

The Machsorim in use in most orthodox congregations in Frankfurt were the "Roedelheim" edition (Roedelheim is a suburb of Frankfurt; a Jewish publishing house was once located there). My Machsor was a "Metz" edition (Metz is a city in eastern France). The "Rodelheim" tradition was often at variance with the "Metz" tradition and frequently I got lost during the service. Frantically turning pages, I struggled to find the right place in my Machsor, while Freddy sneered at my ignorance. Mr. Stern usually came to my rescue. And he did more than just help me along with the prayer book. Sometimes he invited my sister and me to his home to participate in the Havdalah service, which marks the end of Shabbat and the beginning of the workweek. I owe to Mr. Stern that today I can walk into any synagogue and feel more or less at ease.

I liked the Friday evening service welcoming the Shabbat best. The service was shorter than on Shabbat morning and at the completion, when the Hazzan made Kiddush, the three pre-Bar Mitzvah boys were called to the front of the sanctuary to receive a sip of Kiddush wine.

The men had looked upon Freddy's father as being the most learned in the congregation, hence Freddy, the oldest by a few months of us three boys, felt that he too was superior in his Jewish knowledge. During the recitation of the "Amidah," the Eighteen Benedictions or "Shemoneh Ezreh," which is said silently while standing (Amidah means standing) Freddy and I raced through it to see who would finish first. I never won.

I had to admit that Freddy knew more about the "correct" way of being "observant," but I was sure that I knew more about Jewish history and therefore had a better understanding of what it meant to be a Jew. We had many arguments, which at times turned rather nasty. Manfred never took part in these quarrels. His father always deferred to Freddy's father, and he in turn accepted Freddy's guidance.

It is doubtful that in more normal times we could have developed a close relationship with the Sterns. Not only did we differ in religious matters, but also in politics. The Sterns tended toward the right. Ruth, Freddy's sister, was a member of BETAR, the Revisionist Zionist youth organization. BETAR members liked to wear uniforms during meetings, which I thought was aping the Nazis. When Ruth asked my sister to join, she refused. In our home anything on the right was considered anathema.

I think that Freddy and I really didn't like each other very much, and not only because of our differences about the proper way of being Jewish. Freddy's grades in school were better than mine, and neither Freddy nor my parents would let me forget that. Yet after our quarrels and even fights we always had to make up. In this world, I learned, we Jews were stuck with each other, like it or not. The world's enmity toward the Jews always brought us back together.

The Mais' butcher shop was rather extensive, which was perhaps another hint that in the past the Heddernheim Jewish community had been larger and more prosperous. There was a slaughterhouse, a large sausage kitchen, an icehouse, a stable for two big horses, and the large store for the public. During the first couple of years we lived in Romerstadt, the butcher still made home deliveries of kosher meats.

But even before the Nazis banned kosher slaughtering, the butcher had shut down most of his facilities. The Jewish community had become too small to sustain his large operation, and the non-Jewish community, which once patronized the Mais' shop for its high quality meats and sausages, was afraid being seen going into a Jewish store. Occasionally after Shabbat services, Freddy, Manfred and I would not go home immediately but went to Mai's place to roam around in the old stables and slaughterhouse.

Despite the many difficulties the congregation had to face, it kept its orthodox character. Few compromises were made. The "one armed" Mr. Stern, who usually went to services in the city, occasionally reported back on how synagogues in the city were coping. At times, the rabbis there introduced small changes in the service. Some changes were made under Nazi pressure; others were in response to the community's feelings. Thus the main synagogue quietly dropped the prayer for the fatherland. Our synagogue then did the same. One day the congregation decided to have a choir on the High Holidays, just like the large Main Synagogue in the city. With our small membership we couldn't have a male choir as the shul's orthodox character required. So our "choir" was made up of the women and the children, and that, to my horror, included me.

The synagogue, its interior wrecked during the November 1938 pogrom, was destroyed in an Allied air raid, together with a large part of the town. When after the war Heddernheim was rebuilt, many of the old half-timbered houses were faithfully reconstructed; but the synagogue is gone. Only a monument reminds residents and casual visitors that the community once had a Jewish community and a synagogue. The nearby Jewish cemetery is locked. A modern highway, having taken a strip of its land, passes it. Now cars of the prosperous and democratic new Germany roll over some of the old Jewish graves.

CHAPTER 3

SCHOOL

A Troublesome Beginning

In early 1933, less than three months after the German Republic was placed into the hands of Hitler, and less than four months after my sixth birthday, I entered First Grade. This somewhat frightening step in a child's journey toward adulthood was made worse for me by the intrusion into the classroom of revived German anti-Semitism.

As defined in the dictionary the German word "Gleichschaltung" means equalization or leveling. In the language of the Nazis the word had taken on a somewhat different and more sinister connotation: It was the name the Hitler government gave to its policy of "bringing into conformance with National-Socialist ideology" the press, the labor movement, the courts, cultural activities and, of course, the schools.

"Gleichschaltung" included ridding German education of "alien" influences. By this the Nazi education minister meant modern educational ideas, which he attributed to the Jews. In place of these "corrupt" ideas, "folk ideals and virtues" were to be emphasized. In practice this meant the dismissal of all Jewish teachers and teachers who had openly associated with left wing movements. Textbooks reflecting the new ideology replaced the existing, more politically neutral ones. Even grammar books and the arithmetic texts were permeated with Nazi ideology and anti-Semitism. Phrases and expressions such as "dirty as a Jew," "deceitful as a Jew," "noisy like a Judenschule," and others in a similar vein were part of reading exercises in the first grade reader.

Nationalist indoctrination was fed to the first and second grade students together with the alphabet. Germanic legends were presented as history. With Fascist Italy not yet an ally of Germany, much of "history" concentrated on the struggle of the Germanic tribes against the Roman Empire. The ancient heroes overcame the stronger Roman legions by living up to Germanic ideals of bravery and dedication. With pre-Christian traditions resurrected, pageants reenacting ancient ceremonies and rituals of sun worship were organized "to bind today's youth to yesterday's heroes." The ideal German male, the all-male class was told, is a courageous warrior obedient to his leader, while the ideal German woman is the proud mother of a warrior.

The nation's rebirth, guided by the Fuehrer, was to be rooted in these old traditions. Germany, once again beset by external and internal foes, looked to her youth, inspired by the courage and steadfastness of the ancient Germans, to take the lead in the rebirth of the fatherland.

This was heady stuff for young boys. With many of their fathers still suffering from the defeat in World War I and the subsequent economic disaster, this form of national-ism was a balm to festering wounds. A villain was needed to take the blame for the defeat. Heroes, to be real heroes, must have an enemy to overcome, and the greater the wickedness of the enemy, the greater the merit in defeating him. Jews, only recently emancipated and still struggling for full acceptance, filled the bill. And so, a steady stream of vituperations against them accompanied these nationalistic fantasies.

Freddy and I, the only Jewish boys in the class, had to sit through all the anti-Semitic propaganda. Obviously this made school rather uncomfortable for us. Happily, however, we were excluded from participating in the reenactments of ancient Germanic rituals. These took place mostly after regular school hours.

During the first few months our classmates, still overwhelmed by the experience of going to school, looked upon the two Jewish boys only with curiosity. But soon, the unceasing anti-Semitic propaganda fed to them, in and out of school, began to show effect. When class was in session, attacks on us were not much of a problem; the teachers didn't permit any disturbances in the classroom. But during recess and on the way home, life became hell. Freddy and I developed all kinds of stratagems to avoid confrontations. Fighting back was not much of an option since we were greatly outnumbered, and complaining to the teachers was of no avail. Teachers patrolling the schoolyard were too uncertain as to how to handle the situation. None wanted to be called a "Jew lover" and possibly dismissed. Harassment of Jews, not yet official policy, was not discouraged.

I hated school. At times I pretended to be too sick to go to school, but to no avail; my parents would not fall for it. I wouldn't do my homework, and especially I refused to read. Homework turned into an almost daily battle between my mother and me. Since books played an important role in our home, my apparent unwillingness or inability to read was especially upsetting to my parents. In letters to my father my mother complained bitterly about my poor schoolwork. When my father was home I was spanked quite often, and when he was especially angry he used a carpet beater to cane my behind. What really hurt was not the beating itself (it did hurt), but the humiliation of having to go and fetch the carpet beater from the broom closet. When being caned I bit my lips trying not to cry while my sister ran upstairs to her room doing the crying.

Herr Vogt, our homeroom teacher, was a tall man, but then to a six-year-old, a teacher standing in front of the class, a blackboard pointer in his hand, does appear that way. The left side of his face was somewhat distorted, the skin almost purple. Perhaps it was the result of an accident, or nothing worse than an ugly birthmark. Of course I, like most of the boys, found it difficult not to stare at the teacher's face. But we quickly forgot to pay attention to his appearance and paid attention to the teacher himself. He had no problem keeping order in the class of fifty boys. Most of the boys liked the teacher, and none wished to make him angry.

I too liked our homeroom teacher, and I had a special reason for doing so. Herr Vogt, well aware of the situation in which Freddy and I found ourselves, tried to help us as much as possible without jeopardizing his own position. While the class was in session, that was no problem. By keeping strict classroom discipline, he kept the harassment to a minimum. But during recess and on our way home there seemed at first little that he could do.

Most days he walked home right after the last class of the day. A group of boys from our class liked to walk with him, something he encouraged. Since his walk home took him past my house, I too would have liked to walk with him. I figured that the presence of the teacher would restrain my classmates, and I could walk home without being beaten up. I did not dare to walk with the group, so I followed a short distance behind, and as I had hoped, the boys mostly ignored me. After a while I noticed that my teacher made sure that I was walking home just behind the group. If he did not see me at once, he would slow down, giving me a chance to catch up.

He tried to help me in other ways to cope with the situation and to push me to live up to what he thought was my potential. In the classroom the boys were ranked by performance. The better students sat further back in the class, while the poorer students sat closer to the teacher. Herr Vogt insisted that my place was near the last row, although my class work hardly justified that. He spoke to my mother a number of times, trying to find ways to improve my performance. He talked my parents into having my eyes examined. With glasses my schoolwork did improve, but not enough to satisfy my parents.

In second grade there was a noticeable lessening of harassment. A fellow student, one of the top students in the class, explained to me why: The attacks on us did not square with his perception of German heroism. I can't be sure how much this thought really influenced the class's behavior. A better reason for the change was perhaps Herr Vogt's subtle influence. Hitler Youth activities in which the boys became increasingly involved may also furnish a better explanation. The wearing of uniforms, the marching and parading, the hikes and war games, all seemed far more exciting than the daily beating up of two Jewish boys.

As my second school year reached its mid-term mark, school segregation became the law. With that, harassments in school came to an end. But new problems took their place.

Claire

As brothers and sisters go, Claire and I got along fairly well. Of course we quarreled and had fights, and certainly there was rivalry between us. At times we ratted on each other to our parents. But then there is nothing unusual about that.

Perhaps it's only normal for the younger sibling (my sister was 13 months older than I) to think that the parents preferr the older. I certainly thought that my parents, especially my father, preferred my sister. That feeling was reinforced by the attention lavished on Claire during her serious illness and during her recovery.

Claire had entered school before the Hitler era. By the time the Nazis had begun their school "reforms," her first year was almost behind her. The only Jew in an all-girl class, she nevertheless had made good friends among her classmates. While I suffered in school from Jew-baiting almost from the first day, many of my Sister's friends refused to desert her despite the anti-Semitic diatribes to which they too were increasingly exposed. Perhaps girls were less susceptible to Nazi propaganda than boys. Boys seemed to lap up the "warrior ethics and mythology" that the new regime fostered in the schools. But even girls who accepted the Nazi line did not turn to violence against my sister.

At times I blamed myself for these troubles, thinking it was my own fault that my classmates so readily turned against me. Freddy too had problems, but his were far less severe. At the age of seven I came to the conclusion that school wasn't for me.

Early during her third school year, Claire became seriously ill. An infection of the inner ear spread along the ear canal and the auditory nerve. With modern antibiotics not yet available, there was a real danger that the infection could reach the brain. To me, an ambulance at our front door was both frightening and exciting.

With a difficult operation required, my mother's attention became focused on my sister. She spent much time at the Hospital and during the most critical days was with my sister day and night. With my father somewhere in the Middle East and unable to return home quickly, I was farmed out to our neighbors, the F's. (Why not the Jewish family, the Sterns? I can only guess that at the time we had not yet become fully accepted by the orthodox Jewish community.)

My sister's recovery was slow. She had to return to the hospital a number of times and only as summer neared its end could it be said that her recovery was complete. With my parents' attention focused on my sister, I felt pushed aside. Little heed was paid to any of my problems, especially the difficulties I had at school. When I came down with a severe sore throat, my parents dismissed it as an attempt to get their attention and sympathy. Only after I developed a high fever was a doctor consulted. He recommended that my tonsils be removed.

Claire's illness had strained my parents' financial resources. Another operation and hospital stay came as a big blow to them. The high-priced and arrogant but very competent surgeon who had operated on my sister offered to remove my tonsils free of charge. He considered a tonsillectomy trivial, assuring my parents that a hospital stay was not necessary. For my parents this came as a great relief; for me, however, it didn't turn out so well. The great surgeon butchered the job. Perhaps simple operations were beneath him.

The procedure was done when my sister was once again in the hospital for a follow-up operation. While my mother stayed with my sister, a nurse took me to the operating room. There I was placed into a chair, somewhat like a dentist's chair, tied down and covered with a large rubber sheet. Someone put a mask over my face, dripping ether onto it. Scared, I tried to stay awake, but went under quickly.

I came out of the anesthesia before the operation had been completed. When my eyes opened, what I saw was a bloody mess in front of me covering the rubber sheet. I became violently ill, which increased the mess and annoyed the surgeon and his assistants. I wanted to scream, but couldn't. I don't remember what happened after that.

After a brief stay in the recovery room, my mother took me home. As a concession to my feeling rather awful, she took a taxi, despite its high cost. I had always liked riding in a taxi, but this ride I certainly did not enjoy.

As I recovered quickly and my sister still had problems, the episode was shoved aside. Yet I did feel rather resentful of the way I had been treated, especially at the hospital. I hadn't even received the scoop of ice cream the hospital usually gave children recovering from a tonsillectomy!

Claire and I had shared a room. Following her return from the hospital this changed. While my sister was in the hospital "our" room became my sister's room. My parents bought new furniture for my sister, including a real bed. Some of the children's furniture, including the bed, was moved into a small chamber above the stairway. This became my room.

Not that I didn't like my room, I loved it and wouldn't have traded it for anything. But as the younger child I had to do with "hand-me-downs." Even after I had outgrown the children's bed, I did not get a real one. The slightly fire-damaged living-room couch became my bed, while my parents finally refurnished the living room.

I did not make friends easily, at least not as easily as my sister. And what was worse in my parents' eyes was that I did not do nearly as well in school as Claire. Even with her frequent absences due to her illness, she had remained one of the top students in her class.

As I became convinced that I was a disappointment to my parents, my performance at school deteriorated further. My mother blamed my poor schoolwork on my apparent unwillingness to read. Of course I could read and I did, but not in school and not for homework. To stimulate my reading, my parents bought me books they thought would interest a boy. Among these was "Robinson Crusoe." I loved the book and read it in a rather short time. Finally convinced that I could read, they were not all that pleased with the outcome of their effort. Robinson Crusoe became my role model: to be alone and self-sufficient; and I didn't even need a Man Friday.

Much of my free time I spent stretched out on my bed, on the floor or, if the weather was fine, on the back lawn reading. When I was ten or eleven, I discovered "Don Quixote." Now I was no longer Robinson Crusoe happily alone on an island, but a lonely knight facing a world engulfed in evil.

Freddy's Cap

Freddy was very proud of his cap and he took good care of it. One thing Freddy did not like was for his cap to get wet. When it rained, Freddy took off his cap, folded it carefully and put it in his pocket; mine, on the other hand, came out of my pocket and, all crumpled, went on my head. With conditions as they were, Freddy could, of course, not wear a yarmulke in public, so his head remained uncovered. He made me promise never to mention that to his father. I am sure that his parents noticed that on rainy days Freddy's cap was dry while his hair was wet. But they never remarked on it. Apparently they were far more understanding than their son gave them credit for.

In 1935, when I was in second grade, elementary schools became segregated. The Frankfurt school system set up special "Jew Classes" in selected city schools. For Claire and me this meant we no longer could just walk to the end of our street to go to school, but now we had to travel nearly an hour by bus and streetcar. We were lucky, however. The classes to which we were assigned were held in an up-to-date school in one of the newer sections of the city. It was a neighborhood of modern office buildings and equally modern apartment houses, all constructed during the progressive days of the late 1920's. The spacious classrooms were bright and furnished with the latest equipment.

To reduce the chances for confrontations between us, the Jewish students, and the other students during breaks and on the way to and from school, our school day was modified. Jewish classes started when regular classes were already in session, and ended when it could reasonably be assumed that the non-Jewish school children were at home eating lunch.

Segregation had many positive aspects: It eased many of my daily anxieties caused by the possibility of hostile confrontations with the German boys; no longer were the Jewish students forced to listen to the anti-Semitic diatribes that were now part of German education; and it permitted adjusting the curriculum to better meet the needs of Jewish children. Hebrew and Tanach were now regular subjects, making after school "religious" classes unnecessary.

Yet segregation was not a total blessing. Traveling to and from school by bus and streetcar made for a long day and brought new troubles. No longer did I have to deal with hostile German school children; now occasionally adults made trouble for me. "You are Jewish" or "You look Jewish" were remarks I heard many times. What made strangers think that I was Jewish?

At home, among the boys in school, and among friends and acquaintances, "looking Jewish" stimulated many discussions, and even heated debates. But no one could really define adequately what "looking Jewish" meant. Not all German boys were blued eyed and blond, as Nazi propaganda had it; and not all Jewish boys had dark curly hair (Freddy did) or large crooked noses (I did).

Not that I minded looking Jewish; I was rather proud of it. But looking Jewish could be dangerous. So I wanted to know what made me look Jewish. If I knew, perhaps I could make myself look less Jewish if the need arose.

Perhaps we did behave differently in public; there may have been a clue in that.

But there was nothing obvious at which I could point a finger. Once on the way home from school a man came up to me and slapped my face, calling me a "dirty Jew." I was more puzzled than hurt.

Another possibility: Did we dress differently? At first, this also did not seem to provide an adequate answer. The wearing of yarmulkes in public, or showing tzitzit, had long since disappeared. Sure, most of German boys wore at times their Hitler Youth uniforms or parts of the uniform. But not all of them did so all of the time. So what gave us away?

"It must be the cap!" I said to myself.

The swastika and other Nazi symbols were everywhere. Each of the various organizations sported their own insignia, their own uniforms, and often their own distinctive cap. Youth groups, workers organizations, women's auxiliaries, sports clubs, and the like, all could be identified by their insignias and often by the clothing they were wearing. Among boys the cap marked you as "belonging." German boys liked to wear caps that, if not actually part of the Hitler Youth uniform, were made in the same style. What was definitely "out" was wearing a beret or a visor cap of the type that had been popular among workers, especially those who identified with the left. Wearing a cap other than a uniform type cap did not necessarily identify you as being Jewish, but it certainly showed that you did not "belong." And what boy likes to be marked as an outsider?

There were two possible solutions to the problem of the cap: Wear a cap similar in appearance to the uniform cap, or don't wear a cap at all. Wearing a uniform type cap posed a moral question: Not advertising being Jewish that was all right; pretending to be something else was not. It looked too much like being ashamed of being a Jew. The best solution was, therefore, not to wear a cap at all. That was all right for me, but Freddy, being religious, refused to walk around with his head uncovered. So Freddy usually wore a cap, a black visor cap, unless, as I said, it rained.

On his travels, my father often wore a black beret, or Basque cap, especially when on board ship or train. Being rather of dark complexion, when wearing his black beret he was often taken for a Spaniard. Like my father, I too had a Basque cap, but no one ever mistook me for being Spanish. With my cap, I thought I looked even more Jewish. Yet the cap, which I really didn't like, did have one advantage: It could easily be put into my pocket. So, when I went out without my parents, that's where my cap went.

Of course I knew that it wasn't the cap that gave us away, Freddy and me. But with no other handy explanation, it had to do.

Years later, as an adult, and not wearing a hat or cap of any kind, I still heard strangers remark: "You look Jewish."

I still don't know what that means.

An Almost Happy Ending

School was compulsory for the first eight years. After the completion of the first four years of elementary school, the Frankfurt school system provided a number of educational tracks: The minimum track of four years of Volks Schule (Public or Grade School); an intermediate track of six years of middle or high school for a total of ten years of school; and the higher education track of eight years of high school, or preparatory school, gymnasium for boys and lyceum for girls, for a total of twelve years. The intermediate track led to careers in business, teaching, or engineering. The higher education track prepared the student for the university.

With the of end my fourth school year approaching, my parents had to decide whether to enter me into the Jewish secular high school, the Philantropin, or keep me in the Volks Schule for four more years to complete the required eight years of school. My grades were not sufficiently high for me to gain easy admittance into high school. After some discussion my parents concluded, somewhat reluctantly I believe, that it was better for me to finish my education in grade school. Once I had completed school I could take an apprenticeship, most likely in a carpenter's shop, following the tradition of my mother's family. The year before, at the age of ten, Claire had been enrolled in the Lyceum, the high school for Jewish girls, at the Philantropin. The school was rather expensive, and perhaps there was not enough money for both Claire and me to be sent to high school. My low grades provided an argument against sending me there.

I felt deeply hurt that I had to go to a school for the not so bright. Freddy, to my chagrin, had been admitted to the Samuel Raphael Hirsch School, the high school for orthodox Jewish boys. I felt that I might as well resign myself to the fact that I was not very smart, at least not as smart as my sister. I was sure that I was a disappointment to my parents.

The classes for grades five through eight for Jewish children were held in a rather dilapidated school building in an industrial part of the city, a long distance from home. I did not like the long travel, I did not like the teachers, and I did not like any of my fellow students. So far, my school experiences had been rather miserable and I was convinced that I would never be happy in school. I enjoyed reading, especially travel books, and I liked to write. Influenced by my father's travels I decided when grown up I would be a writer of travel books. And for that, I consoled myself, I really didn't need a higher education.

Mrs. Oestreicher (I cannot recall when or how my parents met her) was a teacher in a small but prestigious private Jewish high school, the Hamann Schule. The school's goal was to provide Jewish children, boys and girls, with the high level of education required for entering a university. The school's curriculum was based on one of Germany's most prestigious preparatory schools for boys. Mrs. Oestreicher thought it was not right that my sister attended a Lyceum while I was stuck in a low level grade school.

Mrs. Oestreicher made arrangements with Mrs. Hamann, the school's owner and principal, that both my sister and I could attend her school at reduced tuition.

Thus after only a few weeks in the school for non-achievers, I became a student at a school for high achievers. The classes were small, the teachers excellent, and the children eager to learn.

Yet my parents still thought I wasn't bright enough for the university and for an academic career. But with a good high-school diploma I could gain admittance to a "Technische Hochschule" (engineering college) to pursue an engineering career. Thus my future, although somewhat disappointing to my parents, or at least to my father, seemed to have been mapped out for me.

The nearly two years at the Hamann Schule, which ended with the 1938 pogrom, were the only school years I did not consider a burden, an unenjoyable duty.

Waiting

Despite my problems in school, despite constant fear of violence, despite many stories of Jews disappearing into concentration camps, and despite the tensions caused by numerous international crises, I have good memories of the time from 1935 through most of 1938.

The enactment of the "Nurnberger Gesetze" should have swayed the Jews to exert maximum effort to get out of Germany. Instead, the new anti-Semitic laws caused only indecision and false hope. Each new crisis, and one crisis followed another, gave hope that this time the Western Democracies would put an end to Hitler's aggressions. The period was one of twilight: Not yet fully dark, there was enough light to keep illusions alive that full darkness would not descend upon us. Only few who were willing to see that the clouds that had gathered on the horizon were moving relentlessly forward.

Any belief that the German people would rebel against their criminal government quickly turned out to be but a false hope. The public appeared satisfied: Once again factories were humming and with work for everyone; breadlines had become things of the past. A German army was once again marching proudly, and the multitude enjoyed government-sponsored colorful pageants glorifying the nation. Apparently "Bread and Circuses," the policy of the Roman emperors, could still to do its magic.

Eventually we will have to leave Germany, my father said. Yet he felt no sense of urgency. He wanted to use the time he thought we had to build his business in the Middle East and North Africa. Only when that was accomplished could he assure a decent life for his family. My mother, though less sanguine than my father, followed her husband's lead.

With the discrimination becoming ever more confining, my mother tried to make life for her two children as normal as possible, while not exposing us to too much unpleasantness. Even such ordinary undertakings as shopping were no longer just ordinary. She preferred to go shopping with us in the larger department stores in the city. Dealing with department store sales personnel was much less personal than dealing with the people in the smaller suburban shops, and hence there were fewer chances for unpleasant incidents.

A few times we even went to the Zoo, although some parts of it were closed to Jews. A place that permitted us to feel just a little freer was the new international airport. There, with foreign travelers arriving and departing, the Nazis were not eager to display their nastier side. With the airport café not displaying the sign "Jews are not wanted," we indulged in ice cream and lemonade while watching airplanes land and depart.

I especially liked going to the railroad station to meet my father on his returns from abroad. Usually we waited for him at the gate, but sometimes my mother felt generous and bought tickets so we could go out on the station platform to watch the train come in.

The sounds and smells of the large station, at the time one of the largest in Europe, told of adventures and faraway places: People, jostling and pushing, rushed to catch their trains or to gain sight of just arriving friends or relatives; vendors, peddling drinks, chocolate, and other sweets, tried to make their voices heard above the din; porters, their carts loaded with luggage of all shapes and sizes, many covered with stickers from hotels in faraway places and from exotic shipping lines, threaded their way through the crowd; train dispatchers shouted their commands. My mother had to have a firm grip on my hand and drag me along or I surely would have become lost. I wished I could climb into one of the railroad coaches and let the train take me wherever it went.

The very air seemed to vibrate when the train came into the station. As the huge red painted drive wheels of the engine passed in front of us, it was just a bit frightening, smoke and steam enveloped the platform for a moment. The acid smell of burning coal mixed with the pungent odor of hot oil irritated nose and throat. But no matter, I loved it. Then came the cars: First the baggage car, followed by the sleepers with their mysteriously curtained windows; next the dining car with neatly set tables, and finally the coaches. As the train came to a halt and the doors opened, we stretched our necks trying to spot my father.

Happy to be back once again, my father spoiled his family. Instead of going home right away he took us to a café near the station, one not yet marked with the anti-Jewish sign. There we indulged in coffee and cake with lots of whipped cream before taking a taxi home.

Summer vacations brought some freedom: no school, no homework, and none of the tensions caused by the long daily trips to and from school. We went on hikes in the nearby mountains, where I enjoyed walking along lonely forest trails. There, neither the trees nor the occasional hiker we met cared that we were Jews. Or I played soccer with other Jewish boys, playing at a field where we thought no one would recognize us. And we went swimming.

When public swimming facilities became closed to Jews, the Jewish community prevailed on City Hall to open a segregated facility for the city's Jews. Cooperation between the Jewish community and the City produced one of the finest and largest swimming facilities on the Main River within city limits. Though located at the very edge of the city, for us over an hour's travel, first by bus and streetcar and then a long walk, my mother, Claire, and I went there a number of times, often together with the Sterns. The facility was shut down in 1938; nothing took its place.

It was during those years that my mother's girlhood friends, Dora and Gertrud (they were not Jewish and neither ever married) were frequent visitors at our home, but only when my father wasn't home. Both were very close to us; Claire and I called them Tante (aunt). The three women had been friends for years, dating back to their school days in Mannheim. Through all the troubled times of the persecution and war, both Dora and Gertrud remained my mother's loyal friends. Their friendship lasted to the end of their lives.

Tante Dora was the more frequent visitor. Even during the war she visited us a few times when this was rather risky. Her folks, simple working people, lived in an older part of an industrial suburb of Mannheim. The family was neither anti-Nazi nor pro-Nazi, with the exception of Tante Dora's sister who married an SS man, a flamboyant fighter pilot. (He was shot down over Stalingrad and killed.) No one in the family objected to her relationship with us, not even the SS brother-in-law.

Tante Dora's visits were always fun. She had studied voice and liked to entertain us with folk songs or arias from light operas and operettas, with my mother accompanying her on the piano. When singing folksongs she accompanied herself on the guitar. On her weekend visits, Sunday breakfasts were something special, often lasting until dinnertime. I don't remember all the things that were discussed (politics was out), but Tante Dora was always full of gossip: There were stories about her family; about people she and my mother had known during their youth; or about intrigues in the office where she worked as a typist. But when, over many cups of coffee and many cigarettes, she turned to her latest love affair, I usually lost interest.

Like Dora's family, Gertrud's also came from the working class. Her father was a stonemason. However, members of her immediate family put high value on education. They were all well-read and had many intellectual and artistic interests. Yet their political orientation did not differ much from that of Tante Dora's family.

Tante Gertrud's interests, which she shared with my mother, were literature and Greek and Roman antiquities. She wrote poetry and had a small volume of poems published. In her relationship with us she was more cautious than Tante Dora. An intellectual, she tried to stay aloof from politics.

Tante Gertrud's caution, and her insistence not to get involved in politics, was in part due to her position. She was private secretary to the Managing Director (Chief Executive) of one of Germany's major corporations. (He had been aware of her relationship with us.) After the war, while many German industry and business leaders were removed from their positions for their wartime activities and some were tried for war crimes, Tante Gertrud's boss was exonerated by the Allied War Crimes Court. He was permitted to keep his position.

During Tante Gertrud's visits, Sunday breakfast lasted nearly as long as breakfasts with Tante Dora. But instead of gossip, table conversations were about literature, art and history. Though usually way over my head, the conversations fascinated me. That I became an avid reader was partially due to Tante Gertrud's influence. At a time when my mother still despaired that I would ever learn to read, Tante Gertrude brought me books. My love for books, I'm sure, is at least partially due to her influence.

And so we waited. We waited for my father's plans to mature, or for the German people to come to their senses and depose the hooligans running their country, or for the world to take measures against the Hitler regime.

Years later I asked myself: Had the German people overthrown the Nazis, or had the world taken timely measures against them, would we have remained in Germany? By the time World War II erupted I was sufficiently alienated from the land of my birth that I could no longer see myself living there. I don't know what my parents would have done. But this is an idle question with no possible answer.

As the summer of 1938 drew to a close, the period of relative calm also came to a close. The clouds of war, no longer just a threat on the far horizon, were rapidly gathering overhead.

CHAPTER 4

PRELUDE TO DESTRUCTION

Clouds of War

Gathered around the radio our teacher had brought to the classroom, we listened with fascination to the ceremonies taking place in London, the crowning of King George VI. The pageantry seemed to belong to another age.

In December 1936 King Edward VIII abdicated and his brother assumed the throne. The coronation of George VI took place early in 1937. It was a major event in Europe, a Europe jittery with fears of war. While German and Italian "volunteer" forces were fighting in Spain on the side of the Fascist insurgents under Generalissimo Franco, the Soviet Union and international left wing groups aided the Republican government with fighters and arms. With Germany demanding in increasingly belligerent tones the reordering of the map of Europe, the civil war in Spain looked like a grand rehearsal for the war to come.

The coronation had brought together statesmen from around the world. The gathering had created hope that the world's leaders, especially those from the democracies, would seize this opportunity to begin a process leading to a more stable and peaceful world.

The deposed king gave up the throne of England for love, at first producing a lot of sympathy. But soon stories went around that King Edward's marriage to a commoner and divorcee was not the real reason for his forced abdication. According to gossip, the king was somewhat sympathetic toward Nazi Germany's aspirations, while his brother, now

King George VI, was less likely to stand in the way of a more vigorous British policy opposing the ambitions of the fascist countries. My father saw this as an indication that Great Britain had regained her moral strength, and was ready to cut the bloody dictators down to size.

In March 1938 Germany annexed Austria. The "Anschluss," Hitler's absorption of the Austrian Republic into Greater Germany, was virtually unopposed by the democratic nations of Europe. Only Fascist Italy objected, seeing herself the protector of Austria's independence. Mussolini had sworn revenge for the murder by an Austrian Nazi of the Austrian Prime Minister and Fascist leader Dollfuss in the summer of 1934. Yet soon after the Anschluss, Mussolini changed his position. Following his conquest of Ethiopia, El Duce felt ready to challenge French and British dominance in the Mediterranean, and for that he needed an ally. His pledge to punish the murderers of Dollfuss was forgotten. Already a partner with Germany in support of the Spanish Fascists, Mussolini favored an alliance with Hitler. The German-Italian "Axis" was born.

The news coming out of German-occupied Austria was disturbing. Austrian Nazis, perhaps to demonstrate their allegiance to the Fuehrer, viciously turned against the Jews. These actions could well be seen as a hint of things to come.

The "Anschlusss" was not yet history when Hitler initiated the next crisis. The Treaty of Versailles, in creating the Republic of Czechoslovakia, awarded to the new nation a mountainous area along her border with Germany, known as the Sudetenland. The Sudeten Mountains were to give the Republic defensible borders against the possible reemergence of an aggressive Germany.

Hitler now claimed this area, populated by a German majority, for Germany. The German People, raged the Fuhrer, were demanding that the injustice done by the Treaty of Versailles be rectified. The Sudeten Germans, "oppressed by the Slavic regime" and all their land, must be "returned" to the Fatherland.

In May 1938 the crisis became acute. Germany's war preparations dominated the summer: Reserves were called up, air raid drills were held, food rationing was made ready; by late summer Germany began massing troops along her Czechoslovak border. Nazi propaganda against the Czech people saturated the airwaves; newspaper pages were filled with reports of atrocities the "criminal" regime in Prague was committing against "innocent women and children." Berlin sent weapons and "volunteers" across the border to assist the "beleaguered German population" in defending themselves against their oppressors. The Government in Prague, ignoring the Army's advice to take military action against the insurgents, appealed to the League of Nations and especially to France and England. Hitler threatened war.

Although my father was skilled with his hands, gardening was not his forte. Yet he did love to putter around in the garden. If at home during spring he planted flower and vegetable seeds. Every morning, before breakfast, he was out in the garden looking for seedlings coming up. To the amusement of our neighbors he made his early morning inspections even in the rain, with an umbrella, of course. When my father wasn't home a gardener took proper care of the garden.

Spring and summer of 1938 were different. In spring our gardener failed to show up. Whether it was the international crisis or whether he no longer dared, or wanted to, work for Jews, I don't know. With fewer summer flowers, our garden looked somewhat dismal. But nature, it seemed, wished to compensate us. The climbing roses my father had planted a number of years before to screen off our back patio finally consented to bloom. The scent of the roses sweetened the air (attracting lots of bees and wasps). Our plum tree and the currant and gooseberry bushes were loaded with fruit.

With many sunny days, we enjoyed our outdoors. We didn't, of course, know that it was for the last time.

While the Nazis busied themselves vilifying the Czechs, anti-Jewish propaganda was somewhat tuned down, making life just a bit easier for us, or at least for me. Perhaps having made the alleged persecution of ethnic Germans their just cause, and trying to evoke the world's sympathies, the German government did not want to draw attention to their own persecution of a minority living in their midst.

My parents worried about a possible war and its impact on us and on the Jewish community. The toning down of the hate propaganda against the Jews would not last; war would certainly make it worse. They tried to keep these worries away from Claire and me, but this was nearly impossible. War had become the dominant topic of conversation, and not only at home. Even in school war and its possible consequences were discussed and argued about. In those tense days and weeks of the summer of 1938 my interest in history and world affairs was born. It never left me.

The radio now played an increasingly important role in our home. Much of the day it was tuned to news broadcasts. Concerts and operas, our usual evening fare, had to take second place. With the German radio merely the voice of the Ministry of Propaganda, news was just that, propaganda. My parents turned to French and other European stations.

Listening to the news took on an air of a ritual, especially when my father was home. At news time we had to be very quiet. With foreign news broadcasts frequently jammed it was at times difficult to hear clearly. I too wanted to hear what was going on, but sitting quietly for a long time was not always easy for me. Occasionally my father would miss a few words due to some noise I made. Then he would lose his temper and chase me out of the room.

The war would be over quickly, I was sure. How could the corrupt Nazis hold out for long against the combined forces of the Democracies? Didn't France have the largest army in the world and did they not have the impregnable Maginot Line? And the British, though their army was small, had the world's mightiest navy. Even Nazi propaganda admired the British military. The adults' fears I dismissed; war against Germany would end, like my favorite books, with the victory of the "good guys." How I would relish seeing the arrogant Nazis being beaten! The boys in the neighborhood would no longer dare to yell "Jew drop dead" and beat me up.

Yet war was also frightening. My mother told us stories from the first world war, about cowering in the basement listening to the whistling of falling bombs and the crashing sound of their explosions. I certainly was aware of the Sterns from our synagogue; both brothers had been maimed in the "Great War." If war came, what would the Nazis do to us, to the Jews? My father, I reassured myself, would get us out of Germany in time.

September came but war didn't. Great Britain and France, still preoccupied with problems caused by the Great War and the Great Depression and haunted by fear of communism and gas warfare, opted for appeasement. A series of meetings between Western leaders and those of Germany and Italy culminated in the now infamous Munich Conference.

There the crisis was resolved. The leaders of France, Great Britain, and Italy informed the Czechoslovak government, which had not even been invited to the conference, that they had to cede the Sudeten area to Germany.

The Czechs hesitated. Russia promised military assistance to the beleaguered nation. Poland, coveting a slice of the Republic's land promised to them by Hitler, refused Russian troops to pass through her territory. The Prague government, seeing no way out, capitulated.

"Munich" entered the dictionary meaning appeasement. Chamberlain, the British Prime Minister, and his umbrella became appeasement's symbol. The League of Nations, formed to protect its members from aggression, remained silent.

The Munich agreement delayed the outbreak of war for about a year, giving the European Democracies a year to rearm. Jews too were given one more year in which to escape from the Nazis. With little help from outside, however, far too few were able to take advantage of the reprieve. For the Jewish People "Peace In Our Time" became but a prelude to the murder of six million.

Kristallnacht

November 10, 1938, began like any other fall school day. The sun was not quite up when Claire and I left for school. As usual, my mother had to see to it that we were warmly dressed, had all our schoolbooks, and ate at least some breakfast before rushing off. We were always late and insisted that if we did not leave right away we surely would miss the bus to the streetcar station. And also as usual she handed us our midmorning snack as we ran out the door. What was different that morning from a normal early November day was my father was at home.

At the peak of the "Sudeten crisis," with war seemingly imminent, my father had been in Damascus, Syria. As he had a German passport the French authorities in Syria expelled him as an enemy alien, even though his passport was marked with a "J" (Jude). Surely the French must have known what the "J" meant; it made no difference to them. Earlier, his "J" passport had forced my father to drop Greece from his itinerary. The Greek government refused admittance to travelers having "marked" passports.

By the time he arrived home, "Munich" had happened; the crisis was over.

Being on an involuntary vacation, my father was still in bed when my sister and I went on our way, waiting for my mother to call him down for breakfast. No one had yet turned on the radio.

After the end of World War I and prior to January 1933, many Jews, especially young Jews, left Poland for the more tolerant, liberal, and democratic post-war German Republic. There they found educational and occupational opportunities not available to them in the newly independent Poland. Zionist groups had set up camps and schools to train young people in skills needed to build a Jewish homeland, Eretz Israel. Some of these potential pioneers, having found life in Germany to their liking, opted to remain in their new host country.

In September 1938, a short time after the Munich Conference had brought the world back from the brink of war Germany expelled all Polish Jews from the Reich. By end of October those who had not left "voluntarily" were put on trains to be shipped to Poland.

At the border the expellees were forced to get off the trains and walk across muddy fields the remainder of the way into Poland. Polish border guards refused to let them proceed. With the weather wet and cold, these hapless people found themselves stranded in no- man's land, without food and shelter.

Among the stranded were the parents of Herschel Grynzspan, at the time a student in Paris. On the seventh of November 1938 Herschel Grynzspan walked into the German embassy in Paris and shot a young embassy legate by the name of Ernst vom Rath.

The Nazi propaganda machine went into high gear. The murder had been committed, not by an irate young Jew, but "the Jews." Radio and newspapers screamed, in near hysterical tones, for revenge. "To their murder of Christ," Dr. Goebbels ranted, "the Jews have now added the murder of a young German."

During the night of November nine, two days after vom Rath died in Paris, the pogrom, which became known as "Kristallnacht," got underway.

When Claire and I arrived at our school, we realized something was amiss. The usual noise and chatter of students greeting each other as they made their way to the classrooms was missing. The students stood in the hallway; none had yet gone to their rooms. Most stood quietly, a few talked only in whispers. Claire and I joined our friends and classmates. One boy whispered to me that the nearby synagogue was burning.

A few teachers, all women, stood nearby, also talking in subdued voices. Finally the head of the school arrived, somewhat out of breath. She demanded quiet, though everyone had stopped talking.

"The school will be closed for the day," she announced. "Go home at once, do not loiter on the way, and make as little noise as possible. Your parents will be told when classes resume."

With that we were dismissed. That the school was closed because of a fire at the synagogue made not much sense to me. We did as we were told. Claire and I made our way home without any incidents.

Our parents were anxiously waiting for us. The first reports of trouble came from Radio Strasbourg. During late night of November ninth, the station reported, spontaneous attacks on Jews had occurred in a number of German cities. The station gave no indication of the scope of the violence.

Throughout the morning my father sat by the radio turning the dial. Perhaps he could get more details from other stations; but he had little success. Finally, and somewhat reluctantly, he turned to Radio Madrid.

In November 1938 Spain's capital, Madrid, was still in the hands of the anti-Fascist forces. Radio Madrid's newscasts consisted mostly of anti-Fascist propaganda, hence when the station reported on the scope and violence of the pogrom my parents took the reports with skepticism. As the day wore on and other non-German stations gave more detailed reports, Madrid's reports appeared to have been confirmed.

After a night of burning and looting of synagogues and Jewish-owned homes and stores by rampaging mobs led by Nazi Party officials and storm troopers, the action was now led by police, firemen, and the Gestapo. Firemen now supervised the burning of synagogues, policemen controlled the looting of Jewish stores, and the Gestapo began rounding up Jewish men.

Gestapo actions usually took place at night or in the early morning hours. Hence, when by early afternoon nothing untoward had happened to us, my mother felt it was safe to venture out to see how our Jewish community had fared.

First she went to the Sterns, who lived only about a fifteen-minute walk from us. During the night a stone had broken their living room window and the Succah in their back garden had been demolished; nothing more serious. That seemed somewhat reassuring. But early in the morning the Gestapo had taking Mr. Stern into "protective" custody.

Next my mother rushed to Heddernheim. There the Jewish community had not escaped the fury of the pogrom. Mobs had broken into Jewish homes, the kosher butcher and the synagogue. The Schwelms' home, next to the synagogue, had been wrecked: furniture had been broken, dishes smashed, linen and clothing torn to shreds. Mr Schwelm had been severely beaten.

The synagogue had been vandalized: The eight precious Torah scrolls had been thrown to the floor, trampled on and ripped apart; the Torah silver stolen. The mob had wanted to set fire to the synagogue but the local fire chief had stopped them. He was worried that adjacent half-timbered houses could catch fire. And as morning dawned, the Gestapo came to pick up Mr. Schwelm.

Now worried that the Gestapo may have picked up my father too, my mother hurried home. But at home all was serene. Yet we had not been idle. Under my father's direction, Claire and I had searched the house for anything that could possibly be considered violating one of the many Nazi decrees.

Among the fascinating items in my father's desk was a letter opener, a silver inlaid dagger from Serbia. It could be considered a weapon. My parents had once been members of a book club associated with a now outlawed left wing consumer organization. Some of our books showed the club's imprimatur. I busied myself ripping out the marked flyleaves. That done, I went to the basement to throw the dagger and the ripped out pages into the hot furnace.

I stood by the open furnace door watching the paper quickly turn to ashes and the beautiful dagger slowly turned glowing red. I had liked the dagger, its strange decorations hinting at a far-away romantic world. I buried the glowing dagger under a shovel of fresh coal. Then I went to my room and hid my Zionist flag.

During the hasty and uneasy evening meal my parents discussed possible actions: My father still had a valid travel visa for Switzerland. Perhaps he should leave at once, even that night. But, according to the radio the Swiss had closed her border with Germany; so the idea had to be dropped. Taking refuge with my mother's brothers was rejected. My parents did not want to make trouble for them. But perhaps they could take Claire and me. Giving refuge to two children may be less of a risk for them. And without children my parents could go into hiding, though it wasn't clear to me where they would go.

In the end, they decided that for the moment it was better to sit tight. Yet each of us packed a small satchel: change of clothing, a toothbrush, and other essentials. My mother thought it prudent to be ready to leave home at a moment's notice. Then we listened to some more news and waited.

Shortly before midnight a group of people assembled in front of our house, shouting: "Throw the Jews out!" Although they made threats, no stones were thrown. After the shouting had gone on for a while, my mother stepped outside to see if she could recognize any of our neighbors among the shouters. As soon as my mother opened the door, the crowd fell silent and soon left. A short time later a few children returned to shout obscenities. But they quickly grew tired of it and went away.

Eventually my parents decided it was safe for us to go to bed. I don't think they slept much that night; I fell into a deep sleep. It had been a very long day.

The Arrest

Even though school was closed, I got up early. When I came downstairs to the living room, my father was already sitting in front of the radio. I ate my breakfast in silence, afraid to disturb him. My mother made efforts to act in a normal way, although I think she was not very successful. The atmosphere was one of confused expectations: we were waiting for something to happen, hoping nothing would. If we could get through this day without incidents, I ventured to remark, perhaps the pogrom had passed us by. This produced a curt remark from my father to keep quiet.

With breakfast dishes cleared away, my parents once more examined and re- examined what they should do, could do, and what they must not do. Was there a place for us to wait out the storm? Sooner or later things had to return to some degree of normalcy.

The discussion turned to what to do once the immediate danger was past. My father suggested sending Claire and me to his aunt in Strasbourg, France as soon as borders reopened. She would surely welcome us. But would it be safe for us in France? In case of war how will the French treat refugees from Germany? Or, thinking of World War I, how deep would the Germans penetrate into France? Perhaps business friends in England or in neutral Switzerland could take the two children until arrangements could be made for us to go to Palestine. Reluctantly my father agreed to consider the United States as a possible place of refuge.

Yet after all the talking my parents could agree on only one step: Convinced that from abroad he had a better chance to make arrangements for us, my father would leave Germany as soon as it was possible to do so. In the meantime, we just had to sit and wait.

Windows were shut, curtains drawn. No one was to step outside the house, not even into the garden. Perhaps the Gestapo or the police were not aware that my father had returned from abroad. While my mother busied herself with housework my father returned to the radio to listen to the news. The volume was turned low, hoping our neighbors could not hear it.

The news was not encouraging. Arrests of Jewish men continued. If anyone in the world was doing anything to help the Jews trapped in the Third Reich, there were no signs. Perhaps it was still too soon for the nations to react.

The morning wore on, time moved slowly. I tried to do some planning of my own: If we had to flee or go into hiding, what should I take with me? Which of my favorite books? What other things? I went to my room and rummaged around, but couldn't decide what to pack. I sat on my bed to read, but for once my usual way of escape didn't work. I went around the house restlessly, cursing the Germans with the vilest curses I could think of, though I made sure my parents didn't hear me; I did not want them to find out that I knew these "bad" words. And mostly I tried to stay out of my father's way.

Late in the morning, the doorbell rang. My father turned off the radio. My mother went to answer. She took a quick glance through the glass panel alongside the front door. Two men stood at our doorstep, a policeman in uniform and behind him a man in plainclothes. Slowly, reluctantly, she opened the door.

"Is he home?" the man in plainclothes demanded, as he pushed past the policeman into the house, briefly flashing his Gestapo identity badge. He went directly to my father's study.

My father was waiting for him. After a quick body search (the idea that my father carried a weapon seemed utterly ridiculous to me) he ordered my father to pack a small suitcase with a few overnight things. My father went upstairs.

The Gestapo officer sat down at my father's desk and began to rummage through it. The policeman stood behind him, next to my mother. Both watched in silence. The policeman, an elderly man, kept glancing at my mother, shrugging his shoulders. On the wall near the desk hung a picture of my mother when she was about eighteen. The policeman, pointing at it, gave my mother an admiring smile.

I hovered near the door, just inside the room. Claire may have been standing with me, but I don't remember. I wasn't sure what was expected of me. I felt curious as I watched what was going on, at the same time feeling vaguely guilty for feeling curious and for not doing something, although I don't know what I could have done. Most likely I was expected to stay out of the way.

"Where is your gold, your foreign currency? Where do you hide your weapons, your communist propaganda?" The questions came rapid fire. The Gestapo agent never waited for answers. Probably he didn't expect any.

After rummaging through the desk for a while and not finding anything that interested him, he went to the large bookcase. He leaved through a few books, but soon lost interest. Then he discovered my father's stamp collection.

"Are there any communist stamps," he demanded, "stamps from Russia?" I think this time he did expect an answer.

My father, who had returned to the study, replied with a curt no. Impatiently the man from the Gestapo leafed through pages of stamps. Impatience seemed to be one of his trademarks. Perhaps he didn't really expect to find anything incriminating, or perhaps he didn't care whether he did or not. Satisfied that there were no communist stamps he put the collection aside. (Did he notice there were also no stamps from Nazi Germany?)

He decided it was time to go. He didn't search any of the other rooms for gold, weapons, or communist postage stamps. The three men walked out of the house, the policeman the last one to leave. As he passed by my mother, he gave one more apologetic shrug.

We stood in the open door, my mother, my sister, and I, watching in silence as the Gestapo took my father away. My eyes followed the three men walking down the street. My father, carrying his small suitcase, walked between the two officers like a criminal, I thought with a sense of disbelief. Perhaps my mother felt, like I did, that this wasn't really happening. Any moment now my father would be walking toward the house as if he had just returned from one of his travels.

Slowly, reluctantly, my mother closed the door.

My mother sprang into action. The time for lengthy discussions, for making complicated plans was gone, now it was time for decisions, and she had to make them quickly and by herself. She ordered Claire and me to put on our coats, and out we went. As we rushed down the street toward the bus stop, neighbors who saw us, and who had probably seen my father being led away, gave us only curious glances. There was no "hello," no "how are you." We rushed on.

We took the bus and the streetcar to the city. We walked, ran, to my father's office. There my mother told the people what had happened. (Only two Jews were still employed in the once Jewish firm.) The people at the office promised help. They at once called the company head office in Cologne. People there too promised to do all they could to free my father. They assured my mother that the company had some influence in Berlin. With the German mark not acceptable in international trade, Germany needed to earn foreign currency to pay for her rearmament program. The Ministry of Trade should be able to exert some pressure on behalf of my father.

With that mission accomplished, we rushed home. Perhaps there was news from my father. Nothing. After a belated and rather quick lunch my mother dashed off letters: To my father's associates in Switzerland, England, and Yugoslavia, and to relatives in France. Could they help to get Claire and me out of Germany? Two more letters: one to the American Consulate requesting an application for immigration, the other to friends in the United States. That done, we went out to mail the letters. We went together, my mother did not want to leave her children alone at home or have them go to the mailbox by themselves. Then home again. Any news from my father? Still nothing.

Toward evening, it was not yet quite dark, we heard a car pull up in front of the house. My father? The Gestapo again? We rushed to the window. To our surprise Uncle Max came up the front walk followed by two of his brothers. They had come, Uncle Max explained, to take my father to Switzerland. With his connections, he thought, he could get my father safely across the border. The three brothers had set out the previous day, but a road accident had forced them to return home. Perhaps it had been the hand of fate that had created the day's delay. Who knows what would have happened if they had been stopped by the police with my father in the car. For despite Uncle Max's assurances, the escape attempt could have gone wrong.

Having failed to take my father to safety they offered to take Claire and me with them. My mother rejected the idea. After a while they left for home.

One more time we listened to the radio. Maybe the world leaders were finally reacting to the pogrom. But there were no encouraging reports. Perhaps even now it was too soon to expect anything; or perhaps no one really cared.

A quick dinner and Claire and I were sent to bed. Only forty-eight hours had passed since the start of the pogrom.

Aftermath

The month of November, I remember as always gray, rainy, unpleasant. The blustering winds of October had stripped the trees of their foliage. Fallen leaves whirled like dervishes in the windy streets. The few garden flowers that bravely continued to bloom despite the calendar showing winter on its way fell victim to the first frosty nights. As the calendar pages flipped to the end of November nature was ready for winter.

In 1938 the dismal month of November brought more than the anticipation of winter; to Germany's Jewish community November had brought destruction and disarray: Jewish community leaders, and most Jewish men, were imprisoned; ransacked Jewish businesses were shut, stores wrecked and plundered. Jewish newspapers and magazines had stopped publication. The few synagogues not destroyed by Nazi mobs had their doors barred, schools were silent. With Jews beaten and homes vandalized, fear of violence stalked the community.

As so often in the history of our people, so in the aftermath of the November pogrom: The burden of holding families and community together fell upon the women. During the weeks following the pogrom, with husbands, brothers, and sons in the hands of the Gestapo, the women had to care for and reassure their frightened children; struggle with hostile authorities to learn the whereabouts of their men and try to gain their release; and appeal to the world for help.

With no real information available, any news tidbits about the arrested men, no matter how trivial or suspect, were welcomed and passed along. Few homes had telephones, and with the normal points of contact – synagogues, Jewish stores, the schools – unavailable, the women had to do a lot of running around. Mail was not trusted; many believed the Gestapo intercepted letters.

As the pogrom abated, contact with non-Jewish neighbors was carefully re-established. A few courageous neighbors, mostly women, passed along stories they had picked up from wives or sisters of police or SS officers. These stories provided the first real information concerning the arrested men, although much of what was learned this way was looked upon with skepticism. Even the news that the men were in concentration camps and were to be released soon was treated with caution or disbelief. More credence was given to a rumor that they were being held for ransom: The German government demanded large sums of money for their release. If the world's Jews wouldn't pay up, the men would be sent into salt mines and dangerous munitions factories.

The radio proved useless. German stations kept silent about the arrests. The reports on Radio Strasbourg, Radio Luxemburg, and the BBC were mostly rumors we had already heard. Radio Madrid, reverting to anti-fascist propaganda, told of the mass murder of Jews, stories we really didn't want to hear.

The first reliable information came when a few old and sick men were released. They confirmed that indeed the men were in concentration camps. Buchenwald, Dachau, Sachsenhausen, became familiar names.

Yet what everybody wanted to know they also didn't know: Will the men come home, and if so, when?

Toward the end of November World War I frontline veterans came home. Ruth and Freddy's father, Mr. Stern, was among the first to be released. But he could not tell us anything about my father.

Though pressed for information, the returning veterans told little. A few verbal messages from those who had to stay behind, that was all. Written messages had not been permitted. Upon their release the men had to pledge not to talk about their camp experiences. A violation of the pledge would put them back into the camps, and for the rest of their lives. Few were willing to take that risk.

Though rescue efforts remained spotty, efforts by Jewish communities and by humanitarian groups began to bear fruit. Bringing children to safety was given priority. "Kinder Transporte" – children transports – took children to Holland and England. While hundreds of Jewish children were saved from the Holocaust, hundreds of Jewish families were broken up. Many of the rescued children never saw their parents again. Freddy and Ruth Stern were among those who were brought to England and saved. Their parents did not survive.

While working for my father's release and trying to find a way for us to get out of Germany, my mother did her best to return our days to normalcy. We were used to my father being away, so his absence did not present special difficulties, at least not as far as I could see. Claire and I remained confined to the house much of the day, but again this bothered me little.

But the attempt to return to some kind of normalcy failed. The dreary month of November brought us new troubles: The suburb of Romerstadt, conceived, designed, and built by a Jew, was to be "Judenrein," cleansed of Jews. Now in addition to all her worries, my mother had to find an apartment in the city, arrange for our move, and dispose of whatever we were not be able to take with us. And this had to be accomplished by the end of month, all the time the authorities allowed us. This time my mother called upon her brothers for help. The day before the movers came, Uncle Max showed up with a truck and some help to pick up what my mother had determined we had to give away: The handsome oak furniture of my father's study, my mother's piano, our good china, my railroad set, and many other items. The furniture was sold, giving my mother badly needed cash.

The building boom of the mid and late twenties and the early thirties had failed to completely alleviate the severe housing shortage caused by World War I and the upheavals of the immediate post-war years. With the Nazi government more interested in guns than houses, the housing shortage persisted.

The City's West End, once a middle-class and upper-middle class neighborhood, had retained much of its air of gentility despite the social changes of the 1920s. Of the city's two Jewish neighborhoods, it was considered the "better" one; the East End, the other Jewish neighborhood, was working class. Yet even the "better" West End had not escaped the consequences of the lack of new home construction; even there, large apartments were forced to sub-divide.

Apartment buildings having a majority of Jewish tenants were designated "Jewish" and Jews were restricted to buildings so designated. (Non-Jews living in these buildings were not forced out.) As Jews were being expelled from some city neighborhoods and suburbs and from many smaller towns, a severe shortage of "Jewish" apartments developed. "Jewish" apartments had to be sub-divided again and again and again.

Early December 1938 we moved into one of the "sub-sub-sub-divided" West End apartments. The apartment, on the second floor, had once been luxurious. A wide glass paneled double door led from the stairway into a very large vestibule, still giving an impression of "well-to-do." But the impression was all that was left.

A long corridor connected the vestibule to three rooms in the rear of the apartment, probably at one time the bedrooms. An elderly bachelor occupied one of the rooms; the other two became our new home.

Even though we had rid ourselves of some furniture and many other things, moving from a five room house into two rooms was not all that easy. At first I had fun helping my mother setting up the rooms: trying one arrangement then another, moving things here, moving things there. Moving furniture around gave me an opportunity to show off. Though not yet quite twelve, I wanted to do all the heavy work. With my father not home I felt I was "the man in the house."

The smaller of our two rooms, with a sink and a cooking stove, was our kitchen/living room. The other, a very large room, we divided, using furniture, into two: A "bedroom" for my parents and one for my sister. I did not get a "room" of my own; I had to make my bed on the sofa in the kitchen/living room. Being the younger one I was used to taking second place. And certainly I did not need a room. I had given up many of my things when we moved. I rationalized that I had outgrown them anyway. In our new country, Eretz Israel, everything was new and I would have all new things, including a room of my own.

Nevertheless, that my sister had her own "room" did hurt a bit. At night, after we were all in bed, I could hear her and my mother discuss the day's events. To me it appeared that she had taken my father's place in his absence.

The pogrom had shattered my secure world of home. Within a few short weeks the familiar had become the past: Our home and the streets of Romerstadt; my room and the garden; the synagogue and the butcher shop in the small town of Heddernheim; the horse and wagon of the baker bringing fresh rolls in the afternoon and the young man on his motor-tricycle delivering our groceries once a week. The Sterns, the Schwelms, and all the other members of the congregation had moved away. Our small Jewish community who had taught me so much about being Jewish was no more.

Alfred Herz

A few days after we moved into the two rooms in the "Jewish" West End, the Herz family, an elderly widow and her two bachelor sons, Alfred and Kurt, moved into the front part of the trisected apartment.

The Herz's were from the city of Worms, a city rich in medieval history and legends, both Christian and Jewish. Jews probably came to this southwest German town on the Rhine River during the Roman period. Evidence suggests that Worms had a synagogue as early as the early part of the 10th century CE. A still legible tombstone in the Worms cemetery, perhaps the oldest extant Jewish cemetery in Europe, bears the date 1076. Miraculously the cemetery survived the Nazi era.

No miracle, however, had saved the twelfth-century synagogue, known as the "Mannershul," which had replaced the synagogue destroyed during the Crusades. (Early in the 1700's a women's section had been added.)

Legend tells that the famed Rashi once taught at the synagogue, although he probably never did. The historic synagogue was destroyed during the November 1938 pogrom; only the outer walls remained standing. Still visible on one of these is an indentation, kind of a niche, the subject of one of the legends:

One day, the wife of Rabbi Meir, heavy with child, was walking through the narrow lane between the synagogue and a neighboring house when she heard the sound of hoofs coming up fast behind her. Looking back she saw a rider galloping up the lane.

"Out of the way, Jew!" the rider yelled. Certain that she would be trampled to death by the horse's hoofs, there was no place for her to go to let the rider pass, she pressed her extended belly against the wall of the synagogue, hoping that she could at least save the unborn child. Miraculously the wall gave way, forming a shallow niche just deep enough to save both child and mother. In another version the woman was not the wife of a famous Rabbi but that of a poor and humble man.

I preferred the alternate version, but thought that the first version was far more realistic. Rarely have simple people been able to find a saving niche. After the war the synagogue was restored as a monument to the city's historic past. But the city's Jews are gone. On one of the synagogue's walls a plaque tells where they were murdered.

Mrs. Herz's husband had been a religious man, suspicious of all forms of learning, especially secular learning, but not excluding Jewish learning. His guides to life were hard work, complete honesty, and following Jewish laws and practices as taught by his Rabbi. He hated assimilated Western Jews and had contempt for unassimilated Eastern European Jews. These he considered not religious, but superstitious and dishonest.

A cattle dealer, Mr. Herz had earned the trust of his customers, the local farmers. In a business in which dishonesty was not uncommon, his reputation of honesty was such that the farmers persisted in conducting their business with him even after the government began to discourage doing business with Jews. Mr. Herz died before November 1938 and thus was spared seeing his once loyal customers turn against his family.

Kurt, the younger son, was a stocky man of medium height, always eager to please. Somewhat unkindly I thought of him as the "simple son" in the Passover Haggada. A hard worker, his were the manual tasks in the business: Feeding the animals, cleaning the stables, and other related labors. With all that work, he still found time to help his mother in the house. And without questioning he followed the religious lead of his father.

Alfred, a couple of years older than his brother, was the rebellious son. He was about the same height as Kurt, but rather slim; and while Kurt was usually calm Alfred was rather restless. Impatient with the narrowness of traditions, he was openly irreverent. In defiance of his father and to the dismay of his mother and of the community, he had become non-observant. Nonetheless, it was Alfred Herz who had become the mainstay of his father's cattle business. Like his father he had the farmers' confidence. Already as a very young man (at the time we met him, he was in his late thirties) his father had entrusted him with cattle buying, with negotiations of prices, and with the especially important task of ascertaining the health and quality of the beasts.

As a youngster Alfred had dreamed of becoming a veterinarian, but his father had rejected his son's ambitions. Yet in time, Alfred learned much about taking care of cattle. When a farmer's cow showed signs of poor health, it was Alfred who was consulted and not the local veterinarian. In cases of difficult calving, again the farmers preferred his assistance in trying to save both cow and calf. Alfred never charged for these services.

In contrast to his father's puritanical outlook on life, Alfred Herz believed in finding some joy in the world. He loved music, especially the music from light operas, knowing many of their fetching tunes by heart. Once Hitler was gone, he promised Claire and me he would take us to see all his favorite shows. As a consequence, and despite his importance to the business, there was a lot of hostility between father and son. During the last years of his life the senior Herz refused to speak to his son. And this is the story:

In the late twenties and into the early thirties, until the Nazis ended it all, operettas and light operas had enjoyed great popularity in Germany. Jews had been heavily involved in their financial support, as writers and producers and, of course, as audiences. Taking advantage of his business travels that took him to many parts of the country, the young Mr. Herz found time to attend performances in the larger cities. Once, while attending a performance in the city of Hamburg, it came to him that a lively tune in a popular operetta fitted the Friday evening hymn welcoming the Shabbat. When he returned home, he told the Hassan (Cantor) of their synagogue that he had heard a new melody suitable for Shabbat evening services. Of course, he did not tell that had heard the tune in an opera house. The Hassan showed interest. After listening to the melody he agreed to use it. Perhaps, he thought, his rural congregants would be impressed with his awareness of what was happening in the big cities. After practicing the tune on his violin, he was ready to introduce the melody from the large city congregations to his small rural congregation.

To the astonishment of his father, Alfred came to the synagogue that Friday evening. Alfred figured that no one in the congregation had ever heard the tune before, and he was curious to see the reaction. But he was only almost right. One member did recognize the tune, and with a great show of indignation ordered the bewildered Hassan to stop the service. Now Alfred's father understood why his son had so suddenly decided to attend a Friday evening service.

At the time of the death of the senior Herz, the cattle business had already begun to decline. Still, with the local farmers continuing to do business with them, the widow and her two sons were able to manage.

Kristallnacht brought the business to an end. Rampaging Nazi storm troopers together with local thugs broke into the house. Alfred and his elderly mother were severely beaten, while the younger brother, Kurt, was thrown out of the second floor window into the courtyard. House and stables were looted. And whatever the thugs couldn't take they smashed. And not one of the friendly farmers came to their aid.

With broken bones and broken furniture, scared and hurting, old Mrs. Herz and her two sons arrived in Frankfurt. It was to Alfred that his mother and younger brother looked to take charge and rebuild their lives.

Alfred, however, was suffering from stomach ulcers, aggravated by vicious kicks to the stomach from jackbooted storm troopers. There were many days and especially nights when Alfred was in terrible pain.

I must not conclude this story without first paying tribute to a young German doctor. He came to the aid of the hurt and sick Herz family, treating them free of charge, often providing needed medication at his own expense. Resisting heavy pressure, the doctor continued to attend to the sick in the Jewish community. The Nazis finally solved their problem by having him called to military service.

Despite our own problems and her anxiety about my father, still in a concentration camp, my mother aided the Herz's in their distress and helped them settle into their apartment. While Mrs. Herz and her sons were recovering from their injuries. we did their shopping and helped them in many other ways. Several times, awakened in the middle of the night by their screams from nightmares and pain, my mother rushed to their apartment to calm them and give them their medicine. My job was to run to the pharmacy to pick up prescriptions the doctor had left for them. I hated that. The pharmacist was not very friendly, and many times local boys beat me up on my way to or from the pharmacy.

At first Claire and I did not like Alfred Herz, although I cannot now say why. Perhaps I thought his obvious suffering from pain wasn't manly; I wasn't permitted to complain when I was beaten up by the boys in the street; or perhaps it was his mannerism, so different from the assertiveness of my father or even of Mr. Stern. Yet in time his indomitable spirit and the support he gave us when we needed it forged a friendship between us that lasted until the Shoah brought it to an end.

The Pledge

He was a big heavyset man, easily noticed. He sat quietly in his seat, apparently absorbed in prayers or in his thoughts. He rose when standing was called for and sat down again at the appropriate time. And though on Shabbat he always sat in front of me, I had never heard his voice.

Not that the synagogue had assigned seats. But Shabbat morning services were always crowded and most of the men preferred to sit in the same seat every week. This avoided disputes, and more importantly, it gave assurance that one knew who occupied the adjacent seats. A stranger was looked upon with suspicion; he could well be a Gestapo informer. The fear of informers was not baseless. A few Jews had turned to informing on their fellow Jews. Some did so because they were being blackmailed by the Gestapo; others thought they could buy themselves favors from their oppressor.

Frankfurt's West End had two large synagogues: The Liberal (Reform) West End Synagogue and the Orthodox Unterlindau. A few months after the pogrom, the Jewish community restored the Unterlindau and repaired the fire-damaged roof of the West End Synagogue. The Gestapo then gave permission to hold services: Orthodox services in the Unterlindau and Reform Shabbat morning services in the school auditorium. The West End Synagogue remained closed.

Influenced by the anticipation of my Bar Mitzvah, I attended Shabbat services rather regularly, and I chose to go to the orthodox synagogue. At times I even went to weekday morning minyans, even though this meant getting out of bed very early. My "religious" phase didn't last very long, only about a year. It faded quickly after my Bar Mitzvah.

But it had not been merely my forthcoming Bar Mitzvah that made me turn to the synagogue. I felt a need to identify more closely with the Jewish community, an affirmation of sorts that, contrary to the incessant hate propaganda, being Jewish was good. There weren't many opportunities to openly demonstrate one's allegiance to being Jewish. Attending orthodox services was one of the few still left. Reform just didn't seem Jewish enough to make the point. Or perhaps it was nothing more than one of those phases children often go through while growing up.

Names, sites, places often turn into symbols, and Frankfurt's Festhalle (Festival Hall) became such a symbol. The Festhalle, a large complex for mass rallies, sports events, exhibits, and circuses, now evokes the image of masses of Jewish men being assembled to be shipped off to concentration camps. And on this November day, the Festhalle became a symbol of defiance as it witnessed a great, and unplanned, performance.

The men arrested during the pogrom were assembled at the Festhalle prior to being shipped off to concentration camps. Names, age, addresses, and other personal data were verified, and some of the men were interrogated about business or other activities. The process was slow; the detainees had to stand for hours without drink or food. The rather bored Gestapo and SS officers had plenty of opportunity to harass the men, and they did not let the opportunity go unused. The questioning also did do some good: Overzealous officers had brought in boys younger than eighteen and old men barely able to walk. These were now let go.

Among the men brought to the Festhalle was a former basso from the

Frankfurt Opera. His interrogators, having learned the man's identity, decided to break their boredom with some fun. Taunting him about his past fame, they demanded a performance. Pointing at the assembled people. they told him that this was the first time his "audience" was unable to walk out on him.

He refused. His refusal spurred his tormentors on to further taunting. As he continued to refuse, ridicule turned into threats. Finally, one of the higher-ranked officers had enough of this game. He made the basso an offer: "Sing, and you will be set free. If you don't, who knows what will happen to you."

The basso gave in. But first he made a pledge: This would be the last performance of his life; never would he sing again. And so he stood in front of his tormentors and his captive audience of thousands and sang.

For his "performance" he chose the aria of Sarastro, the high priest in Mozart's "Zauberfloete" (The Magic Flute). The priest, proclaiming love for all mankind, urges forgiveness for one's enemies. Dismissing treachery and revenge as unworthy, the priest stretches forth a helping hand to those unable to live according to these high ideals. Those, however, unwilling to accept these teachings joyfully, the priest declares in the aria's final words, do not deserve to be counted among humanity. Witnesses reported that his powerful voice filled the huge hall.

It was a great act of defiance. In throwing their inhumanity into their faces, he could well have expected the wrath of the Gestapo. Some of the older policemen on duty hid their faces so not to reveal the tears in their eyes. Even the coarse SS men fell silent; and the Gestapo for once kept their word to a Jew: They let the Basso go.

At first I admired this act of defiance; but then came second thoughts: Why had the opera star not left Germany when it had still been possible? Taking advantage of their reputation many artists, scientists, and other intellectuals escaped from the Nazi tyranny by going to another country.

But there had also been those whose faith in German "Kultur," admired around the world, blinded them to reality. They believed the German people's pride in their country's cultural achievements would bring this barbarism quickly to an end. Faith in Germany's "Kultur" did cost many their lives.

My father told of an encounter in Haifa with a Jewish doctor from

Germany. The man, a Zionist, well educated, bemoaned the lack of culture outside his native land. He wanted to transplant Germany's high culture into his new country, Eretz Israel. But this admiration for Germany was not confined to German Jews. Many around the world, Jews and non-Jews, saw in Germany only the land of Goethe and Beethoven.

Ridiculing this faith in Germany, my father delighted in reading aloud, mostly to my mother, passages from Nietzsche. My father had bought his Nietzsche in Switzerland. It was not one of the expurgated versions sold in Germany. In some of his critical essays, this German philosopher, much admired by the Nazis, treated the German people with sarcasm, even contempt. When he spoke of the "Herrenvolk" (Master Race) it was not the Germans he had in mind: The German people, Nietzsche wrote, were incapable of playing a leading role in the world.

Stranded

Barely a month had passed since the "Kristallnacht" had interrupted our life and destroyed many of our illusions. Settled into our two rooms in a "Jewish" building many of life's routines began to return. I have few clear memories of the months we lived in the two rooms, and few of those are pleasant.

In spite of all the problems confronting my mother, she tried hard to turn the two rooms into "home" and create for her children a feeling of normalcy. Of course Claire and I had to help with household chores: washing and drying dishes, dusting, vacuum cleaning, etc. We did most of our jobs willingly, but without enthusiasm.

One job, however, did cause friction between my mother and me: Taking out the trash before bedtime. "Back home" I hadn't minded taking out the trash in the evening. Walking down the dark garden path to its very end where the municipal garbage bins stood, I had let my imagination roam. I didn't just walk in a garden, but along a jungle trail with all kinds of interesting plants along the way and strange creatures lurking in the dark. Now I hated taking down the trash. No longer did I encounter strange things on the way that stimulated my imagination, but strangers, residents of the building, to whom I had to be friendly. Nearly every evening my mother and I had a fight: I wanted to wait till morning, while my mother insisted it had to be done before I went to bed.

Late morning, December 8, 1938: Jewish schools had not yet reopened. Claire and I were at home with my mother. The doorbell rang, three rings. Few people knew our new address, so who could be calling on us? The ringing had certainly been for us: One ring for the old bachelor, two rings for the front apartment, the Herz family, and three rings for us. My mother went to the entrance hall to see who rang, Claire and I trailing behind. She opened the door and gasped. Looking past her, I saw a strange looking man standing at the threshold.

In my eyes my father had always appeared as a very respectable figure: Tall, important looking, self-assured, sun-tanned, a full mustache, well dressed. The man at our door was nothing like that: His head was shaven, his face, unadorned by a mustache, was stubbly and ashen gray. His suit was dirty and did not fit him very well. A terrible odor came from him. An air of uncertainty was about him.

Was this my father? I was in shock. My mother must have sensed my reaction, for she quickly made me run back to the apartment to do something or get something, though I can't recall what. She and my father walked more slowly down the long corridor to our rooms.

While my father took a bath in the one bathroom we shared with the other families on the floor, my mother finished baking the planned birthday cake. We had a double celebration, my sister's birthday and my father's safe return.

Like other released prisoners my father didn't tell much about his experiences in the camp, though gradually a few details did emerge:

At Buchenwald concentration camp, where my father had been sent, water for the prisoners was strictly rationed. With barely enough for drinking, washing oneself was limited to the barest necessity. Laundering one's clothing, or rather rinsing it since the inmates had no soap, too had to be suspended. Apparently the guards at the camp didn't care how dirty the men became; as everyone knows, Jews are dirty.

My father's group had included two young men, barely eighteen. Some of the older men, including my father, gave some of their meager food rations to the always-hungry youngsters. My father, who had only one partial kidney, received an extra ration of water on the camp doctor's recommendation. He took a chance with his health and gave his extra water to the two boys.

When released, my father was given a train ticket to Frankfurt and a warning: "Be out of Germany within two weeks or you'll be back in the camp, this time for life." Unaware of our eviction from Romerstadt my father went directly to our former home. Finding the house locked and empty he went to the local police station. There he received our new address.

With the world teetering at the edge of war, clearing the many hurdles that obstructed the way out of Germany became ever more difficult. Certainly it was not possible for us to leave together, not within two weeks. Getting my father to safety was, of course, most important. He also thought that from outside he had a better chance to get his family out quickly.

He still had a valid visa for Switzerland and could leave immediately. Yet he decided to take the risk and delay his departure by two weeks. This permitted his employer, who was willing to help, to arrange a three-month business trip to Cyprus, Egypt, and Iraq, countries that played a role in his plans for our future. The trip would also keep him on salary for at least that length of time and hopefully give him the opportunity to arrange for the escape of his family.

These were busy days for my father. To give the trip legitimacy, a collection of merchandise samples had to be prepared, meetings with customers had to be arranged, prices established. And he had to obtain police permission to travel to the city of Cologne, where the company's headquarters were located. And so, my 12th birthday, January nine, was forgotten.

"Couldn't you stay home for my birthday?" I pleaded. "You were home for Claire's birthdays."

This produced an angry response from my father. He would have slapped me had my mother not intervened. Of course my request was rather childish. Yet all my pent up resentments, past and present, were compressed in my remark: Why hadn't we left Germany a long time ago? Why did I have to put up with being beaten up in the street? Why did my sister have the larger room in our home and even now she had a bed and a "room" while I had to sleep on the couch in the living room? How could my father save us from the Nazis if he couldn't even postpone his trip for a few days?

What I saw was that he was leaving on a business trip just as usual, while I didn't even have a proper home. Perhaps my disappointment also reflected my mother's unspoken skepticism that my father could get us out of Germany before war closed all doors.

On January 13th my father left for Switzerland on his way to the Middle East. I did not see him again until March 1947, eight years later.

At first my father's letters from Egypt were encouraging. But soon problems developed. In the increasingly tense atmosphere, his German passport made it difficult for him to move freely, though he did make a short trip to Iraq.

A family reunion in Egypt, even for a short time, had to be ruled out. Egypt did not grant visas to refugees unless they had lots of money. Going to Palestine too had to be dismissed; Britain had shut the door to Jewish refugees. There was one hope left: The island of Cyprus.

My father asked a business friend in Cyprus, Mr. Kyriakides, for help. Mr. Kyriakides willingly obliged. He suggested bringing my mother and her two children to Cyprus as his houseguests. Once the three of us were in Cyprus, my father would make arrangement for Claire and me to go "temporarily" to Palestine to attend school. This the British authorities permitted. Without children my mother could obtain a visa to Egypt to visit her husband. Once this had been done, sufficient time should have been gained to work on a more permanent arrangement.

Once a month the British governor invited prominent Cypriot business leaders to Government House to discuss the island's economy and other local issues over dinner. Mr. Kyriakides, a frequent guest at these dinners, thought the monthly dinner presented an opportunity to enlist the governor's help in expediting visas for the three of us. Friends of my father's on a Moshav in Eretz Israel were ready to make arrangements for Claire and me to go school there. Everything seemed in place; all we had to do was to wait for the necessary papers to arrive. I was eager to start packing

To go to Cyprus, to Eretz Israel, perhaps to Egypt and see the pyramids! I felt superior to children who had only one choice: America. Stories circulating in our community told of difficulties refugees were encountering in the United States. Immigrant women had to work in factories or clean other people's homes for leftover food to feed their families. I was horrified: my mother washing other people's laundry, scrubbing their floors, and we having to live on food other people threw away? That would never happen to us: my father knew how to take proper care of his family.

In March 1939, as Germany dismantled the Republic of Czechoslovakia, Hitler readied his next move: Political and territorial demands on Poland. The Munich arrangement for "Peace in Our Time" was crumpling fast. This time no hasty conferences were called to save the peace: London prepared for war. Cyprus, placed under military control, was declared a closed military zone. And with peace unraveling, our plan for escaping from Nazi Germany also unraveled.

I suspect my mother never had much faith in my father's plans. Not saying much to her children, she kept working on an alternative: going to the United States of America. But this too seemed rather hopeless. She applied for an interview at the US consulate, the essential first step in the lengthy process leading to an immigration visa. The appointment she received was three years hence. Even with war threatening, the US consulate in Stuttgart, the consulate to which we had to apply, failed to speed up the procedure. (US consulates in Berlin and Cologne were more helpful. The State Department insisted that applications for immigration must be processed at the nearest consulate.) There was little chance Hitler would keep the peace for that long.

After my father left we rearranged the two rooms, making them just a bit more comfortable for the three of us. Claire moved in with my mother, taking my father's bed, while I took my sister's "bedroom."

In the meantime Jewish schools reopened. Claire and I returned to the school of Mrs. Hamann, but the school was no longer what it had been. Some students had left the country, and several of the male teachers had not yet returned from concentration camps. The school's curriculum too changed: Academic subjects were dropped in favor of more practical ones, subjects which presumably could be of help in starting a new life elsewhere. English took on highest priority. But by the end of the school year Mrs. Hamann had given up; the school closed its doors.

Not unexpectedly my father lost his job. Management had done its best to keep him on the payroll as long as possible. But with the increase in preparations for war, Germany's trade with the Balkans and the Middle

East was rapidly drying up. The company could no longer justify employing a Jew. The lack of an income now was added to my parents' woes. With war nearly a certainty and with no hope for getting out of Germany in time, our fortune had hit rock bottom.

For my mother, the situation was desperate. She did receive some financial help from relatives but this could tide us over for only a short time. But there was no money for school – schools were not tuition free – so she broke the law and kept Claire and me home; nor was there money for paying rent. The Frankfurt Jewish community, already overburdened with problems, could not help.

With reluctance my mother considered breaking up the family. Claire and I would live with her brothers' families while she reconverted to Christianity so she could get a job. Once established, she could take Claire and me back. But this meant giving up being Jewish and that, she thought, would not be good for her children. So she dropped the idea.

Just as we were stranded in Germany, my father was stranded in Egypt. But in his case, war came to his rescue. Fluent in German and French, and with a smattering of English, the British intelligence services recruited him for reviewing German mail that had ended up in British hands. He quickly advanced to section supervisor.

Unaware of these developments we still believed, or wanted to believe, that his business activities were continuing. How else could he take care of us once the war was over and provide a good life for us outside Germany?

Giving up was not my mother's way. Having rejected breaking up the family, she now made a fateful decision: Our family's fate was tied irrevocably to the fate of the Jews in Germany. And so she set about making a new life for us within that community.

* * * *

As the winter of 1938/39 turned to spring, my mother had succeeded in making new arrangements for us, arrangements she hoped would see us through until Germany's defeat. That Germany would eventually be defeated, none of us dared to doubt.

PART II

THE CLOSING DOOR (1939-1941)

CHAPTER 5

THE HOUSE OF MRS. LEVY

The Arrangement

The House of Mrs. Levy fitted well into the neighborhood in which it stood. Located at the intersection of a busy thoroughfare and a less-traveled residential street a short distance from the Frankfurt Opera, it projected quiet elegance. The five-story building was rather typical of the upper middle class residences in this part of the city. They date mostly from the period between the Franco-Prussian war of 1870/71 and the beginning of World War I, a period of growing prosperity for the German middle class. This newfound prosperity was a result of the emergence of German industry and trade as important factors in the world economy. German business spread German wares around the world, German shipping lines plied the oceans, and German products were gaining a reputation for quality. The City of Frankfurt had played an important role in the expansion of the country's international trade and its Jewish citizens, despite lingering anti-Semitism, had played a key part in the city's economic growth.

Mrs. Levy's husband, an investment banker, made his fortune during the years of instability that followed World War I. Apparently a shrewd businessman, he made a considerable amount of money, both during the runaway inflation and the subsequent fiscal restructuring. Even when, in 1929, the world's economy collapsed and the resulting depression kept the world in its grip for several years, Mr. Levy continued to make money. Inevitably his success led to talk that his business practices went at times beyond what was strictly ethical or even legal. Whether this talk had any foundation in truth, or whether it was just envy or vicious anti-Semitic gossip, I wouldn't know.

The high rate of unemployment and long bread lines had turned the political climate in Germany away from the freewheeling and dealing prevalent in many business circles during the period of the Weimar Republic. When political parties on the far right gained strength, and they singled out Jewish businessmen as the culprits in the economic collapse, Mr. Levy thought it prudent to leave Germany. He departed for the United States, leaving his wife behind (I know of no children) to cope with the developments as best she could and defend, if possible, that portion of their fortune he had been unable to transfer out of the country.

Apparently Mrs. Levy had managed quite well. She succeeded in holding on to her property and to some of the remaining money, and she did this at a time when the Nazis were busy plundering the Jews of what they possessed. Her apparent immunity was such that even the pogrom of November 1938 didn't touch her; the rampages against the Jews bypassed her house. How she was able to achieve all this was well beyond my comprehension. Having seen Mrs. Levy operate and manipulate people, her success really shouldn't have been all that astonishing. I always stood somewhat in awe of Mrs. Levy.

Before the Nazis "cleansed" German culture from "alien," meaning Jewish, influences, Mrs. Levy had been an impresario at the Frankfurt Opera. When Jews were purged from German cultural life, she too lost her position. Mrs. Levy was not a person willing to remain idle for very long. With the investment bank closed, Mrs. Levy converted the offices of the bank, on the ground floor of her house, into rooms for boarders. Her boarders, retired Jewish personnel from the Opera and Theater, were people with enough money to pay what Mrs. Levy charged. One operation, however, was not enough. Other rooms in the spacious house were converted into classrooms, and Mrs. Levy opened a private school, The Heinemann Institute.

How my mother met Mrs. Levy and entered into her orbit I do not recall, or perhaps I didn't really know. With hopes for leaving Germany in the near future having been dashed and with my father no longer able to support his family, my mother, rejecting breaking up the family, had to find a way to sustain the three of us until it was possible to leave Germany. Hopefully, the world crisis would abate long enough to provide us with a window of escape. The arrangements she made with Mrs. Levy were to give us the needed respite. In spring of 1939 we moved into the house of Mrs. Levy.

At first my mother worked as general help, but soon Mrs. Levy placed her in charge of the complex household. In return for her services she received a small cash payment, we were given an apartment in the attic rent-free, and Claire and I attended Mrs. Levy's school without paying, the tuition also being considered part of my mother's remuneration. My mother's duties included supervising the help, assisting in the kitchen, and even cleaning toilets if the regular cleaning lady fell behind in her tasks. Together with the cook, my mother assisted Mrs. Levy in planning the daily meals for the boarders and other members of the household.

Claire and I too had to do our share. Claire helped my mother in the kitchen and with various household tasks. Keeping the yard and the sidewalk swept, taking care of the hot water furnace and later, during winter, the heat, made up my assignments. In addition I had to be available to run errands for the boarders. The three of us were certainly kept busy.

For us to live in her house and attend her school had several advantages for Mrs. Levy: We were available twenty-four hours a day, seven days a week. The tasks Mrs. Levy kept finding for Claire and me usually took precedence over attending classes.

I didn't mind the work. Sweeping the yard and sidewalk was boring but not strenuous; it gave me plenty of time to daydream. Taking care of the furnace was the job I liked best. At times, after shoveling fresh coal into the furnace, I stood for a moment at the open furnace door watching as little blue flames danced their ballet on top of the fresh coals as they heated up. Aware that keeping the fire door open was wasteful, and taking pride in doing my job well, I reluctantly closed the door to return to my schoolwork or some other task Mrs. Levy had for me. I would have liked to sleep a little longer in the morning and not get up so early to tend the furnace even before I had breakfast. Sometimes I did oversleep; then my mother had to do my job.

Mrs. Levy collected people. Her collection included her boarders, employees who came daily to do their jobs in the house or the school or both, and some whose roles were not as clearly defined. The majority of Mrs. Levy's people had been associated with the Opera or the Theater. No longer able to find employment in their profession, they found Mrs. Levy ready to help.

Mrs. Levy did not give anything away for free. All or nearly all the people in her house were in some way of use to her. Although most appeared grateful, a persistent but not openly expressed opinion held that she was merely exploiting people for her own ends. Yet I sincerely believe that on final judgment day the good she did will far outweigh all her selfish motives.

Among the boarders was a well-known opera star; that is, well known before the Nazis had ended her career. In the Levy household, however, she was still a star. The best room had been assigned to her and she was permitted to have her meals served there rather than eat in the common dining room. Although I can no longer recall her name I remember her quite well. She was a little old lady with very curly hair. She accepted her special treatment with royal grace. She had many errands for me, though I cannot recall what these involved.

I disliked running errands for the boarders. Even tips, or an occasional present, didn't appease me. So I tried to avoid the boarders as much as possible. My obstinacy became an irritant between my mother and me. But it wasn't the only irritant.

In the past Mrs. Levy's school may have provided a good education. However, when Claire and I became students there, her "Institute," as she called the school, had become a farce, a school in name only. The "Institute" had few students and few qualified teachers. How Mrs. Levy had managed to keep her license to run a school is difficult to understand. The government, to be sure, cared little whether Jewish children learned anything or not. But why did the Jewish community allow the school to continue to operate?

Of the school's so-called teachers I remember three, all former members of the Opera. An opera singer was our music teacher. I am sure she had a beautiful voice, but she was not a teacher. She and I feuded constantly. Insisting that I had a terrible voice, she asked me not to participate in singing. Of course I resented this. Being rather bored in class I became disruptive and disrespectful. My behavior became so bad that my mother had to be called to discipline me, further increasing the tension between my mother and me.

I rather liked our art teacher, a former costume designer at the opera house. She thought I had talent. Impressed with her art of costume and clothing design, I resolved to become fashion designer when I grew up. The third of the teachers I can recall was little Mr. Heiman. He deserves a story all of his own.

My mother didn't have much time off from work; even Shabbat was a busy day for her. Although most housework ceased, the kitchen was especially busy. Shabbat dinner was more elaborate and formal. Only Sunday afternoons did my mother have some free time; then, with a few hours to ourselves, we were an almost normal family.

Following lunch, and with her work done for the day at least until supper time, my mother came upstairs to our attic apartment, bringing with her a few slices of cake from the Shabbat table she had put aside for us. Sitting in the small living room around our large dining room table we had brought with us from our home in Romerstadt, we enjoyed coffee and cake and talked or listened to the radio. This "coffee," though not real coffee but roasted grains, succeeded in evoking the "good old days" of relaxed Shabbat and Sunday afternoons.

(With Germany's economy on war footing, real coffee was no longer available. But thanks to an arrangement my father had made, on rare occasions we did enjoy real coffee. Once in a while his former Swiss business partner would mail us a package of cheese, chocolate, and a small amount of coffee.)

Our friendship with old Mrs. Herz and her two bachelor sons, Alfred and Kurt, which began in the shared apartment in the West End following the November pogrom, now deepened. After recovering from the severe beating he had received during the pogrom, Alfred had become our steady guest during our Sunday afternoon time off. Following our move to the House of Mrs. Levy, his visits became a "tradition." Only extraordinary circumstances could make us skip a Sunday afternoon. We talked about what was going on in the community, and exchanged news and rumors about the present and stories from the past. To dispel the gloom that so often hovered over us like an unwelcome specter, Mr. Herz entertained us with humorous stories from his travels as a cattle dealer.

Sunday afternoons were quiet oases, a calming moment in the struggles of the week, a small reassurance that life was not all bad. Yet these afternoons were also a reminder of what I had lost and of what I had imagined life could have been if we had escaped Germany in time. And so at times I rebelled against what was happening to me. I wanted to be rid of my responsibilities, wanted to be a child again free to play.

Once again I wanted to feel the stillness of the early summer mornings, a stillness interrupted now and again by the chirping of a bird, the buzz of a bee just passing by. Once again I wanted to smell the sweetness of the summer blossoms drifting into the open window of my room. And most of all, I wanted once again to have a home.

Interesting People

Mrs. Levy's house was full of interesting people: The boarders, the employees who came daily to do their jobs in the house or the school or both, and a few who were neither residents nor employees. All, in some way, had their life interrupted by the Nazi regime.

How Mrs. Kahn and her deaf-mute daughter – she was in her early twenties – fitted into the Levy household I don't know. They did not live in the house, nor were they employees of Mrs. Levy. The daughter did occasionally help out in the kitchen and at times served meals to the residents; but most of the time she just hung around. What her mother did at Mrs. Levy's I never figured out.

Towards the end of World War I a new form of warfare was introduced: Air raids on cities. One evening, so the gossip went, Mrs. Kahn, then sixteen years old, was alone in her home with her uncle when an air alert was sounded. Uncle and niece went down into the basement shelter. Nine months later the girl gave birth to a deaf-mute baby. I never quite believed this story, dismissing it as just a morality tale, the meaning of which wasn't at all clear to me.

Miss Kahn appeared always cheerful despite her disabilities. She made herself understood using sign language and by making peculiar throaty sounds, which most people in the house had learned to interpret. Taking advantage of not always being immediately understood, she was given to playing tricks on the unsuspecting, and occasionally did other, mostly harmless, mischief. Yet some of the time, I thought, the mischief was not totally intentional.

And then there was Mr. Bender. Mr. Bender had no useful function in the household other than that of being Mrs. Levy's lover. Their relationship posed a few problems. For a starter, Mr. Bender was not Jewish. Sexual relations between a Jew and a non-Jew – if not married to each other – violated Nazi Germany's racial laws. The punishment for a violation ("Rassen Schande" – Racial Shame – was the term used) was the concentration camp for the Jewish partner, and for the non-Jewish partner, jail. To make the story read even more like a plot from a novel, Mr. Bender was married and his wife was Jewish. And even if that was not enough of a complication, Mr. Bender liked young girls. This habit of his was to become a real problem in the House of Mrs. Levy.

Mr. Bender, a tall and handsome man, had earned a very brief footnote in the history of the immediate post-World War I period in Germany. Following the armistice in 1918, the German Empire collapsed and the Kaiser fled the country. Chaos spread through the land. Provinces of the former empire hastily established confederations, declaring their independence from the newly formed Republic of Germany. Many of these mini-states printed their own money, collected taxes, established courts of law, and some even organized their own armies.

A discharged army officer, Mr. Bender collected a few fellow ex-officers and a troop of leaderless soldiers still willing to take orders from officers of the defunct Imperial Army. With his troops, Mr. Bender marched on Darmstadt, a city southwest of Frankfurt, seized city hall and proclaimed the "Independent State of Hessen-Darmstadt," with himself as president. (Before the unification of Germany in 1871 there did exist a principality by that name.) After ruling his "state" for about two weeks he was arrested, convicted of sedition and jailed.

(A pre-1933 German novel, "The Captain of Koepernick" tells of a similar plot. The fictional story took place in a small town near Berlin. Apparently Mr. Bender's coup was not such an unusual event in those days. The Nazi banned the novel.)

The courts of the Republic treated former officers of the Imperial Army with leniency, and Mr. Bender did not remain in jail for very long.

However, the courts did ban him from entering politics again. Mr. Bender had to find new things to do.

First he married money, not an uncommon practice among Imperial Army officers. What was uncommon was that the woman he married was Jewish, though she did come from a wealthy assimilated family. Having thus achieved a degree of financial security, he proceeded to indulge in new hobbies: Writing and lecturing on astrology, and after Hitler came to power, chasing after young girls, preferably in their mid-teens. It was not likely that his Jewish wife would make trouble. Though attractive, Mrs. Levy wasn't that young anymore. But I'm sure that her money compensated for her age.

Miss Kahn openly suggesting going to bed with Mr. Bender. Not that she was enamored with him she was just curious why people made so much fuss about sex. She thought he would do for her to find out. Was she serious, or was this just another instance of her peculiar sense of humor? Mrs. Levy did not think this was very funny and tried not to give the two any opportunities. Mr. Bender also appeared to be trying to avoid Miss Kahn. Most likely he did not wish to annoy Mrs. Levy, or perhaps he was more pretense than action.

I paid no attention to Mr. Bender's predilection of chasing after young girls, nor did his past political activities or his present involvement with Mrs. Levy interest me.

What did interest me was Mr. Bender's cosmology. The universe, he explained, is a hollow sphere or shell without an outside. The inner surface was the surface of the earth, while the sun, the moon, and the planets, as well as all the stars, filled the space within sphere. The vast distances of the universe, as computed by "conventional" astronomers, were merely optical illusions.

I thought that his theory was pure nonsense. As had become my wont, I turned to books to find arguments against it, only to find out how little I knew. So in a way his crazy ideas stimulated my interest in science and mathematics.

Of course, there was tension between Mrs. Levy and Mrs. Bender. Though Mrs. Bender was not part of Mrs. Levy's entourage, she frequently came to the house. Maybe she hoped that she could prevent her husband from spending time in Mrs. Levy's bedroom. Mrs. Levy never ordered her out of the house. Occasionally she was even invited to the dinner table. Circumstances, however, moved against Mrs. Bender. When nightly curfew was imposed on Jews, she was forced to return home early in the evening, while her husband, not being Jewish, could stay away from home as late as he pleased. Some evenings my mother had to take a mid-night snack for two to Mrs. Levy's private apartment.

As the summer of 1939 drew to a close, war became ever more a certainty. And when it came, the many changes it brought, and especially to the Jewish community, did not pass over the House of Mrs. Levy.

War

In September 1939 Germany invaded Poland. World War II had begun. What we had hoped for, and feared, finally happened: England and France had decided to challenge German expansionism. How long would this war last? How quickly would the Nazi regime collapse?

Poland's army was no match for the Wehrmacht. The Polish defenses were quickly breached by German armor, while the German Air Force, the pride of the Nazi regime, established a new high for brutal warfare: Indiscriminate bombing of cities from the air.

We paid little attention to the fighting in Poland. We did listen to the daily war bulletins, but it was not the war in the East that interested us, but the war in the West. With Germany fully engaged in the conquest of Poland, we expected action by France and Great Britain. Apparently so did the Germans. Germany withdrew her troops from the border into the fortifications known as the "Westwall." French troops did indeed cross the border occupying a number of evacuated German towns and villages. That done, they halted.

For years the radio had been our main source of information from the world out side Germany. Freedom of the press had died in Germany with the Enabling Act of 1933, the decree that placed all news media under the control of the Ministry of Propaganda. To learn what was happening in the world, we had to turn to non-German radio stations. Radio Strasbourg was my father's favorite station. News broadcasts were in French and German.

Occasionally we also listened to Radio Luxembourg, which broadcasted in three languages, German, French, and English, and to the BBC.

My parents had bought their first radio in 1929. With the use of an outdoor antenna we were able to receive stations from the remotest corners of the world. However, progress in technology had brought problems. By 1937, a few of the most critical vacuum tubes had become weak, and reception, except for local stations, had become difficult. Replacement tubes were no longer available.

Our conspicuous outdoor antenna was a clear give-away that our listening was not confined to local stations. My father was afraid that this was no longer safe for us; a new radio had become a necessity.

This was a simple enough problem in normal times, but these were not normal times.

No longer could we just walk into a store to buy a radio. More and more stores, especially the better stores, displayed the sign: "Jews not wanted here." And this included the stores that carried the type of radio my father wanted. Of course, my parents could have taken the risk and gone into a store that displayed the anti-Jewish sign. But in the prevailing atmosphere of fear and suspicion it was more prudent not to draw attention to oneself. The type of radio my father was looking for would without doubt have aroused the curiosity of the store clerk.

Mr. F, our Nazi neighbor in Romerstadt, had been fascinated by our old radio and would have liked to try his hand at rebuilding it. Though well acquainted with the city's radio and hobby shops he too found it impossible to get the needed replacements. Understanding our situation only too well, Mr. F surprised us by offering to obtain a radio for us. He had good connections, he said, and could get us an excellent set, and at a reduced price. So he did, and we got just what my father had wanted.

As tension grew in the world, the German government increasingly discouraged listening to foreign broadcasts. No longer could we just turn on the radio at news time; listening to the news became a ritual. Windows were closed, the volume turned low. Then we crowded around the radio.

Keeping us informed of what was happening in the world was not the radio's sole function. Seeing a play, attending a concert, or even going to the movies had been severely restricted and eventually prohibited to Jews. The radio had to be theater and concert hall. In the evening after dinner, with the dishes cleared away, we frequently sat around the radio, this time the sound turned to a proper volume, to enjoy an opera or a concert. When my father was not at home, Claire and I, at times together with (Jewish) friends, listened to international soccer games. Again the windows had to be closed, this time for a different reason: Every time the German team scored a goal, the whole neighborhood erupted in cheers; but when a goal was scored against Germany, the only cheering came from our house. When, following "Kristallnacht" we were forced from our home we had to give up many things, but our precious radio went, of course, with us.

War made listening to foreign news broadcasts even more important, but also more risky. Listening to broadcasts from enemy countries was punishable by jail or even death; and for Jews death was a certainty. Though always worried, the risk failed to deter us.

In the evening, a short time before Radio Strasbourg came on the air with news in German, the routine in the House of Mrs. Levy was interrupted. My mother, my sister, and I went upstairs to our living room, followed by several of the pensioners, those who didn't mind climbing the many stairs. A few minutes before news-time, all chatting in the small, and now rather crowded, room ceased: It was time for my important act.

Our receiver had developed a problem: The station selector was broken. As Jews, we couldn't just walk into a repair shop to have it fixed; yet we couldn't let the dial sit permanently on Radio Strasbourg. The Gestapo could walk into a Jewish home whenever they pleased, so there was always the chance for a visit. For our protection our radio's dial had to point to a German station.

Changing stations was a delicate operation. After opening the back of the set, I very carefully moved the dial from the inside while my mother or sister watched the front, listening to the speaker. After I reached the right station and the sound was clear, the radio was closed again.

During this procedure complete silence prevailed in the room as the "audience" seemed to be holding its breath. When the news finally came on and the sound was clear, and I had neither electrocuted myself nor caused any damage to the set, sighs of relief broke the silence.

But the exercise was for nothing, the news was always disappointing: The hoped for report of a German defeat on the battlefield failed to come.

With the news over, the process was reversed; the dial was returned to a German station.

Early morning on September the ninth, 1939, the day of Yom Kippur, we heard a knock on the door. When my mother opened the door two Gestapo agents marched into the room.

The intruders announced that they had come to pick up our radio. A new regulation, which had come into force that very morning, forbade Jews from having radios in their homes. The agents admired our set: "With this you can receive stations from all around the world," one of them remarked.

"I wouldn't know," was my mother's response, "I thought it was forbidden to listen to foreign stations."

He picked up the radio, "Your contribution to the war effort."

"This set will be given to soldiers on the front," his buddy added.

He wants to keep it for himself, I thought. For days afterwards I worried: Had I returned the station selector back to a German station, or did it still show Radio Strasbourg?

By the end of September, Warsaw fell; Polish resistance collapsed. Nazi Germany and Communist Russia, now allies, divided the defeated country. We were deeply disappointed. The West had done nothing. The French troops that had occupied a number of small German border towns and villages withdrew. The war entered the period that became known as the "phony war."

For us, however, the war was far from phony. New prohibitions were imposed upon the Jews.

"Cowboys and Indians" And Light Switches

Not only did I love books, books fascinated me. I liked to read, but reading was not all there was to books. Books were to be collected, looked at, leafed through; books represented adventure, entertainment and, of course, knowledge. And books were a refuge. I could retreat into a book and for the moment forget the problems, the turmoil, the fears of the day.

Mrs. Levy's private suite included a large oak paneled room, serving as both dining room and library. Two sets of iron grilled French doors at the far end of the room gave it an air of elegance. Yet neither the room's formality and elegance, nor the large table - it could seat at least forty diners - impressed me. What did impress me, and interest me, were the books. One of the room's long walls was completely covered with shelves, from the room's double door entrance to the room's far end, and from the carpeted floor to the high ceiling. Thousands of books must have filled these shelves.

How I would have loved to spend time in that room! Just to be there, all by myself, looking at the books, taking a book off the shelf here and there, only to return it to its proper place. I promised myself that when I was grown up I too would have a large library.

Most of the books in Mrs. Levy's library were of no interest to me. They related to her work at the Opera. Hundreds of librettos shared shelf space with books on music and music history, and books on the development of the opera shared space with books on stage settings. But the library also included several books on travel and exploration, books on history, some books on science, and collections of short stories from around the world. Very little "light" literature could be found on these rows.

Mrs. Levy, who had learned about my fascination with her library, granted me permission to borrow her books. But being Mrs. Levy, she imposed conditions: Borrowing books was to be a reward for having done my assigned jobs and my schoolwork, and having done them well. Also, I could not just browse in the library, which is what I really wanted to do, or select books myself. Mrs. Levy would do the selecting, selecting books she thought suitable for me. Among these would be some difficult books, and I would be required to write book reports. These reports would be considered homework and one of the teachers of her school, or perhaps Mrs. Levy herself, would grade them,. With reluctance and the urging of my mother I accepted these conditions. I wanted the books, so what else could I do? But after having written two or three reports, I realized that no one paid attention to them. I gave up writing reports, and as I had suspected no one asked for them.

The "good" reading provided by Mrs. Levy's library was fine, and I enjoyed many of the books she had selected. But I also wanted to read "boys' books," that is, adventure books. Especially late in the evening after a miserable day, I longed to escape into a world where the good guys were always the winners. Luckily, I found a source for that kind of reading.

Among the teachers in Mrs. Levy's school was Mr. Heimann, a former stage electrician in the Frankfurt Opera. He was a skinny little fellow, perhaps no more than four and a half feet tall. He was married to a big and sloppy looking wife. Rumors had it that she beat him regularly. I thought that this was just vicious talk, although they did make an odd-looking couple.

Little Mr. Heimann was supposed to teach us about electricity, how electrical motors worked, etc. But Mr. Heimann was not a teacher, at least not in the sense of a schoolroom teacher. Although his class was small, he found it impossible to maintain order or to teach us anything. Attending his class was mostly a waste of time, which eventually even Mrs. Levy had to admit. The "course" was dropped.

As was customary in the House of Mrs. Levy, no one had just one job. In addition to his questionable teaching position, Mr. Heimann was also the house maintenance man. Already while he was still a teacher, a special relationship had begun to develop between us. Perhaps this was because I was a boy – the classes consisted mostly of girls – or perhaps because I showed at least some interest in what he was supposed to teach us.

Mr. Heimann suggested that I become his helper. I readily accepted. Mrs. Levy approved and so did my mother.

At first I just followed him around the house, handing him a tool now and then or holding the ladder for him, but mostly I just watched what he was doing. After a while, he started to instruct me on how to do simple jobs: fix a light switch, replace an electrical outlet, splice wires, and the like. He taught me the "dos" and "don'ts" of electrical work. After I had gained some skills, he let me do some of the work, but only under his supervision. He showed me how to work safely with hot wires in an emergency. Mr. Heimann had not been a good classroom teacher, but now he was a very patient and practical private instructor. He never reprimanded me when I made a mistake or hadn't quite listened to his instructions.

In the basement was a large walk-in vault, part of the defunct banking operation. Mrs. Levy thought the vault could serve as an air raid shelter. A bit cramped, perhaps, having to accommodate all the residents of the house, but its thick reinforced concrete walls and ceiling would offer good protection. The vault was well ventilated and if the need arose, the heavy steel door could be opened and closed from the inside. Mr. Heimann was given the job to clear out the vault and ready it for its new function. He asked me to help.

With fascination I watched Mrs. Levy spin the dial on the vault's door as she entered the combination. With the proper numbers entered, she turned the large hand-wheel. To my disappointment, no mysterious squeaks and rumbles came from the large, massive hinges as Mrs. Levy slowly opened the heavy door.

Another disappointment: Though the door was open the vault still couldn't be entered: Another door, made of heavy steel bars, barred the way. Mrs. Levy produced two very large keys; turning first one then the other she opened that door too, removing the last barrier between the safe's contents and us.

All mystery evaporated. I don't know what I had expected, but all that was revealed were stacks of old ledgers and file folders and boxes full of paper. The one item of possible interest was a telephone switchboard, half hidden under piles of outdated records.

The vault's contents weren't all that exciting to Mrs. Levy, she didn't even bother to enter. Remaining in the doorway, she briefly surveyed the mess.

"The papers will be burned. The switchboard must be dismantled and all the copper saved. The copper has value in wartime." With these orders the adventure of the locked vault came to an end.

Mr. Heimann and I went to work. Paper and cardboard went into the furnace. With that done, we began taking the old switchboard apart. This proved to be a more interesting task. While dismantling the switchboard and collecting the copper and other useful materials, Mr. Heimann became once more my teacher. He explained the workings of relays and switches, and how telephone operators made connections. I'm sure I did not understand all that he explained, but working together enhanced the bond between us. And I learned that Mr. and Mrs. Heimann once had a son.

One day Mr. Heimann invited me to the Heimanns' apartment. There he took me to a room that had once been his son's. Their son, their only child, had been Mr. Heimann's pride and joy. A few years before, at the age of thirteen, the boy had died. (Mr. Heimann never told me the cause of death.) Since the boy's death, the room had remained locked. Nothing in it was ever touched, except for an occasional dusting which only Mrs. Heimann was allowed to do. It was as if the room were being kept in readiness for the boy's return. Indeed it was a great honor to be admitted into that room.

In one corner of the room stood a neatly-made bed. A table and chair, probably for doing homework, a cabinet, which I assumed contained the boy's clothing, a shelf filled with toys and a bookcase completed the room's furnishing.

I hardly saw the things that were in the room. My attention had become focused on the bookcase full of books: Adventure stories, "Cowboy and Indian" stories, science fiction. I must have stood there, my eyes wide open with surprise and delight, my heart pounding with hope that I would be allowed to have some of these books.

I could borrow books, Mr. Heimann said, one at a time. He had only one request: I must take good care of the books, returning them unmarked and undamaged.

Only Mr. Heimann himself could take books down from the shelves and put them back again. They had to be returned to exactly the same spot from where they had been taken. In this room, he explained in a quiet voice, nothing must ever be changed.

A Houseful of Girls

Following the outbreak of war, the Nazis speeded up "cleansing" Germany's small and mid-sized towns of Jews, concentrating them in a few large cities. Most Jewish institutions, including schools, were closed. The Philantropin, Frankfurt's remaining Jewish school, not counting Mrs. Levy's, had to absorb students from many parts of the country. Homes had to be found for these children.

Mrs. Levy, never slow in taking advantage of a situation that could bring her a profit, offered her house as a boarding home for girls. The Jewish community agreed, not really having much of a choice. But, the community heads insisted, the girls had to attend the Philantropin, and not Mrs. Levy's private school. She agreed. Her school couldn't absorb that many students anyway. Late in the summer of 1939 the House of Mrs. Levy became filled with girls. Their ages ranged from six to fifteen.

The arrival of the girls brought many changes and problems to Mrs. Levy's house: My mother's workload increased; Mrs. Levy's school faded further into the background; the boarders no longer occupied center stage; and the predilection for young girls of Mrs. Levy's boyfriend, Mr. Bender, could no longer be ignored.

Everyone in the house was very busy, even Mrs. Levy. Mr. Bender, however, did not cut down on his visits. Nearly every afternoon, with Mrs. Levy busy, he could be found roaming the hallways. Encountering one of the fourteen and fifteen year old girls, some of them rather good-looking, he tried to trap them to give them a quick hug, a touch, or even a kiss. A sort of cat-and-mouse game ensued, as my mother and some of the other women in the house kept a wary eye on his comings and goings, not to let him have any opportunities for his little games. Mrs. Levy did not take his behavior very seriously, looking at it as harmless.

For me these weren't happy days; I had become an outsider. No longer was I free to roam around in the house, walk into the kitchen to talk to my mother to see "what's cooking," or listen to the gossip.

Though not yet quite thirteen, I now had to take care of myself. I still had to do my tasks in the house, taking care of the hot water, sweeping the yard and occasionally helping Mr. Heimann, but except for a greater demand for hot water, my workload essentially remained the same. Much of my free time I had to spend alone. Even at mealtime I was now by myself. My mother and Claire had their meals with the girls, while I had to eat in our attic apartment.

Food rationing, which had become general with the war, provided the Nazis with opportunities to erect additional barriers between Jews and the general public. Ration cards issued to Jews were marked with a "J" and could be used only in the special "Juden Laden" ("Jew Store"). The store was open only from late afternoon to half an hour before the eight o'clock curfew for Jews. No longer part of the Levy household, I had my own ration cards, and worst of all, I had to do my own shopping.

I hated shopping. In late fall the weather usually turns rather nasty. Cold winds and rain or icy drizzle, or even light snow, made it unpleasant to go out. The fall of 1939 was no exception. Once or twice a week I found myself trudging to the store through dark evening streets, with all streetlights turned off because of blackout, feeling miserable and lonely. By the time I got to the store it was already crowded with people on their way home from work, hurrying in order not to be caught by the eight o'clock curfew. Lines were long, customers impatient, and the German store clerks rude. And more often than not, the store was short on supplies.

People jostled and cursed trying to get to the front of the lines before supplies ran out or it was time for the store to close. I wasn't very good at pushing and shoving. It was easy for the store clerks to ignore a boy or for the other shoppers to shove him aside. So occasionally I ended up with nothing. Then I had to come back on another day for a repeat performance. Or, having run out of patience, I bought something that was still available rather than what I wanted, wasting precious ration points. As I said, I hated shopping.

Not infrequently I had to do without breakfast, not getting out of bed in time. After quickly doing my morning duties, I rushed to school. Lunch I usually ate in the kitchen of the girls' home, even though I wasn't supposed to be there. The cook, a friendly woman, always had something for me.

But for dinner I was on my own. The attic apartment had no kitchen, so I had to do my "cooking" on two hotplates. The easiest for me was to make soup from a can or a powder, with a few bits of vegetables thrown in, if I had any. I ate the soup with a slice of my rationed bread. Occasionally I did a bit better; the cook or my mother gave me some leftovers from the kitchen, which I only had to warm up. However, with food supplies shrinking, leftovers became rare. Once in a while I felt adventurous and concocted something of my own.

I didn't mind these evening "meals" alone. Eating alone had its advantages: I did not have to mind my manners and I could read while eating. Cleaning up was of course a nuisance. However, with only one pot, one plate, one cup, and a few pieces of silverware, it wasn't a big deal.

In the evening, as the house became quiet, I put the furnace "to bed," preparing it for next morning. Then up to our rooms in the attic. There I read until about midnight when my mother came upstairs.

It was the only time when we had a chance to talk. But not for too long; now she was tired after a long day, and she had to be the first up in the house, very early in the morning.

Friday evenings were different. Mrs. Levy opened the large dining room, a white tablecloth was spread over the long table and the table was set with nice china. All the staff in the house joined the girls for the Shabbat meal. I too was invited, sitting at the table with the staff. After lighting the Shabbat candles, Mrs. Levy made Kiddush (Sabbath blessings). In unison we recited the blessing over the bread.

With the meal over and the dishes removed, we sang the Birkat Ha'mazon (blessings after the meal), the older girls taking turns leading, followed by more singing. As the evening wore on, there was less and less singing and more and more talking. Finally Mrs. Levy gave the signal that it was time for bed. The girls, the younger ones first, slowly and reluctantly filed out of the dining room saying "good night" to Mrs. Levy and my mother on the way out.

It was time for me to retreat to our rooms under the roof.

Hineni

"Hineni." "Here I am." The cantor's voice, intoning these words, betrayed pain and anguish as he pleaded for forgiveness.

On Rosh Ha'Shana (Jewish New Year) and Yom Kippur (Day of Atonement), following the reading of the Torah at the completion of morning services, the cantor, or Hazzan, leaves the sanctuary, formally re-entering prior to the start of Musaph. The Musaph service, or "additional service," recalls the "Korban Musaph," the special Temple sacrifices on Shabbat, the High Holidays, and the day of the New Moon. After the destruction of the Temple in Jerusalem the "additional sacrifices," as they were called, were replaced by the "additional service."

Upon re-entering the sanctuary the cantor slowly makes his way through the congregation to the reader's desk in front of the Aron Kodesh, intoning "Hineni," the special prayer for the cantor. It is a very solemn moment. The Hazzan, humbling himself before God, asks for forgiveness, first for his own sins and shortcomings, and then for those of the assembled congregation.

Cantor Grosz reciting "Hineni" was high drama. His voice could be heard even before he emerged through the doors in back of the sanctuary. After passing through the door, he took a few steps and paused. For a moment he stood in silence, his head bowed. Then he resumed his walk, his voice, full of pain and sorrow, now filling the sanctuary. One did not have to understand these words; his voice said all there was to be said. Now and again he slowed his progress, even stood still for a moment, his voice dropping to a mere whisper as if overcome by emotion. During those moments no other sounds could be heard in the packed sanctuary; the congregants appeared reluctant even to breathe. Then, apparently having regained his strength, he resumed his slow walk and the power of his voice filled the synagogue once again.

But Bar Mitzvah lessons with Cantor Grosz were quite a different matter.

Early November, accompanied by my mother, I went to see Rabbi Neuhaus, then the rabbi of the remaining Orthodox congregation in Frankfurt. He asked about our family, the whereabouts of my father, and about my Jewish education. When the conversation turned to my mother's conversion, I was told to wait outside his study. After that he talked to me for a while, with my mother waiting outside.

Finally the Rabbi decided it was high time to start preparing me for my Bar Mitzvah. My Parashah (portion of the week) would be B'shalach, also known as Shabbat Shirah, the Shabbat of Song.

B'shalach ("send out") tells of the trials of the People of Israel after Pharaoh "sent them out of Egypt." Trapped between the Sea of Reeds and Egypt's army in hot pursuit, Pharaoh had once more changed his mind. Israel could see only destruction: Be killed by Pharaoh's soldiers or drown in the sea. The people despaired but were saved by the faith of a few: The waters parted to let them pass through; they did not part for the Egyptians, drowning Pharaoh's men, horses and chariots.

Rescued from one danger, the Israelites found themselves in the desert, but without food. Where was there a land that would receive them? Despairing once again, they were ready to return to slavery. Once more they were saved, only to have to face yet another enemy, Amalek. This time Israel fought back and destroyed the attackers. Yet Israel had paid a high price: Many of the weaker among the people were killed.

Three times the Children of Israel faced disaster and three times they were saved. Will we be saved? The sea had not parted for us.

But at the moment I had to suppress this thought, having to face a daunting challenge: Bar Mitzvah lessons with Cantor Grosz.

Twice a week, from mid-November until my Bar Mitzvah day in mid-January, two boys and I met with the cantor to learn our "Parashah" and practice the "trop" (the melody for reciting the Torah). Once a week I also had to meet with the Rabbi for lessons in Judaism.

Cantor Grosz was a very impatient man. Mistakes were not easily forgiven. Simple mistakes, not hitting the right tone for the trop, earned a sharp rebuke, often accompanied by remarks doubting the "sinner's" intelligence or ability to ever learn his Torah portion adequately. He was convinced that we would never learn it correctly. A larger mistake, like misreading a word or mispronouncing it, sent Cantor Grosz into a tantrum. Rapping the offender on the head with his knuckles, he told him which animal the offender resembled the most.

It was indeed no great pleasure to be a student of Cantor Grosz. The three of us took great care to be very well prepared for each lesson.

As November's unfriendly days turned into the bitter cold of December, a new problem put my Bar Mitzvah into question.

Bar Mitzvah

In December 1939, the city was hit by a severe diphtheria epidemic, lasting for about two months. Schools throughout the city were closed, including the Jewish school, the Philanthropin. Even Mrs. Levy's school had to suspend classes.

At first the epidemic appeared to have skipped over the House of Mrs. Levy. Although the girls were on an enforced school vacation, they had to remain at Mrs. Levy's house. The health authorities had placed the house under quarantine. All the children, and that included me, had to be inoculated against the disease. My Bar Mitzvah lessons too had to be interrupted.

With the girls apparently unaffected by the epidemic, Mrs. Levy prevailed on the teachers of her school to return to work. They did, though this may have violated the quarantine. Classes were set up, which Claire and I joined. For the first time since we were enrolled in Mrs. Levy's school, schoolwork superseded our house duties. Once a week the Philanthropin mailed homework to the girls, which they did under the supervision of Mrs. Levy's teachers. Claire and I too had to do the assignments.

Mrs. Levy opened her large music room, and a class in music appreciation, conducted by a former opera star living in Mrs. Levy's house, was added to the school day.

With the one exception of music appreciation, I didn't like this arrangement. Being the only boy among all these girls was embarrassing. Also, I had become rather used to the lackadaisical way of Mrs. Levy's school. Now I had to do real schoolwork.

However, the House of Mrs. Levy did not remain immune from the epidemic. At first a few girls did come down with the disease, but as the cases were not severe, they were not taken very seriously. The infected girls were placed into isolation, and the daily routines continued as before.

But the disease was not that easily banished. It spread, and more serious cases developed. School was discontinued as Mrs. Levy's house turned into a virtual hospital. The staff and those among the older girls not infected (including Claire) were now kept busy caring for the sick. Those with the most severe cases had to be taken to the hospital.

I too caught the disease. For a few days I was in bed in our attic apartment with a high fever. My mother looked after me in the little spare time that she had. The doctor finally insisted I had to be moved to the hospital. Barely eight weeks before my Bar Mitzvah day I entered the isolation ward of the Jewish hospital.

My first week in the hospital's isolation ward was rather miserable. Confined to bed with persistent high fever, and with no visitors allowed, I felt that I was living inside a cocoon. The one bright spot were visits by a young nurse, a friend of Kurt Herz, who worked in the ward. She looked in on me as often as she could to cheer me up. For a while she was my only contact with the outside world.

By the second week the fever dropped and I could get out of bed, or rather was ordered to get out of bed. The hospital was understaffed. The nurses had trouble keeping up with their duties. Ambulatory patients had to make their own beds, help clean their rooms, and otherwise be of help.

I too was asked – told – to do my duty: make my bed, change linen, and sweep my room twice a day before the floor was mopped with antiseptic. One night, the fever returned and I was sick. The night-nurse had no sympathy; she made me clean up.

Much of the six weeks that I spent in the hospital, I was alone in the room and my duties were not all that bad. But twice I had roommates disturbing my peace.

My first roommate, a little boy no older than four, was rather spoiled. At least I thought so. I had to feed him, bathe him, make his bed, and make sure he used the potty. Once I hadn't paid attention, and the head nurse made me clean up. After that I made sure he used the potty. To keep him quiet, I read him stories or played games with him. In no way did this arrangement please me. It prevented me from reading. Every time I picked up a book the little boy started to scream; and every time he screamed, a nurse came rushing in to reprimand me for not paying attention to the little tyrant. After a week or so, he was released. Once more I had some peace, but not for very long.

My second "roommate" was a baby barely six months old. She was less of a problem for me than the little boy. The poor little girl suffered from diphtheria in the eyes. Twice a day her mother came to breastfeed her. When the baby was being nursed I had to turn my back, which didn't bother me at all. I usually had my nose buried in a book. Nights, however, were a different matter. The baby had trouble sleeping and cried much of the night. Nurses came running in and out of the room trying to calm her. I pretended to be asleep despite the disturbances. I was afraid if the nurses noticed that I was awake, they would ask me to carry her around or give her a bottle. Eventually the baby girl was moved to another room and once again I could enjoy being alone.

The winter of 1939/40 had been discouraging. Hitler's Germany, together with her new found ally, Stalin's Russia, seemed to be able to do anything they pleased, while the French-British alliance appeared helpless.

After occupying part of Poland under the agreement with the Germans, the Soviet Union proceeded to move her defensive line as far west as possible by acquiring additional territory. The three Baltic States, "asked" to be incorporated into the Soviet Union, were occupied by Russian troops.

Next, to increase the defensive depth for Leningrad, the Soviets demanded a strip of land from Finland.

Hitler was not happy with Russia's actions; they complicated his plans for invading the Soviet Union.

The Finns refused to yield the land. Stalin resorted to force. In the West, the public demonstrated sympathy for little Finland's heroic defense against the Russian colossus, demanding military assistance to the beleaguered Finns. We feared that the Western Allies would come to an accommodation with Hitler and turn against Russia.

If lack of progress in the war against the Nazis and the diphtheria epidemic weren't sufficient to make us feel miserable, there was more. The winter was one of the coldest on record in recent times, at least in our area.

During my second week in the hospital I was finally allowed to have visitors. But no visitors were permitted inside the isolation ward, so my visitors had to stand in the snow and bitter cold and talk to me, or rather shout, through my partially open window. Visits were rather short.

All items that visitors had brought – books, a few cookies, a letter from my mother – had to be given to a nurse who would bring it to me. Nothing was allowed to pass directly between my visitors to me. Letters I wrote to my mother had to be sterilized before being mailed.

My mother did come to my window a few times, but she was far too busy with the many sick girls to pay much attention to me. Alfred Herz was my most faithful visitor, coming twice a week. He kept me informed of what was going on at home and in the world and even managed to bring me a newspaper now and again, or an interesting article cut out from a paper. (Jews were not permitted to buy newspapers; the few papers that found their way into the community were precious, even though they were full of propaganda.) When he couldn't come on his regular visiting day he sent his brother Kurt.

When not being bothered by the little boy or the baby, I read. I devoured as many as three books a day. The small library in my room was soon exhausted, and I demanded that every visitor bring something to read. Mrs. Levy came to my aid. She made sure that I was well supplied with books. To my regret, all the books I received had to be left behind in the isolation ward.

My Bar Mitzvah lessons had, of course, been suspended. Without a

Humash (book of Torah) available in the isolation ward I couldn't even practice by myself. I thought my Bar Mitzvah would have to be postponed. But a sympathetic nurse came to my rescue, bringing me a Humash. Of course it had to remain in the isolation ward; the ward finally had a Humash of its own.

As the year 1939 neared its end, the epidemic subsided. Many restrictions were eased, though schools remained closed for a while longer. With the quarantine lifted from Mrs. Levy's girls' home, my sister came for a visit together with a few of the girls. Finally, test results showed I was free of the disease. After a brief waiting period I finally left the hospital. The date was January fifteen, five days before my Bar Mitzvah day.

I pleaded with my mother and Rabbi Neuhaus for a postponement. But the Rabbi refused to hear of that. Perhaps he felt there were not many chances left for having a Bar Mitzvah. No one could be sure how long the Nazis would permit Shabbat morning services.

Every day for several hours, a young Rabbi, newly hired as assistant Rabbi, worked with me. He was full of praise for how much I had learned on my own while in the hospital. I didn't really believe him. I thought he just didn't want to discourage me. Anyway, he reported to the Rabbi that I was ready; my opinion to the contrary was of no account.

On a mild mid-January day, January 20, 1940, Shabbat B'Shallah, my Bar Mitzvah finally came. The Underlindau Synagogue, usually crowded, was even more crowded that day. Alfred Herz came with his brother Kurt to give me moral support. My mother, Claire, and to my embarrassment many of Mrs. Levy's girls, crowded into the upstairs women's section.

I sat in my usual seat, nervously waiting for the Torah reading to begin. Just before the second Aliyah (calling up to the Torah) (being a Levy I was the second to be called to the Torah) the young assistant Rabbi signaled me to come to the Bimah. I went up wearing a borrowed and rather threadbare tallit. I said the blessings without stumbling over any of the words, which rather surprised me. What happened after that I don't recall.

With services over I quickly left for home. Convinced that I had made many mistakes, I didn't want to listen to the insincere congratulations I was sure I would receive. But especially I wanted to avoid the girls.

My mother had arranged a little party for me in our small attic apartment. Alfred Herz showed up and so did a few friends of the family.

Mrs. Levy had been most generous. Despite the food rationing she had instructed the cook to bake a large birthday cake for me.

Rabbi Neuhaus gave a very moving sermon. (So I was told; I hadn't heard a word of it.) He praised the courage of boys who in these difficult times celebrated their Bar Mitzvah, thus affirming their faith in God and their allegiance to the Jewish People. In the latter remark, I thought, he had me in mind.

Only years later did I learn that a sour note had crept briefly into "my day." On her way out of the synagogue my mother was approached by Mr. Stern from Romerstadt. We had not been much in contact with the Sterns since their children left for England on a "Kindertransport." But instead of congratulating her, he expressed astonishment that I had a Bar Mitzvah, and in the orthodox synagogue. Then he complained that he had not been given an Aliyah. My mother felt rather hurt.

I'm sure that my Bar Mitzvah must have been painful for him, not being able to be at his son's Bar Mitzvah. My father couldn't attend my Bar Mitzvah either, but to Mr. Stern that didn't mean anything. We weren't religious and my father never came to the synagogue.

Perhaps we should have arranged for an Aliyah for Mr. Stern. But after we had been forced out of our homes in Romerstadt, Mr. Stern had shown little interest in helping me. My mother surely could have used some help in arranging for my Bar Mitzvah. Yet instead of taking pride in how much he had taught me during the days at the Heddernheim Shul, he let bitterness set the tone.

About a year after my Bar Mitzvah the Nazis ordered all synagogues closed. Jewish religious services were outlawed.

Vladivostok, A Last Door Of Escape

Time was running out for Europe's Jews. I am not sure how much we were aware of that, though we were very much aware that few countries were willing to come to our rescue. Great Britain closed the doors to Palestine ever tighter. The hopes of many to go to America were frustrated by cumbersome bureaucratic procedures aggravated by anti-Semitism among consular personnel. Isolationist sentiment still ran high in the United States.

The story of the journey of the ship "St. Louis" in spring of 1939 has been told in books and articles. Yet the story needs to be told again and again, for it tells of the difficulties Jews had to face in trying to escape from the Nazi onslaught.

Among the unfortunate passengers were friends of ours, a middle-aged couple. They had reached the gate of America, had looked up at the Statue of Liberty and had seen New York City's famous skyline, yet had to live through the nightmare of the Holocaust. Luckily they survived. This is their story of the unhappy voyage:

In spring of 1939, the "St. Louis" left Hamburg, Germany for New York. Among her passengers were a large number of Jewish refugees. Many had paid for the journey with what money was left to them after the Nazis had confiscated all their possessions. In New York, a number of the refugees, including families with children, were denied debarkation. Our friends too had to remain on board. The denial to land stated that the refugees had not fully complied with all immigration requirements. Our friends had been well aware of this. As the shortcomings were all in paperwork, they had believed, that this could be taken care of in New York. After all, the whole world was aware of the peril in which the Jews in Germany found themselves.

No one wanted to believe that the Immigration and Naturalization Service (INS) could be so cruel as to send refugees back to the land of the Nazis for purely bureaucratic reasons. Perhaps the refugees would be kept at Ellis Island until all details had been satisfied. Being a detainee on Ellis Island, no matter how uncomfortable, would still be better than being a Jew in the Third Reich.

Assisted by American Jewish organizations, our friends tried to come to some arrangement with the INS, but to no avail. With the ship overstaying her time in New York, the captain had no choice but to start his return journey with some of the Jewish passengers still on board.

Trying to find safe harbors for his Jews, the ship's captain made a number of port calls in the Caribbean islands before embarking on his homeward journey. At first he had no success. Only after entering European waters did he manage to disembark some of his unhappy charges. Aided by local Jewish organizations and grudging sympathy from officials, a few families with children were permitted to land in France and England.

The refugees who had to remain on board had only one choice: Go back "home."

One place of refuge had remained open for a while: Shanghai. The city, not yet occupied by Japan, accepted all refugees who could pay for their passage. No immigration visa was required; a valid passport, even one stamped with the "J," was sufficient. But going to Shanghai was a step of desperation. Although little direct information reached us from there, rumors abounded, most of them rather discouraging. The rumors, we learned after the war, had not all been false; they had described the conditions of the refugees in Shanghai quite accurately.

The refugees were not permitted to work. Few aid organizations were available to assist them, and the local Jewish community was too small and poor to be of much help. Despite these discouragements, a number of Jews decided to take their chances with the uncertainties of Shanghai rather than with their near certain fate in Hitler's Germany. Shanghai, they believed, was only a brief stopping point while arrangements for going elsewhere were being made. For most it didn't work out that way. After the Japanese occupied the city, the conditions became worse. The hapless refugees, now harassed by the occupier, lived in abject poverty until America's victory over Japan liberated them.

After Great Britain and France declared war on Germany, leaving by ship was no longer possible. But with the United State still a neutral country, those who had valid US immigration visas could still go to the States – if they could find a way out of Germany. One route, complicated and expensive, was via neutral Switzerland. From Switzerland it was possible to go by train via France and Spain to Portugal. There the traveler could finally board a neutral ship to New York.

Obtaining the necessary transit visas was difficult. The Swiss, fearing that some would not move on, were wary of issuing transit visas. Like many countries, they were not eager to add to their number of Jews.

The Hitler-Stalin pact of 1939 had created a new opportunity for going to America. During the so-called period of "friendship and cooperation" an escape-hatch had been opened for those whose papers were in order, who had the necessary funds to pay for the expensive journey, and who possessed sufficient courage and stamina for the long journey across Siberia and the Pacific Ocean.

The journey started in Berlin, where the traveler boarded the train to Moscow. The Soviets were not very welcoming to visitors and once the train had crossed the border into the Soviet Union the traveler's movements became severely restricted. In Moscow the passenger transferred to the trans-Siberian railroad for the long trip to the port of Vladivostok at the Sea of Japan. The journey through Siberia took several days, during which the passengers remained confined to their now-sealed railroad car. From Vladivostok the trip continued by ship across the Pacific to San Francisco.

In March 1940, Mrs. Levy departed for America via Moscow and Siberia to join her husband in the States. Wishing everyone well, she turned the operation of the girls' home over to my mother and also asked her to take charge of the liquidation of the "House of Mrs. Levy."

Mrs. Levy had made arrangements to have her personal possessions, including some furniture, shipped to the States. She asked my mother for one more favor: to take care of the packing and shipping. From the things not shipped, we could pick what we wanted for ourselves. Finally I had a chance to romp freely through Mrs. Levy's library. I took a few books, but unfortunately they were lost during the war.

A few days after Mrs. Levy's departure for Berlin, a large shipping container arrived, and with it a packing crew and an official from customs. The customs man's job was to assess the value of the goods being shipped. The government wanted to make sure the "Reich Flucht Steuer" (escape tax) was being collected.

The customs official was a strange man. Balding, middle-aged, and rather short, he did not look very impressive, even in his green custom inspector's uniform trimmed with gold braid. He paid little attention to the packing, spending most of his time in the kitchen sipping a cup of (ersatz) coffee while talking with my mother. Occasionally one of the packers would interrupt to ask him to inspect an item or confirm an assessment. The packing crew soon realized that the inspector had little interest in making assessments, so they ignored him. Whether this was to the advantage of Mrs. Levy or to the Germany treasury I wouldn't know.

In conspiratorial whispers the customs inspector confessed that he was a member of the Seventh Day Adventists. This religious sect, outlawed by the Nazi regime, had seen many of its members go to jail or even to concentration camps. Strangely, this man had escaped detection, but even stranger, he had kept his government position even though he was not a member of the Nazi Party. At least that's what he said.

We speculated about his motives for telling my mother his secret. Perhaps what he told her was not all true, though Mr. Herz thought that it was. Mr. Herz suggested, half seriously, that what the customs man had in mind was to convert my mother, marry her, and adopt Claire and me, thus saving us spiritually as well as physically. I thought he was a Gestapo spy trying to find some secrets hidden in the house. Most likely he just needed to talk to someone, and my mother was a good listener. Yet she thought that the situation was somewhat delicate and had to be treated with great caution. We knew absolutely nothing about this man nor had we any clue about what motivated his behavior. We did not know what he knew about us.

We were rather relieved when the packing was completed and both the strange customs official and the packers left. I don't know if the container ever reached its destination in America; I don't even know whether Mrs. Levy made it all the way to America to rejoin her husband.

With Mrs. Levy safely on her the way, Mrs. Bender took revenge on her husband: She denounced him to the Gestapo for having had a liaison with a Jewish woman. Mr. Bender was arrested and disappeared.

Mid-April the girls left and the House of Mrs. Levy was dissolved. We too packed up our belongings and moved on. The Jewish community had hired my mother to set up the new home for the girls.

I lost track of most members of the House of Mrs. Levy: The pensioners, Mrs. Kahn and her daughter, the employees, the teachers, and little Mr. Heimann and his big wife. Most of them, if not all, fell victim to Germany's policy of genocide. And without the protection of her Aryan husband, Mrs. Bender became just another victim of the Holocaust.

In just over one year after my father's departure for Egypt, and with all efforts to get us out of Nazi Germany having failed, my mother had succeeded in making a new life for us within the Jewish community. No longer just a passive member, she now took an active part. She saw this as the only way, despite the many risks, to let her children have a chance to know where they belonged.

There was, of course, no way of telling how long this new life of ours would last. We hoped that a rapid end to the war would reunite us with my father in Palestine or Egypt, or any other place except Germany, and that once again he could take care of us. But should this war drag on, we thought, what then?

Ominous stories were coming out of German-occupied Poland: Stories of Jews being concentrated in large ghettos and in slave labor camps, and stories of mass killings. We struggled to retain our faith in the Western democracies. But with an apparent lack of action, our doubts increased: Was the West really willing to destroy the Nazi tyranny?

CHAPTER 6

SEPARATED

A Small Bag of Potatoes

With a sigh of relief we looked at the calendar: April. Spring had finally arrived.

The first winter of the war had brought many difficulties: Record-breaking cold, a diphtheria epidemic, general food rationing with special restrictions for Jews. Spring renewed hope: With the sky clearing and the snow melting away, perhaps the time had come for the Allies to take decisive action against Germany.

Yet spring also brought new challenges, especially for me.

Mid-April of 1940, after we left Mrs. Levy's house we moved our few belongings to the city's East End, traditionally a Jewish neighborhood. There, on Sandweg number seven, the new Jewish Home for Girls was to be located. My mother's task was to ready the house for the arrival of the staff and later, in early summer, the arrival of the girls.

The arrangement the Jewish community had made with my mother did not include an apartment, not even a couple of small attic rooms as we had at Mrs. Levy's. Like the other senior members of the staff, my mother had a room in the home. My sister would be rooming with the other young girls, fifteen to seventeen year olds who were no longer permitted to go to school under the Nazi law. These girls would be employed as helpers at the House for Girls. For me, there was nothing.

We were given a small room in the attic for storing some of our things my mother and sister could not accommodate in their rooms: A few pieces of furniture, some pots and pans and dishes and a few other things we weren't quite ready yet to dispose of. And, of course, many books, books we refused to give up. We arranged the attic space into a "living room" to give us a place to which we could at times retreat for some much needed privacy. There I slept until more permanent arrangements could be made for me prior to the arrival of the girls, scheduled for mid-summer.

Perhaps Hitler had fallen victim to his own propaganda, feeling sure that this war, unlike World War I, which lasted over four years, would be short. With Poland defeated in a lightning campaign, the Germans had talked themselves into believing that England and France would see little to be gained by continuing the war. Hitler was convinced the two countries would come to terms with the new order in Europe. The Fuhrer promised to be generous and make no territorial or other demands on the British Empire. He was less generous toward the French, demanding the "return to the fatherland" of Alsace-Lorraine. Although the Western Allies had shown little inclination to fight, they showed no inclination to accept the German conquest of Poland or give in to Germany's demands.

With his plan to bring the war against the West to a successful completion before striking out at the Soviet Union failing, Hitler began to show increased irritation with the Allies. To counter the nation's disappointment in not achieving the promised quick conclusion of the war, the Ministry of Propaganda tried to divert the people's attention away from the failure to adequately prepare the country for a long war. Banner headlines screamed of new international crisis, real or imagined, while anti-Jewish propaganda, somewhat less strident during the initial phase of the war, was stepped up. "International Jewry," the newspapers asserted, was behind the obstinacy of France and Britain. The Fuhrer, who would have preferred "peaceful solutions to Europe's problems," found himself once again "reluctantly compelled" to use military force to counter the "Jew inspired" violence against the German people.

The unusually harsh winter, together with inadequate economic planning, had caused serious food shortages as winter stores became depleted. Especially serious was a potato shortage, potatoes being one of the most important staples in the food basket of Germany. Although potato rationing was not imposed, in the spring of '40 the government, to its embarrassment, found itself compelled to restrict the distribution of potatoes. Shoppers could buy only a limited quantity and had to show their ID and ration cards. No potatoes were to be sold to Jews. Both identification cards and ration cards of Jews were marked with a "J."

Much work had to be done. The kitchen had to be cleaned, supplies received and stored, and the rooms for the staff made ready as the furniture arrived. Most of the work had to be done by the three of us.

As in the House of Mrs. Levy, Sunday afternoon was our time to relax. After a brief lunch, the three of us sat down to enjoy a cup of (ersatz) coffee with cake and talk. Despite the rationing of flour and sugar, my mother still managed to bake for the weekend. Alfred Herz, now having a longer walk, again joined us.

It was a Sunday not much different from other Sundays. As he sometimes did, Mr. Herz had stopped for a brief visit at his cousin's home a few blocks from the house on the Sandweg before coming to us. Upon leaving his cousin, she handed him a small bag of potatoes. I can't recall how many potatoes were in the bag; I'm sure there weren't very many, most likely three, one for each of the Herz's.

When it was time for Mr. Herz to be on his way home, my mother added a small piece of cake to the bag of potatoes. As I often did, I went with him for a short distance, enjoying a brief walk. Mr. Herz had a good half to three quarters of an hour walk to reach home, and because of the eight o'clock curfew for Jews, I could accompany him only a short part of the way.

To be caught in the street after curfew time, eight o'clock in the evening, could have serious consequences. Any policeman or Nazi Storm Trooper could make an arrest. Even ordinary citizens had the right to challenge a Jew being in the street and detain him until a policeman arrived to make the proper arrest. Any arrested Jew, no matter for what reason, had to be turned over to the Gestapo. This was far too great a risk to take. Hence the curfew was diligently obeyed.

A short block from the House on the Sandweg was a major street intersection, always very busy. I liked to avoid the intersection with its many people, some in a hurry, whom I didn't mind, but others apparently just hanging about. I was far too likely to be cursed at, spat at, or even pushed. Yet there was really no way for Mr. Herz and me to avoid the intersection. Sure, we could have gone a long way around, but this would have taken far too much time.

I would have liked to take a shortcut through a park, wander around among its tall trees, oaks, beeches, and other trees whose names I didn't know. But all parks were off limits to Jews.

Mr. Herz and I hadn't yet walked far. We were ready to cross the intersection, when we noticed a man idly watching the traffic of people. His beige trench coat was a clear give-away that he was an agent of the Gestapo. We saw no reason to worry about encountering a Gestapo officer, but for a Jew any encounter with a member of the Secret Police had the potential of turning unpleasant or worse. There was no way for us to avoid him.

I could have gone home, leaving Mr. Herz to deal with the situation by himself. That thought never occurred to me. Besides, the agent had spotted us and came toward us with a few quick strides. Stopping in front of us, he blocked our way. Very correctly he showed Mr. Herz his identification. He didn't ask for ours.

"Where are you going in such a hurry," he demanded. Mr. Herz started to explain. Interrupting, he pointed at the paper bag Mr. Herz was holding. "What's in there?"

Mr. Herz told him: A piece of cake, a few potatoes, gifts from friends for his sick mother. The word "potatoes" triggered a sharp reaction. He grabbed the bag out of Mr. Herz's hand and looked into it.

"Potatoes!" he nearly screamed. "Where did you Jews get potatoes?"

Again Mr. Herz explained: The potatoes came from his cousin. They were left over from last fall when Jews were still permitted to buy them.

"Let's go and see that cousin who has too many potatoes." I was told to come along. The three of us marched off, Mr. Herz leading the way.

Mr. Herz rang the doorbell. A frightened looking woman, who must have seen us coming, opened the door almost immediately. Her husband stood behind her. The man from the Gestapo pushed his way into the apartment past the woman and her husband. This time he did not bother to show his identification.

"So, Jews have potatoes to give away," he started out "while Germans have to do without. How come you have so many potatoes?"

Once more the explanation: The potatoes were left over from the previous fall. Now the Gestapo man became abusive, calling the old couple lying Jews, dealers in the black market, spicing his remarks with a few of the standard anti-Semitic epithets. Though frightened, the old woman stuck to her story. Her husband, still standing behind her, kept nodding his head in confirmation.

"Let's see your hoard of potatoes" was the Gestapo man's next demand.

Down into the basement we went. I trailed behind, having been ordered to come along and not to try to run away. I wondered how this would end.

In a corner of the basement stood a wooden crate, nearly empty. A few rather miserable looking potatoes was all there was of the "hoard." They could very well have been stored there all winter as the woman claimed. I rather doubted that's where Mr. Herz's potatoes had come from. But the man from the Secret Police seemed satisfied.

Back upstairs Mr. Herz was ordered to go home. He hesitated, looking at me. The Gestapo man repeated his order. Still Mr. Herz hesitated. The loudly ticking grandfather's clock showed time was well past the curfew. A short pause, then the Gestapo agent instructed Mr. Herz to go home as quickly as possible, take the shortest route, and not stop anywhere. If stopped, he should explain that the Gestapo had detained him. Mr. Herz left. A perfunctory search of the old couple's apartment and the Gestapo agent was ready to leave. The Gestapo man turned to me: "You come with me. I'll take you home. Lead the way."

We walked out of the house leaving a rather relieved husband and wife behind. We walked quickly, and for a while in silence. As we passed a closed and boarded-up synagogue he slowed his pace and began to ask questions.

I can't recall all that he asked, but eventually his interest turned to the whereabouts of my father. I told him my father was in Egypt.

"He ran away and left you all behind." There was a sneer in his voice. I didn't respond. He changed his tone, trying to sound friendly.

"In Egypt," he commented with interest, "the land of the pyramids. You must be receiving very interesting letters from your father."

No, I said, we didn't get any mail at all, only an occasional letter via the International Red Cross, as was permitted. With all seriousness I explained to him that it was not permitted to receive mail from Egypt, which was in the hands of the British. The Red Cross "letters" were really only brief notes of the type "I am well, hope you are well."

I have no idea whether the guy was listening to my babbling. By the time I was finished with my explanations we had reached the building where we lived.

(Of course we did receive letters from my father, illegally, via Switzerland. Since mail was being censored, the letters omitted all references that could possibly reveal my father's whereabouts.)

With my Gestapo escort a few steps behind me so that he couldn't be seen right away, I rang the bell. My mother opened the door almost immediately, as if she had been waiting for me. Before I could open my mouth she started to scold me for staying out past the curfew.

(Mr. Herz had warned my mother. With considerable risk to himself, he had stopped at our apartment before going home. He reached home without any further incidents.)

The Gestapo man stepped forward. Flashing his ID he told her that he had detained me. He did not explain why. Brushing past my mother, he headed for the kitchen. There he began the inquisition.

"You have too much food!" This was his opening statement.

"I know," he continued in a calm voice, like explaining something to someone not very bright, "I know because I know that you are giving away food."

My mother feigned astonishment, wondering out loud what made him think so. "You have too much food," he repeated. He seemed to like this statement, repeating it several times during his questioning.

Then in a tone conveying patience: "Just tell me where it's all hidden."

My mother, the patience in her voice matching his, answered that she had not known that giving a piece of left over cake to a sick old woman violated any laws.

His eyes surveyed the large kitchen. One long wall was lined with cabinets, still empty. In the rear of the kitchen a door led into a walk-in pantry. The pantry door stood open, revealing rows of shelves, all still bare.

But the man from the Gestapo was not easily defeated. Sarcasm now replaced the patience in his voice:

"Quite a lot of space for keeping black market food. You must have excellent sources. So tell me, where is it all hidden?"

My mother explained. There were no hidden supplies. This house was going to be a boarding home for schoolgirls. Within a few weeks the staff would arrive and soon thereafter the girls. By then the now empty shelves and cabinets would be filled with pots and pans and supplies.

Did my mother's explanations satisfy him? Standing near the large table in the center of the kitchen, his face now revealing uncertainty, his eyes surveyed the many cabinets. One more time he looked into a few of them, carefully examining their back walls. Was he looking for a secret door? Nervously I had watched his search, wondering what would have happened if some of the supplies had already arrived. Finally he gave up. Without a further word he left.

On the large table in the center of the kitchen stood a bag of sugar. It was far more sugar, a rationed item, than my mother could readily justify having. (The sugar had been left over from Mrs. Levy's house.) The man from the Secret Police had never noticed the bag.

Exiled

We walked up to the house that was to be my home for the coming year, my mother and I. In my hand I carried a small satchel containing clothing, a few other personal items, and a book. I had fought bitterly against this separation from home, although the small room in the attic of the house on the Sandweg, the new boarding house for girls, hardly qualified as "home." With my mother and my sister not only working there, but also living with the girls, I would have to take care of myself. This was not considered appropriate for a boy of thirteen.

I had to admit that once the girls had arrived at the House of Mrs. Levy I really hadn't belonged there any more either. Still, our attic apartment, no matter how small, had created at least the illusion that I still had a home, that we were still a family. Now that illusion was gone.

I saw my "banishment" to the home for boys as just one more step toward the break-up of our family. First, following the pogrom of November, we had lost our home, then my father left us for Egypt, and now my "exile." Staying together as a family had been an anchor of stability. This anchor was now being cut loose.

Certainly my mother would have it much easier without me; perhaps it would be better if I weren't around at all. Surely I must be a burden for her, an anchor tying her down. Claire at least could be of help at the girls' home; but I, what could I do?

Of course I was exaggerating as I stood waiting for the door to be opened. But my feeling of misery was real enough.

Gleaming white, handsomely modern, the building of the boys' boarding house, the Floersheim Stiftung (Foundation), gave the impression of being far removed from the world of pogroms, mass arrests, and official persecution. It stood there, an island of stability and continuity, in sharp contrast to the makeshift appearance of the boarding house for girls where my mother worked. Further strengthening this impression of aloofness from the present, this Jewish house, Am Dornbusch, was located in a good middle-class suburban neighborhood of garden apartments and well-kept single homes with neat little gardens, from which Jews had been expelled some time ago.

On one side the Floersheim Stiftung was separated from its neighbors by its walled-in play yard; on the other side, by high shrubbery. Behind the building was a large garden which, from late spring to early fall, provided the home's kitchen with a small crop of vegetables and the Shabbat table with flowers.

Inside the house a similar atmosphere of having remained untouched by the turmoil of the times appeared to prevail. "Appeared" is surely the right word to use: Neither high shrubs and walls nor closed doors were able to prevent the problems on the outside from impacting life on the inside. Still, the institution's leaders made brave, or perhaps foolish, attempts to preserve that air of gentility and elitism that the founder of the house had thought essential for the proper upbringing of boys destined to become leaders in the community, in business and in intellectual fields. I quickly decided that I hated this place; I only could see arrogance and pretentiousness.

The Floersheim Stiftung had been a well-endowed educational institution for non-religious Jewish boys. Here a select group of thirty-two first to fourth graders had lived, studied, and played under a rigid code of conduct in an environment of near luxury. The foundation's admission policy had favored high achievers and boys with good upbringing. After completing their four years of elementary education the boys were ready to enter any one of the country's most prestigious gymnasia.

Following Kristallnacht, the then headmaster moved the institution to England. He took with him the resident boys, several members of the staff, and part of the endowment's funds. What had remained in Frankfurt were the facilities, funds sufficient to allow the institution to continue to function, its educational precepts, and the housemother, Miss Caspari.

When the Nazis prohibited higher education for Jewish children and all Jewish schools in the city were closed with the exception of one school, the elementary school of the Philantropin, the Floersheim home also had to close its school. The resident boys now had to attend school with ordinary students. However, they could stay at the home for the full eight years of "Volksschule," thus remaining exposed, at least to some degree, to the idea that they were part of an elite.

Soon, however, other changes invaded the home, finally destroying the idea that this place was for a small elite only. With the Philantropin the only Jewish school in a large area of southwest Germany, the Jewish community had to find accommodations for out-of-town boys and some boys with no proper home in the city. The Floersheim Stiftung had to accept its share and expand beyond thirty-two residents. It was my bad luck that I became number thirty-three.

I certainly did not measure up to the past admission criteria. And, being the harbinger of coming changes, I was resented by Miss Caspari and even by some of the older boys.

Despite her title, housemother, Miss Caspari, a thin, almost emaciated looking, middle-aged spinster, was not a motherly figure. Backed by Mrs. Floersheim, the headmaster's wife, she made every effort to retain the air of exclusiveness of the original institution.

The institution's rigid pre-war dress code was still in force: During the day a house jacket, a blue blazer, had to be worn inside the house. For post-Bar Mitzvah boys, coat and tie were obligatory for Shabbat dinners on Friday evening and Saturday noon. Mrs. Floersheim insisted that I meet the dress code.

I did not have a coat acceptable for Shabbat, as I had outgrown my Bar Mitzvah suit. Jews were denied clothing coupons, and without them I could not buy the prescribed suit and house jacket. Besides, my mother didn't have the money. So how could I satisfy the requirements? And not any house jacket would do. It had to be of a specific blue and tailored to a specific cut. It had to be worn indoors at all times; being in shirtsleeves was not acceptable. To me the jacket symbolized the Stiftung's outdated attitude.

For several days and nights my mother worked hard to make the needed clothing. She dyed some old linen for the all-important house jacket and, using material from suits my father had left behind, made two pairs of slacks for me. Yet despite my mother's efforts I failed to satisfy the home's standards. This earned me the resentment of Miss Caspari.

With some of the boys arrogantly looking down on me because of my not quite proper jacket, I felt rather miserable, until a few months later other boys sent by the community arrived. They too didn't have the proper house jackets and they too failed in many other respects to fully conform to the dress code. The obnoxious code was finally relaxed.

In keeping with the past, the midday and evening meals were rather formal. (With the boys rushing off to school, breakfast was a bit more relaxed.) Mrs. Floersheim and Miss Caspari ate with the boys. They sat at the head table, with their favorite boys next to them. On a signal from Miss Caspari everyone sat down and the kitchen help started to serve the food. Mrs. Floersheim and Miss Caspari were served last. No one was allowed to start eating until Miss Caspari picked up her soup spoon or her knife and fork. On that signal conversations had to stop; talking was not permitted while eating. At the completion of the meal no one was allowed to leave the table until Miss Caspari again gave a signal.

Occasionally the "start eating" signal was delayed. Miss Caspari had to have two slices of bread with her meal. But these were not ordinary slices of bread, they had to be to Miss Caspari's exact specifications: Paper thin and lightly buttered. Only the cook could slice the bread thin enough for Miss Caspari's satisfaction. Once in a while the slices were not of the proper thinness or too much or inadequately buttered. When that happened, Miss Caspari refused to give the signal to start eating. The cook was summoned to the dining room to be reprimanded. Only after the cook had personally delivered the proper slices of bread could the meal begin. The cook, a big good-natured woman, took these episodes in stride.

Not even Miss Caspari's favorite boys, though they all sat at the head table, were all equal. Favorite among the favorites was an obnoxious freckle faced six-year old who, in Miss Caspari's eyes, could do no wrong. Her "bridegroom," as she called him adoringly, could violate almost any of the house rules. Talking during lunch or dinner was not permitted, but this prohibition did not apply to the little "bridegroom." While we ate in silence his mouth kept going, and not just from chewing his food. He delighted in picking on one of the boys, aiming nasty remarks at him. His victim couldn't of course respond. Yet I can't recall that anyone ever tried to get even with him.

Mrs. Floersheim spent most of her day in the office and had little direct contact with the boys. Yet she seemed to be fully aware of what was going on, even to the minutest detail. A strict disciplinarian, she set the tone of the home. She made the rules and determined the punishment for violations or for "improper behavior." Except for the cook, everyone, including the help, stood in awe of her.

For Shabbat, the dining room was transformed. The ordinary oilcloth table covers were replaced with white linen; the head table was decorated with flowers; and instead of the ordinary tableware. the tables were set with china. The boys had to put on their Shabbat best; those of Bar Mitzvah age or older had to wear coats and ties. Mrs. Floersheim lit the Shabbat candles. Mr. Floersheim made Kiddush and said the blessing over the challah. Everyone received a piece of challah from Mr. Floersheim after wishing him, his wife, and Miss Caspari "Good Shabbos."

With Mr. Floersheim present in the dining room – he did not eat with the boys during the week – the atmosphere felt a bit more relaxed. Although he too did not encourage table conversations among the boys, at least the world didn't come crashing down on the head of the boy making a brief and quiet remark to his neighbor. Occasionally Mr. Floersheim even started a conversation by asking questions about school, a boy's family, or what the Rabbi said in his sermon.

With dishes removed, Miss Caspari called on a few boys to recite grace after the meal. Among those selected was always at least one whom Miss Caspari disliked.

She never made a secret about whom she liked and whom she didn't. If that poor fellow made a mistake in his reading, Miss Caspari not only pointed it out with sarcastic remarks, but she did not object to some sneering and laughing among the boys. Although I was among those she disliked, I was seldom called upon to read; apparently she believed that I read Hebrew fairly well.

Post-Bar Mitzvah boys and those close to their Bar Mitzvah had to attend Reform Shabbat morning services, which were held in the school's auditorium.

Shabbat dinner, which was served as soon as everyone had returned from services, followed the same routine as the Friday evening meal, with candle lighting omitted, of course.

I rather liked Mr. Floersheim. He had once been my homeroom teacher, and I remember him as a good teacher. He also remembered me, and apparently also in a positive way.

The home had a fair-sized library. It was rather underused, as reading was not encouraged. Reading, Miss Caspari said, was a solitary activity, with the reader excluding himself from the group. She preferred group activities, which, she claimed, were a necessary preparation for life. Reading too was made into a group activity. The older boys read bedtime stories to the six- and seven-year olds, or small groups got together to read and discuss a book. Every Sunday morning after breakfast the boys were assembled in the large day room. There, for about two hours, Miss Caspari read to us from books she had selected.

When the Floersheim Stiftung had to take in more boys, the existing bedrooms were no longer sufficient. Even after single beds were replaced with double bunks, the available bed space was still inadequate. Mrs. Floersheim decided the library had to go. The bookshelves were replaced with triple bunks.

Mr. Floersheim asked me to help him pack up the books. I happily agreed. Packing the books went slowly. For Mr. Floersheim it seemed almost painful to take the books off the shelves and put them into boxes. At times he would open a book to read to me a passage, or he would talk to me about a book and its author. He made a list of books he thought I should read. As we thus worked together, he was not the head of a boys' home, but a lover of books. When our task was finally, and sadly, completed, he rewarded me with a number of books.

Among the books was a three-volume historical novel, "Ein Kampf Um Rom" (A Battle For Rome). The author, Felix Dahn, a late 19th century

German nationalist much admired by the Nazis, relates the story of a small band of Roman pagans rising in revolt against the Christianizing of Rome by invading Barbarians, who attributed their victory over the Imperial Roman legions to their newly acquired Christian faith.

The pagan revolt was not so much against Rome's Germanic rulers, but against the corrupting influence of their new religion. Behind the façade of a loving Christ lurked a plot to strip Roman society of its masculine republican virtues of honesty, strength, and self-reliance and replace these with a slave morality of submission to corrupt and cruel rulers.

Of course the revolt failed. The small heroic band of pagans was prepared to fight to the end but were saved by Viking ships. The Vikings took the survivors of the battle for Rome to the hidden fjords of Norway, there to wait for the time when they would be able to return to Rome to liberate her from the oppressive slave morality. Rome, once again free, could resume fulfilling her destiny.

Why did Mr. Floersheim give me this novel to read? I didn't just read it; I gobbled it up. In this hapless band of defeated pagan warriors, fighting against greed and corruption, I saw myself, and I saw the Jews, resisting the Nazis. Sometimes it is better, the story seemed to say, to admit defeat and live rather than fight on and die. ("Massada" was not yet part of the Jewish consciousness.) Was that what Mr. Floersheim was trying to tell me? Not to keep fighting what I couldn't change, battles I couldn't win, but to persevere until better opportunities came along? Or perhaps he did, like I, simply enjoy a good yarn.

Sunday was free time. After breakfast/lunch and straightening out our room I could escape from the boys' home; that is, if Miss Caspari approved. I was sure Miss Caspari, aware of how important these Sunday afternoons were to me, was only too ready to take this privilege away for even the most minor infraction of one of the many house rules. A few times she succeeded in doing so.

As soon as I received permission to leave, I was on my way to the Sandweg girls' home to see my mother. It was a long walk, an hour, or perhaps even longer. I went straight to our room in the attic, which I still considered home.

I made myself comfortable lying on the couch or, in defiance of Miss

Caspari, put my feet on a chair to wait for my mother to come upstairs. As before my "exile," Mr. Herz would join us.

Occasionally my mother couldn't come upstairs right away and Mr. Herz and I were alone for a short time. With my mother not there, I felt free to air my discontent. Mr. Herz listened patiently as I poured out all my anger. He urged me not to let my anger make me see everything as hopelessly dark, that this "exile" was only temporary. And he asked me not to turn against my mother. She was carrying a heavy burden all by herself. In this hostile world she was doing the very best she could for her children, and not for herself.

At about six o'clock in the evening it was time for me to start on my way back to the boys' home. I had to be sure I got there before eight, the time when Jews had to be off the street. I left the small attic room feeling somewhat reassured that I was, after all, not alone.

Settling In

Gradually I adjusted to being in the boys'home, though the adjustment didn't come easily and it was never complete. What helped was that the home too had to make major adjustments as conditions in the Jewish community changed, and that these changes were made as reluctantly and incompletely as I made mine. What finally eased the pain for me was that I made two good friends and that I fell in love.

A rigid code of behavior and an equally rigid code of honor set the tone at the Floersheim Stiftung. The codes, held over from the days when the boys ranged in age from six to ten, demanded that the younger boys obey the older ones, and that no boy ever told on another. After Jewish high schools were forced to close, the boys ready to leave fourth grade were permitted to remain at the home through eighth grade, now the end of school for Jews. Eventually the boys at Floersheim Stiftung ranged from first through eighth grade. The code, however, remained unchanged.

The senior boys were expected to look after the younger ones. Their duties included supervising the washroom in the morning and before bedtime, making sure that shoes were shined every Friday before Shabbat, and handing out punishment for misbehavior. Only the most grievous of transgressions had to be reported to the adults.

Giving responsibilities to the boys was certainly not wrong, and 'ratting' is universally abhorred. Yet the result of the code wasn't always good. The tone in the home tended towards the bullying of the younger boys by the older. Victims of the bullying had little recourse but to accept it; the code of honor prevented them from complaining to the heads of the home. And both Mrs. Floersheim and Miss Caspari closed their eyes to the abuse.

When I entered the Floersheim Stiftung only three seniors were in residence: Leo, Walter, and Nathan. Each had a specific role: Walter was in charge of the first and second graders, Leo looked after grades three through seven, and Nathan was the designated bad guy.

Walter and Leo exhibited contrasting modes of leadership, reflected in their relationships with their charges: Walter was obeyed and adored; the boys called him "Papa;" Leo was obeyed and disliked. Walter listened, explained, and talked things over with his charges; Leo gave orders and doled out punishments.

As the fourth senior boy I upset this arrangement. Mrs. Floersheim wanted me to share responsibilities with Leo, but Leo objected. He felt the new arrangement as a threat. He saw me as a rival for his position as the "head boy." In school I did much better than he did, and he was very much conscious of that. And he was of course aware that Mr. Floersheim's chief interest was how well the boys were doing in school.

Leo made sure that I didn't harbor the idea that I was his equal. Within a day or so after my arrival, he took me aside to make clear to me what his position was and what he expected mine should be: I would be tolerated, he couldn't do anything about that, but I would have no role to play as a senior boy. I didn't belong here. My clothing wasn't up to par and as I was poor I wouldn't have the proper standards of behavior.

That I was "poor" seemed obvious: No loose change jangled in my pocket; my mother couldn't afford giving me an allowance. But except for showing off, none of the boys, with all the coins in their pockets, had any need for money. Jewish boys simply didn't have opportunities to spend it.

Leo had decided that I would be another Nathan. "Nathan the Fat," a heavy boy of medium height, was generally despised by the boys. Those who did not actually dislike him ignored him. Nathan never gave up trying to ingratiate himself with Leo and other boys favored by Miss Caspari, but to no avail. Miss Caspari also did not like him and made no secret of it. He was the butt of many jokes and tricks. I think he was the most punished boy in the home.

I didn't like Nathan either, but once I felt more at ease in my new environment I occasionally came to his defense. This didn't do him any good, but it did get me into trouble.

Miss Caspari insisted that Nathan lose weight. During meals we were permitted to ask for a second serving, but not Nathan. A few times I asked for seconds, though not actually wanting it, but to give it to Nathan who sat next to me. I succeeded a few times before getting caught. It cost me a weekend visit to my mother. Nathan was moved to another table.

Aware that I was not well accepted in the home, Leo tried to impress me with his position as leader: He ordered me around, or at least he tried. But he quickly learned that I was not another Nathan, that I felt no need to ingratiate myself with anyone. I used an old and simple method of defense: blackmail.

Leo was not only a bully, he was also rather lazy: he never did his homework. As he was one of my classmates this provided me with the leverage I needed.

Every day on our return from school, Mr. Floersheim asked about homework, and just as regularly, Leo would reply we had none. Under the code of honor, his classmates had to support his lie.

Leo was afraid that if he continued to harass me, Mr. Floersheim would someday discover that we did have homework assignments. To prevent this from happening he left me alone. After I made it clear to him that I had no ambition to replace him as the 'head boy' we got along with each other fairly well.

Actually, the problem with homework was exaggerated. Walter also did his homework even though he supported Leo's claim. Of course Mr. Floersheim knew better. Yet he never said anything.

Objecting to the emphasis on leadership I argued with much conviction and with just as much ignorance that the 'leadership principle' was typically German and not at all Jewish. Jews did not behave like sheep; they decided for themselves what was right and what was not.

Yet the idea that a few boys had to be the leaders permeated the relationship among the boys, both in the home and in the classroom. In our eighth grade class a few boys were considered the leaders, and though I wasn't sure who designated them, certainly not the teachers, they never seemed to object. When the so-called leaders asked me to become part of their group of three or four, my answer was an emphatic NO. This did not make friends for me among them; they enjoyed the air of authority. Mrs. Floersheim, and especially Miss Caspari, aware of my attitude, accused me of avoiding responsibility.

Eventually I made two good friends. Both were a bit younger than I and they were quite different from each other.

Gert Hayum, a short wiry boy a grade below me in school, was the son of a vintner and innkeeper. Gert's father had somehow managed to keep both his inn and his vineyards in operation. How this was possible is hard to explain, but stranger things happened in the Third Reich. Perhaps he had the protection of some Nazi bigwig who liked his wine.

Of all the boys in the home, Gert came closest to the ideal the founder of the institution had set: He was bright, his parents were wealthy, he was well brought up, and he excelled in sports. Yet he was considered an outsider, just like I was, reluctant to conform to the home's mode of life. Miss Caspari disliked him. She even resented that his grades were the best in his class; perhaps the boys she disliked had no right to be good in school. Gert, in turn, disliked being at the home. What he missed most, he told me, was helping his father in the wine cellar and playing soccer.

I have trouble remembering the name of my other friend because no one ever called him by his real name. (I think it was Kurt Levy.) He was known only by his nickname, Moby Dick.

Moby Dick was a husky boy of medium height and one of the most good-natured boys one could meet. Everyone liked him, even Miss Caspari. Why he chose to be friends with Gert and me, the two non-conformists, I cannot explain.

With more boys entering the home, Miss Caspari could no longer supervise all the boys by herself, though she was loath to admit this. Nevertheless, the Jewish Community insisted that the boys' home hire an assistant, and Mrs. Floersheim overruled Miss Caspari's objections. The assistant was placed in charge of the younger boys.

Miss Caspari's resentment only increased when the woman who showed up was not only charming and bright, but also young. The young woman's influence began to exert itself almost immediately, especially on the older boys, who responded positively to her. Relieved of some of the burden of having to supervise the younger ones, the older boys markedly decreased their bullying of the younger ones. And the new supervisor's willingness to listen to the boys' concerns and not be constantly preoccupied with enforcement of rules further improved the home's atmosphere.

Miss Caspari's assistant was in her early twenties and rather tall, and I thought her very beautiful. I fell madly in love. It was a strange feeling, both exhilarating and embarrassing. Of course, I had to keep my feeling a secret; I did not even reveal it to my friends. I don't know if the young woman suspected my feeling toward her, but we did strike up a friendship of sorts. She convinced me it would be better to accept my situation and make the best of it. After all, it was only temporary until the end of the school year. If I really tried, I could get something positive out of this experience.

I don't recall how much I actually listened to her admonishments, but the very fact that I could talk to her, and even more that she was willing to listen to me, was itself satisfying.

Stories were beginning to circulate about Jews being sent to labor camps, where they had to work under the most dismal conditions. We tried hard to ignore all these stories and rumors, but to no avail.

Gert had an older sister whom he adored. When a hundred young unmarried Jewish women from various parts of the country were rounded up for work in a munitions factory near Berlin, his sister was among them. She was then just eighteen. My friend was devastated. We both felt rather depressed. Reaching the conclusion that at best only one of us would survive this war, we made our 'wills', leaving our favorite books and our most precious possessions, whatever they were, to each other.

I never felt happy at the Floersheim Stiftung, but because of my two friends and the young woman it had become possible for me to settle down and complete my "year of exile" at the boys home without feeling miserable all of the time.

Two Rabbis

I had some very definite ideas of what it meant to be Jewish. According to my perception there were three types of Jews: Religious Jews, secular Jews, and Jews who did not want to be Jewish. Of course I couldn't help being aware of the "Liberals." The large and rather impressive Reform Temple, known as the West End Synagogue, had been only half a block from the temporary apartment into which we moved following our expulsion from our home after Kristallnacht. But since the Liberals did not fit readily into my scheme of things, I ignored them.

By religious I meant Orthodox. The Orthodox, I thought, were simply behind the times. They hung on to outdated ideas and rituals, had failed to grasp modern science, and misunderstood history. Nevertheless, it was primarily the Orthodox who maintained our connection with the Jewish past. They represented continuity as the Jewish people moved through history, and it was they who had prevented the Jews from adopting too many non-Jewish practices.

The secular Jews (I considered myself among them; my "religious" period had ended some time ago) were nationalistic Jews, that is Zionists. These Jews had adopted modern, liberal ideas, and had distanced themselves from most of the old superstitions without divorcing themselves from the Jewish past. In a sense they represented the future. They saw the Jews living in their own land, a nation among nations. Basic to this idea was retelling Jewish history as 'history' and not as religious experiences.

And then there were the self-haters. These Jews blamed the Jews for all the misfortunes that had befallen them throughout history. Full of bitterness against the fate that had made them Jewish, they believed that Jewish 'chutzpah', that is, collective misbehavior, separatism, and especially resistance to modernity, were the primary causes of anti-Semitism. Jews had become obsolete. These self-haters blamed the Jews for not being allowed to just walk away from the Jewish people and to be rightful members of the German Nation. The only solution to the "Jewish Question" was the full integration of the Jews into the host society, and thus their disappearance as a distinct people. The methods by which this goal could be achieved were conversion and intermarriage. Leftists among them saw the solution in the ideology of Communism.

Now I had to rethink my ideas. I had to concede that my three categories were inadequate, that they were far too simplistic. No longer could I dismiss the Liberals, or Reform, as irrelevant. Being Jewish, I had to admit, was far more complex and difficult to understand. Not only was this so because of the hostilities from without, but even more so because of the divisions and hostilities within.

The Floersheim Stiftung was neither orthodox nor secular and certainly not Zionist; it considered itself traditional yet liberal. The boys saw themselves as Jews because their parents were Jewish; no other explanations were needed.

Like Catholics and Protestants, Jews kept certain traditions, although not all kept all the traditions, or kept them in the same way or to the same degree. Keeping traditions, at least those not in conflict with modern knowledge, created an identity. Having an identity was important, and our identity was being Jewish.

One of the traditions being kept at the home was for the older boys to attend Shabbat morning services. Before Kristallnacht, they had attended services at the city's large Reform Temple. Now, with the Temple destroyed, they attended the Reform services held in the school's auditorium.

Never having attended Reform services before, I found it a new experience. The service, conducted primarily by the rabbi and not by the cantor, was indeed strange to me. The prayers were mostly said in German or sung by a mixed choir accompanied by the auditorium's organ. In addition to traditional synagogue melodies, much of the music used was from works by Jewish composers, music no longer performed in Nazi Germany.

Brachot and the weekly Torah portion were read in Hebrew. The rabbi, together with the cantor, chanted a shortened Mussaf Amidah. I missed the challenge of racing through the Amidah trying to finish at the same time as the Hazzan. With the Rabbi having the main role in the service, the cantor's part seemed to have been leading the choir.

Although I sneered at the use of the organ, just like in a church, I did enjoy the music. Frequently after the service, the blind organist continued to play for a while, now switching from Jewish composers and traditional synagogue music to Bach. I would have liked to stay for a while and listen, but could not remain for very long. Even the more relaxed Shabbat atmosphere did not permit showing up late for lunch.

Among us boys, we had many long and often heated debates about the synagogue services. Several of the boys, Leo of course being one of them, made fun of the Orthodox service. Many of their remarks sounded to me very much like anti-Semitic slurs. I, in turn, ridiculed the Reform. With traditional prayers shortened and even the weekly Torah readings abbreviated, the Shabbat service was rather short. Contemptuously I called Reform Jews "abbreviated Jews."

Even more than the services themselves – in all honesty, I preferred the Reform services, they were shorter, but I would never admit this out loud – it was the impressions I had of the two Rabbis, the Rabbi of the Orthodox synagogue and the Rabbi of the Reform, that exerted the most influence on my perception of Orthodoxy and Reform: The Orthodox Rabbi seemed uncompromising, stern, serious; the Reform Rabbi accommodating, relaxed, theatrical.

Rabbi Neuhaus, the Orthodox rabbi of my Bar Mitzvah, was a heavy-set man of medium height, who, with his gray beard, had "rabbi" written all over him. Usually he wore a hat, even in the synagogue. In his office, however, his head was covered by a large black yarmulke (skullcap). During services he did not wear a robe but an ordinary, somewhat crumbled looking suit. He wrapped himself into his long Tallith (prayer shawl), or at least tried to do so; it kept sliding off his shoulders. I was fascinated by his constant pulling and tucking at his Tallith, trying to keep it in place.

Except for an occasional sermon, he took no active part in the service. Once in a while, during silent prayers, he read out a word or a short passage in a loud voice, maybe to emphasize the importance of the word or passage, or to remind everyone of the right place in the Siddur; or, perhaps, he just wanted to make sure everyone in the congregation was still awake.

But what was most impressive about Rabbi Neuhaus was the way he looked at you, especially at the boys. When he focused his eyes on you, you were at once possessed by a feeling of guilt: What did I do wrong?

Rabbi Zaretzky, the Reform rabbi, was a tall and handsome man. His manner was always friendly, yet he seemed aloof. Throughout the Shabbat morning service he stood behind the reader's desk on the bema in front of the Aron Kodesh. He never sat down. He wore a long black robe, his head covered by a tall miter-like hat. His tallith, always neatly folded, was draped across his shoulders. It never slipped off. After reading the shortened weekly Torah portion he explained the text, trying to put it into modern, historical terms. His sermons spoke of tolerance and understanding. He never reprimanded the congregation for being insufficiently observant of Jewish laws and traditions.

Rabbi Neuhaus survived the Holocaust in Theresienstadt. Rabbi Zaretzky vanished in the camps.

A Strange Encounter

Act one, scene one: A bench in New York City's Central Park. The time: Early afternoon, late fall. The trees are mostly bare; a few lonely leaves still hang on the branches. Leaves cover the ground; some are dancing in the cold breeze.

The few that had fallen on a lonely bench at center stage had remained there, apparently protected from the wind. Otherwise the stage is empty.

A young man, or rather a boy of about sixteen, enters. For a moment he pauses, looks around, perhaps to make sure he is alone. He brushes a few leaves off the bench. He sits down, taking as little space as possible. He hugs himself against the chill wind. His thin, threadbare coat is quite inadequate against the autumn chill. He talks to himself.

Scene two: A young woman, somewhat older than the boy, enters. She looks around, perhaps looking for another bench. After a moment's hesitation she sits down on the only bench, seating herself as far away from the boy as possible. He stops talking to himself huddling deeper into his coat. They sit in silence. They avoid looking at each other. Then the young woman opens the bag she is carrying and takes out a sandwich. She offers part of it to the boy.

I'm not sure why I am telling this story, or what it is that compels me to do so. The events had completely slipped my mind but suddenly, unprovoked, they had made their appearance, though vague and incomplete. The story, as it emerged, doesn't have a proper plot, nor does it describe a situation of great importance. I wanted to dismiss it, banish it to a corner of memory where disconnected fragments of past happenings are kept. Yet the story refused to be put back. So I gave in and tell what I remember.

One day a Mr. Auerbach showed up at the boys' home. He introduced himself as an actor and playwright. He was working on a play, he said, a play that centers on a Jewish boy, a refugee from Europe, who finds himself alone in a strange city, New York, in a strange country, America. Mr. Auerbach was searching for a boy to play the part of the young refugee. It was important to him that the boy he will cast in the role matches the boy's character as he had shaped it in his mind. He had come to look for a suitable candidate.

The fourteen and fifteen year old boys were summoned. Mr. Auerbach gave a brief synopsis of the play's first act. Not quite sure how the play would develop, he told us in general terms about some of his ideas. As I hadn't listened very well most of his presentation went past me. I really wasn't interested in acting.

Following the briefing, Mr. Auerbach spoke with a few boys individually, of course starting with Leo. Certain that I wouldn't be asked, I returned to my seat and picked up my book, sure that Mrs. Floersheim and Miss Caspari had already decided who would get the part, the author's opinion notwithstanding. However, Mr. Auerbach rejected all candidates and could not be persuaded to change his mind.

Disappointed, he was about to leave when someone stopped him, pointing at me. I don't remember who it was, but I suspect it was my friend Gert. Once more I had to interrupt my reading. With Mrs. Floersheim and Miss Caspari watching and the rejected boys staring at me, the playwright looked me over. After a short moment's thought he asked a few questions. Then, with a somewhat dramatic gesture, he thrust a few sheets of paper into my hand.

"Read this. Next Sunday, two o'clock in the school's auditorium. Be on time!" Without a further word and without saying goodbye, he put on his hat and left.

I received a few dirty looks from the rejected would-be actors. Miss Caspari looked annoyed, while my friend Gert Hayum tried hard not to burst out laughing. I returned to my favorite corner in the room to resume reading, not the book I had left there on the chair, but the script from Mr. Auerbach.

The following Sunday, Mr. Auerbach was alone in the large auditorium. He had taken a seat in the front row facing the stage. Apparently absorbed in his script, he appeared not to have noticed my entrance. A chair, which I presumed represented the park bench, stood on the otherwise empty stage.

Somewhat hesitant I approached Mr. Auerbach. Without taking his eyes of what he was reading and without a word of greeting, he ordered me to go up on the stage. After a brief, and to me awkward, moment he told me to sit down and start reading from the script I had brought with me. I did as I was told and began to read the opening soliloquy. I had not read more than a few sentences when he interrupted me:

"No good! No good!"

I stopped reading, feeling relieved, yet a bit disappointed. I waited, ready to be dismissed. I had known that I would not be good at this. Now I could go back to my book and, after some initial kidding, forget about the whole silly thing. But instead of dismissing me, Mr. Auerbach came up on the stage, took the sheets I was holding out of my hands replacing them with new ones.

"Try this." Then he returned to his seat.

I realized that the "no good" had not been in reference to my reading, but to the script. I read the new lines. He interrupted me a few times, changed a word here and there, asked me to repeat some lines over and over again, all the time taking notes. I can't recall how long this session lasted. I was getting tired, but, I had to confess somewhat reluctantly, I was not bored.

The second rehearsal a week later did not differ much from the first, at least at the beginning. Again Mr. Auerbach made changes to the script. After a while his attention shifted from the script to me. He instructed me on the use of my voice, when to pause, when to speak faster, when slower; he told me how to sit, how not to look stiff, to shift around in my seat. And as he described the boy's emotions, I gradually began to feel some empathy for this lonely boy on a lonely park bench in New York.

When I came for the third rehearsal, a second chair had been placed on the stage. For nearly an hour we followed the same routines of the previous two sessions. Mr. Auerbach was still making changes to his script.

After a brief pause during which Mr. Auerbach worked on the script and I relaxed on the "park bench" a young woman showed up. Without greetings or an introduction, she joined me on the stage, taking her place on the second chair. We began reading our dialogue, or rather I read while she seemed to know her lines by heart. Silently I made excuses: I had more lines to remember than she, and the constant changes the author was making made it difficult to remember any of the lines.

As the session ended Mr. Auerbach expressed satisfaction with my progress. He regretted that we couldn't have any rehearsals for some time; he would be busy with writing and rewriting. He would let me know when rehearsals will resume.

"In the meantime, learn your lines." With that I was dismissed.

Though all exit doors were closed, the Jewish community continued to discuss and debate emigration. Nearly everyone that I knew wanted to leave Germany as soon as this was again possible, though I realized that there were others who did not feel that way. Many were afraid of leaving Germany; they feared entering a new and unfamiliar world.

Perhaps this was what Mr. Auerbach's play wanted to convey: Fear of starting life anew with a different language, different traditions, different mores? Or perhaps he wasn't quite sure what he wanted to say. Perhaps all he wanted to do was to tell the story of a boy growing up during a difficult time.

These questions were on my mind as I began to see myself as the young man on the park bench in New York, alone in a strange world, seemingly belonging nowhere.

I will never know what Mr. Auerbach had in mind, how his play was to have progressed, or how it was to have ended. Mr. Auerbach never called to resume rehearsals. Perhaps he had given up on his play.

At the war's end, Mr. Auerbach was not among the survivors of the Holocaust.

CHAPTER 7

EIGHTH GRADE

Back to School

Following the enactment of the racial laws of 1935, the "Nurnberger Gesetze," school for Jewish children was gradually eliminated. The first move in this campaign against Jewish children was segregation. In 1935, special "Jew classes" were set up in selected elementary schools. A few years later, school for Jewish children was limited to eight years of elementary school. Finally, in 1942, educating Jewish children was outlawed. The murder of Jewish children, infants, girls, boys, was the final chapter of the campaign. One and a half million Jewish children were put to death by Germany.

Frankfurt's Jewish community had been proud of its excellent schools. The Orthodox were served by the Samson Raphael Hirsch School, while more liberal and secular oriented families sent their daughters to the Lyceum of the Philantropin and their sons to the Philantropin's Gymnasium. A number of private schools, among them Mrs. Hamann's School for bright children, which my sister and I had attended, further served the community's needs.

By 1940, the Philantropin, by then the sole Jewish school left in Frankfurt, had become a mere shadow of its former excellence. Two maladies afflicted the school: A shortage of good teachers and a discouraged student body. Despite these difficulties, the school made valiant efforts to maintain a positive learning atmosphere. However, their efforts were not always crowned with success.

Under the guidance of the school's principal, Mr. Speier, and with the efforts of a few dedicated teachers, the school tried to provide a good education and to instill in the children a sense of self-worth, countering the constant drumbeat of denigration of the Jews. They spoke about contributions Jews had made to the sciences, to literature, and to the arts, although mentioning this was against the official educational policy. While German students remained ignorant of Heine and Mendelsohn and were taught that Einstein was a second rate scientist, Jewish children were aware of Jewish contributions to the arts and sciences. (Heine's poems had been very popular in Germany and could not simply be eradicated. The most popular of the poems were republished with "Author unknown.")

But with exits firmly closed, two questions, or rather accusations, were on our minds: Why am I still in Germany and why are you still here? We had little respect for our teachers, who, like ourselves, were "left behinds." Like our own parents, they had lacked the foresight or courage to leave, or they had simply refused to see the coming catastrophe. Mr. Weil spoke in glowing terms of his son, a professor at the University of Cincinnati. So why was Mr. Weil still in Germany?

In the spring of 1940, I started my final school year, eighth grade. Not having attended a regular school for some time, adjusting to the large class and to the conventional teaching was not easy for me. At the Hamann School, with its elite student body, its excellent teaching staff and its less formal classroom, my attitude toward school, which had not been very good, markedly improved; I had enjoyed school at least some of the time. But after "Kristallnacht" came Mrs. Levy's school, which had hardly been a school at all. And much of what I had gained at the Hamann School, including an improved attitude toward school, I lost again

Being far behind in a number of subjects, I had a lot of catching up to do, which did not improve my negative attitude toward school. Besides, it was my last year in school, so I figured, why bother? And for what future should I prepare myself? These thoughts were probably merely rationalizations. I just didn't like going to school.

I was a rather indifferent student, or at least that what my homeroom teacher, Mr. Weil, called me. Perhaps indifferent wasn't the right word to use; uneven would have been more accurate. At times my schoolwork was good, occasionally even very good, but in general, I put little effort into it. I liked writing and I was rather knowledgeable in geography, hence the two subjects didn't demand much effort. Yet both got me into trouble.

A strange relationship, I thought of it as a "feud," had developed between Mr. Weil and me. He thought that I could put more effort into my schoolwork, while I thought that he was picking on me. I did a lot of daydreaming in class, which surely must have annoyed him. I recall a number of occasions when he called on me while my thoughts were far, far away. I usually came out of my reverie when the class, normally quite noisy, suddenly became very quiet. On several occasions Mr. Weil accused me of making fun of him, although I don't think that I ever acted with disrespect toward him.

I discussed this "feud" with my classmates. Some thought I was only imagining it; others, though agreeing with me, dismissed it with a shrug. A few claimed, and I think correctly, that on many occasions Mr. Weil favored me.

We had been given an assignment to describe a small incident or experience that we thought of as important. Instead of doing as I was told (I never liked to talk about myself and besides, I thought nothing ever happened to me that could be of any interest to anyone else), I wrote a fictitious story. Apparently the story had been interesting and fairly well written. It received the highest mark.

The trouble began when Mr. Weil asked me to read my composition to the class. At first the class was listening quietly and with apparent interest. Then someone started giggling, and soon the class was filled with laughter. Mr. Weil stopped my reading. Asked what was so funny, one of the boys explained that my story was not a true story, but was all made up. (I never figured out how he knew.) Mr. Weil became furious, not at the class, but at me. He charged me with disrespect and he accused me of sneering at him. I was dumbfounded. I wish I could recall what I wrote, but I have not the slightest fraction of a memory.

My father's travels had awakened my interest and had provided opportunities for me to learn more about the world that lay beyond the borders of Germany. My reaction to the Nazi persecution further strengthened my interest in other lands. Denying that Germany was my homeland, I had to look elsewhere for a country I could call "home."

Wherever and whenever Jews got together, the conversation sooner or later turned to the question of where to go. Most of the people I knew looked toward the United States for their future home; I saw it in the Middle East.

My reading also reflected my interest in geography. I liked travelogues and preferred adventure stories and historical novels in which the action took place in countries other than Germany.

Thus, through reading I had gained much information about different parts of the globe, although, I'm sure, not always with accuracy and reliability. At home I spent hours poring over the maps in our large world atlas, trying to identify countries and the areas referred to in the books and stories. All this had given me a fair knowledge of geography, and self-assurance bordering on arrogance.

Our geography teacher was one of the few younger teachers in the school. He had lived in the United States for a few years, but returned to Germany. Life in the States had not been to his liking.

Americans, he said, were obsessed with "race." Freedom applied only to white people. Even in New York with its mixed population "Negroes" were discriminated against. In the United States, in order to enter a profession or obtain a good job, one had to prove that one did not have "Negro blood."

What had concerned him most, however, was the "low cultural standard" that prevailed in the States. Europe's cultural and intellectual life was far superior to America's. And that was especially true for Germany.

He was convinced that most Jews from Germany who had immigrated to the United States would eventually return "home" as disappointed in America as he had been. He admitted that at the moment Jews had it difficult in Germany. But, he assured the class, this was temporary. Germans were a decent and cultured people, and once the undesirable elements among the Jews, financial swindlers and crooks, had been weeded out, once again life would be good for Jews, as it had been prior to 1933. Hitler's mission was to cleanse Europe of communists and criminal elements; and unfortunately, among these were many Jews.

We ignored his malicious remarks about the Jews and paid scant attention to his disparagement of America. The United States was our greatest hope for rescue. There was an enduring faith that the great democracy would eventually open her door to us, or at least intervene in Europe to end the Nazi terror.

But it was neither his views on America nor his attitude towards Jews that led to a clash between the teacher and me. At the first day he announced his grading policy. To deserve the highest grade, "Very Good," or "A," a student had to know more than the teacher; he was sure not one of us would qualify. To earn a "Good" ("B") the student had to know as much as the teacher, but he thought that we wouldn't be willing to study hard enough to achieve this. Many, he was sure, would never pass.

His words were a challenge. I thought his grading policy highly unfair. I made no secret of my opinion, which annoyed him, and he didn't make a secret of that. I was convinced that my knowledge of geography was superior to anyone else's in the class; most of my fellow students agreed with me. Thus encouraged, I took every opportunity to make him aware of my determination to achieve the impossible grade of "A."

The offshoot was that my relationship with the teacher became tense, not at all a normal teacher/pupil relationship. What began as a contest deteriorated into antagonism: I tried to prove I deserved the highest grade and he tried to prove that I did not. Had I been a little smarter, I would have recognized that in this contest I could not possibly come out the winner. With less hostility on my part, I may even have achieved my goal.

As the school year neared its end, the teacher announced that he had already decided on the grade each student would receive. Since the class had not been very attentive, grades would not be very good. However, he was willing to give us a chance to improve them. To those willing, and he didn't encourage anyone to do so, he would give a special oral examination. The examination, he assured the class, would not be an easy one. A number of boys decided to go for it. Still convinced that I could obtain the highest possible grade, I too signed up for the special exam.

On the day of the examination, maps and charts were set up in front of the classroom. One student at a time was called to the front of the room. Using the maps and charts, the student had to answer questions the teacher put to him or her, and, if necessary, explain and justify the answer. A wrong answer and the student had to sit down. The number of questions a student was able to answer correctly determined the final grade. The examination went rather quickly; few students lasted very long. He had reserved me for last. As I strode up to the front of the class, with my confidence unimpaired, tension in the room became palpable.

I had listened carefully to all the questions and answers. I felt sure I wouldn't have any problems. And so it seemed. The first questions he had for me were hardly a challenge; I answered them easily. My cockiness increased. Although the questions became tougher, I was still holding my own. We made our way through Europe, Africa, Asia, and on to America. I hadn't been very interested in America, and hence the twin continent constituted my weakest area. Stepping up to the map I had to show the location of the major cities in the United States, follow the course of major rivers, identify mountain ranges, industrial areas, etc. I was beginning to get shaky, but still hung in there. With the class watching in silence, the teacher drove on relentlessly. Ordered away from the map I had to name all forty-eight States. I sat down, defeated. I felt humiliated.

I did receive a "B," which was sort of a victory, but it did not satisfy me. (I think only one other student received a "B," though it had been more easily achieved.) Some of my classmates pointed out that in accordance to the teacher's own words, I knew as much as he did. This admission by a teacher, they suggested, should satisfy me. It was the most anyone could ever expect from a teacher.

During the recess that followed the examination in geography, I still felt all tensed up and furious. When I saw that the geography teacher was on school-yard duty, I went up to him and said in a very loud voice so that I could be heard in the yard, that I had earned the highest grade and that he was well aware of that. He slapped my face.

The Hebrew Teacher

Time and again I had to learn a bitter lesson: Jews were far from a united people. It seemed so much easier to blame fellow Jews for the misfortunes that had befallen our people in the course of history than to blame our enemies who were out to destroy us.

We boys had many angry debates about the shortcomings of Jews and how the Jewish people had contributed to their pariah status in the world. Self-doubt, self-loathing, even self-hatred had become far too common among us. I felt certain that the attitude shown by my classmates reflected the attitudes in their families. But it was not only that. The incessant hate propaganda had its impact, creating doubts in many of our minds. Seeing ourselves as powerless to fight the Nazi slander, our anger had turned inward. What was needed was an outlet for this anger, a symbol representing the "guilty Jew" at whom we could lash out. And our Hebrew teacher, Mr. Messer, seemed to be ready made for this role.

Hebrew was divided into Modern Hebrew, Ivrit, and "Old Hebrew," the language of the Tanach and the prayer book. In "Old Hebrew" the class read excerpts from the various books of the Hebrew Bible and the Siddur (prayer book). Guided by the teacher, we learned to read with the proper pronunciations and gain some sense of the meaning of the passages without actually attempting to translate them. There was little effort to develop a Hebrew vocabulary or grammar. The class in Ivrit, the language of Eretz Israel, was conducted by the school's principal. He learned while teaching.

Mr. Messer, once professor of mathematics at a university in one of the Baltic Republics, taught "Old Hebrew" to an all-boys class. I'm sure that we could have learned much from the old man, especially Hebrew, in which he was fluent.

The class showed little interest in what he had to teach. At best, most looked at Hebrew as one of those courses one had to suffer through only because the school administration said so. Yet the class was in no mood to be tolerant. A sizable minority of students displayed hostility toward the teacher, much of it due to boredom, much of it due to prejudice. His mannerism, his long beard, the Yiddish-accented German, typified to them the "Jew" as portrayed by Nazi propaganda.

Sadly, far too many Jews in Germany had accepted this cartoon of the "Ost Jude," the Jew from Eastern Europe, too readily, blaming much of the anti-Semitism in the West on the Jews from the East. And those students who did not express open hostility toward the teacher closed their eyes to the prejudice of the others.

The students were inattentive, noisy, and rude. They made fun of his accent, his patient attempts to keep order in the classroom, and the gentle way in which he admonished the "children" for their misbehavior. I saw him as a kindly old man who was completely out of his milieu. More used to being treated with respect by the students at a university, he was at a loss on how to handle restless and angry teenagers.

Since learning anything in his class seemed nearly impossible, I withdrew and used my time to do my homework from other classes, or just daydream. Once I made a sketch of the old man's face. The fellows in the class thought the sketch was very good, but in a fit of disgust I tore it up. Now I regret having done so.

I don't recall what triggered the incident; was the class especially rude, or was I upset about something else? In any case, my feeling of anguish for the old man did not produce my usual withdrawal, but turned into a rage as I watched our teacher's ineffectual way to control the class. Suddenly jumping up, I leaped on top of my desk and started to berate the class for its behavior. Shouting and laughter stopped; the students looked at each other with embarrassment. With my anger spent I sat down again.

The room had become very quiet. Mr. Messer, standing in front of the class, looked bewildered. He seemed to be trying to say something, but for a moment words failed him. Finally recovered, he reprimanded me for my outburst, doing so in his usual kind and gentle way. Then he resumed the lesson. For the next few minutes, until the bell rang, the class was well behaved.

When the class met again, the episode seemed forgotten. The students were as ill-behaved as before. I resumed my daydreaming.

The Punishment

Mr. B. was supposed to teach "Religion" and "History." "Religion" was a required subject in the local school system: Protestantism in the Public schools, Catholicism in Catholic schools, and Judaism in Jewish schools. So called "Free- thinkers," upon the sworn statement from their parents, were exempt from "Religion." Jewish schools, like Catholic schools, did not grant exemptions, all students had to attend classes in "Religion."

Teaching history presented difficulties that would have challenged the most experienced history teacher. What the Third Reich promoted as history was not what a Jewish school would have wanted to give to their students, yet to teach anything at variance with the official line was far too risky for both the teacher and the school.

"Religion" had its own difficulties. Our Hebrew teacher, Mr. Messer, was certainly knowledgeable and could have taught the course well, but that was not his assignment. I suspected that the school feared that delving too deeply into Jewish history and thought could stray into forbidden territory, contradicting the official line that Jews were a parasitic people without any original ideas. Post-Biblical Jewish history, the Talmudic era, the Middle Age, the Enlightenment and subsequent emancipation, and the recent Zionist revival had to be avoided. An ignorant teacher seemed much safer.

While "History" consisted primarily of remembering names and dates, "Religion" was confined to reading and briefly discussing somewhat simplified stories from the "Old Testament."

Mr. B, the teacher (I don't recall his name) was a big man, coarse in appearance. He gave the impression of being more at home in a cow barn than in a classroom. A sloppy dresser, he often came into the room with his shirt partially unbuttoned and not properly tucked into his trousers. A few times he stood in front of the class with his fly unbuttoned (producing lots of giggles). He was verbally abusive and frequently physically abusive as well. Pummeling an offender with both his large fists was his preferred method for disciplining a boy, and as most of the boys were generally not well behaved, his fists saw plenty of action. No one, however, was ever seriously hurt.

He didn't hit girls, but his choice of punishment was even more upsetting, at least to the boys. The young lady being disciplined had to stand in front of the class facing the boys. She had to remain standing there for several minutes, and the better endowed the girl, and the tighter her sweater or blouse, the longer she had to remain standing there. A few girls claimed that the teacher had on occasion touched their breast "unintentionally." I cannot attest to the truth of these assertions. I suspected that the girls who made these statements wanted to further the antagonism between the boys and the teacher, while drawing the boys' attention to what they had.

We were only too eager to believe what we were told. I'm not all that sure that many misdeeds of which the teacher was accused actually happened, although many of them certainly did.

A few of the boys and girls, I among them, had suffered little from the abusive behavior of the teacher. Why he never picked on us, of that I am not sure; most likely we did show some interest in the little he had to teach.

What I find more difficult to understand is that no one ever complained to her or his parents, to our homeroom teacher, or to the principal. Even those who never had to suffer his abuse never mentioned it to anyone outside the classroom. That the school administration was completely unaware of what was going on is also difficult to believe. And if they knew that something was wrong, why was no action taken before the situation got out of hand?

Gradually the boys, or at least a majority of them, which included the class leaders, concluded that some action against the teacher had to be taken. We, the boys, decided we could no longer tolerate the teacher's behavior. We had no choice, we told ourselves, but to protect "our girls" against the teacher's abuse. Many of the girls were in support of our decision.

Though our indignation ran strong, the call for action was vague. We had no definite ideas of how to proceed, what form this "punishment" should take. A few preparations were made, but these were along the line of playing a few disruptive pranks. We had given no thoughts toward the possible outcome of our action, nor did we consider how the teacher would react. We certainly were unprepared for what happened.

Along two of the classroom's walls hung large portraits of famous men, scientists, writers, thinkers. Each framed portrait was suspended on a single long wire from a picture rail mounted just below the high ceiling. The portraits hung there like so many pendulums. And indeed, giving a picture a push sent it swinging just like a pendulum.

The day of the action finally arrived. We had posted a lookout in the hallway, to signal when he saw the teacher approach. As soon as we received the signal, we set them swinging. Then we all sat quietly in our seats.

The "action" appeared not to have been very daring; it was more like a harmless and rather silly prank. Had the teacher simply ignored the swinging pictures or laughed at it, the pictures would have swung themselves out and the episode would have ended right then. Instead, he ordered the boys sitting nearest to the wall to stop the pictures from swinging. The order was ignored. The teacher repeated his order, threatening punishment. His order was no longer just ignored, but each portrait was given an additional push to keep it swinging. Now shouting his demand, the teacher's language became vulgar and abusive.

The class feigned astonishment: "Swinging portraits? What swinging portraits?"

The pictures kept swinging. We held our breath, waiting for further reaction from the teacher. We didn't have to wait long; it came like an explosion. The teacher turned violent. Was that the reaction we had hoped for? Shouting nearly incoherently, he attacked the boy nearest to him with his fists. But instead of avoiding the fists by diving under the desk, the usual reaction, the boy ran to the rear of the room with the teacher in pursuit. Now several boys were out of their seats, running wildly through the room, challenging the teacher to try to hit them. The girls, who up to this time had been quietly observing the action, began to scream, some yelling encouragement to the boys. The teacher, more and more hysterical, charged around the room, first after one boy then after another. Bedlam reigned.

Once, charging past me (I was in my seat), he screamed at me that he had not expected I would participate in anything like this. I ignored him. Later it occurred to me that his words were a plea for help.

A boy, apparently pushed by the teacher, fell to the floor. Hastily an already prepared "bloody" bandage was put around his head. One of the girls yelled: "He is dying! You killed him!" The "dying" student screamed in "agony."

The teacher fled in panic, slamming the classroom door behind him.

Pandemonium stopped. The room became very, very quiet, no laughter of triumph, no shouts of satisfaction. This, I felt, was not what had been intended or expected; we had never thought about the possible outcome of our action.

Perhaps we had believed that we could control the action, to bring things to a halt before the situation got out of hand. The teacher was not the only one who had lost control; so had we.

Our bravado was gone. We were embarrassed, feeling ashamed and guilty. A few students, with perhaps too much imagination, were sure the teacher had left the room to kill himself; others thought he had gone insane.

Quietly we straightened out the room, took our seats, and waited. Barely a sound could be heard in the classroom. Minutes passed.

The door opened. We held our breath. The school's principal entered. Without uttering a word he strode to the front of the room. I had expected a lecture on classroom behavior, or some punishment, or whatever. I couldn't imagine what would be appropriate in this situation.

The principal, in a calm voice gave a brief summary what the day's lesson should have been, gave homework assignments, and dismissed the class.

At least among the boys no one wanted to talk about the incident; we didn't talk about it amongst ourselves nor did we discuss it with others. I too wanted to forget this "punishment action." For a long time I kept seeing the man's ashen face, could hear his plea for help, and picture his panic-stricken expression as he fled the classroom. It was not a pleasant memory.

A day or so later the teacher returned. We were on our best behavior and so was he. He put a hand on neither boy nor girl and managed to restrain his abusive language, but then there was little need for reprimanding anyone. The truce lasted for the remainder of the school year.

The Class Of '41

With my classmates I had a rather ambivalent relationship. The Floersheim boys kept themselves apart, and at first the boys in the class had looked at me as being one of "them." But once they understood that I did not identify with the boys from the home, their attitude changed. The class leaders, a small group of three or four, even asked me to join their group. I said no; I felt far more comfortable being an outsider. I had made one good friend, and for me that was sufficient.

In mathematics I sat next to a tall quiet boy much liked by the teachers. Neither Schlesinger – I don't remember his first name – nor I were big talkers, so at first we hardly said a word to each other. We were both good in math and soon we found ourselves competing for the highest mark in the class. But after a while (I think that Schlesinger made the first move), we agreed that this rivalry was rather silly. If we cooperated we both could achieve the highest possible score. And so we did and together we were at the top of the mathematics class.

Our friendship lasted to the end of the school term. It was of great help to me in finally coming to terms with the school and with life in the boys' home; it was assurance that I did not always have to be alone. I hope that during the brief time we knew each other I was able to be of some help to him. Like most of the boys and girls in the class, he too was swallowed up by the Holocaust.

For Jewish youth life was very confined. We had few outside stimulations; we couldn't visit a museum, attend a show or go to a concert. We had none of the places that teenagers like to frequent: movies, sports events, dance halls. For us there was no dating. Not that we didn't like girls, but where would you take a date? The school did arrange some after class activities: ball games in the schoolyard, students' art exhibits, classes in handicraft. But usually, after the last school bell of the day, students and teachers went home as quickly as possible.

So much of the time we turned to fantasies. Most of the boys in my class had selected a "girlfriend," that is, a girl you would like to take out on a date if that were possible. We made a (meaningless) agreement that once a boy selected a girl, no other boy was allowed to talk to her without permission. Another rule was that the girls in our class could not be selected as a "girlfriend." These girls were classmates or even friends, but not "girl friends."

I had my eyes on a pretty dark haired girl, a about a year younger than I. I still remember her name, Judith Salomon. Almost every day after classes were over I would check that she was all right. If I did not see her right away, I would check with her brother, whom I knew fairly well, about her well-being. I don't think I spoke many words with her.

One day, checking up on her after class I noticed some math problems on the blackboard, which apparently she had written. I noticed several grievous and uncorrected errors. I felt very disappointed, and my ardor for her quickly cooled.

After that I saw her only once more: She and her brother were climbing into a cattle car on their way to extinction.

A small group of boys at the Floersheim Stiftung, myself included, could not go home even during school vacation. Having little to do, we did dare to go on hikes in the nearby mountains, being careful to select out-of-the-way trails where no one would recognize us as Jews.

As the day of graduation approached, we could only see a bleak future ahead: Few ambitions were left to nourish, few dreams to dream. With Nazi Germany winning the war a real possibility, a sense of futility had invaded our classroom. Although only a few among us believed in Germany's victory, many feared a stalemate. England and France would grow tired of this war, and opt for an accommodation with Germany. The Austrian "Anschluss" and the rape of Czechoslovakia were still fresh in our minds. When in early summer the German Wehrmacht easily overran France, the possibility of such an end to the war seemed not far-fetched. And, if the war ended without a defeat of Germany, what would happen to us? No one in the world seemed to care. When the last class session was over, we said brief good-byes and left.

About a year later, after the school was forced to shut its doors, a small group of us boys from eighth grade who had remained in contact, decided to have a last visit to the school for a "farewell party." Breaking into the closed building we went on a wild rampage. We turned over desks, spilled ink, and wrote stupid and obscene comments on the blackboard. Roaming undisturbed through the deserted building, we looked into various rooms that had been closed to the student body, including the principal's office. We found nothing of interest to us.

Continuing with our "tour" we finally discovered something: A locked area on the building's top floor. We forced the lock without too much difficulty. What we had found were laboratories for physics, chemistry, and biology. When the high school was closed, the science labs were no longer needed. The doors remained locked.

We broke in, not even feeling guilty, and rampaged through drawers, cabinets, and closets. In one closet we found school supplies: paper, pencils, notebooks. We looted the closet. The supplies I took (stole) lasted me a long time. With stationery items not available to Jews during the war my loot came in handy. I don't know if anyone ever investigated the break-in. Most likely no one cared.

Eventually the building of the Philantropin was taken over by the Wehrmacht and turned into a hospital. After the war it was returned to the Jewish community. The small left over community, with few children, had no use for the large school. The building was sold to the city. Once again a school, it houses an art institute and a school for music. A plaque in the entrance hall commemorates the school's founder and the teachers who perished in the Holocaust.

Among my classmates there were few, if any, survivors.

CHAPTER 8

A THREE DAY WAR

Breaking A Rule

The rules were simple: Try not to be noticed, avoid confrontations, if attacked don't hit back, attempt to get away. Not only were we outnumbered and without recourse to police protection, but the authorities quite often encouraged violence against us. As Jews, we were fair game. What else could we do but duck? Jews had followed these rules for centuries. In Nazi Germany, the old rules had regained their validity.

Yet once we violated one of the rules: we fought back.

A Brief Skirmish

The boys' home was about an hour's walk from school. For the most part the walk was along a broad tree lined boulevard, one of the major arteries fanning out from center city connecting it with the suburbs. Emerging from one of the old city gates the boulevard first passed through a section of town consisting of public and business buildings and stores, with a few apartment houses here and there. Gradually, as the boulevard moved further away from the city's center, apartment houses became dominant, and as the boulevard reached the suburbs it had become purely residential. Streetcar tracks ran along the center of the street for part of the way.

Several schools, public and private, had found it advantageous to locate where the boulevard changed from mixed business/residential to residential. Among the schools was the large Jewish Philanthropin.

To prevent unpleasant encounters between Jewish students and those from neighboring schools, the Philantropin's school day began about half an hour later than the others, when it could be assumed that their students were safely inside the classrooms, and we left school for home when other school children could be expected to be at home eating their dinners.

To further reduce the possibility of incidents, the Floersheim Stiftung had prepared rules of behavior for the way to and from school: Don't loiter on the way and do not talk loudly with lots of gestures; never bunch up, walk in small groups of no more than four but never walk alone; take the most direct route although stay on main streets if possible; do not take short cuts through side streets.

The rules posed no special problems. Most of us didn't want to walk alone anyway, preferring to go with friends. Although no one liked to wait for laggards, the older boys were responsible enough to make sure that no one walked home alone. Once one of the boys insisted with great bravado on walking alone. He turned up late for lunch with his nose bloodied.

Staying on the main boulevard also was no problem: it was the most direct route, at least for most of the way. However, on the way home we often did take a shortcut. As the boulevard reached the suburb where the home was located, a dirt road branched off, providing a shorter route. The dirt road, used mostly by local farmers through whose fields it passed, skirted a major intersection where several local roads met the boulevard. The heads of the home were aware that, when it was not raining, we used this shortcut. They had voiced no objections, not even the meticulous Miss Caspari.

Most school days Gert Hayum and I walked home together, and most days we were also the last to leave school. We preferred to remain at school as long as time permitted to do at least some of our homework so we could avoid doing it at the home. This was especially true for me. Leo never did homework, asserting that none had been given and "solidarity" demanded that I did not contradict him.

Homework was, however, not the only reason why at times Gert and I stayed a bit longer at school. An ardent soccer player, Gert couldn't always resist joining a game being played in the schoolyard. And if a goalkeeper was needed, I too would join in, goalkeeping having been my favorite position.

A soccer game was being organized in the schoolyard as Gert and I were leaving for home. The boys were short of players and a goalie. Surrendering to temptation, we agreed to play for "just a few minutes." By the time we finally left the game, we were in danger of being late for lunch. Showing up late in the dining room was a house-rule violation, which had serious consequences. For me this could mean not visiting my mother on the weekend.

We made good time, and when we reached the dirt road short cut, we felt we could relax a bit and catch our breath. We changed from running to a fast walk.

As we slowed down, we noticed that we were being followed. We didn't know for how long the two boys on their bicycles had been trailing us. Though feeling a bit apprehensive, we continued our fast walk, ignoring them.

Suddenly we heard a loud yell. Turning around we saw them speeding up, aiming their bikes at us. We stepped aside to let them pass. As they did so they shouted a few anti-Semitic vulgarities and threatened to "get us." As there was nothing especially unusual about this, we ignored the two bikers.

But they couldn't be ignored. After having passed us, they turned their bikes around and again came at us at high speed. Once more we sidestepped them. This game was repeated several more times.

Whatever motivated us, I cannot be sure; most likely we were simply fed up with the harassment. In any case, we discarded the rule of not hitting back and took action.

As our attackers came at us once more, instead of jumping aside we grabbed the bikes' handlebars while giving the front wheels a vicious kick. The boys took a nasty spill. By the time they got themselves off the ground, we were making our way through the wheat field alongside the path. We felt sure that the boys would not follow us into the field with their bikes and that they would not abandon them to give chase.

We made our way home. Lunch had already started. Somewhat out of breath, we dutifully reported the incident, admitting that we had left school late, though "forgetting" to mention the soccer game. Hardly believing our ears, we were told to wash up and take our places at the table. We neither received a reprimand nor did Miss Caspari make her usual sarcastic remarks.

With lunch over and before being dismissed, Mrs. Floersheim reiterated the necessity of not loitering on the way home from school and using only main thoroughfares. From now on the dirt road shortcut must not be used.

Gert and I dismissed the incident as just one of those street troubles all too familiar to Jewish children. Not fighting back may have been wiser though less heroic. Had we taken the time to first discuss what to do, we probably would have kept a cooler head and escaped into the wheat field without first knocking our assailants off their bikes.

Next morning we went to school as usual, the incident seemingly forgotten. But as we were ready to leave school for home, we received a stark reminder that not everyone had forgotten the previous day.

Fighting Back

A basic creed of Nazi ideology was the "Fuehrer (leader) Principle." The principle stated that within a nation only a small number were born to be leaders. The majority were destined to be loyal followers. In theory, leadership qualities became apparent early in a boy's development. Once recognized, these qualities had to be encouraged and nourished. One way was to enroll the boy in one of the elite schools, schools specially designed to develop incipient leadership qualities. Such an elite school, the Muster Schule (Model School), was located not far from our school, the Jewish Philanthropin.

The day after the dirt road incident, Gert and I decided not to hang around at the school but to leave for home at once. As we made our way to the exit gate, a somewhat agitated and puzzled school principal blocked our way. He was calling all the boys from the Floersheim Stiftung together. A large group of boys, presumably students from the nearby Muster Schule, had gathered outside the gate demanding revenge. The previous day, they informed the teacher who went to investigate, two of their fellow students had been beaten up by two students from the "Jew School." The two assailants, they claimed, were from the Jewish boys-home. (How did they know?) No one, they threatened, would be permitted to leave the schoolyard unless the two "dirty Jews" were turned over to them for punishment.

Our principal, Mr. Speier, and the teachers took these threats seriously. They felt helpless in the face of German aggression, even if the aggression came only from boys aged twelve to perhaps sixteen.

We told Mr. Speier of the previous day's incident. He made no comments, at least not to us. We stood by as the staff discussed what to do. Acceding to the demand and turning us over to the boys outside the gate was out of the question. No one even suggested it, and Gert and I didn't volunteer. One of the teachers recommended, sensibly I thought, that everyone should remain in school for a while, using the time constructively: Doing homework or even some extra studying. Within a short time, he argued, the boys at the gate would grow tired of this and also get hungry, and depart. His suggestion was ignored.

No one thought of calling the police. Jews did not look toward the police for help. Nor did a policeman show up to investigate despite the crowd building up outside the school's gate.

We, the senior boys from the Floersheim home, finally made our own decision. After a brief discussion during which Leo, our presumed leader, had remained uncharacteristically quiet, we agreed that all the Floersheim boys leave together as one group in violation of the rule. We reasoned that seeing us together would discourage the boys from the elite school from attacking. A few of our classmates volunteered to come along to make the group look larger. We rejected their offer.

We told Mr. Speier our plan. He neither raised objections nor agreed with it. But he and a few of the teachers offered help. The teacher who had talked to the boys outside offered to talk to them again. Perhaps they would let the sixth and seventh graders go home unmolested. After all, it certainly could not have been one of them who had aroused the ire of the boys from the elite school. The departure of the younger ones may create a brief diversion, sufficient to give the Floersheim boys a chance to slip away.

Mr. Speier opened the school's main entrance, located on a side street, for us, which was usually off limits to students. Hopefully, by the time our besiegers noticed our departure, we should have put sufficient distance between them and us to discourage the "Muster" boys from giving chase.

We organized ourselves. The youngest and smallest were to go first, with the oldest and strongest forming the rear, providing a protective screen for the others. Then we left. Unfortunately, the boys from the Muster Schule were alert and noticed at once that we were leaving. Abandoning their siege position, they gave chase. At least this permitted everyone else to go home.

Seeing our enemies rushing toward us, we halted. We had two choices: run or fight. Running meant that each one would be on his own. The quicker ones would certainly get away, and just as certain, some would be caught and beaten. We decided to fight.

After instructing the youngest to keep moving, we faced the approaching enemy. A few brief scuffles, and even briefer fisticuffs, and to our surprise, our attackers withdrew. We resumed our homeward march, hoping that the boys from the elite school had no stomach for a real fight. We moved fast, but didn't run.

Our enemy, however, had not given up. After a short pause, they resumed the attack, using a new tactic. Now instead of rushing at us all at once, they resorted to brief forays, apparently trying to capture one or two of us for a beating.

Every time they rushed at us we halted to face them, remaining in a tight group. Our defense was successful, spoiling their attempts to take a captive.

Every attack produced a few fistfights, which were, however, not too serious. From their behavior we concluded that our adversaries were not eager for a real fight and so we relaxed. But apparently we had relaxed a bit too soon: Our attackers finally succeeded in capturing one of our boys. As they dragged him off to give him a beating we counter attacked. This they had apparently not expected. Caught by surprise they released the captive almost immediately and withdrew. And then something snapped.

Instead of being satisfied and resuming our homeward trek, we continued to press the attack. Though unplanned the attack was effective. Now the roles were reversed: They had become the defenders, we the attackers.

Our counterattack was far more ferocious than their attacks had been. To my astonishment, it was Moby Dick, my cheerful, non-aggressive friend Moby Dick, who led the charge. With fury he went after our withdrawing foe, knocking several boys to the ground. We followed closely behind him, wildly swinging our schoolbags, kicking and punching anyone within our reach. The elite boys' withdrawal turned into flight. With us in hot pursuit, they ran back to their school and into the schoolyard, closing the gate behind them.

We stood there, in front of their closed gate, staring at the elite boys, not quite sure what to do next. The obvious action would have been for us to return to our homeward march; but at this moment we seemed no less confused by the turn of events than our enemy.

Of course the siege of the Model School by a bunch of Jewish boys could not continue for long. So far, people in the street had ignored the fight. Fights between groups of schoolboys were not all that uncommon and none of their concern. Most likely they had not realized that one of the fighting groups were Jews. Shouts from behind the closed gate soon alerted the passersby to that fact. Now some man began to interfere. Cursing the "dirty Jews" and using other, choicer epithets, they threatened our parents, our teachers, and of course us, with unspecified actions if we did not stop at once molesting the boys from the Muster Schule. This brought us back to our senses. We withdrew.

We had not yet moved very far when we realized that our enemies not only had regained their composure but also had received reinforcements. Once more they followed us as we retreated, at first cautiously, keeping a safe a distance between us. But soon, with their courage having returned, they resumed the attack. We continued to move along at a steady pace, stopping at times to repulse an attack, hoping that our pursuer would tire of this game and go home.

But then the fight turned uglier. We had come to an area where sections of road had been torn up for repair work on the streetcar tracks. Workers at the site, who apparently had been watching the approaching fight, shouted encouragement to our pursuers while mocking and cursing the retreating Jews. Suddenly, among the shouts we heard far more ominous words: "Stone the Jews!"

Along the work site there were piles of crushed stones, ballast for the streetcar tracks. Urged on by the workmen, the boys, some no longer only from the elite school, began pelting us with stones.

An amazing sight indeed: A main city thoroughfare, with sidewalks filled with busy people and with trucks and cars going by and even a clanking streetcar passing, yet stones were flying. Though the stones could easily have injured passersby or could have damaged vehicles, the workmen kept urging the boys on: "Stone the dirty Jews! Chase them away!" Now and again some people stopped, watched briefly, then moved on quickly. No one protested, no one wanted to get involved, and no one seemed willing to alert the police. Not a single policeman was in sight.

Against flying stones we had no defense; we began to run. At times we slowed down, using our school bags as shields against the flying stones, to give the smaller kids a chance to get further away. Bobbing and weaving like boxers to avoid being hit by the stones, we gradually drew our enemies away from their piles of ammunition. Unavoidably we did have some "casualties." A few boys were hit, but no one in the face.

As the battle moved away from the street repair site, our attackers ran out of missiles to throw at us. We kept running for a while longer, convincing at least some of our pursuers that we were fleeing in panic, which, of course, could be expected of "cowardly" Jews. Thus encouraged, they gave chase. As we slowed down they caught up with us, but to their regret. Angered by the stoning, we were not gentle. Grabbing a few of them, we gave them a thrashing. Once again our opponents withdrew to a safer distance, this time a few with bloody noses.

With the latest attack thus repulsed, the battle finally ended. The enemy followed for a while longer, keeping a safe distance. Soon their number began to shrink as more and more of them drifted away. We made our way home, feeling rather pleased with ourselves. We had dished out better than we had received.

Confrontation

Following the delayed lunch, the senior boys were summoned to the office to discuss the situation with the Floersheims and with Miss Caspari. Expressing our opinion, we didn't think that the confrontation was behind us. Mrs. Floersheim and Miss Caspari, looking rather undecided, didn't disagree. The suggestion to skip school for a few days, until after the weekend, was rejected.

Finally, Mrs. Floersheim made a decision. We would go to school but walk home together. The home's maintenance man would escort us. The presence of an adult would surely restrain the students from the Muster Schule.

Though we were skeptical we had no choice but to accept Mrs. Floersheim's orders.

The maintenance man was middle aged, rather gruff looking and not very friendly toward the boys. He took his orders from Mrs. Floersheim, and at times from the cook, doing everything in sort of a sullen way. He also took care of the routine garden work. Once I had asked to help him with his garden work, but he had wanted none of it. After that, I never liked him.

The following day, with classes over, we assembled at the school's main gate where the maintenance man was waiting for us. Also waiting for us, at some distance away, were our adversaries. We started walking home. Our escort, pushing his bicycle, followed behind us, and further back were the boys from the Muster Schule and their friends. They made no move to attack, and after a while faded away. Apparently Mrs. Floersheim's suggestion had done the trick. Our escort remained with us a while longer, but with no apparent danger in sight, he mounted his bike and pedaled away without saying a word.

Not trusting the peaceful air, we refused to relax. We stayed close together, shepherding the younger boys ahead of us. We watched our backs and went cautiously past intersections, fearing a surprise attack. With some relief we approached the major intersection where we had to turn off the main road to enter the side streets leading to the boys-home.

What we saw at the intersection made us come to a halt.

A group of young men, not boys, blocked our way. How many there were, I do not know, I didn't count. But it was a large group outnumbering us. Though they made no hostile moves as we approached, they certainly did impede our progress.

After a brief moment, one of them approached us. In an almost polite tone he identified his group as students from the nearby Technische Hochschule (College of Technology.) They had come to demand retribution. The previous day, he asserted, we had without provocation attacked and beaten students from the Muster Schule. His group was honor bound to deal out appropriate punishments.

In his speech the spokesman tried to sound reasonable. He didn't use anti-Semitic slurs and almost seemed to ask us to understand their position. With the preliminaries over, he stated their demands: Turn over to them a few of our comrades to receive a thrashing; that would be our punishment. As soon as we had agreed to their demands they would select the boys to be beaten. Everyone else was then free to go. He concluded with a little sermon: He hoped that we had learned our lesson and would no longer be tempted to attack students from a neighboring school.

What to do? Not only were we outnumbered but we were confronted not by boys our own age, but by young men perhaps eighteen or twenty years old, or even older. A few looked as if they were on study leave from the military. No way could we fight them. Should we accede to their demand and turn over a few for punishment to protect the majority? Perhaps they would be quite reasonable, select only a small number, or accept volunteers. Hopefully the beatings would be token ones only.

We decided to stall, gain some time, although we weren't sure what to do with the time gained.

Leo, having found his courage, now stepped forward as our spokesman. He asked for time to permit us to discuss the situation. Again they proved to be reasonable, showing no signs of making a hasty move. We let more time go by.

Feeling somewhat encouraged by their reasonable tone, we turned down their demand, but requested that they let the youngest proceed home unmolested. We thought that without having to protect the younger ones, we would feel freer to put up a good fight. Also, back home the kids would report what was happening. Someone could perhaps think of a way out of this situation. The request was rejected.

The waiting game resumed. No one made a move. We just stood there confronting each other. Then one of us noticed that each student from the Tech School had a bicycle; and not one of them had put his bike aside. Now obviously one could not fight very well holding on to a bike with one hand. Conclusion: our adversaries were not prepared for a fight. We, on the other hand, were.

We decided to continue to wait. Time, we felt, was on our side. Sooner or later, growing tired of this game, they would become willing to compromise. Perhaps they would give us a "severe" warning and let us go. Or, someone at the home realized that we were late and came to investigate.

And then a miracle!

Mr. and Mrs. Floersheim had a son, perhaps in his early twenties. He never wanted to have anything to do with the boys, not even the older ones. Even on Shabbat, when both his parents shared the Shabbat meal with us, he refused to sit at the common dinner table.

As we stood at the intersection confronted by a mob of college students, he came by on his bicycle and, as usual, ignored us. We hoped he would report what he had seen, although we really weren't sure. If he did report, then most likely help would be on the way soon. We decided to continue with the waiting game.

As the young Mr. Floersheim rode by, one of the college students yelled: "Here goes one of them!" (How did he know that? How much did these guys know about us?) Mr. Floersheim sped away. A number of the students, eager to give chase, tried to get on their bikes, but they stood so tightly packed together that it took a few moments for them to get free, mount their bikes and go after the quickly retreating young Floersheim. A bicycle race began.

Mr. Floersheim won the race; he made it safely to the boys' home. What he reported there, if anything, I do not know.

With the attention of the Tech School students momentarily diverted as they watched the bike race, we acted. With the biggest and strongest in the van, we formed a wedge and attacked, catching our adversaries by surprise. As during the brief altercation with the two bike riders a few days before, we did not attack the students, but their precious bicycles. And we got the same reaction: With several bikes knocked to the ground, the Tech Students seemed more concerned with protecting the bikes than in blocking our way. We broke through. Once through, each one of us was on his own, running the short distance to the home.

We hoped our enemies would ignore the smaller kids who could not keep up with us and go after the bigger and older boys. They did ignore the younger and smaller boys.

The students, recovering, mounted their bikes to give chase. They quickly caught up with us, but then weren't quite sure what to do. Get off their bikes and fight?

I don't think many of them liked that idea. A few rode past us to block our way and resume the confrontation. But lack of coordination or planning on their part worked to our advantage. By the time they had themselves organized, the first from our group were only a few steps away from the doors of the Floersheim Stiftung.

A number of our pursuers did get ahead of us and tried to block our way. But with one final effort we managed to knock several of them off their bikes. A few fistfights, one final spurt, and we were all safely inside the house.

Although some of our boys had sustained bruises and scratches and one had a bloody nose, we felt that once again we had succeeded in preventing any one of us being seriously beaten.

A few of the Tech students, joined by students from the Model School, laid siege to the Floersheim home. Riding their bikes up and down the street, they shouted anti-Semitic epithets and bragged about what they would do to the Jews. The reasonable tone, shown earlier in the confrontation, had given way to expressions of hatred.

Mr. Floersheim

As we assembled in the dining room for the noontime meal, everyone tried to act normal. But this time Miss Caspari did not need to enforce the no talking rule. Preoccupied with thoughts and fears of tomorrow, no one felt like making conversation.

With our bravado of only moments earlier evaporated, we felt apprehensive about what might come next. Though outnumbered, we had been able to deal with boys our own age; we even had managed to get past a group of young adults. We doubted that we could do so again. The Tech School students would surely not have forgotten the humiliation they had received from a bunch of Jewish kids. If they became better organized, we no longer would be able to stand up to them.

Following the uneasy lunch, there was another council of war. Previously rejected options were resurrected and rejected again. The next day was Friday, and the best strategy was to skip a day of school. Yet we were afraid that this would only postpone a confrontation till Monday.

It was argued to just let the first and second graders go to class, the enemy would certainly not attack them. Or perhaps the opposite; only the big boys would go to school. Unhampered by the need to protect the younger ones, we could fight it out. We, the older boys, didn't like that idea. We had looked to Mrs. Floersheim to provide us with answers, but this time she was unable to give us any.

No one had paid the slightest attention to the Old Man, which wasn't at all unusual. Mr. Floersheim had remained in the background, not saying anything. But with everyone else seemingly unable to come to a decision, he took charge.

He did something very simple: He phoned the police. After a brief conversation he called all the boys, not just the seniors, into the large day room to give his instructions. There would be no further discussions, now he told us what to do: No skipping of school; tomorrow, Friday, we will be going to school as usual. The one deviation from the normal routine will be that we will go home together. That was all. Then he told us it was high time to do our homework

Friday morning came, and we did as we were told. We went to school the way we always did, although I doubt that any one of us paid much attention to what was happening in the classroom. We were worried, yet at the same time relieved. We were worried that whatever Mr. Floersheim had arranged with the police would not work, and relieved that someone had taken charge. During recess there was brave talk about fighting as best we could against the overwhelming odds, to give the enemy a good account of ourselves. Not one of us believed that we would get away as easily as we had during the previous two encounters. To everyone's credit, there were no recriminations. Our unusual unity remained intact.

When, at the end of the school day, we walked somewhat reluctantly out of the schoolyard an elderly policeman was waiting for us. He escorted us home. There were no incidents on the way. Our policeman remained with us until the last boy was safely inside the house.

During the evening some boys, presumably from one of the schools involved in the previous days' events and perhaps joined by some local youths, demonstrated outside the home shouting dirty anti-Semitic slogans, promising revenge, and throwing trash into our yard. I think that our neighbors complained about the noise, and the demonstration ceased.

The following Monday normalcy returned: We went to school without special precautions and without any incidents; the unity among the boys was gone as the younger and less popular boys were again being bullied by the older ones; Miss Caspari once more favored the boys she liked; and Mr. Floersheim retreated to his passive ways, leaving all decisions to the two women.

For a brief moment we had the illusion that it was possible to fight back. The battle with the boys from the elite school and even the confrontation with the older Tech School students had ended well for us. We were never again molested on the way from school.

Yet questions remained: Why hadn't the police intervened sooner? Had the police really been unaware of the street battles? I was sure that the police did not like street battles unless organized or at least sanctioned by the Nazi Party.

If the incidents had been officially instigated why did they end so quickly once Mr. Floersheim, a Jew, called the police? The more normal police reaction would have been to blame the Jews for the troubles: Mr. Floersheim, the teachers, the school's principal.

No answer to these questions will ever be found. The story of our "three-day- war" must end with a question mark.

****

In June 1942, with the closing of the last Jewish school, the Floersheim Stiftung too came to an end.

Mr. and Mrs. Floersheim, Miss Caspari and her lovely assistant and all the boys, from the top boy Leo to the boy on the bottom of the totem pole, Nathan the Fat, my two friends Gert Hayum and Moby Dick, all vanished in the death mill of the "Final Solution." Perhaps somewhere in the world there are a few survivors who have fonder memories of the boys-home than I have.

PART III

THE DESTRUCTION (1941 – 1942)

CHAPTER 9

THE BOYS OF THE ANLERNWERKSTAT

An X-Rated Story

Although Hitler failed to bomb Great Britain into submission, the war progressed favorably for the Germans. In June 1941, following the spring campaign that brought the Balkans under the domination of the Nazi/Fascist Axis, the expected German invasion of the Soviet Union got underway. Once again the German forces advanced quickly. By the end of summer they were deep inside Russia, bringing millions of Jews under the rule of Hitler. With no Allied victory in sight, our future looked grim indeed.

1941 was a most difficult year for me. Early in summer, with school behind me, I had to make two decisions: What I should do and where I would live. Concerning what to do, the decision wasn't difficult. Not many options were open.

The Jewish trade school in Frankfurt, the "Anlernwerkstatt" (Trainee Workshop), had once been part of the international organization of ORT (Organization for Rehabilitation through Training). Near the turn of the century, ORT had established schools and camps, mostly in Western Europe, providing vocational training for poor Jewish youth. Germany became the focal point of the effort. The program's stated aim was the rehabilitation of boys from the ghettos of Eastern Europe by teaching them "useful skills," rather than see them live a "religious but parasitic life." Among the "progressive" Jews in Europe, including many Zionists, were those who saw the "unproductive life of Talmud-studying" Jews as a major contributor to the rise of modern anti-Semitism.

Under the Nazi regime the Anlernwerkstatt could no longer be affiliated with the international organization. However, the government permitted the Jewish Community to continue to operate the workshops and to pursue their original purpose of training Jewish youth in the crafts. With education for Jewish children now limited to eight years of elementary school, something had to be done with the boys fourteen to eighteen years old. The Anlernwerkstatt provided a solution. Here the youngsters could learn skills useful in Eretz Israel or any other place in the world where Jews could take refuge.

After only the briefest of brief discussions, I was enrolled in the carpentry shop. Carpentry was a family tradition. My maternal grandfather had been a carpenter and so had several of his sons. Sawdust, as the saying went, was in my blood.

But the second question, where I should live, did pose a problem. My mother and Claire worked and lived at the home for girls, but we had no home to which I could return after I had to leave the Floersheim Stiftung. The small attic room in the building that housed the girls' home, to which I had escaped on Sunday afternoons to relax away from Miss Caspari, was ruled out. For a boy of fourteen to live by himself was not considered proper.

The Anlernwerkstatt provided a solution to that problem too. Associated with the shops was a dormitory for out-of-town apprentices. Although I was not from out of town, arrangements were made for me to move into the dorm.

The dormitories of Anlernwerkstatt were managed by a Mr. Simenauer and his wife. The Simenauers had one son who, if not quite retarded, did at times act in strange ways. The apprentices had given him the nickname "Bee." No one ever knew what he was doing; he always seemed to be just "buzzing around."

But the son was not the only Simenauer whose behavior, at least in my eyes, was somewhat odd. Perhaps Mr. Simenauer had at one time been a calisthenics instructor, at least that's the impression he left with me. Seeing life mostly in terms of the needs of the body, physical fitness and bodybuilding were his obsessions. He liked to show off his well-muscled body. Quite frequently, he could be seen after his shower (a cold one, of course), jogging naked through the dormitory's hallways. At other times after a shower, he beat and rubbed his body with an especially rough towel until his skin was a glowing red. This, he asserted, stimulated blood circulation and good blood circulation was the secret to a healthy body. Only a healthy body could produce a healthy mind. For other problems of growing boys, such as the emotional upsets caused by their sexual development and the need to find their place in the world, he showed little understanding.

Assigned to a room without regard to age, I found myself with seven boys two or three years older than I who had roomed together for at least one year. For teenagers, two or three years can be a huge difference in attitude and maturity. Not that I was a puny kid, I was fairly tall although somewhat skinny. I did not fit well into this room.

The room, like all the rooms in the dorm, was Spartan. Furnished in the style of army barracks, it had four double bunks, a table with a couple of chairs, and steel lockers for our clothing, nothing else. More like a prison cell than a boy's dorm, I thought. And in one way even worse than a prison: The dormitory had no recreational facilities, no day room, no library, and no reading room. At the end of our long workday, after the evening meal and an occasional bit of housekeeping, there was nothing for us to do but to sit in our rooms until time for lights out. Obviously, this provided plenty of opportunities for nonsense.

Jon (pronounced Yon and probably short for Jonathan) was the undisputed leader of our room. Jon was a tall muscular guy, obsessed with sex. Not that he was chasing after girls, no, his interest was simply SEX: sexual techniques, sexual varieties, and sexual "expression" (pornography).

After the evening meal, when we were in our room with nothing to do, Jon took charge, giving lectures on his ideas on sex. Just lecturing wouldn't have been so bad, but for Jon verbal descriptions, no matter how detailed, were not sufficient. He insisted on demonstrations. With some of the boys in the room participating, he gave demonstrations of homosexual techniques, or with one of the boys acting as a girl, how to make a girl submit. Forcing a girl to have sex, he asserted, heightened sexual enjoyment for both partners. I don't know if Jon's talks were based on actual experience, or just fantasies taken from pornographic literature. I suspected the latter.

Occasionally he conducted contests, masturbating contests: Who could masturbate the longest, ejaculate the most semen, or shoot the semen the furthest; and other inane things.

On Fridays, before Shabbat, Mrs. Simenauer, a small mousy woman, went from room to room dropping off fresh bed linens and towels. It was on my first Friday in the dorm when Jon decided to play a "trick" on Mrs. Simenauer. On his orders everyone in the room would undress completely and start masturbating. The idea was that when Mrs. Simenauer entered the room with her arms full of linen all the boys would stand there stark naked with the penises fully erect.

And so it happened. Mrs. Simenauer dropped off her linen and the young men did exactly as Jon had ordered them to do. Mrs. Simenauer did not say a word, did not scream, nor seemed shocked. She simply ignored the demonstration. Perhaps seeing this kind of behavior appeared not all that strange to her.

I found all this rather upsetting. None of the other boys in the room, however, ever voiced objections or at least I was not aware of any. But then, Jon didn't tolerate opposition. He did not mind at all enforcing conformity. Mr. Simenauer, who must have known about these goings-on, never interfered. He apparently preferred to ignore what was happening, or perhaps he thought this was all part of the normal development of boys.

Though Jon insisted that everyone in the room participate in his games, I refused to do so. During my first week in the room Jon didn't pressure me into joining in. This changed in the second week. One evening Jon announced that he had decided I could no longer exclude myself from the room's activities. He wasn't asking me to take part, he emphasized he was telling me. And he was ready to enforce his demand using what he called "physical persuasion." In front of the assembled room I had to choose: participate in this evening's sexual demonstrations or receive a beating and then be forced to take part.

I refused, mentally preparing myself for a beating or worse. I knew that physically I was no match for Jon, but decided to fight back the best I could. Taking him by surprise, I managed to land a few good blows before he had me pinned to the floor ready to proceed with whatever he had planned. The other boys in the room just stood by watching. Suddenly Jon pulled me off the floor and shook my hand:

"You have more guts than I had expected of you. From now on," he promised, "I will leave you alone. If you want to participate, you are welcome; if not, fine. It's your choice."

That seemed to end the episode, but not for me. I was shocked. Jews, I had believed were supposed to be different and didn't act like that. I had been just too unprepared to deal with the situation effectively. I also felt that in time other attempts at coercion would surely be made, if not by Jon, perhaps by others in the room. Besides I really didn't want to watch these evening activities.

The following Sunday I gathered my few belongings and took them with me on my weekly visit to my mother. Without telling her why, I announced that I would not return to the dormitory. From the tone of my voice she must have realized that there was no sense in trying to argue with me or even to ask why. She approached the head of the girls-home, Betina Falk, better known as Schwester Oberin. (Schwester Oberin, which means chief nurse, is not only a position, but also a title.) Well informed of what was going on within the community, she agreed that the dorm was no place for me.

After having lived in the dorm for not quite three weeks, I moved into our small room in the attic. For the first time since our eviction from our home in the Romerstadt I had a room of my own.

Learning A Trade

The shops of the Anlernwerkstatt were housed in an old factory building in a decrepit part of the inner city, a neighborhood of neglected tenements, dirty workshops, and partially empty factory buildings and warehouses. Here and there were a few cheap bars and seedy looking brothels.

The L-shaped three-story building sat in back of a large courtyard fronted by a rundown tenement now serving as the dormitory for the apprentices. The top floor of the old factory housed the carpenter's and cabinetmaker's shop, the shop in which I was enrolled. On the floor below were various smaller workshops: a locksmith shop, a plumbing shop, a workshop for tool and dye makers, and a shop for constructing light machinery. The ground floor was used for assembling heavier machinery and electrical motors. An annex, the wing making up the shorter leg of the L, provided space for a barber and a shoemaker.

Services we take for granted in modern life, such as shoe repair, haircuts, electrical and plumbing household repairs, were no longer available to the Jews of Frankfurt. Jewish businesses had been forced to close and the non-Jewish businesses had been coerced into not serving Jews. The craftsmen and the boys of the Anlernwerkstatt had to fill this gap.

Our "barber," one of the boys of the Anlernwerkstatt, had learned his trade as a child, watching his uncle cutting hair. He was kept busy cutting the hair of the apprentices and anyone else's in the community willing to trust his hair to a fifteen year-old.

Because shoes were rationed and Jews did not receive shoe rations, the shoe-repair shop, one shoemaker and one apprentice, should have been very busy. But the shop received little material for fixing shoes, so the shoemaker and his apprentice kept themselves occupied with giving good advice on how to keep one's shoes in good shape.

Although the Anlernwerkstatt's electrical and plumbing shops tried to serve the Jewish community, the long working hours and the strictly enforced early curfew imposed on the Jews left little time for the electricians and plumbers to make house-calls. Jewish households had to fix most problems by themselves, doing so with various degree of success.

Words can trigger memories and the word "plumbing" awakened a story that I feel needs telling. It's the story of a man who had the courage to defy the Nazis. Not many were willing to challenge the Nazis, yet this man did; and he did so not for reasons of political ideology –I didn't know his political orientation – but for reasons of human decency. I don't know if anyone in Frankfurt or among the few Jewish survivors remembers him. If not, let the telling of this story be his memorial.

The man's name was Knoblauch. Mr. Knoblauch (he was not Jewish) had a plumbing business in the old part of the city. He was a very tall, heavy-set man, (I was always amazed how this huge man could crawl under the narrow space under a sink to do his work) the kind of man who makes up his mind as slowly as he spoke and who does not like to be told what to think or do. He thought it was unwarranted interference in his business to tell him to whom he could provide services and to whom he could not. Refusing to bow to the Nazi Party's demands, he openly and defiantly provided plumbing services to Jewish homes. To emphasize his objections to the Nazi policy, he let it be known that his Jewish customers paid less for his services than non-Jews. Under the law Jews were paid lower wages then others, he argued, so they also had to pay less for his services.

One day, while walking along a street in the older part of town, not very far from where Mr. Knoblauch had his home and shop, I noticed the words "Jew Lover" painted in large letters in the middle of the road with an arrow pointing up the street. Throwing caution to the wind, I followed the direction of the arrow. After a short distance the words and the arrow were repeated. I continued to follow the arrow's direction. Once more I saw the words "Jew Lover," but this time without an arrow. I stood in front of Mr. Knoblauch's home and shop.

Eventually Mr. Knoblauch was forced out of business. No longer did anyone dare to use his services. I don't know what eventually happened to this stubborn plumber.

Two master craftsmen were in charge of the Anlernwerkstatt's woodworking shop. The more senior, a highly skilled cabinetmaker, had overall responsibility. He loved working with his hands, looking down on those in the trade who relied on machinery for their work. These, he asserted, were not really craftsmen but machine operators. The other master craftsman, a general carpenter, believed in doing a job with the best tools available, including the use of machines. First year apprentices were under the supervision of a young journeyman who was not much older than the apprentices.

Under normal circumstances most of the boys would have gone on to high school, and many would have followed a career requiring some form of higher education. Forced by circumstances into a profession they had not chosen, a number of the boys showed little interest in their work. This lack of dedication to their work made the supervisor's job not an easy one.

Walter Lilly, a first year apprentice, and I belonged to those whose interest in our "chosen" trade was marginal, although, I'm sure we did not quite know what we wanted to do with our lives. We had become friends and, to the annoyance of our journeyman supervisor, and that of the two masters, we spent much of our time discussing subjects of more interest to us than learning how to use the tools of our trade: History, religion, science, and philosophy. Or we occupied our minds and time arguing about books we had just read.

Among the most debated books that made the rounds among the apprentices were two concerning the Jewish uprising against Rome: The writings of Joseph ben Matityahu (Josephus Flavius) and the historical novel "The Jewish War" by Leon Feuchtwanger, based on the writings of the Roman/Jewish historian. (The books were on the Nazi list of prohibited works.) Josephus' defense of Judaism against pagan criticism and disdain, and the willingness of the Jews of antiquity to fight their oppressors, including mighty Rome, impressed us. Jews had not always been helpless victim; Jews did fight back.

Although Walter and I were not the only ones who engaged in these discussions, we received most of the blame for work interruptions, and probably rightfully so. Our foreman had little patience with the two of us and ignored us as much as possible. We were given the least interesting and challenging work, which only increased our boredom. I did not gain many skills in woodworking, but rationalized that I was furthering my education in Jewish history and Jewish thought. And how could this be bad?

One topic not much discussed among the apprentices was politics, at least not openly. We did exchange war news and rumors, and passed along any stories on anti-Jewish actions. The sources of the stories, however, were never revealed. It still amazes me how accurate much of the information turned out to be.

We also knowingly passed along false rumors. At times we indulged in a silly and somewhat dangerous game: A few would concoct a story and pass it along as a rumor recently picked up. Then we waited to see how long it took for these rumors to come back to us as "facts."

When the Anlernwerkstatt was organized it had been for the training of boys only. After the closing of all Jewish schools, the Jewish community had first followed a more traditional way: While the boys went to the Anlernwerkstatt to learn a trade, fifteen to eighteen year old girls were sent to children's homes and old age homes to be trained in household chores. But these positions had become very limited, and work had to be found.

The Nazis did not permit Jews of working age, fourteen to sixty-five, to remain unemployed. To protect the unemployed girls against being shipped off to work camps or factories, the Anlernwerkstatt was opened to a small number of female apprentices. The carpentry shop took two girls. My friend Walter Lilly became interested in one of them at the expense of his interest in books. Our stimulating discussions soon faded away.

At about that time I was taken under the wings of one of the most senior of the apprentices, a very serious, and rather religious, young man. Being the top apprentice in the shop, he was given the most interesting and challenging work, and the right to pick himself a helper. To my great astonishment, and an even greater boost to my ego, he asked the master to assign me to him as his helper.

(Later I learned that the head of the girls-home had once again taken interest in my welfare. An acquaintance of the young man, she had prevailed on him to look after me.)

Finally I began to acquire some basic skills in woodworking. But it was almost too late: The Gestapo had other plans for the boys of the Anlernwerkstatt.

The Judenstern

The "Jew Badge" has a long history in Europe. Contrary to propaganda and popular mythologies, Jews do look like human beings. The authorities, in the past as well as in the 20th century, were faced with the problem of mistaking a Jew for a non-Jew, or vice-versa. Requirements for Jews to wear distinctive garb, hats or insignia had been common practice during the Middle Ages. A badge was apparently first introduced in 13th century France. Early Jew Badges were in the shape of a circle or a wheel. A yellow badge shaped like a disk was probably first introduced in Germany. The "honor" belongs to the Nazis for taking the world back to Medievalism.

In June 1941 Hitler made his fateful move: Germany invaded the Soviet Union. The attack on the Communist empire, long planned, was to achieve German dominance from the Atlantic to the Pacific and from the North Pole to the borders of India and China. With World War II entering its new phase, the Nazi plan for wiping out the Jews of Europe went into high gear.

In September 1941, all Jews living under the domination of Germany were ordered to wear a yellow badge. The badge – the "Judenstern" (Jewish Star), the "Yellow Star," or simply the "Star" – had to be worn on the left side of an outer garment, at about the place of the heart. It had to be clearly visible and it had to be firmly sewn to the garment; just pinning it on was not sufficient. Not wearing the badge in public, trying to conceal it while wearing it, or not wearing it in the proper manner were criminal offenses. Violator of the rules could expect severe punishments. There was no need to ask what that meant. For Jews the Nazis had only two penalties: Death or the concentration camp; and the concentration camp most often led to death.

The badge, a Magen David on a yellow cloth, was inscribed with the word "Jude." (In countries under German rule the equivalent word for Jew was used.) The lettering of the word "Jude" was supposed to resemble Hebrew letters. The badge was about four inches across.

No one was willing to defy the new regulation and refuse to purchase the badge. But wearing it in the prescribed manner was a different matter. All kinds of clever and not so clever schemes of concealment were thought of and a few were even tried. None proved at all practical, several were clear give-aways, and some downright silly: Walking with arms folded across the chest, for example.

Popular among both women and men, especially during cold weather, was to wear a loose scarf, falling across the badge. A more common scheme was to carry a package in the crook of the left arm concealing the badge. Both of these methods allowed the badge to be quickly revealed if one suspected a Gestapo agent or a policeman was watching.

Occasionally a few brave, or foolish, souls did venture forth without wearing their yellow star; some of these failed to return from the outing. Most complied fully with the regulation; the risk for not doing so was simply too great.

Some refused to conceal the badge, not out of fear, but out of pride. The "Jew Badge" was not as a badge of shame, as was intended, but as a badge of honor. Once, passing two women on the street, I overheard one saying: "He is wearing his star with pride."

Our fear that being publicly marked "Jew" would expose us to unpleasant incidents or even violence failed to materialize. If there was an increase in open hostility it could not have been very significant. I cannot say that I noticed an increase. I had always been readily recognized as a Jew, although I could never figure out why; the wearing of the star changed little for me.

At first people just stared. We received many curious glances, even a few embarrassed ones. In a short time, however, most people became used to seeing a few Jewish Stars in the street. Most ignored it, or perhaps they did not want to see it.

If the purpose of the "Judenstern" had been to further isolate the small Jewish population, that purpose was indeed achieved. With the introduction of the badge, most Jews avoided as much as possible going out into the street. Few went just for a walk. Neighbors, who before the Star still had said an occasional "hello," acted as if they did not see you. The badge made it virtually impossible, or at least much riskier, to go to a remote neighborhood in the city to shop in stores off limits to Jews or to shop for vegetables not requiring a ration card. What before the "Star" could have caused merely an unpleasant incident, with the "Star" could have a fatal outcome.

With the German invasion of the Soviet Union, I took up a new hobby: tracking the progress of the war on maps. I was convinced that the end of Nazi Germany had come. Any possibility of an accommodation with Nazi Germany was gone. Even when the Germans won battle after battle, though disappointed, I kept my faith. I read as much as I could on Napoleon's Russian campaign.

Carefully tracing the progress of the war on my maps, I looked for even the smallest hint of a German setback. Obviously, my interest was more than just a hobby. For us the progress of the war was a matter of life and death.

Every Sunday afternoon I walked to the newspaper building in center city to read the news bulletins and military dispatches posted there. Without radio or newspapers, the posted bulletins were the only news sources available to us. Although most of the bulletins were lies and propaganda, valuable information could be gleaned from them, especially when carefully tracing the battlefront on detailed maps. Now with the "Judenstern" on my coat, I no longer dared to be seen reading the bulletins.

Collecting news and then interpreting and analyzing what I had collected occupied more and more of my spare time. Every scrap of newspaper I found I read, any rumor I heard, every small news item passed along by word of mouth, I noted down. Every evening, before going to bed, I would take out my maps and notes and compare the newly gathered information against what I had previously recorded. Of importance were place names mentioned in military dispatches, in news items, and even in death notices. (When the war started to go badly for the Germans, place names were removed from the death notices of fallen soldiers.)

My diligence finally paid off. Early in winter 1941/42 I had picked up a not unusual news item: German artillery, it said, had pounded the Russian city of Rostov. Looking at my map and notes, I noticed that only a few months earlier the Germans had announced the capture of that city. Either the previous report had been false, or the Russians had succeeded in pushing the Germans out of the city. After further study of the reported battle lines I became convinced that indeed the Russians had succeeded in halting the German advance and had launched a successful counter attack. It was the Wehrmacht's first major setback.

Excited, I told my conclusion to anyone willing to listen. When a few weeks later the Germans reported a Russian winter offensive and a partial German withdrawal to "straighten out the defensive lines," I considered my interpretation of the events confirmed. And with that I established a reputation as a "war analyst."

Collecting war news became easier. Jewish neighbors brought me all kinds of information and rumors they had picked up. Some even brought me scraps torn from newspapers, scraps that may have bits of information of some significance. Though much of what I obtained was of little use, the accumulated intelligence eventually produced a fair picture of the war's progress.

The first Russian success was short lived. In spring of 1942 the Germans resumed their offensive and penetrated even deeper into Russia. But the winter of 1941/42 showed that Germany was not able to achieve a quick victory over the Soviet Union. And when in December 1941 the United States was finally drawn into the war, for the Germans victory had slipped out of reach.

Tough times lay ahead for us, but the German military reverses gave us hope that the end of Hitler's Germany had begun.

The Feudal Lords

The Gestapo's nearly absolute power over the Jewish community and over the individual Jew had removed all constraints from the Gestapo agents. In dealing with their Jewish subjects they were the lords, there were no courts of appeal. The individual officer was arrogant, intimidating, arbitrary, and often brutal, and in his better moments, merely condescending.

"Gestapo Muller," chief of Gestapo headquarters in Berlin, was a name familiar to most in the Jewish community. The name was like a bugaboo with which to frighten little children. Yet the local Gestapo head – I can't recall his name – though less well known and less powerful than his chief, was for us much more frightening. Few who called to his office at the Lindenstrasse – Gestapo Headquarters in Frankfurt – ever returned home.

Ordinarily Jews had little direct contact with the Gestapo or any other German authority. Day-to-day dealings were via a liaison officer, Herr Holland. An employee of the Frankfurt office of the Secret Police (he was a member of the civilian branch of the SS and liked to wear his black uniform when in his office at the Jewish community), Herr Holland was an ordinary bureaucrat. Yet in fact, though not in title, he was the head of the Jewish community; and he liked to see himself that way. He usually referred to the community as "meine Juden" (my Jews).

Gestapo officers were not subtle in letting it be known that Herr Holland was not one of them, that he had no real power. Even in his fiefdom, the Jewish community, his power was determined by what they were willing to grant him at any given moment. Of course he resented their patronizing attitude. What irked him the most was that he had to take orders from Gestapo officers of lower rank, and that he had to do so in front of "his Jews." The friction between Herr Holland and his Gestapo colleagues and bosses frequently put him into a foul mood. And who had to pay the consequences? The Jews, of course.

As the de facto head of Frankfurt's Jewish community, Herr Holland was also the boss of the Anlernwerkstatt. This job he enjoyed very much.

He liked to stroll through the shops like a lord surveying his domain. His interest, often a nuisance for us, turned out to be rather advantageous to the Anlernwerkstatt, especially to the woodworking shop.

Herr Holland had a hobby: designing furniture; and his position provided him with the opportunity to indulge in this hobby. He had designed a living room/dining room suite for his home. Now he ordered "his shop" to implement his designs and to do so under his personal supervision. He thought himself very good at designing furniture. He was especially proud of the breakfront for his dining room. He personally installed the cut glass sliding doors.

So proud was he of "his" cabinetmakers that he offered the shop's services to other members of the Gestapo and SS. None were interested; they preferred obtaining good furniture by plundering Jewish homes.

Herr Holland's frequent visits to the shop used up a lot of the master's time, who could not, of course, ignore his visitor. Even more upsetting to the master was Herr Holland's insistence that they review the detailed design drawings, made by Herr Holland's own hand, together. Many hours were spent in discussing the selection of woods and finishes and other, rather minute, details.

Herr Holland, accompanied by the master, loved to watch the apprentices as they worked on his furniture. When he thought progress was satisfactory he was happy, forgetting for a moment that we were the despised Jews. And if the work went particularly well, he even indulged in some light banter with some of the senior boys or the master, who did not like any sort of banter. But if the work did not turn out well and progress was slower than he had expected, and especially if one of his designs did not come out quite the way he had imagined it, he could become abusive and threatening. Gone was the joviality, and we were again the lazy Jews who could not be trusted.

Behind his back the apprentices made fun of Herr Holland's interest in cabinet making and his tastes. Even our master, who rarely made any comments about anything other than things related to our work, made contemptuous sounds about Herr Holland's childish delight in glossy surfaces and shiny brass knobs.

At times our contempt for SS-man Holland got the better of us and could have landed us, and the masters, in deep trouble. I recall one incident of particular recklessness: Someone in the group had taught us the words and tune of the Communist anthem, the "International." During one of Herr Holland's frequent visits, one of the boys started to hum the International, which was picked up by others in the shop. Soon most of the fellows on the floor were either humming or whistling the forbidden tune. It was like waving a red rag before a bull. We were lucky; Herr Holland either did not hear us, which is difficult to believe, or he did not recognize the melody, which I also can't believe. Maybe he was just in a good mood and thought this was just stupid teenage behavior.

Before the Anlernwerstatt could make Herr Holland's furniture. he had to solve one major problem: How to obtain the woods and material needed. Under the restrictions of the wartime economy the Jewish workshop did not receive any allocations of lumber and other necessary items, such as glue, finishes, sandpaper, etc. In fact, the lack was a persistent problem, making it difficult at times to keep the operation going.

Herr Holland solved the problem in a typical Nazi fashion: Corruption combined with the extra-legal status the Gestapo enjoyed in the Third Reich. The Jewish Anlernwerkstatt became a defense sub-contractor. To the astonishment of our neighbors, military trucks showed up at the shops, unloading lumber. Soon the trucks came regularly, delivering material and picking up finished goods.

The deals Herr Holland had arranged were advantageous all around: The defense contractors paid only for material and not for labor (the staff was paid by the Jewish community, the apprentices did not get paid at all), thus making a nice profit; the military got quality work; we received what we needed, including new tools and even machines; and Herr Holland got custom made furniture for free.

Not that the work for the military was always interesting. Indeed, much of it was rather dull. There weren't many carpentry skills one could learn from making ammunition boxes. Occasionally, however, more interesting work did come our way: Once we received an order for cabinets for field hospitals; another time we made prototypes for cabinets, tool chests, and workbenches for mobile automobile repair shops.

The other shops of the Anlernwerkstatt did not have a share in Herr Holland's interest in the crafts and hence they benefited less from the association with Herr Holland than did the carpenters. In his mind these were auxiliaries to our shop, or worse, just a service to the Jewish community. Yet they too benefited.

The shop that benefited most from "our" war work was the machine shop. To meet the delivery schedules our master had to overcome his bias against the use of machines. The shop was modernized with machinery made by the machine shop. The other metalwork shops were kept busy making parts, such as brackets, hinges, etc., needed for "our" military products.

In a way the arrangement provided an additional benefit for the apprentices: We learned to use power-tools.

The arrangements Herr Holland had made for the workshops did not last very long. Perhaps, after he received his free furniture, his interest in the shops waned. Eventually the destruction of the Jewish community forced the workshops to shut down.

Herr Holland did not enjoy his furniture for very long. In an Allied air raid a bomb hit his apartment. The furniture the shop had made for him was destroyed.

The Gestapo had their own uses for the boys of the Anlernwerkstatt. They needed labor for the various "actions" against the Jewish community that got underway during the fall of 1941, signaling the implementation of the infamous "Final Solution to the Jewish Question." The boys of the Anlernwerkstatt were readily available to do the many tasks involved in the liquidation of Frankfurt's Jewish community. The Gestapo's use of the boys increased the friction between Herr Holland and his Gestapo bosses. Once I overheard Herr Holland shouting that these were "his boys" and only he could tell them what to do.

In mid-winter winter 1941/42 the government ordered the confiscation of all Jewish prayer books, all copies of the Tanach and the Talmud, and any books in Hebrew. Also ordered to be seized were Hanukkias, Tephillin, Tallisim, etc. The decree made it illegal for these items to be held in private hands. After the war, when the Jewish people no longer existed, the items were to be exhibited in a Gestapo museum of a "depraved people that history had destroyed."

Jews were ordered to turn over to the Gestapo all "Jewish items" they had in their possession. Agents going from house to house were to pick up "donations" to the planned museum. Homes of those not cooperating would be searched and the residents suitably punished. Most Jews cooperated with the collectors of the "donations" to avoid having their homes searched. One could not be sure what a Gestapo search would produce.

The local Gestapo sprang into action. Collecting teams were organized, made up of Gestapo officers, SS troopers, Nazi Party auxiliaries, and the boys of the Anlernwerkstatt. The actual work was done by the boys, of course: they carried the collected items to trucks and then unloaded the trucks at the Gestapo warehouse.

The day the operation got under way was rather cold. Light snow had fallen during the night, making the sidewalks slippery. Snow from a prior snowfall was still piled along the curbs. The conditions made our work difficult.

I had been assigned to a team of three Anlernwerkstatt boys, two elderly Storm Troopers and a Gestapo agent who was in charge. The troopers and the Gestapo man were not very enthused about their assignment. Rather indifferent and bored, they were not very thorough in the collecting effort. They kept telling us to hurry up, looking forward to a drink in a warm bar. Also they were rather ignorant and had only the most vague idea of what to look for, readily accepting the few items that were offered to them. However, judging from the volume of items brought to the warehouse, other teams must have been more thorough in their effort.

The action took several days. Taking advantage of the knowledge of what was being collected and the collection dates enabled us to warn people, allowing them to hide at least some of what they wanted to protect. My mother hid a number of books and other items, several of which survived the war and are now in my and my sister's possession.

The winter of 1941/42 was not yet done with the boys of the Anlernwerkstatt. In January, a heavy snowstorm lasting nearly a week brought the city to a virtual standstill. Army troops and prisoners of war were sent into the city to help the city's sanitation department with snow removal. The Gestapo too wanted to make a contribution to the effort. Their contribution: The Jewish apprentices.

We worked alongside the city sanitation workers, the war prisoners, and the soldiers. While the sanitation workers and the prisoners of war mostly ignored the group of Jewish boys, the young soldiers did not:

To break the boredom of the work they made a sport of harassing us. They taunted us with obscenities and curses, sang anti-Jewish Nazi songs celebrating the destruction of the Jews, and occasionally even interfered with our work. When they dumped several loads of snow on the sidewalk we had just cleared, our city foreman, who had ignored the behavior of the soldiers, finally complained to their sergeant. The worst of the harassments stopped.

The ordinary soldier was not alone in enjoying tormenting the Jews. Once a young lieutenant, checking up on his men, assured us in a friendly but loud voice that we would not have to shovel snow much longer. Soon we, together with all Jews, would be dead. His men greeted his remark with loud laughter.

Our workday started early in the morning when it was still dark. We worked late into the evening, ending the day when it was dark again, getting home just before curfew time.

For over a week we worked in center city, clearing major intersections and thoroughfares. We worked a long day in very cold weather and even during heavy snowfall. While others, sanitation workers, soldiers, prisoners of war, were given regular rest periods during the day when they had the opportunity to warm themselves and eat some hot soup, the Jewish boys were given only a noon break. Rushing home, about half-an-hour each way, we quickly ate a warm meal and if possible changed into dry clothing.

The city workers, soldiers, and even the prisoners of war, had been issued warm waterproof outer clothing and boots; we had to do with whatever we had. We certainly were not prepared working for days in the cold and in deep snow. Especially our shoes were a problem. After the first couple of days our shoes were soaked through and could no longer be dried out overnight. Since Jews couldn't buy shoes, most of us owned only one pair of boots. Surprisingly, not one of us got sick, or even caught a cold.

We, the apprentices of the Anlernwerkstatt, we were a proud bunch. I recall few, if any, complaints. We never permitted ourselves to show signs of weariness. Perhaps much of this was just youthful bravado, but we felt that we were ready to take whatever the Nazis would dish out.

Our real test was yet to come: When the orders came to liquidate the Jewish community of Frankfurt, the boys of the Anlernwekstatt were forced to work for the SS and Gestapo loading the trains that took the

Jews to their final destination: Ghettos, concentration camps, the camps of death.

A Poem

"Love and Death," a connection often celebrated in romantic literature, occupied much of our minds. But for the boys of the Anlernwerkstatt approaching the threshold of adulthood, these thoughts were not just literature, for us they reflected reality.

One of the apprentices, a quiet boy about a year older than I, had composed a poem, a poem about love and death. The poem, rather lengthy and, at least in parts pornographic, was not badly written. I am sure that the poem's sexual fantasy largely accounted for its popularity among the apprentices. Most likely much of the poem was an expression of the not unusual teenage "angst" that goes with growing up. Yet, I also believe that there was more to this poem than mere descriptions of lovemaking or an expression of the anxieties caused by the awakening of sexual feelings.

The poem's hero, a teenage boy, struggles with his sexual awakening. Afraid of being alone with his girlfriend, he nevertheless tries again and again to be alone with her.

Eventually the two do find themselves alone. After a brief hesitation he kisses and touches her. The warmth of her lips and the feel of her body arouse his desire.

Unbuttoning her blouse, his eyes delight in the beauty of her breasts. But his eyes' delight is quickly overwhelmed by an even greater delight as his hands touch her. The feel of her breasts vanquish all hesitation; desire wins.

The girl, at first resisting his advances, gradually surrenders to his ardor and the pleasure of his touch. With his kisses covering her body, her desire merges with his.

As their ecstasy reaches its highest point they hear a knock on the door. Torn between feelings of joy and guilt the young couple, covering their nakedness stares at the slowly opening door.

Death enters.

Since the war's end, volumes have been written about how much the world knew about the extermination of Europe's Jews. When the young apprentice wrote his poem we were not fully aware of the extent of the killing process, yet we sensed that death was stalking us. So we mourned for the lifecycle experiences that were being denied us: The cautious interplay between boys and girls as they learned to deal with their feelings, the joy of weddings, and the celebrations of births.

All these did not exist for us. What remained of the lifecycle events was only the final one: When the last synagogue was forced to close its doors, almost the only Jewish religious institution still functioning was the cemetery.

The mass deportations were in progress. Trainload by trainload, Frankfurt's Jews were being shipped like cattle to what for most was their final destination. The fellow apprentice, the boy standing at the next workbench, would most likely be gone soon. We knew for us time was running out.

And so the poem's conclusion rang all too true: Even if we were granted the time to experience love's ecstasy, death would surely follow, death by the Nazi executioners or in hopelessness, by suicide.

The poem revealed a fear shared by nearly every one of us: Fear of missing out on life, that before we could taste its full measure, for us life would be over.

Of course not all the boys expressed themselves that way. Sure, some were tempted to surrender to despair; others fantasized about escape, convinced that any attempt would end in failure, hence in death. I knew of an apprentice who had disappeared together with his family. Other stories told of family suicides, of failed attempts to hide.

We engaged in many, often passionate, discussions about how to react to what was happening. Usually these debates began late in the afternoon as work was slowing down and we were getting ready to clean up before leaving for home or the dormitory. Obviously, with arguments occupying our time, cleaning up did not progress very rapidly. Eventually our foreman and the masters had to put a stop to the debates. They too had to be home before curfew.

Cleanup interrupted the debates only briefly; we continued our arguments in the street, on the way home. To passersby it must have looked odd to see two or three boys or young men (more than three would have been a violation of the law) wearing the Jewish Star, earnestly arguing, at times wildly gesticulating, as they walked along the street. We knew, of course, and were reminded of it many times, not to be in the street any longer than necessary, never to loiter, and most of all, never to attract attention. But these were emotional issues, deeply felt although we pretended our discussions were purely intellectual. So at times we forgot the rules.

The apprentices reflected the make-up of Frankfurt's shrinking Jewish community. Among the hundred or so boys only a small minority tried to remain observant; another small group considered itself Zionist; but the majority was far less certain in their beliefs.

Many of the observant boys understood suffering as a necessary part of Jewish existence in exile and saw in our present predicament nothing unusual. Mostly preoccupied with long, to me convoluted, arguments about which Mitzvot (good deeds) had to be kept even under present circumstances and which could be compromised to save a life, they rarely participated in our passionate discussions. Some, trying to impress us with their knowledge of the writings of the Sages, dismissed as inconsequential any of our arguments that to them seemed to be insufficiently grounded in Jewish learning. I suspected that at times they misquoted the Sages, or made up quotes, just to score points against the ignorant.

The religious boys had to face many difficulties. Religious leaders had been among the first victims of the Nazis. Except for the orthodox Underlindau Synagogue, religious institutions were closed before secular ones: The religious Samson Rafael Hirsch High School before the secular Philanthropin; the orthodox Rothschild Hospital, before the non-religious Gagernstrasse.

With Jewish religious services outlawed the last synagogue was closed. Even meeting in homes Minyan was forbidden. And the Gestapo could, and did, enter Jewish homes at will. Shabbat was an ordinary workday. Jewish books were hidden. The orthodox boys, having few opportunities to continue learning. had to make do with what little knowledge they possessed and what they could learn from their parents. But many parents were themselves struggling with their faith, with the apparent absence of God.

The boys, holding stubbornly to their beliefs, expressed their anguish and feeling of abandonment by turning against the few religious leaders remaining in the community. I was friendly with one of the orthodox apprentices, a tall gangling fellow. Today's rabbis, he asserted, were not "real rabbis," they had nothing of the greatness of the sages of the past. Despite my urgings, he refused to elaborate on his opinion. "You won't understand," was his reply.

I leaned toward the Zionists and would have liked to associate with them. But most of them were far too doctrinaire for my taste. I thought that they were just about as narrow-minded as their religious counterparts. Like them, they blamed the catastrophe facing us on the Jews themselves. They saw the present as a terrible historical necessity. They argued that without anti-Semitism the Jewish people would never have roused themselves to leave the ghetto, adopt modern ways, and redeem the Land of Israel.

Yet the few Zionists among us gained much strength from their belief in their goal: the building of a Jewish homeland. They were the most diligent in their work, looking at the present as a preparation for the future. The skills we were learning were the skills needed to rebuild our ancient homeland.

They understood that not all of us would be permitted to survive, thus obligating the survivors to carry the extra burden of doing the work of those who would no longer be privileged to participate in the reconstruction of Eretz Israel.

Lacking the faith of the faithful, nor having the zeal of the Zionists, the majority could not easily escape into what I called, with a bit of arrogance, "ideological day dreaming." Yet we too had to fight despair. We berated those who contemplated suicide as the only escape. Killing ourselves was only doing the Germans' work for them. Let the Germans be guilty of our murder. We pledged to do all in our power to survive. Survival was to be our revenge.

Yet we could do little against what appeared to be our inevitable fate. Realizing that the feeling of helplessness drove some to self-destruction, I had to find a way to protect myself from becoming a victim of despair.

What disturbed me was the rage I felt building up within me. Would this rage ever burn itself out, or will it keep smoldering deep inside, eventually distorting my life? I found it difficult to mention the words

"German" or "Germany" without a feeling of hatred. I was afraid that if I succumbed to this hate, I would end up being no better than a German.

I tried to become uninvolved, to look at events only from a perspective of history, and therefore with detachment. Seeing current events from the position of an observer of historical developments made the present less personal, turning it into an intellectual experience, and hence less threatening. However, with the worsening situation, this protective shield soon lost its adequacy.

I wanted to escape the feeling of despair and helpless anger by hiding from the terror and the nightmares, even if only for a moment. Again I looked to books to provide me with a refuge. I read nearly anything I could get my hands on. Much of my free time I spent lost in a book.

As the destruction of the Jewish community entered its final phase, the Jewish workshops, too, reached its end. The deportation trains took away the staff and more and more of the apprentices. Soon too few were left to make the workshops a useful tool for the Gestapo. The Nazis had certainly no interest in Jewish youngsters learning a trade for their future. The decision had already been made: For us there was to be no future.

For the apprentices whose time had not yet come, all that was left was to wait for the notification to be deported, hoping that the victory of the Allies would come before the dreaded call.

The refrain to this tale is no different from the refrains to most of the others: The poet, the master craftsmen, the apprentices, all vanished in the Holocaust. Like tumbleweed, they had just blown by on my way to where I did not yet know.

CHAPTER 10

TRANSPORTS

The Markthalle

In the year 1941, on the nineteenth day of the month of October, the Nazis took the first step in annihilating of the Jews of the City of Frankfurt.

They rounded up the Jews not in the darkness of the night to ship them off to the camps and ghettos; this took place in the light of day.

They did not hide from the public eye what they were doing; the Jews were marched through the streets of the city for all to see.

The loading of men, women, and children into the trains did not take place at an out of the way railroad siding; the Jews were pushed and kicked into the railcars in one of the city's major industrial areas where thousands of good citizens worked.

And what did the citizens of this proud city do? Did they protest? Did they put obstacles in the way of the agents rounding up the Jews? Did they offer succor to those being taken away?

A few watched in dismay, many with glee, most averted their eyes.

With the German military campaign against the Soviet Union, the hate rhetoric against the Jews gained in shrillness. The Jews, the Minister of Propaganda Dr. Goebbels ranted, must and will pay for the sacrifices the German people were forced to make in their struggle against the Jewish/Bolshevik world conspiracy. The task destiny had given to the German People was to rid the world of the Jewish pest. In the new world order to emerge from the victory of German arms there will be no place for Jews.

Ominous stories were coming out of German-occupied Eastern Europe. In Poland and in areas of Russia that had fallen into German hands Jews were being rounded up and concentrated in ghettos and labor camps.

In early fall, rumors began to circulate that the Jews in Germany and elsewhere in occupied Europe would have to share the fate of their eastern compatriots. An "Aktion" against the Jews was being planned, although what that meant was not clear.

The issuing of night passes to personnel at the Jewish community office made it clear that the rumors of an impending action were not just rumors but that something serious was going on. The personnel ordered to work long hours into the night, past the curfew time for Jews, had been warned not to talk about what they were doing. However, it did not take long before word got out that a list of people was being prepared. List for what?

First the talk was that young people would be shipped to labor camps to work in dangerous ammunition factories, or that they would be sent into salt mines.

Soon a new word emerged: "Umsiedlung" (Resettlement). Jews would be moved into self-governing ghettos in Eastern Europe.

An article in an illustrated German weekly reported on life in a "self-governing Jewish settlement" in German-occupied Poland. A reporter, who had visited the "settlement," reported to the German people on how Jews were coping with the "autonomy" granted them by the occupation government.

In the ghetto, the article said, Jews had been given the chance to live in accordance with the "laws and traditions of the Talmud." Photos showed beggars, who could be seen everywhere in the dirty streets, vying with starving children for scraps of food, while rich Jews, their heads covered with skullcaps, enjoyed themselves in nightclubs, indulging in food, drink, and prostitutes. In their own autonomous settlement, the article concluded, "The Jews are at least stealing only from each other and not from the German people."

We took the article as a hint of what lay ahead for us: Starvation, dirt, and corruption. Only the corrupt had a chance to rule in the ghettos; the Nazis would see to that.

Finally, after a number of nerve-wracking rumor-filled days all speculations came to an end: The "list" was made public. Those whose names appeared in the list were to prepare themselves for "Umsiedlung."

The order included instructions on what the deportees could ship to their new "home" and what they could carry with them on the train. They were given date and time when to report to assembly points.

The order made the point that the list had been prepared by Jews. Jewish leaders, not the Gestapo, had selected those who would be "resettled."

To most people, I presume, "wholesale produce market" conjures up a picture of a bustling place where produce, often packed in colorful crates and boxes, arrive from farms, from neighboring countries, or from seaports to which ships had brought exotic fruits from faraway places. During early morning hours, trucks would pick up the fruit and vegetables brought in by rail during the night and deliver them to markets, stores, large institutions, and warehouses. Smaller retailers would come with horse and wagon, and the owners of even smaller stores would come with their pushcarts to see what they could pick up cheaply before what was left was given to orphanages and other charitable institutions. Stevedores, unloading the trains, would be rushing from here to there, pausing at times for a quick smoke while telling each other off-color jokes.

In my mind "wholesale produce market" conjures up quite a different picture: Here people, the city's Jews, were herded into waiting trains; here the pride of German manhood, the SS, kicked helpless old people, women, and children with their heavy jackboots or shoved them with the butts of their rifles.

The Grossmarkthalle (or simply the Markthalle), Frankfurt's wholesale produce market and distribution center, was a long ten-story structure with a multilevel basement underneath. A railroad track, sufficient to accommodate a long freight train, ran along the full length of the building. An open area adjacent to the track provided space for trucks and carts waiting their turn to be loaded. A ramp, for use by hand trolleys or small electrical carts, led down into the large basement complex, which provided space for storing potatoes, beets, cabbage, and other fruits and vegetables suitable for being held over the winter months. On the building's roof, reminding us of the ongoing war, light anti-aircraft guns were visible.

Across from the Markthalle building, facing the parking area, was the kitchen for the city's school lunch program. There, early in the morning after the arrival of fresh produce, hot lunches were prepared for the school children of the poor.

These were the facilities the SS took over for the four major "transports," as we called the "Umsiedlungsaktionen" (Resettlement operations), the operations that emptied the city of its Jews. In four "transports," taking place over a period of ten months, the nearly thousand-year history of the Jews in Frankfurt came to a virtual end.

I wonder what happened to the Grossmarkthalle. Can one still hear, echoing off its walls, the curses of the SS, the weeping of the children, the cracking of the whips, the screams of the desperate? Will it remind the good people of the city what they had permitted to be done?

For me, the Grossmarkthalle of the City of Frankfurt will always stand for the murder of the City's Jews: From here the city's Jews, the children, the women, the men, the old and the young, the feeble and the strong, were sent to their death. For the boys of the Anlernwerkstatt forced by the SS to provide the labor needed for the operations the experience had been traumatic. Few ever wanted to talk about it.

My memory of the days of the Markthalle has many gaps; many hours spent there remain unaccounted for. Perhaps the mind blotted out some of the worst incidents. Yet one question kept haunting me for a long time: Who did we help, the SS or the deportees?

The Helpers

We stood in the dining room of the Anlernwerkstatt nervously awaiting Mr. Simenauer. About twenty boys, ranging in age from fourteen to about eighteen, instead of going to work as usual had been ordered to assemble in the dining room to receive instructions. We had been asked by the Gestapo, Mr. Simenaur said, to be helpful to the deportees during the forthcoming "Umsiedlungsaktionen:" What being "helpful" meant was not explained. Then we went to our workbenches to await further orders. We didn't do much work that day.

On the morning of October 18, 1941, I went to the Anlernwerkstatt a little earlier than usual, not to work at my carpenter's bench but to join the other selected apprentices in the Anlernwerkstatt's courtyard to await our orders.

Mr. Simenauer and Mr. Schwarcz, director of the workshops, greeted us. After brief "pep talks" by the two men, we were divided into groups of four, though no one told us what these groups were supposed to be doing. Then, while the other apprentices arrived to begin the day's work, we waited.

By mid-morning large moving vans arrived. We were ordered to board the vans, one group of four boys to each van. Still puzzled about what was expected of us, we climbed into our assigned vehicles and off we went. Riding around the city in a moving van almost seemed like fun.

When our van came to a halt in front of an apartment building in which Jewish families lived, we finally learned our mission. Supervised by the two SS men accompanying each van, we were ordered to collect the luggage of the deportees and the household items they were permitted to take with them: small kitchen utensils, pots and pans, hand tools, (non-electric) sewing machines, and even a few small pieces of furniture.

Despite some friction here and there about what to take, the collecting of luggage and the other items went reasonably well. The two SS men of my group, though rather short tempered with the deportees, were not unfriendly to us.

A strange relationship developed between the SS men and us. To our surprise working closely together with the mostly young troopers created a rather informal atmosphere. Of course they were in charge, but they treated us almost like "Kameraden." A Jew could not speak to an SS officer without first asking for his permission to address him. This rule was quickly dropped as being impractical. We talked to them without even addressing them by their rank. During breaks we ate together, with the SS providing the food.

We felt rather uneasy about this relationship which was made worse by the strain that developed between some deportees and us, though most of the deportees tried their best to keep their composure and not take their anxieties out on us boys. Yet some were clearly hostile, calling us Nazi lackeys.

What people were allowed to take with them depended on the interpretation of the rather vague rules by the SS man in charge or on the mood he was in.

Some people, noticing our apparently easy relationship with the SS, tried to enlist our help in arguing with the man in charge about taking a disallowed item. At times this led to angry outbursts by the SS. We, of course, had to pay attention to the orders of the troopers no matter how whimsical and inconsistent. So we ignored the sometimes tearful pleas.

The occasional bad feeling between the deportees and us was not all the deportees' fault. We were young and rather scared, so at times we were short-tempered with the people making demands on us that we thought were unreasonable. I'm sure that we could have taken some small risks. Later in the day, with the van loaded, we proceeded to the Grossmarkthalle to transfer the luggage and the household goods to a railroad freight car.

Time was well past our curfew time, when the job was finally done. Before being dismissed for the day, we were handed curfew passes good for two days and told to report to the Markthalle early next morning. Again no one told us what to expect.

The following morning we reported to the Markthalle as ordered. Mr. Simenauer was waiting for us, but he was not alone: Herr Holland was with him. Though we had not seen him until that morning, we had expected that Herr Holland would be in charge of the Anlernwerkstatt boys. He called us together to give us instructions, though I had the feeling he really didn't know what we were supposed to be doing.

Apparently we were much too early. It was the first hint that the operation wasn't all that well organized.

When the SS troopers finally showed up, they started to give us instructions. Herr Holland protested that we were "his boys," and we would receive our orders from him. At first the SS troopers ignored him. But as he continued to argue and even tried to interfere, they ridiculed him, rudely suggesting that he liked boys, especially circumcised boys. They didn't mind mocking him even in front of us Jews.

Finally he stopped arguing, though he remained present during the operation. He stood watching, looking somewhat forlorn. We would have been amused, if we hadn't been so scared.

Mid-morning the moving vans returned. We were ordered to go to the homes of those being deported to pick up mattresses and bring them to the Markthalle. Back into the moving vans, again accompanied by two SS men, and back to the homes of the deportees. As it was nearly time for the deportees to report to their assembly points, we had to hurry.

After returning to the Markthalle with the loads of mattresses (the mattresses remained on the trucks), we once more stood around doing nothing. This time we had to wait for the SS troopers to finish their midday meal, served to them by the school system kitchen across from the Markthalle freight yard. The troopers seemed in no hurry.

Finally the leader of the troopers called us together. Now, we thought, we'll find out what we were supposed to be doing. But to our astonishment the officer ordered us to the kitchen:

"There is food left over; go help yourself."

There was plenty of leftover food: beef stew and bread. And we did help ourselves. To the amusement of the SS, we ate until not a bit of food remained in the pots.

This easy relationship between the apprentices and the SS troopers did not survive the initial phase of the transport. The brutal behavior of the SS towards the deportees worsened as the operation progressed, deteriorating further with each transport. Their brutal behavior toward the deportees quickly spilled over into their behavior toward the boys.

When we left the kitchen, the joking and laughing SS men were no longer joking and laughing. While we had been gorging ourselves on the food left over by the SS, groups of deportees had begun to arrive and were herded into the Markthalle basement. Gone was the easygoing joviality of the troopers, their almost friendly attitude toward the boys of the Anlernwerkstatt. We were given orders in harsh tones to the accompaniment of vulgarities and anti-Jewish epithets.

We were ordered to unload the mattresses from the trucks and take them into the Markthalle basement. An area had been cleared for the deportees to spend the night while waiting their turn to be "processed" (whatever that meant). In the morning they would be boarding the train.

A brief word about the mattresses: A mattress consisted of three equal sections, which together formed the mattress for a bed. (Actually a bed's mattress was made up of four sections, but the fourth, a wedge shaped section used as a head rest, played no part in this story.) The mattress sections had no innersprings, but were stuffed with various materials. The cheapest mattresses contained straw, medium priced mattresses were filled with cotton wool or similar material, while the most expensive ones contained horsehair. The firmer the mattress, that is, the more solidly stuffed and the better the material it contained, the higher the cost and the heavier the mattress. Not many cheap mattresses were among our load.

In unloading the mattresses from the trucks, each boy had to take the three mattress sections on his back and proceed, that is run, down a long ramp leading into the basement. In the basement, after running through several narrow corridors, the mattress carrier finally reached the large hall-like area where the deportees were being assembled.

The delay in unloading the mattresses had created a problem, and the boys of the Anlernwerkstatt had to pay the penalty. Taking mattresses into the basement at the same time that deportees were being herded into it created traffic jams on the down ramp and in the corridors. Every time a group of people arrived, we had to get out of the way and wait. Why other ramps into the basement were not used, I don't know. Perhaps this was just another sign of poor planning.

The commander became increasingly irritated with the slow progress and the confusion. Cursing Jews in general and us boys in particular, he ordered us to work faster and faster: "Run, run, run! You damn Jews you are holding up the operation!" It wasn't the last time we were accused of slowing down progress.

A few hundred sets of mattresses had to be unloaded. And so we ran, for a couple of hours, from the parking area down the ramp into the basement, and through the long corridors to the assembly area, carrying mattresses on our backs. The mattresses grew heavier and heavier as time went on. Of course, we also had to run back to the trucks.

For the SS troopers, the unloading of mattresses was rather boring. Much of the time they stood around with little or nothing to do, so a few decided to make the operation a bit more entertaining. Armed with sticks – I saw one who had a fancy walking-cane – they posted themselves at an intersection of two narrow corridors, waiting for a boy to come running by with mattresses on his back.

As the mattress carrier came around the corner, unable to see the troopers, one of them would jump from his hiding place to trip the runner with his stick. If the boy went down, the troopers laughed uproariously, kicking the downed boy with their heavy jackboots until he got up. Then, waiting for help to put the mattresses back on his back, he had to endure their taunts while blocking the way for the next mattress runner. This did not speed up the operation. A boy on his way back from his mattress run had to help to unblock the jam.

Luckily, the game came to a quick end. Either the troopers got bored with it, or were ordered to stop delaying the operation. With the exception of a few bumps and bruises, none of the boys was hurt.

We had been ordered not to speak to the deportees, not to give them food or drink, and not to accept anything from them. The deportees too had been told not to talk to the boys, yet this order was hardly enforceable. As we dropped off our mattresses, people did talk to us, mostly making demands. Some did not like the mattresses that were given to them, a few even asked us to find their own mattresses for them. Others wanted to change location to be closer to friends.

We refused all requests, except one: Requests for water we did try to satisfy. And this got us into trouble.

I can't recall how we obtained drinking cups, whether they were smuggled in or deportees gave them to us. We didn't have very many, and in retrospect our efforts turned out to be rather futile.

For those of us who had obtained a cup, the trick was to fill it with water and deliver it before picking up another load of mattresses. Some tried rather unsuccessfully to fill their cups on their mattress run. This presented the SS with an opportunity for a new game: knocking the cup out of a boy's hand spilling the water on the floor. Soon the floor became wet and slippery, making it more difficult to run with a load of mattresses. Few people received water; most cups were lost.

I managed to bring water to a few people. Not that I had devised a clever stratagem; I simply had good luck. I had noticed that the SS men supposedly watching us were not paying any attention to me. Picking up a couple of cups I quickly ran back and forth between the faucet and the deportees. After a few successful runs I thought that I was tempting my luck. I returned to the loading platform to pick up more mattresses.

By the time all mattresses had been put in place, the sun had set. To my relief, the mattress carriers were sent home.

On the third morning, before the sun was up, we were back at the Markthalle for the final day's operation: the boarding of the train. During the night a train of old passenger cars had arrived. Now our task was easier. Before the boarding began we placed buckets of drinking water into the compartments and loaded loaves of bread into a freight car attached to the train. (We stole a few loaves, quickly dividing them among all the helpers.)

As the people started to emerge from the Markthalle basement and the loading began, we had to get out of the way. So we stood around watching.

The SS became increasingly impatient. The deportees, tired and scared, pushing and shoving, and being pushed and shoved as they made their way to the railcars, never moved fast enough for the cursing and kicking troopers' liking. The closer the operation came to completion, the more abusive the SS became.

Finally, the younger boys, I included, were ordered to go home even before loading was completed. The older boys had to stay behind to clean the basement.

We didn't want to go. We had worked long and hard; sending us home before everybody was being dismissed seemed to be telling us that we "couldn't take it." But we had no choice. And despite my protestations, I felt rather relieved.

Casual remarks made by SS officers during the operation made it clear that more "transports" were in the offing. Of course we couldn't know what the Nazis were planning, but in our mind there was no question, our turn too, would come.

Yet, hardly admitting it to ourselves, we searched for reasons why some people had been chosen for deportation and not others. Had it been at least in part their fault? If we could figure out the reasons, perhaps we could avoid deportation.

At the same time some among us felt guilty for not having been selected. A few boys even toyed with the idea of volunteering, jumping on the departing train to go with the people, or heroically take someone's place.

A Not So Funny Joke

Again the rumors, then the curfew passes for the personnel at the Community Office and the nights of preparing the "list." The Gestapo preferred nights for doing this kind of work. And, also as before, useless speculations about who would have to go this time made the rounds in the community. When the day of the second transport came, the boys of the Anlernwerkstatt interrupted their work once more and reported to the now familiar Grossmarkthalle.

The second mass deportation differed in several ways from the first. Perhaps the authorities had felt that the operation had been too gentle to the Jews, had taken too much time, and had required too many resources. The head of the local SD (Sicherheitsdienst – Security Service – the uniformed branch of the Gestapo) now in charge ordered the operation speeded up: No more "coddling of the Jews."

The new rules required fewer preparations, and hence the boys of the Anlernwerkstatt had less work to do: No mattresses had to be taken to the Markthalle, the people had to stand or sit on the bare floor while waiting to be processed; no more extra luggage had to be picked up, the deportees could take only what they themselves could carry; and no bread had to be loaded onto the train, each person had to bring his or her own food. This time there were no old passenger cars, now it was cattle cars. Again we placed buckets of water into the cars, but not for drinking water; the half-filled buckets served as toilets.

Our tasks were fewer, but there were also fewer of us. Although many apprentices were at the Markthalle, they were there not as helpers, but together with their families, as deportees.

The SS did not wait for the arrival of the deportees to harass us, the harassment began at the very outset of the operation. Now the orders were always "run, run, run" even if at the moment there was nothing for us to do. We were given neither food nor drink, nor rest breaks. Only about noon were we permitted a short break. We ran home for a quick bite to eat and then back to the Markthalle. We all made it back in time; no one wanted to find out the punishment the SS leader had in mind for those returning late.

We also had fewer illusions and much less optimism. "Resettlement" was a word now rarely heard. Stories told by German soldiers serving in Poland and Russia had found their way into our community. Stories told of harsh labor, of filthy ghettos, of starvation. They gave the first hints of mass killings of Jews.

In dealing with the deportees, the SS troopers were less patient and behaved far more brutally than during the previous transport. These officers were no mere bureaucrats or soldiers mindlessly executing orders. Their joking and laughing gave them away; they were enjoying the power they were permitted to exercise over people. They indulged themselves in their ability to instill fear. Fear showing in the eyes of their victims was cause for amusement; and the more their victims showed fear, the more biting their jokes and the louder their laughs.

In winter darkness comes early. The SS leader had been pushing hard to get the deportees settled in the basement before complete darkness, and time for black-out; after all it was war.

With the deportees finally in the basement, our first day's work seemed done. Mr. Simenauer, again in charge of the boys at the Markthalle, now asked for permission to release the younger boys, those aged fourteen and fifteen. The answer was no, not yet. So we stood in the dark cold night, hungry and tired, wondering what the SS had in mind for us.

Finally, a low ranking SS man showed up, carrying a rifle. He told us that he had been placed in charge of us and we must follow him.

We lined up and were counted. I don't recall how many of us there were, perhaps ten, perhaps one or two more. Having been counted we were told to wait. Then he left. We stood waiting, wondering what would happen next.

Then, out of the darkness, our SS trooper reappeared. After counting us once more, he marched us off into the Markthalle basement, but away from the area where the deportees were spending the night. He marched us around in the dimly lit catacomb-like basement, through narrow corridors, down some stairs, up others, making right turns, left turns. I soon lost all sense of direction.

"Halt!" Our guard shouted the order. "Line up! Against the wall!"

We stood in the dimly lit corridor uneasily watching him. Once again we were counted. Reassured that he still had the same number of boys he had started out with, the SS man addressed us:

"You Jews," he began, "you Jews cannot be trusted. If I let you go, you will be telling all kinds of stories about what happened here today. Of course, these will all be lies."

He paused. Taking the rifle off his shoulder and fingering the trigger he continued:

"Of course I cannot let you spread false stories. They would only frighten people unnecessarily." He paused, again fingering his weapon.

"My commanding officer ordered me to shoot you, all of you. This is not something I'll enjoy doing. But," he shrugged his shoulders, "I'm a soldier."

Re-shouldering his rifle, he ordered the march to resume. Though feeling increasingly anxious, I was not yet really frightened. I refused to believe that he would shoot us. But what did he have in mind, what were his orders?

Having already lost all sense of space, I now lost all sense of time. I wasn't sure how long we had been marching around; minutes, perhaps hours? We had entered a corridor even more dimly lit than the ones we had been passing through, but it seemed to me, not quite as narrow. I couldn't be sure, there wasn't much light.

Again he ordered us to halt. Once more we were lined up against the wall; once more our guard counted us. Again his rifle came off his shoulder and again his finger seemed poised at the trigger. Slowly he walked along our line like an officer inspecting his troops; or, I thought, a warden looking over his prisoners before the execution.

Is he really going to shoot us? I still refused to believe it, but I wasn't quite so sure anymore. Don't be scared, I urged myself, though my heart was beating just a bit faster; my mouth felt dry. I wanted very much to talk to the boys standing next to me, but didn't dare. None of the boys said anything.

It was very quiet down in the basement. Only the slow measured steps of the SS man broke the stillness as he walked away into the near darkness. What was he going to do? All kind of thoughts raced through my mind: Would he just keep us here in the basement till morning? Perhaps there would be some tasks for us to do before being allowed to go home. Or, a frightening thought, we wouldn't be allowed to go home at all. The SS would put us on the transport, going with the deportees wherever they were going. No one but the SS would know what had happened to us.

Maybe, I forced myself to think more hopefully, he was just trying to scare us so we wouldn't talk about what we had seen. Perhaps this was all it was.

Our guard kept walking. I strained my eyes as they tried to follow him into the darkness. Was his rifle pointed at us?

Then I saw his figure vaguely visible against a less dark, grayish background. At the same moment I felt a waft of fresh air. I realized we were standing near the end of the corridor. Perhaps there was a door leading to the outside and he had opened it.

He turned toward us: "Out with you Jew boys! Hurry up! Go home! No loitering on the way!"

We rushed through the door into the cold fresh air. We ran as fast as we could.

His laughter, echoing off the basement walls, followed us into the night.

In the morning we reported back to the Grossmarkthalle to do whatever tasks were still left for us to do.

Stories in the Night

We stood in line facing the cattle cars, now closed. We stood in silence, waiting, our work done. The train, loaded with its human cargo, also stood in silence, waiting. I tried to envision what it must be like inside these nearly windowless boxes. What were these people doing? Were they standing, or perhaps sitting on the bare floor, exhausted from yesterday's ordeals, from the long sleepless night in the Markthalle basement, from this morning's brutal loading? What were their thoughts as they waited for the train to begin its journey, not knowing where it would take them? Were they hoping that it would never leave, praying for a last minute reprieve, a miracle?

Had we done the right thing? Perhaps we should have done more to help the deportees; perhaps we should have refused to participate in the operation, and to hell with consequences; or have heroically sabotaged the transport.

The SS troopers, gathered near the front end of the train, also stood waiting, though not in silence. I could hear them talking and laughing. I wondered about the thoughts of the soldiers manning the anti-aircraft guns high on top of the building. They had been watching the loading of the men, women and children through their field glasses.

The third transport had started out no differently than the previous operations: Long nights at the Jewish community office preparing the list; the call on the boys of the Anlernwerkstatt to assist in the operation; the march of the deportees under armed guard to the Markthalle; and their waiting and "processing" in the Markthalle basement.

Finally evening had come. With no more deportees arriving, our day's tasks seemed done. I longed to go home, wash up, have a quick dinner and go to sleep. Let sleep hide the events of the day. But it was not to be.

Mr. Simenauer, again in charge of the boys, had received permission to release most of the boys for the night. A small group of about six had been ordered to remain behind on standby, I among them. (Why me? I had just turned fifteen, one of the youngest.) As we weren't permitted to go home for a bite to eat, nor was food provided, we assumed our vigil would be short.

We stood in the large, now nearly empty yard with no shelter from the cold night air. No one would tell us how long we had to remain. Mr. Simenauer tried to learn from passing troopers what we could expect. They either didn't know or refused to tell. Our request for permission to find a more sheltered spot was denied.

Around midnight the SS officer in charge came strolling over to us. Now we would find out when we could go home. Or perhaps he would permit us to go to a more sheltered area, away from the cold night wind. Maybe he had some tasks for us. Anything was better than just standing here doing nothing. Or, I dared to hope we would get something to eat. The officer joined us.

He introduced himself. His name was Weigand. Officer Weigand, a big man towering over us, was in a most jovial mood. Greeting Mr. Simenauer in a friendly manner he included us with a sweeping gesture of his hand. The night, he said, reminded him of the time when he had been a mere recruit in the Waffen SS undergoing basic military training. Reminiscing, he spoke about his time in a training camp somewhere in the north of the country. He told stories of nights of drinking, of fights, of hazing. One phrase he kept repeating over and over:

"Can you imagine," he said laughing, "a thousand young men and not a single woman!"

I didn't want to listen to his stories, his bragging, the dirty jokes. Soldier's talk, I thought, but why tell these tales to us? Why this joviality, this pretense at camaraderie, camaraderie with Jews? On a mere whim he could harm or even kill anyone of us, or all of us. Yet he kept talking, joking, even engaging in some light banter with Mr. Simenauer.

I had seen Weigand in action during the day and during earlier transports. I recalled his swaggering, his bullying, his cursing of Jews; I had watched him kick helpless people. I had heard him order his men to beat people not moving fast enough for his liking. His enjoyment of unrestricted power had been there for all to see. So what was behind this friendliness?

I didn't think his stories were interesting, his vulgarities and dirty jokes amusing. Fortunately, Mr. Simenauer knew when to guffaw, when to chuckle, when to laugh. (Perhaps he appreciated the dirty stories.) We chimed in following Mr. Simenauer's lead, wanting to make sure that Weigand got the impression we were appreciating his stories. If he thought otherwise, the consequences could well have been bad for us.

Eventually the officer ran out of jokes and dirty stories. A brief pause, and without uttering another word he walked away into the darkness. We remained standing in the empty yard, shivering, waiting for morning to arrive.

Gradually the night's darkness yielded to the morning's light. In the darkness it had been possible to imagine that there were no waiting cattle cars, that there was no Markthalle with hundreds of people locked in its basement, to think that all this was not real, that it was nothing but a bad dream. With light returning, reality reasserted itself. With apprehension we waited for the activities to resume.

With the return of daylight the apprentices released the evening before also returned. I had hoped that we who had waited all night would be released. But even before all were back, we were already at work.

The sun was barely over the horizon, when the first deportees came up from the Markthalle's basement, moved along by the shouts and curses of the SS. We opened the cattle cars' heavy doors. Loading began.

The deportees emerged in small groups. Each group was ordered to form a line in front of a car. An SS officer counted the number of people. I can't recall how many people were assigned to a car, but a loaded car seemed crowded. With the proper number reached, the people were ordered to climb in. Any excess was ordered to join the line in front of another car or form a new one.

At first the loading of the people into the cattle cars proceeded in a quite orderly fashion, and I wondered what we were doing here. But then the procedure broke down.

The cattle cars standing on the rails were fairly high off the ground, quite appropriate for the transfer of cattle and goods from trucks. But for people it was not that simple. Especially the elderly found it hard to climb up into the cars. A loading platform or loading ramps would have been helpful; their lack slowed the loading, aggravating an already tense situation.

The deportees had to carry their luggage themselves. Often being reluctant to let go of it, even for a moment, made it more difficult for them to climb up into their assigned car. And families with small children had additional difficulties: handling their suitcases and their frightened children.

The SS officers driving the deportees out of the Markthalle basement at an ever-faster rate either weren't aware of the loading difficulties, or they simply didn't give a damn. People arrived at the train at a faster pace than the SS men supervising the loading could handle.

Loading turned chaotic. Families became separated as children lost sight of their parents, spouses of each other. Children were crying, while screaming parents tried desperately to find them. The SS tried to solve the problems in their usual manner: First by shouting – "move, move, faster, faster" – and cursing, then, if this did not help, by threats, and finally by the use of violence. Some SS men resorted to pushing people along using the butts of their rifles, others used sticks, and many used the SS man's favorite method, kicking with their heavy, hobnailed jackboots.

We, the boys of the Anlernwerkstatt, were no heroes. We did not perform any great heroic deeds. Most of the time we were just scared, trying our best to stay out of harm's way. No one had given us clear instructions of what we were supposed to be doing. Some troopers prevented us from aiding people climbing into the cattle car, or from helping them with their luggage or even their children. ("These damned Jews are quite capable of doing it on their own; a swift kick will convince them that they can.") Others cursed us for not doing enough, accusing us of slowing down the loading. I have no clear recollection of what we did during the early stage of the loading.

Yet somehow we tried to do what we could. Taking risks we helped people, even if ordered not to do so. At times we stepped between a distraught deportee and an SS man's boot. We had become rather adept in avoiding the heavy booted kicks. Not sure of what we were supposed to be doing, many times we did the wrong thing, aggravating the confusion. All the while Weigand kept shouting to speed up the loading, adding to the chaos.

What eventually allowed us to be of more help to the deportees was that the SS, understaffed or not properly led, lost control. Apparently they had assumed fear would make people docile and move along swiftly. Many were frightened, some in a state of near panic; but hysteria did not speed things up.

Taking advantage of the increasing confusion, we, the young apprentices, went into action. Whether we acted spontaneously or if someone organized us, I don't know or can't recall. Ignoring orders, or even violating some, we gradually gained control of the loading process.

The most risky and frustrating task was to bring some order to the line-ups at the cattle cars. We tried to keep families together, or with more difficulty, reunite families that had become separated. But our efforts were at times hindered by the attitude of some of the deportees. Perhaps out of fear or mistrust they were often reluctant to cooperate with us. Some refused to change places in the line, as we urged them to do, or to surreptitiously exchange cars to allow us to reunite parents and children who had become separated. Admittedly, we were often rather brusque, perhaps having picked up some of the mannerisms of the SS, something that did not help in gaining the deportees' confidence.

With loading finally completed, the doors of the cattle cars were slid shut. We, the helpers, were ordered to form a line alongside the train, facing it. A few moments of nervous waiting, then officer Weigand addressed us. He reminded us of his warning not to take bribes from the deportees in order to help them, and not to accept gifts for having done so. (What could the people possibly have given us?) And we had been told not to accept any notes to friends and relatives left behind. Accepting a note was a most serious offense.

"I know you violated these rules. I'll give you one chance to surrender what you have. If you do, there will be no punishment. But if we have to search and do find something, the punishment will be severe."

My heart was pounding. I tried to look calm, even bored. Deep inside my pockets were a few scraps of paper with hastily scribbled notes from deportees to friends and neighbors. I had not read the notes. I wondered what punishment Weigand had in mind.

We looked straight ahead, not one of us moved, not one of us surrendered anything. Weigand now ordered his men to search us. To my great relief the search seemed rather perfunctory. Nothing was found until the officer searching Jon did find something. What the SS man found on Jon was a streetcar ticket. I don't know what the ticket was doing in Jon's pocket. Jews were forbidden to ride streetcars. I'm not sure that the ticket was even valid.

The officer showed his find to Weigand. The jovial Weigand of the night before strutted over to Jon. Standing face to face with Jon (they both were about the same height) he shouted obscenities, demanding a confession. He wanted to know who gave him the ticket and why. (Was Weigand grandstanding in front of his men?) Jon remained silent.

"The whip!" Weigand ordered. "Twenty-seven lashes!"

No one had worked harder than Jon. Big, strong, and apparently unafraid, Jon could always be found at the most serious trouble spots. Usually coarse and loud-mouthed, Jon had helped people quietly and with patience. Now he was being singled out for punishment.

An SS guard took Jon behind our line. There, Jon was whipped. Jon did not make a sound. The SS man counted out loud. Silently I counted along: Twenty-seven lashes and not a whimper from Jon. The whipping continued: twenty-eight, twenty-nine, thirty. I lost count as the SS man no longer counted aloud.

Finally a whimpering sound, apparently coming from Jon, and Jon retook his place in the line. Later he told us that the SS man had whispered that if he gave just one whimper he would stop. I don't know if Jon told the truth, he liked to brag, but no matter, at the moment Jon was our hero.

We stood in a single line facing the closed cattle cars. We stood in silence. An SS officer walked slowly along the length of the train placing padlocks on the doors.

A railroad worker, trailing behind him, checked the locked doors. All was ready, waiting for the locomotive to arrive to take the train away.

We stood waiting for what seemed to me a long time. Into the near silence sounds from the city intruded. They seemed far off, coming from another world.

From somewhere a church bell announced the hour.

At last the locomotive arrived and was hooked to the train. The sounds coming from the black engine, echoing off the Markthalle walls filled the air drowning out all others. The engine, as if impatient, noisily ejected clouds of steam into the air: Valves hissed and throbbed rhythmically; acid smoke belched from the engine's stack.

How did it feel to be the engineer of the train of the damned, to be Charon the Ferryman? I wondered about the train's crew. Did they know what their train was carrying? What did they tell their wives, their children, their friends, when they returned to their homes?

Near the impatient engine the SS leader conferred with the train's conductor. How much longer? Orders were given. A uniformed railroad official, together with a worker slowly walked the length of the train, once more checking couplings and door locks. With his inspection over, the official made his report to the dispatcher.

The dispatcher raised his signal. The engine's whistle gave a few blasts. For a moment steam and smoke enveloped the front of the train and the men standing there. Drive wheels spun, slipping on the rails; car couplings clanked as metal hit metal with the engine's initial pull. Slowly the train began to move. Wagon by wagon the train passed before us. Finally the passenger car carrying the SS guard moved by. The operation was over.

I felt no longer hungry. What I wanted was not to think, just to let my mind go blank. I wanted to run home, bury my head into my pillow, and sleep.

Kaddish

Early in the morning on the day of the fourth transport, a shrunken group of boys from the Anlernwerkstatt assembled in the yard of the Grossmarkthalle. We had expected to be again greeted by Mr. Simenauer – his name had not appeared on the deportation list – but to our surprise, Dr. Martha Wertheimer was waiting for us.

Doctor Wertheimer, her doctorate was in economics, had been a journalist. In early 1933, when the press came under the control of the Nazi Minister of Propaganda, she lost her position at a local newspaper. An ardent Zionist, Dr. Wertheimer now devoted her time to saving Germany's Jewish youth from the Nazi menace.

During the early thirties, when no one had yet thought of extermination as an answer to the "Jewish Question," Dr. Wertheimer was convinced that the Jews in Germany, especially the young, were at risk. Concentrating her efforts on counteracting the pervasive propaganda that pictured Jews as inherently corrupt, she promoted youth groups with the purpose of strengthening Jewish self-esteem and self-reliance. Once she realized that to save Jewish youth from destruction they had to leave the continent, Dr. Wertheimer turned to promoting going to Eretz Israel. After a visit to Palestine, she organized youth groups for Aliyah. Preaching Zionism, she urged people to pack up and leave before it was too late. And if they wouldn't or couldn't go, they should at least let their children go.

Following the November '38 pogrom she escorted a group of youngsters to Palestine. Despite the urgings of friends in the Kibbutz movement not to return to Germany, she insisted on going to organize another group. There were still young Jews to be rescued. Eventually she paid for her decision with her life.

Enraged by the way the Anlernwerkstatt boys had been treated during the Markthalle operations, Martha Wertheimer accused Mr. Simenauer of having failed the boys by not vigorously protesting the behavior of the SS. She was especially incensed by the way the younger ones had been exposed to the viciousness, vulgarity, brutality, and sexual explicit language of the SS. By his failure to protect the boys he had forfeited his right to be a leader of youth.

How she managed to convince leaders of the Jewish community, and more importantly, the SS, to place her in charge of the boys, I do not know. Having achieved this, she proceeded to convince the head of SS detachment to release the boys under the age of sixteen.

Together with the others under sixteen, I protested our dismissal. The boys of the Anlernwerkstatt, we argued, saw themselves as one group. We all had been forced by the Gestapo to do tasks for them; age had never been a consideration. Certainly, we, the younger ones, had carried our load. Letting the older boys do all the work and take all the abuse made us feel as deserters. Though we admitted to being scared, wondering what the SS was up to this time, we were sure that we could take anything the SS was ready to dish out. We had more than proven ourselves during the last three operations.

Dr. Wertheimer, however, refused to listen to our arguments. In her most autocratic manner she ordered us to leave at once. Yet despite our protestations most of us were rather relieved, I certainly was. I had little desire to go through yet another Markthalle experience.

Yet even Dr. Wertheimer hadn't been able to protect the boys from the brutality of the SS. The abuse of the deportees and the helpers had worsened with every transport, and the fourth transport was no exception. At least two boys had to be sent home after beatings by SS men. The day after the transport had left, a very shaken Martha Wertheimer spoke to us, apologizing for her failure to do more to protect the boys.

It was for quite a different reason that the fourth transport was a great blow to me. A few days before the transport, Mr. Herz came to the kitchen at the home for girls. I don't think he had ever come to the kitchen before and certainly not on a weekday. So we knew that he had come to say good-bye. His name and the name of his brother were on the dreaded list. Their elderly mother had to stay behind alone.

Despite the past year's many changes, my mother had managed to preserve our Sunday afternoon moments of relaxation. Not the turmoil besetting the community, nor the increasing restrictions imposed on it, had stopped Mr. Herz from coming to our (or, as I thought of it, my) attic room in the House on the Sandweg. Every Sunday afternoon we sat over cups of ersatz coffee to discuss the war's progress, the deteriorating situation of the Jewish community and, by stressing whatever positive events we could think of, "recharged our batteries."

Following each transport we had tried to convince ourselves that it had been the last one. Surely the Germans needed all their railroad equipment to move troops and ammunition to their widespread battlefronts. The past winter had not been a good one for the Germans: severe setbacks on the Russian front and virtual standstill everywhere else. Increasing call-ups of men, and even women, to the military were straining the economy. Food and other shortages made life more difficult for ordinary people.

But we also knew that we were only trying to deceive ourselves. Despite military setbacks the Nazi regime had not given up on destroying Europe's Jews.

We knew that eventually all of us would be summoned to board the trains of cattle cars. Yet each time another deportation list was issued and the name of a good friend appeared on it, it came as a terrible shock.

As Mr. Herz was saying his goodbye, I noticed his badly worn shoes, his only pair. (To buy shoes one needed a ration card. "Jewish" ration cards did not qualify for clothing, including shoes.) I ran upstairs to my attic room to I pick up a pair of boots, good boots, almost new. I had wanted to save them for the day the war was over. I wanted to leave Germany with a good pair of boots on my feet.

I handed Mr. Herz my precious boots. (His shoe size was the same as mine.) Of course he refused to take them. Being a sick man, he was convinced he would not survive, not even the train ride. "Dead people don't need boots" was his comment. My mother finally convinced him to accept the shoes.

Before leaving he asked me to do him a favor. Mr. Herz was not a religious man but now he begged me to say Kaddish for his mother upon her death. The sick old woman probably had not much time left. I gave my promise.

Then he left. I hadn't cried when I lost my friends, and I hadn't cried during any of the other transports, no matter how bad it got. But this time I sat alone in my small attic room with tears running down uncontrollably. A part of my small world had come to an end.

A few weeks after the fourth transport's departure, a terrible story began to circulate. The military frequently quarreled with the executioners of the "Final Solution" over the use of the rails, a contest the military usually lost. For once, however, they had prevailed. The engine of the deportation train was diverted to an urgent military need; the cattle cars, with their human cargo, were left standing on a siding. Here it remained unattended, the people inside the locked cars receiving neither food nor drink. Two or more weeks passed before an engine became available. It took the train directly to the crematorium of one of the death camps. No one in the train was still alive.

Was this story true? We received it via a German soldier from the Russian front who worked on the railroad. Other terrible stories we had received that way had far too often turned out to be the truth.

(The fourth transport took place in 1942. According to Yad Vashem's records Kurt Herz died in 1942 in the Majdanek concentration camp. Yad Vashem had no information on his brother, Alfred.)

In spring, after the closing of the last Jewish school, the girls were sent home. The home on the Sandweg changed from a home for the young to a home for the old.

Lonely old people like Mrs. Herz, and elderly couples too feeble to take care of themselves, people who had been left behind when the members of their family were deported, were now "warehoused" where once the young girls had been. The Nazis did not want to waste precious rolling stock transporting people to the death camps, people who with practically no medical care and little food would die soon anyway.

Yet some of these old people were stubborn; using all the feeble strength left in them they hung on to life; and a few did succeed. But many more did not have the strength, or desire, to live. Under the compassionate direction of the head of the former girls' home, "Schwester Oberin," the staff, including my mother and my sister, took care of them until death freed them from loneliness and misery.

Not long after Mr. Herz and his brother boarded the train of the fourth transport, old Mrs. Herz died. The time had come for me to honor my pledge to Alfred Herz.

Schwester Oberin, who knew of my pledge, saw to it that I was given the opportunity to make good on it. When the cemetery people picked up old Mrs. Herz's body, Schwester Oberin prevailed on the men to delay the interment long enough for us to get there.

When the time came for the interment – Jewish funerals were prohibited; the dead were unceremoniously interred – Schwester Oberin went with me to the cemetery. The cemetery was (it still is) in one of the city's suburbs. It was a long walk, nearly two hours. Schwester Oberin was a tall slim woman with a long stride. I never saw her walk at a slow pace; I doubt that she knew how. As the two of us rushed to the cemetery, her flying black nurse's cape seemed like wings; I had trouble keeping up with her.

When we arrived, the coffin had already been lowered into the grave and the gravediggers had begun to back fill. We waited for them to finish their work. Stepping up to the grave, I began to recite Kaddish. Since we had no prayer book (prayer books had either been confiscated or were in hiding) I had to say Kaddish from memory, which I did not quite manage to do. Schwester Oberin helped me along, whispering the words into my ear. The two Jewish gravediggers stood by passively.

The fourth transport, the last transport to leave from the Grossmarkthalle was also the last transport in which the boys of the Anlernwerkstatt served as the workforce for the SS.

Until they too vanished into the unsatiable Moloch of the extermination camps, the remaining leaders of our community kept up the struggle for the people. At great risk to themselves, they frequently intervened with the Gestapo trying to ease the pressure on individuals picked on for special harassment for no apparent reason.

CHAPTER 11

CONFRONTATIONS

A Room in the Attic

After moving out of the Anlernwerkstatt dormitory, I settled into the small attic room in the house on Sandweg seven, the dormitory for Jewish girls, where my mother and sister worked. The events of the Grossmarkthalle were still a few months in the future. The Jewish community, though sharply restricted in its activities, was still functioning as a community: The school, the Philantropin, still provided boys and girls with the basics of education, including a Jewish education, and the Anlernwerkstatt still taught Jewish youngsters useful skills. And a majority in the community still believed that they had a chance to survive the war.

A steep, narrow and somewhat dark stairway ascended from the building's top floor to my abode in the attic, a small room and a very small lavatory. The room was under the roof and only the center part, about the width of the two narrow dormer windows opposite the entrance door, had a level ceiling. To the right, in a narrow space under the steeply sloping ceiling, stood my bed. When I was in bed, my feet nearly touched the ceiling. On the opposite side of the room, also under the sloping ceiling, was a somewhat larger area. There we stored stuff from our previous homes: a few small pieces of furniture, many books, some pots and pans and other items for which we had no other space, or any need at the present, yet which we didn't want to discard. Someday, we were sure, they would again find their place in a real home.

Unfortunately, when we had to move once again, we discovered that the roof over the storage area was not in very good shape, and during heavy rains or when the winter's snow melted, water had seeped into it. A number of the storage boxes had soaked up much of the water, damaging several books beyond repair. Among them were some of my favorites.

Heavy curtains suspended from the sloping ceiling, together with a piece of furniture, separated the "living room" from the storage area. The dining room table with its four chairs from our former home in the Romerstadt took up most of the space. My "kitchen," a couple of kerosene hot plates sitting on top of a cabinet, took up what little space remained under the level ceiling. A small coal stove for heating the room stood at the head of my bed under the sloping roof.

The attic's small lavatory was all right for washing hands, but for bathing, its faucet and small sink were quite inadequate. In the room's storage area I kept two tubs: a small one, for every day, and a somewhat larger one for taking a "bath" before Shabbat. During the week I took water from the lavatory sink. Only cold water was available. On Friday afternoons, however, I went down to the home's ground floor kitchen to fetch warm, or rather not so cold, water for my "bath." It took three buckets to fill the larger of my two tubs.

Much of my free time I spent alone in my room. My mother, busy with her many duties, had little time for me. Late in the afternoon, coming home from the Anlernwerkstatt, I made a quick stop in the kitchen of the girls' home where I could usually find my mother at that time. After a quick hello assuring her that I was all right, I climbed up the many steps to my room for a quick dinner eaten in the company of a book.

The room under the roof was my refuge, the place where I could hide. Here I could ignore a hostile world, hoping that the world would ignore me. Stretched out on my bed, staring at the low slanted ceiling, I would let my imagination roam to wherever it wanted to go.

I pictured myself as a writer, living a lonely existence way above the turmoil of life, composing a masterpiece on the history of the world. Occasionally I would climb through one of the narrow windows to sit on the sloping roof. There, close to the drifting clouds, with the noise from the street below barely reaching me, I imagined myself alone on a faraway island where no one could touch me.

And it was to this lonely little room, crowded with the remnants of our once beautiful home, that I retreated after a Markthalle operation to sleep off the horrors of the experience.

Yet even during the period of the Markthalle life went on. Between transports, we tried to impose some normalcy on daily life, to treat the transports as brief interruptions. Much of life's time is taken up by the routine and by the seemingly trivial. If it hadn't been for that, all of us would, most likely, have been driven into insanity.

We also tried to bring some pleasantness into life; and one aspect of that was Shabbat.

Late Friday afternoon, clean after my "bath" and dressed in clean clothing, I went to the ground-floor dining room to join the staff. A few moments later the girls would file in, also freshly washed and groomed, wearing their best dresses. As they made their way to their seats, they wished "Good Shabbos" to the staff, including me. To my great embarrassment, a few of the girls, subtly emphasizing their budding femininity, would linger near me for a moment. A glance from Schwester Oberin, ever watchful, moved them along.

I enjoyed these Friday evening Shabbat dinners, the only time during the week that I had a real cooked meal. The cook, together with my mother, exerted great effort to make the meal something special despite the increasing severity of food shortages and the restrictions on what was available in the "Jew store."

After the meal the girls recited the "Birkat Ha'mazon." There was always some slight competition among them concerning who could read or chant Hebrew faster and better, but it was in good spirit. Guided by Schwester Oberin the competition stayed within friendly bounds and the younger girls, when making a mistake, did not have to feel embarrassed. Grace-after-meals was followed by singing and lots of girl chatter. By then, most of the staff including my mother had left for the kitchen to clean up.

As the evening wore on Schwester Oberin gave the signal that it was bedtime, though bedtime was a little later on Shabbat eve than during the week. Eighth graders and older were allowed to remain in the dining room a bit longer. When the seventeen or eighteen year old girls who had kitchen duty returned to the dining room after having finished washing dishes, it was time for more singing and even dancing. For me it was the signal to flee.

Sundays, with the Anlernwerkstatt closed, I could sleep to nearly noon. Even after waking up I didn't have to get out of bed immediately but could stay in bed for a while reading. But then I had to get up in a hurry, wash and dress, eat my rather indifferent lunch and quickly do my weekly housecleaning.

Mid-afternoon my mother and Claire came upstairs for their two hours off from work. Most Sundays Mr. Herz joined us for his once-a-week visit. Over coffee (ersatz, of course) and perhaps some cake left over from the Shabbat table we discussed the latest war news and spicy community gossip.

The fourth transport brought all this to an end. Illusions about being able to wait out the war in relative quiet were brutally destroyed.

The time had become as gray as the slates of the roof slanting away from the dormer windows of my small attic room, slates discolored from the ravages of time and from birds just passing by. My friends, with whom I had argued about profound things, the pretty girls, whose smiles had embarrassed me, all had vanished into nothingness as if they had been but pictures in the mind.

A Last Pesach

To Dr. Martha Wertheimer the Anlernwerkstatt, the one Jewish institution in Frankfurt still permitted to teach the young, was of obvious interest. That higher learning was closed to Jews did not disturb her all that much; what did disturb her was the Jewish leadership's apparent lack of interest in Jewish (meaning, Zionist) values. Determined to instill in the boys a sense of pride in being Jewish and a sense of worthiness in working with their hands, she made the apprentices of the Anlernwerkstatt her special concern.

But she did more than just instill pride and courage in the young, she fought for them. She dared to argue with the authorities, Jewish or Gestapo, and many times she won her points.

With Shabbat outlawed, Saturday had become an ordinary workday, but not for Dr. Wertheimer. She insisted that the shops close early in the afternoon. Mr. Schwarcz, the head of the shops, consented to an early closing but only if she could get the Gestapo's permission. And to our astonishment, the Saturday workday was reduced by a few of hours.

On Shabbat afternoon, after cleaning up, a group of apprentices assembled in the dormitory's dining room for Martha Wertheimer's Zionist Oneg Shabbat. How many among us were Zionists I do not know; I doubt there were many. But this didn't matter. We didn't have much to keep us occupied on a free afternoon; so many came.

Usually the get-togethers began with a discussion of Zionism, its philosophy and history, the movement's past and present leaders and its achievements in creating a Jewish homeland in the Land of Palestine. Dr. Wertheimer told stories about her experiences in Eretz Israel, about life on Kibbutzim and in the only all-Jewish city in the world, Tel Aviv.

As the afternoon wore on, many of the boys drifted away. By the time the discussion part of the Oneg (Sabbath celebration) was over, only a few were left. I usually stayed with the small group that had remained. We formed a circle sitting on the floor. One of the fellows had an accordion and, accompanied by this instrument, we sang mostly militant Zionist songs Dr. Wertheimer was trying to teach us. After a while, still in the spirit of Zionism, she challenged us to join together in dancing the Horah. A few boys did respond, although the dancing didn't always go very well.

With the dancing our Oneg Shabbat neared its end. Time was getting late and those not living in the dorm, including Dr. Wertheimer, had to hurry home before curfew. Also we had to leave the dining room, which had to be readied for dinner.

I'm sure that the Nazis were aware of our Shabbat afternoon activities. At least on one occasion a Gestapo officer was in attendance, quietly sitting in the back of the room. Martha Wertheimer was not intimidated by his presence. I wondered what he told his colleagues.

Once the mass deportations got underway, lectures on Zionism and the building of a Jewish homeland had become irrelevant, at least for the moment. Our concern was survival. So the topics changed from developing Eretz Israel to staying alive in ghettos, labor camps, and concentration camps.

Dr. Wertheimer tried to encourage us by comparing life in our "Egypt" to the primitive conditions under which the early pioneers colonized the land. With few resources, little water, and beset by diseases and marauding

Arabs, the young pioneers not only survived, they laid the foundation for a new Israel. She lectured on the importance of cleanliness (a topic which apparently needed stressing), insisting that under even the most adverse conditions keeping clean helped to keep both body and spirit healthy.

Of course, neither Dr. Wertheimer nor anyone else could envision what was in store for us. We still had some illusions left, though they were steadily being eroded. Our experiences at the Markthalle and stories from camps and ghettoes that filtered into the community left little room for optimism.

Pesach had been my favorite holiday. Now with the holiday approaching, I once again recalled the delicious cakes my mother used to bake. Usually, by the third day of Pesach, my father had become tired of eating matzah, so cake took their place on the daily table. Of course we still ate matzah, especially for breakfast when eating matzah with coffee had become an established "ritual."

For "Matzah Coffee" we had especially large cups. First a piece of matzah was carefully broken into the cup; next two lumps of sugar were placed on top of the pieces of matzah; finally, hot coffee was poured very slowly into the cup, pouring it over the lumps of sugar. If done correctly, by the time the cup was filled the sugar had completely dissolved. With milk added, the concoction was ready. In eating loud slurps were permitted. All this seemed like a very long time ago.

Rosh Hashanah and Yom Kippur I thought of as holidays of introspection. But who needed all that self-examination when evil seemed to be victorious? How terrible were my sins compared to the sins the powerful were committing? What divine punishment could there be for us when we were already in hell? What we needed was not self-denigration but assurance that the world was not all evil; what we needed was the strength to resist despair and confidence in the rightness of being Jewish.

Pharaoh had ordered the killing of all newborn Jewish boys; the new Pharaoh demanded the murder of all Jews. Pesach was the promise that the Pharaoh of the present would not triumph, that this Pharaoh will be destroyed as the Pharaoh of the ancient days. And Pesach was the promise that the Jewish people will survive and that the Zionist dream, the return of the People to Eretz Israel, will not remain an idle dream.

In 1941, the baking of matzot was no longer permitted. Hungary, though friendly with Germany, had not yet entered the war on the side of the Nazis. She still enjoyed some degree of independence and the Jews there were not yet quite as suppressed as those in Germany. The Jewish community of Hungary had obtained permission to provide matzot for the Jews in Germany. The quantity of Hungarian matzot was very limited, but what we received was sufficient for one Seder night.

Hungary's Jews, however, were not spared. Soon they too found themselves in jeopardy and for us Pesach '42 looked like a Pesach without matzot. Martha Wertheimer thought otherwise.

Despite the mass deportations and food restrictions, Dr. Wertheimer decided that the Anlernwerkstatt would celebrate Pesach, and celebrate with matzot.

She organized a matzah bake. What we had available for baking matzot in no way met the requirements for "Kosher for Pesach:" not the flour, not the oven, not the bowl for preparing the dough. Did it matter? Our answer: An emphatic NO! In a sense, the slivers of "matzah" we managed to produce were more authentic than those produced in modern bakeries.

The religious boys berated our effort. But we rejected their arguments, calling the objectors "sticklers for ritual correctness." Let them worship form and ignore substance! We reasoned. Our Seder did not commemorate the end of slavery, the going forth as a free people to the Promised Land. We were certain that the waters would not part for us to let us escape the murderous hordes of the present Pharaoh. This Pesach was in preparation for going into slavery or even death. Yet it was a Pesach of affirmation, a belief that this Pharaoh will also be destroyed. Even if there was no future for us, there will be a future for the Jewish People.

Mr. Schwarcz, the head of the workshops, granted Dr. Werheimer's request and excused the apprentices who wished to help baking matzot from their work.

Though it was somewhat unusual for me to volunteer for any kind of extra activities, I volunteered.

On the morning of the day before Pesach Dr. Wertheimer and her matzah baking crew took over the dormitory's kitchen. Mrs. Simenauer, the wife of the head of the dormitory, in charge of provisions, agreed to give us a small quantity of flour. After thoroughly scrubbing the kitchen and burning a piece of chometz "the size of a walnut," we were ready to start baking matzot.

The preparation of the dough, adding water to the flour, rolling out the dough, cutting it into proper matzah size, and placing the matzot into the hot oven, all had to be done within eighteen minutes. Tradition had decreed that eighteen minutes after mixing water and flour fermentation began, making the dough unsuitable for matzot. After a few arguments, we reached the decision that the one tradition that must be kept was the eighteen-minute requirement.

Rolling out the dough with a rolling pin would never do, we could not possibly do this within the eighteen minutes. The process of baking matzot had to be continuous, uninterrupted: making the dough, rolling it out, cutting the rolled out dough, and feeding it into the hot oven. How could we do this? For a moment we were stymied. Then someone came up with a brilliant idea: Use a mangle to roll out the dough. (A mangle is a machine for ironing large pieces, like bed sheets. The dorm had a large hand-operated one. By not heating the rollers we hoped to be able to produce thin sheets of dough.) The mangle was brought to the kitchen and thoroughly cleaned. The cook prepared a small badge of dough. The lump of dough was passed through the mangle, and out came a fairly thin sheet of dough. The idea worked!

We went to work. The cook prepared a batch of dough, apprentices fed the dough into the mangle, others turned the wheel, and a couple of boys cut the emerging dough to the proper size and pushed the raw matzot into the pre-heated oven. Dr. Wertheimer, timed the process with a stop watch: just under eighteen minutes.

After each batch of matzot, all equipment was cleaned and a fresh batch of dough prepared. With all this hard work we did not produce a large amount of our matzot. The war-rationed flour Mrs. Simenauer had allotted to us had been rather small.

Next came the preparation of the "Seder Plate." Jews did not receive eggs or meat rations, so we neither had an egg nor a bone. We had no wine and not even one Haggadah. (Haggadot, like all Hebrew books, had either been confiscated or were hidden away.) The cook had given us some greens for the bitter herbs (marror), and we had no shortage of salt water, but that was all. As evening approached, in defiance of the Gestapo a group of boys guided by Martha Wertheimer, celebrated the Passover Seder.

Sitting on the floor around our symbolic Seder Plate, we recited the Brachah over unleavened bread and ate our small piece of "matzah." No one asked the "Four Questions;" we had only one silent question: Who in this room will survive? Yet we solemnly pronounced "Next Year in Jerusalem."

First we sang the traditional songs, but soon changed from the familiar to the aggressive: Songs of defiance, mostly from the Zionist left, asserting that despite all difficulties, by working together a new home would be built in Eretz Israel.

As afternoon turned to evening, the songs became less aggressive and more sentimental. Lauding the special beauty of the Land of Israel now set the mood. After a while Dr. Wertheimer urged us to join in dancing the Horah. There was some poor dancing and worse singing and, even without wine, a lot of laughter.

With the dancing I moved to the sidelines. Feeling more and more depressed, I wondered what I was doing here. The work, the baking of matzot, even the cleaning up had a purpose. But this singing and dancing seemed too much like whistling in the dark and, like whistling in the dark, it failed to dispel fear.

With curfew approaching it was time to end the festivities. Everyone rose and standing in a circle holding hands we sang "Hatikvah" ("Hope," the Israeli anthem).

Then, with what for most of us turned out to have been the last Pesach, our Seder was over.

Why Should the Cook Commit Suicide?

Suicide was the one escape hatch still available to us, and many in the community were tempted to take this way out—and some did. Stories coming from the East, stories of enslavement and mass killings, fear of incarceration and concentration camps; the specter of Gestapo cruelties and the daily exposure to harassments, together with lack of medical care and a near starvation diet had created an atmosphere of hopelessness. It was a daily battle to keep spirits up.

The following story is the story of a suicide that did not happen. It is not the story of a failed suicide, but the story of a woman, who, defying the Gestapo's urgings, refused to kill herself.

Why did the Gestapo urge the cook to commit suicide? It is futile to even ask. The Gestapo people had their own perverse reasons for doing things.

Early in spring of 1942 with the closing of the last Jewish school in Frankfurt, the chattering and laughter of young girls at the home at the Sandweg was replaced by the gossip of old people and often by their silence. The home had become a place for the old who, for various reasons had lost home and family and were no longer able to take care of themselves.

I still slept in the small garret room, though now I didn't spend much time up there. In the home for the aged I was freer to move around. No longer did I have to prepare my own meals and eat alone in my room; now I ate together with the kitchen help. And thus I got to know the cook.

The cook was a fairly tall woman, although it was hard to tell how tall she really was. Her shoulders were stooped, her head drawn in as if she wanted to protect herself from some danger. I thought that at one time she must have been rather good-looking, but not much was left of any good looks. Her deeply lined face and her always disheveled gray hair gave the impression, at least to me, that in her past there was a really sad story. Her age? Perhaps in the late 50s or early 60s. I was convinced that she was younger than she appeared.

The cook fascinated me. The way she looked, stood, walked reminded me of the witch in "Hansel and Gretel." I could readily see her riding a broom. An aura of mystery seemed to surround her, although I could not give even one good reason why I felt that way.

She was not very talkative. She worked well with my mother who shared kitchen duties with her. The curfew imposed on Jews prevented her from coming to work early in the morning (she did not live in the home) and forced her to leave before the evening meals were completed. Preparing breakfast was my mother's job. Cleaning up after supper was left to a group of girls working and living at the home. Supervising the girls was one of my mother's many jobs.

The cook was always friendly to me. Sometimes, when no one was watching, especially not my mother, she would give me a second serving of soup or an extra piece of bread, and that at a time when food portions had to be carefully measured and counted. Yet even her friendliness made me feel a bit uneasy.

Among the many problems that beset the Jewish community in Frankfurt was the lack of medical care. Non-Jewish doctors were not permitted to treat Jews and when the last Jewish doctor committed suicide, together with his whole family, the community found itself without a doctor.

The burden of looking after the sick in the community now fell on Schwester Oberin, the head of the old age home. A professional nurse, Schwester Oberin had some medical training. A neighborhood pharmacy had been designated by the Gestapo to serve the Jews, though without a doctor's prescription the pharmacist could dispense only non-prescription remedies. Luckily, the pharmacist respected Schwester Oberin and was willing to discuss health problems with her, give advice and recommend non-prescription drugs.

Two remedies were in constant demand: Charcoal pills against diarrhea and a salve against skin infections. Diarrhea was a persistent problem, and many of us suffered from skin rashes and infections, most likely due to vitamin deficiencies.

That we didn't have a medical doctor is, strictly speaking, incorrect. Among us lived an elderly man who had once been a doctor. Sometime in the past, probably during the 1920's (before the Nazis came to power), his medical license had been revoked. The reason for the revocation was something adults talked about only in whispers and never in front of children. I suspected that he had performed abortions; but I wasn't supposed to know about these things.

The ex-doctor looked very much the part of a man who had come way down in life, who had sunk to the bottom of society. His suit, and it appeared to me that he was always wearing the same suit day in day out, looked rather threadbare and not very clean. Not that any one of us had any good-looking clothing. Most of what we had was old, worn, often ill fitting, and not always very clean. But next to him we looked well dressed. Usually unshaven and looking unkempt, he had the air of a derelict.

And this doctor, if I may call him that, and the cook lived together; and they weren't even married to each other!

Not surprisingly, the home for the elderly was a house of gossip: Stories of suicides, of people disappearing or dying mysteriously filled the conversations during breakfast, lunch, and dinner and much of the time between. Speculation about what was happening in the war, about new and amazing weapons that the West would soon unleash against the Nazis and thus end the war, quickly made the rounds. "True" stories about secret deals between Germany and Switzerland (or Sweden, or some other neutral country) to exchange Jews for money, food, or raw materials excited the old people. Other stories were more frightening: The Gestapo, it was rumored, was plotting new diabolical actions.

Usually I paid little attention to this "old folks" talk. Hence, when I heard that our cook had been summoned to the notorious Lindenstrasse (Gestapo headquarters) I dismissed it as just another product of the rumor mill. Why the cook? Despite the fascination she had for me, I felt sure, in my saner moments at least, that she was a quite ordinary person, and not at all interesting or mysterious.

The rumor turned out not to have been false; the cook had been summoned to the Gestapo. A Jew called to appear at Gestapo headquarters seldom returned home. To our surprise and relief the cook did.

Returning from the Lindenstrasse late in the afternoon, for she had been at the Gestapo nearly all day, she went directly to Schwester Oberin's office. My mother was called in. The door to the office remained closed for a long time. When the cook finally emerged it was close to curfew time and she had to rush home. My mother and Schwester Oberin remained in the office for a while longer. Dinner was very late that evening.

Of course I was curious and pestered my mother to tell me what was going on. At first she refused to talk about it but then she relented:

The Gestapo had urged the cook to kill herself. Asserting that she had nothing to live for, it would be best if she simply ended her life. If she needed help, the agent mocked, the Gestapo was willing to assist her. The choice, however, was hers. If they gave a reason for the suggested suicide, my mother did not tell me, or perhaps she didn't know; or the cook may not have reported all that the Gestapo said. The cook promised Schwester Oberin that she would not kill herself.

Although I was not satisfied with what my mother told me, she refused to say anymore. And, as the cook continued to show up for work, after a few days I shrugged off the incident.

Before a week was up, the cook was again called to the Gestapo. The previous scenario was repeated: A day at the Gestapo followed by a conference with Schwester Oberin and my mother behind closed doors.

The Gestapo had repeated their "suggestion" of suicide. Again the cook held firm, promising Schwester Oberin to defy the Gestapo. During the next three or four weeks the cook was repeatedly called to the Lindenstrasse and urged to commit suicide. Then, without a prior hint, the cruel game appeared to have ended. After several weeks went by without summonses, sighs of relief could be heard in the house. The kitchen routine returned to normal.

The feeling of relief had been premature. Now I received a really big scare: My mother was summoned to the Gestapo office, not the cook. For more than three hours she had to listen to Gestapo's harangue: Only the cook's suicide would end the summonses:

"Urge her to kill herself." The officer told my mother. "You must help her out of her misery. She has only way out: death by her own hands."

Then the episode ended: No more summonses, not for the cook, not for my mother. Had the cook won the contest? I don't know. Just about everyone in the home had theories about the "why" of this game. All had been worried about what could happen to the cook and to my mother.

I continued to pester my mother for more details. I was sure many mysterious things had been discussed behind Schwester Oberin's closed door. After a while, however, doubts began to set in. Perhaps there really was nothing more to the story than what met the eye. New dangers, new catastrophes pushed the cook's story out of my mind.

Eventually the cook and her ex-doctor friend became just ordinary victims of the Holocaust.

The Tzaddik

We called him the Tzaddik. I don't recall his real name, although I can still picture him: A little man with a wrinkled face and a sly smile. He liked to tell stories and propound on philosophy. Always an optimist, he was strong in his conviction that the evil Nazi empire could not last very long. He preached courage and hope. And I can almost still smell him; he gave off a terrible odor.

The Anlernwerkstatt had been closed; the girls had left the House on the Sandweg, now a home for the aged; and the first transports were behind us. He showed up one day with his pushcart to collect kitchen refuse. On his pushcart he carried two barrels filled with the foulest smelling brew. He explained, in a conspiratorial whisper, that he had a secret formula, he had developed it himself, for converting kitchen refuse into fodder for swine. The fodder he sold to farms on the outskirts of the city.

His operation was quite remarkable. Jews were prohibited from conducting any kind of business, let alone doing business with Gentiles. Yet he was able to collect refuse from both Jewish and non-Jewish homes and sell his product to farmers. To make this story even more intriguing, he had the protection of the National Socialist Farmers Organization, the Nazi organization to which all farmers had to belong. Within the Nazi scheme of things, the organization was fairly influential. Food production rated a very high priority.

Whatever the truth about his secret formula may have been, the farmers had strong faith in the potency of this foul smelling concoction. They swore that it fattened their pigs better than any other fodder available. The Nazis preferred not to upset the farmers.

The Gestapo, of course, did not like this. The Jewish community was their exclusive fiefdom and they did not readily tolerate interference from anyone, not even from Nazi Party organizations. Our Tzaddik had been taken into Gestapo custody a number of times. Using threats, and even promises, they tried to make him reveal his secret formula, but without success. A few days in the Gestapo lock-up and the old man would reappear, his sly smile still on his face, to once again prepare his "secret formula" and trade it to farmers for money and protection.

The Tzaddik had become a regular visitor to the house on the Sandweg, or more specifically, to its kitchen. On Friday afternoons he would show up, all washed and clean (the odor was still with him, though a bit less pungent), wearing his Shabbat suit and a fresh white shirt with a tie, not to collect garbage, but to talk.

He seated himself at the large kitchen table during the kitchen's most hectic time, when the cook and my mother were busy preparing the Shabbat dinner. From the meager rations, together with whatever unrationed vegetables were available to Jews at the moment, they did their best to make a meal that broke the monotony of the week. It was no easy task. There wasn't much variety in the market basket available to Jewish customers, usually beets of one sort or another and occasionally a few potatoes. There were red beets and a type of beet used as winter fodder for cattle. These were boiled, fried, mashed, or prepared in any other innovative way the cook and my mother could think of. Beet recipes had become a favorite topic of discussion in the community.

The beets, I thought, tasted terrible. Not only did they have to be prepared with lots of imagination, they also had to be eaten with an equal amount of imagination.

Ignoring the activities around him, he made himself comfortable at the kitchen table, slowly sipping the cup of "ersatz" the cook had poured for him. With the second cup in front of him, he was ready to talk. I tried to join him as often as I could. (I don't remember what I was doing at the time, but apparently I did have time off, at least on some Friday afternoons.) Finding an out-of-the-way corner in the kitchen, I got my own cup of "ersatz." Sitting quietly I listened to his talk. Most of the time I was his only audience. Everyone else was too busy to listen.

His discussions, or rather monologues, were not primarily about fodder for swine, although he usually started out by relating his latest adventure with the Nazis, amused by their stupidity. With these preliminaries out of the way he became serious, turning to the subjects he favored most: history and philosophy.

The world was a good place, and evil was bound to be defeated. That, he asserted, was the lesson history taught us. His greatest concern was that the young among the Jews would be misled by the incessant propaganda against the Jewish People and by official falsifications of history. In time, he feared, we would lose pride in being Jewish and with it, faith in our future. He had taken it upon himself to counteract the anti-Semitic propaganda, to correct its misleading information. He emphasized the great contributions Jews had made to civilization: To the sciences, the arts, and especially to ethics.

His strongest ire, however, was directed against the Nazi racial theories.

The Nazis not only misunderstood, but worse, they distorted and misused Darwin's theory of evolution. He tried to explain the true meaning of Darwin.

Without fail, this last topic led him to his favorite subject: the impact of geography on mankind: on history, on political development, on the evolution of ethnic groups, and on national cultures. He refused to use the word "race." To him, race was a Nazi concept without any scientific validity. The wide-open spaces of Russia, often covered with snow during the long winters, had formed the character of the Russians and influenced Russian art: the Russian inclination toward autocracy and the melancholy beauty of her literature. Similarly, the unlimited horizon of the American continent had produced a society that was open and progressive.

His lectures usually ended with an optimistic prediction: The free society of the United States of America would not tolerate for long the evils besetting today's world. One day, he was sure of that, America would put an end to the satanic Nazis.

One gray rainy afternoon the Tzaddik came for the last time to sip his Friday cups of "ersatz." I don't recall what he discussed, and it is quite possible that I wasn't there, having to work that day. This then is the story of his end as I was able to piece it together:

By the time he finished his second cup of "ersatz" the rain had stopped. Keeping his large umbrella folded, he said his usual good-bye and Shabbat Shalom and went out into the street. As he walked toward his home, not very far away, a young man in a Storm Trooper's uniform came towards him. Rules required that a Jew had to step off the sidewalk until the uniformed Nazi passed. Whether our Tzaddik did not do so, or did not do so quickly enough, I cannot say. In any case, the Nazi punk pushed the old man off the sidewalk, knocking him into the gutter. He fell into a rain puddle. The Tzaddik lost his temper. Getting up, he broke his large folded umbrella over the Nazi's head. Two German soldiers, witnesses to the incident, came to the "aid" of the Storm Trooper. Together the three young men gave the old Tzaddik a severe beating. Then they dragged him to the nearest police station. The police turned him over to the Gestapo.

A few days later the Jewish Community office was told to pick up the body of the old man for burial. I presume his "secret formula" had died with him.

The Dregs of Society

One spring day of 1942, a short time after the fourth transport had pulled out of the Grossmarkthalle and the Anlernwerkstatt had closed its doors, I nervously reported to the Jewish community office to apply for work, as the law required. I hoped no jobs were available, at least not immediately. However, hanging around the old age home doing nothing would not have pleased my mother.

Jews from age fourteen to sixty-five, male and female, were forced to work. With the exception of the few who, with Gestapo permission, staffed the Jewish community office, Jews could work only as low-level unskilled laborers in accordance with the rules set by the local Gestapo. The Gestapo determined where Jews could work and what working conditions had to be met.

Employing Jews was cheap. Not covered by labor regulations, Jews could be worked as many hours as the employer wished; were paid at a rate fixed at about one third of the legal minimum wage; did not receive pensions, health insurance or overtime pay; and had no access to grievance procedures. However, good political connections were required to obtain Jewish laborers. Jews made good workers. Believing, falsely as it turned out, that being employed protected them from deportation, they worked diligently.

Using Jewish labor also had its disadvantages. Chief among these was that Jews had to be segregated: Preferably, Jews worked as a separate group away from other workers. Another, seemingly trivial regulation forbade Jews to listen to radio broadcasts. It was customary to have loudspeakers in work places and lunchrooms playing martial music and, at least while the war was going well for the Germans, giving war bulletins at regular intervals. Jews had to be kept out of earshot of the radio. And of course, Jews could not eat lunch together with the other workers.

Jewish employees could number no less than five. The Transports and the not so infrequent arrests of Jews for violating one of the many Gestapo rules at times reduced that number below the minimum. The employer either had to requisition additional Jews, or dismiss those remaining, causing disruptions in the work place. And the Gestapo could and did at times order Jews away from their regular employment for special Gestapo projects and actions, further aggravating the unreliability of Jewish employees.

Consequently, most Jews worked in large factories where the segregation rules could be more readily implemented. However, smaller enterprises could also take advantage of cheap Jewish labor, that is, if they had a "special in" with the Gestapo or the Party. Then they did not have to follow the rules to the letter.

To my disappointment I didn't have to wait, a job was waiting for me. I had been afraid that I would have to work in a factory, so I felt relieved that the job I received was outdoor work.

My employer was a small agency supplying laborers to the City's Department of Parks for seasonal work and special projects. The agency's owner was a young man who, having been wounded early in the war, had his military service behind him and was now free to make money. Having a brother-in-law in City Hall, he set himself up as a city contractor, and being a member of the Nazi Party he had no problem hiring cheap labor, including Jews, for his enterprise.

Employing Jews made good business sense: Charging the City full labor rates, including overtime premium, he paid his Jews only in accordance with the special "Jewish" wage scale, which excluded the overtime premium. (The standard work-week was 48 hours. However, we worked a 54-hour week plus six to eight hours overtime.)

I was assigned to a crew of ten laborers doing maintenance work in city parks: trimming shrubs, cutting grass (by hand with a scythe), sweeping and repairing walks, and preparing flower beds. Though the day was long, the work was not very strenuous. And when the weather was fine it was pleasant to work outdoors.

The foreman, an elderly city employee recalled from retirement due to the wartime manpower needs, was a quiet man. At the start of the workday he gave his instructions, and assuming that everyone knew what to do, left us alone, working by himself somewhere nearby.

Our work crew of ten was made up of five "asocials" and five Jews, four middle-aged men and me. "Asocials" were people with minor police records: vagrants, habitual petty criminals, drifters, prostitutes, and the like, people about whom one reads occasionally in newspapers, perhaps in novels, and in detective stories. Most, if not all of the group's "asocials" had spent time in jail and were on probation. Like the Jews in the group, they did not dare to complain too loudly about long hours or poor working conditions. An "asocial" who accumulated an unsatisfactory working record, or was caught in another crime, usually wound up in a concentration camp. But unlike Jews, "asocials" were German citizens and could claim the few rights German citizens still enjoyed.

Among our group of "asocials" a hierarchy of sorts had evolved. The unofficial leader of the crew was a retired pimp. He had achieved his leadership position by the force of his personality; even our City foreman acknowledged it. His deeply lined face and nearly white hair created the impression of a kindly old man. But one soon realized that he was neither old, nor had he always been very kind. Middle aged and watched by the police, he had mellowed a bit.

Next in line was a habitual street brawler, a fellow who once had delighted in bar brawls. He was reputed to have beaten up policemen who tried to interfere in this type of entertainment. Out of jail on good behavior, he always went for the toughest jobs, showing off his strength and demonstrating that he could work harder than anyone else.

The third ranking member of the team was a "madam" of uncertain age. I don't remember much about her. She was not very friendly and never said very much. Everybody on the team treated her with respect, which may have been due to her being a close friend of the pimp.

A hunchback was number four. When called to military service, the examining doctor had determined that his hunchback was hereditary. In accordance with the Nazi laws of eugenics, he was sterilized. Embittered, he took to petty crime. Despite his deformity, he was as strong as an ox. Being rather short tempered none dared to cross him. Of the group's fifth member, probably also an ex-madam, I have no recollections.

The Jewish team members were all former clerks and salesmen with Christian wives and children, although they themselves had not converted. All their lives they had considered themselves as Germans. Now, having to wear the Jewish Star and having to do manual labor, they felt resentful. I wasn't sure against whom their resentment was directed.

At first the Jewish contingent included a young man who refused to consider himself Jewish, though he had to wear the Jewish Star. Knowing next to nothing about Judaism or Nazi ideology, he even appeared unaware of anti-Semitism. He did, however, know a lot about the German military. He knew all about ranks, insignias, arms, military organization and what not. One day, he hoped, he would be able to rip off his Jewish Star and become a German soldier. He soon left the team. Perhaps his wish had been fulfilled and he had exchanged his Star for the uniform of a Nazi soldier. His replacement was another intermarried Jewish man.

Our non-Jewish co-workers, though not unfriendly, mostly ignored us. They did their work, we did ours; little communication between us was required and none of us was given to small talk. However, a problem did arise: what to do at lunchtime.

A city-provided construction trailer followed us from place to place. Every morning when we arrived at our work-site, it was waiting for us. The trailer stored the tools and bad weather clothing provided by the City. (The Jews on the team did not receive the City's bad weather gear.) Equipped with a table, a bench, a few chairs, and a stove, it also served as the crew's lunchroom.

And that was the problem: Because Jews could not eat lunch together with non-Jews, the five Jewish workers had to eat their lunch elsewhere.

Of course we could eat our lunch sitting on the grass in the park – not on the park benches, these were off limits to Jews – or have our lunch at a different time. But our foreman kept finding reasons for rejecting all suggestions as impractical, although I can't recall his reasoning. And since no one really objected to eating together, a form of token segregation was finally agreed upon: The Jews sat at one end of the table, the "Aryans" at the other. The foreman never ate lunch with us. He went home for a much longer lunch period.

Being the youngest on the team – I was then fifteen – the duty of readying the "lunch room" for the mid-day break fell on me. About an hour before lunchtime I went to the trailer to light the stove for warming up the lunch pails the workers had brought with them, put on water for "coffee," swept the trailer, and arranged the segregated seating around the table.

I hated the job. There were always complaints, mostly coming from my Jewish co-workers: The lunch hadn't been heated properly, being either not hot enough or too hot; there was not enough hot water in the pot for coffee; the trailer hadn't been properly swept; or whatever the complainers could think of. I gladly would have given the job to one of them, but our leader the pimp insisted that the job belonged to the youngest.

About three quarters of an hour by train from Frankfurt's main station is the town of Hoechst, an industrial suburb dominated by a complex of chemical plants of the industrial giant, and supporter of the Nazi regime, the IG Farben Corporation.

Also located in Hoechst, somewhat away from the chemical plants, was a large hospital. And, next to the hospital, in a wide-open field that once had been sown with wheat and rye, an underground bombproof hospital had been constructed. Now the backfilled ground above the hospital was to become productive land once again. Our young Nazi boss received the contract for doing the work.

In late summer our team of "asocials" and Jews had to give up the easy work in the parks for the backbreaking work of removing the coarse rock-filled backfill and replacing it with good soil.

The contract involved "heavy labor" entitling the workers to premium pay and, more importantly, to supplementary ration supplements. The young Nazi, the company's owner, insisted that the City provide these benefits to all his workers, including the Jews. Apparently the City complied.

What he did with the premium pay I do not know, we didn't see it. However, the ration coupons he passed on to his Jews, who could not use them in the "Jew" store. Their wives, however, who did not wear the Jewish Star and did not have "J'" ration cards, could use them when they did their regular shopping.

For my mother, it was a bit more complicated. As a convert, my mother did not wear the Jewish Star. However, our household was considered "Jewish" and hence she too received "J" ration cards and had to shop at the "Jew" store. Once in a while she took my "heavy labor" coupons to a regular store. Most store clerks, though perhaps somewhat suspicious, accepted the coupons without questions. Occasionally a clerk did ask to see her regular ration card, which, of course, she wouldn't show him.

With the new job a new relationship developed between the "asocials" and the Jews. No longer did we just work alongside each other, now in violation of the rules, we worked as a team. I suspect that this change was not only due to the work but also to location. Working outside the city and out of the public's eye, violating the rules of segregation was less visible.

For removing the unwanted dirt from the site, French prisoners of war had laid a narrow gauge track for small dump cars of the type used on construction sites and in mines. No machinery for digging up the backfill was available; all work had to be done with picks and shovels. Even large boulders had to be dug up with hand tools, broken up with a sledgehammer and shoveled into the dump cars.

The work was hard, the weather was still hot, and there was no shade in the open field. But I didn't mind that. To the contrary, I became a bit of a show off. I prided myself in being able to keep up with the "tough" guys in doing the heavy work. I looked down on my fellow Jews who found it difficult to cope with the heavy tasks. Their muscles were sore, their backs hurt, and their hands were blistered.

Inspired by what I perceived as Zionist ideals, I looked with contempt on their "Bourgeois weaknesses." I was the "new Jew," the Jew who one day would redeem the Land of Israel "with the strength of his hands and the sweat of his brow."

As a consequence, the tension that had been lingering between my Jewish co-workers and me, ever since their complaining about the temperature of their lunches and my resentment of their complaining, came out into the open. The men, old enough to have been my father, resented having to work with a fifteen-year old boy on equal footing, a boy they perceived as ill mannered. They ordered me around, asked me to do this or that for them: bring them a drink of water or clean their tools at the end of the day, while they sat down for a spell to catch their breath and rest their sore muscles before departing on their long way home. Sometimes I did what they asked, but most of the time I curtly refused.

The petty criminals showed considerable tolerance toward these middle-aged Jews. The pimp finally put an end to our squabbling. He made it clear that I was a member of the team and was not to be ordered around. Next he gave me a lecture, asserting that at my age the body was not sufficiently well developed to take the constant heavy strain. He expressed concern that I could do permanent harm to myself. He made sure that the heaviest work was assigned to the "asocials."

No longer able to show off in front of the other Jews, and no longer having to listen to their orders and unfriendly comments, our relationship did improve, though it never became warm.

The pimp did more than promote peace within the group. While the "asocials" could buy refreshments at a kiosk in the hospital, the Jews could not. When he was sure no one was watching, the pimp would share a bottle of the cool drink with us, or at times would bring a bottle for us. His kindness was a violation of the law and, being on probation, any law violation was high risk. I am not sure we appreciated what he did.

Shortly after we started the work at the hospital, the team gained another member, also an "asocial." The young Polish prostitute never did much work, being occupied much of the time servicing her clients, which she had no problem in finding. The soldiers of a heavy anti-aircraft battery, positioned on the grounds adjacent to the Red Cross marked hospital buildings, kept her busy. And if they were not enough of a clientele, the French prisoners of war handling the dump-cars had their turn while waiting for us to load the cars.

No one on our team resented her not doing her share of the work. The pimp and the others made sure that her clients did not abuse her and that she did not get herself into trouble with our boss who showed up once in a while.

As the hot days of summer faded into the cooler days of fall, the heavy work was behind us. What remained to be done was to spread topsoil over the now clean backfill and prepare the ground for seeding or planting. I didn't see the job's completion; I received a new assignment away from the team in violation of the rules.

Not far from the hospital the city's parks department operated an experimental garden. Here new fruit and vegetable hybrids were being developed. The hybrids of tomatoes, peppers, cucumbers and others I don't recall were expected to produce more and better fruit during Germany's short growing season than did the ordinary varieties. A gardener, also a retired city employee called back to work, was in charge and needed a helper. I was to be the helper.

The work the old gardener gave me was light: weeding, cultivating, tasks like that. I was a willing worker and an interested helper. The old man responded positively to my eagerness to learn. He showed me how to transplant seedlings, how to spot plant diseases, and how to prune so that only the most vigorous stalks would bear fruit. And he showed his appreciation of my work by giving me some of the experimental fruit. The few green peppers, some ripe tomatoes, and a couple of cucumbers, produce not available in the "Jew" store, were a welcome addition to our monotonous diet. I was sorry when the job came to an end.

I had enjoyed the outdoor work, even the hard work at the hospital. And what I had enjoyed just as much, or perhaps even more, was the train ride from the city to the suburb. For as long as I can remember, I had thought of travel by rail as romantic. Even this relatively short ride had its romance.

I had to leave home for the station early in the morning, even before the end of curfew, and as Jews were not permitted to use public transportation, I had to walk to the station located at the other side of town. In my pockets I carried two special permits: One allowing me to be in the street before the end of curfew, the other permitting me to use the railroad.

The train was never crowded and despite my Jewish Star I had no problem finding a window seat. I loved watching the scenery go by: villages just waking up as the train rushed past, fields of grains and vegetables, patches of forest, and the complex of the switching tracks as the train approached a station. I always felt sorry when the ride reached its destination. But soon the war put a damper on my enjoyment.

Following the United States' entry into the war, Allied air activity over Germany increased. As welcome as this was, for me it created a problem.

From the railroad station to my home was about an hour's walk along one of the City's busiest streets. Apparently the American flyers enjoyed disrupting the late afternoon and early evening hours when the day-shift workers were on their way home and did some last minute shopping. Quite often I too found myself walking home in time for the early evening visits by the Americans.

One late afternoon I was hurrying home from the railroad station when the sirens sounded an alarm. I was still quite a distance from that part of town where I could find shelter in a Jewish home.

No one but air-raid wardens and policemen were allowed in the open during an alert. With Jews not permitted in public shelters, what was I supposed to do when caught by an alert on my way home? I did the only thing I could do: I kept walking.

A policeman stopped me and ordered me off the street. I told him that I was on my way home, and there was really no other place where I could take shelter.

I'm sure he was quite aware of that. He responded not by giving me instructions, but by cursing the Jews. After having apparently run out of curses he aimed a kick at me. Thanks to skills developed during my Markthalle experiences I managed to avoid his heavy jackboot. Taking the kick as a signal of dismissal, I walked away. I reached home as the "all clear" sounded.

Paralleling the main street was a narrow street that passed through a section of town reputed to be a "red light" district. I had never walked through that part of town with its unsavory characters. After the incident with the policeman I decided not to follow the main thoroughfare but walk through the dingy and unsafe streets of ill repute. Not one of the districts seedy citizens ever bothered me, not even during air-raid alerts.

I felt at ease among the dregs of society.

The "Puff Boys"

The plundering of Jews began as soon as the Nazis took power and continued through all the years they ran Germany and ruled much of Europe. Even toward the very end, when hardly anything still in Jewish hands was worth taking, the looting didn't stop. In this enterprise the Gestapo and the SS had the advantage over other Nazi organizations, but all tried to grab whatever they could.

Frankfurt's large Jewish hospital, the Gagernstrasse Hospital, had stood unused for some time. The expensive operating room equipment, the beds and furnishings of the wards, the pots and pans in the kitchen, all the many things found in a modern hospital were still there, little had been removed. The complex stood deserted, its equipment and furnishings gathering dust.

The Wehrmacht, having to deal with ever increasing casualties, requested that the former Jewish hospital be made available to the military.

But the Army's medical services wanted the buildings only, not what was in them. The City, now the owner of the hospital, hired an auctioneer to dispose of everything inside.

The Gestapo, ever helpful, ordered the Jewish community to assist in clearing out the hospital. Six boys, fifteen- and sixteen-year old former apprentices from the Anlernwerkstatt, were selected for the job. I was among them. An "older" Jewish man, a young man in his twenties, led the work gang.

Herr Puff, the auctioneer the City had obtained, was a big jovial man. But this job turned into a severe test of his joviality. The Gestapo, ignoring legal niceties, had decided that Jewish property, even former Jewish property, was theirs for the taking. Gestapo agents and their buddies from the SS roamed freely through the hospital complex and ignoring the auctioneer's effort to take inventory, and their agreement with the City, took what they wanted.

At first Herr Puff tried to list what the Gestapo people took. But with the Gestapo people becoming threatening and abusive, he quickly gave up. However, the Gestapo was not so readily forgiving. They continued to harass him and had some good laughs making fun of the auctioneer's name. (In the local slang a "Puff" is a brothel.)

Herr Puff tried to guess what interested the looters and remove these items before the Gestapo could get their hands on them. Assuming that the Jewish boys were working for him, he ordered us to start loading his trucks even before inventory had been completed. But his effort was frustrated. As far as the Gestapo was concerned Jews worked for them. When they ordered us to load their trucks before the auctioneer's, that's what we did.

One of the hospital's facilities was a luxuriously furnished convalescence pavilion. Here patients who could afford it could live comfortably during their convalescence after full hospitalization was no longer required. The pavilion provided individual apartments furnished with quality living room and bedroom furniture and with many handsome decorative items. Everything went into the SS vehicles as Herr Puff stood by helplessly.

The men from the Gestapo and their SS buddies were not the only looters robbing the City. Herr Puff did some looting of his own. Some of the items we loaded on his trucks also failed to make it to the auction inventory list.

Seeing the looting, we decided that we too could take part in this game. Being poorly supervised, it was not difficult for one of us to get lost occasionally to scout around in the large hospital complex for anything worth taking. There wasn't much for us to take, of course. What we did take had to be small and easily concealable. I'm sure that some of what we ended up taking, we took solely for the sake of taking something on the sly.

On one of my forays, however, I did find something well worth taking a risk of smuggling out of the hospital compound: I discovered a fully equipped shoe repair shop: Small tools and sheets of synthetic material for soles and heels. The closing of the Anlernwerkstatt had deprived our community of many services that one takes for granted in today's society, including shoe repair. Losing the shoemaker's shop had been especially serious. With Jews not permitted to buy shoes and unable to have their shoes repaired, most of us walked around with run down heels and holes in the soles.

With the tools and the material, I figured, I could fix my shoes myself. Hiding what I selected, I managed to gradually smuggle my loot out of the hospital.

Thanks to Herr Puff's mode of operation, removing our loot undetected did not pose much of a problem. Moving vans took large items such as beds, cabinets, operating room equipment, etc., to his warehouse. But for the myriad of smaller things a wagon was used. The wagon Herr Puff provided was a large four-wheeled flatbed that had to be pulled by two people. Whenever the wagon was fully loaded, two of us took it to the auctioneer's warehouse. It was easy to conceal a few small items within the load and drop them off on the way. A few trips and my shoe repair tools and materials were safely at home.

Night raids by the Allied Air Forces on German cities were on the increase. Often hundreds of bombers, sometimes as many as a thousand, would drop their loads on a city. But the Allies also staged smaller raids, nuisance raids and diversionary raids involving only few aircraft. During some of these brief raids a large number of small incendiary bombs were scattered over a wide area. These stick-like bombs could break through the roof of a building and lodge themselves in the attic floor, or at times even penetrate to the top floor before bursting open. The bomb's chemicals, when exposed to oxygen, generated an intense fire, hot enough to ignite any flammable material within a radius of a couple of feet. The bomb's chemical fire could not be put out with water; it had to be smothered, preferably with sand.

Our work at the hospital was nearing completion, when it occurred to someone that at night the hospital buildings were unprotected. A few incendiary sticks could well start a conflagration.

(I don't understand why the military, which wanted the hospital buildings, did not guard them at night. But the Army remained uninvolved throughout the cleanout operation.)

The solution: Let the "Puff boys" patrol the buildings at night. This time the Gestapo co-operated with Herr Puff: they issued us night passes. After our day's work was done, we rushed home for a quick dinner and then back to the hospital to assume our night watch. Equipped with firemen's helmets and flashlights we were supposed to inspect all buildings every two hours, even if there was no alert. During an alert or air raid we were to patrol continuously.

A few cots, a table and a number of chairs were set up in one of the hospital wards. There we could rest between patrolling. In the morning we were to rush home for a quick breakfast and then back to the hospital for our regular tasks.

During the first evening we dutifully did what we had been ordered to do: We checked the deserted buildings. But we had another reason for doing our duty: we wanted to make sure that the Gestapo and the SS had left the hospital compound. Once sure that we were alone in the large complex, we conducted no further patrols.

The leader of the "Puff boys," also in charge of the night watch, was an interesting young man. After returning from our one and only night patrol, he gathered us around to tell us about his past activities. Accompanied by his guitar he related to us, in songs and stories, about the efforts of a group of young enterprising Zionists to bring Jews to Eretz Israel in defiance of the British:

A ballad which he sang for us and which he tried to teach us to sing told of a small group of young people trekking through the "Wilds of the Balkans," guided by local peasants and bandits to Greece. At a deserted spot on the Greek coast, the young adventurers boarded small boats. Aided by smugglers in avoiding British patrols they made their way to Palestine.

The ballad concluded with the joy felt by all when the Land of Israel finally appeared at the horizon.

But the ballad was not all joy. Each of its stanzas ended by cursing those who doubted the rightness of the Zionist enterprise and by damning the cowardly and corrupt (Jewish) bourgeoisie who again and again had tried to thwart the young pioneers from fulfilling their dream: building a new socialist homeland in the ancient but beautiful land between the Jordan and the Sea.

It was indeed a strange picture: A bunch of fifteen and sixteen year old Jewish boys wearing the Jewish Star together with German firemen's helmets showing the swastika, singing a left wing Zionist song in the midst of Nazi Germany.

His stories did not end, of course, with the fulfillment of his Zionist dream. When Italy seized Albania and invaded Greece, the organizers of the treks realized that time was running out. They decided that a final group would go, this time including the leadership still in Germany. They had acted too late.

When German and Italian forces attacked Yugoslavia, the young Zionists were hunted down by the Yugoslavian police and jailed. The newly installed fascist regimes of Croatia, Bosnia, and Serbia turned the Jews over to German and Italian forces. Those handed over to the Germans were "repatriated" to Germany and released into Jewish communities; those turned over to the Italians were taken to southern Italy and imprisoned.

With that our leader's story ended.

But that isn't the real ending of the story; the story ended with an ironic twist: The young pioneers "set free" by the Germans perished in the Holocaust, while several of those jailed by the Italians were freed by Allied Forces invading Italy.

Herr Holland

I didn't mind at all being unemployed. After my job with the gardening company had come to an end I didn't have a real job for a while. Occasionally, I did some work at the Jewish Community or the Sandweg old age home, or, less pleasantly, was called by the Gestapo to do some task for them. And as long as my mother worked at the old age home, which provided room and board for her and her two children, there was no real need for me to be gainfully employed. So I spent much of my time immersed in books, waiting for the Nazis to be defeated and the war to come to an end. Then, hopefully, we could go to Palestine to be reunited with my father.

However, I had to have a real job, one approved by the Gestapo. As regulations required, I reported to the community office to see Mrs. Kahn. It was her duty to assign jobs from a Gestapo-provided list.

Usually this was no big deal, a mere matter of routine. But to my horror and consternation, instead of sending me off to a job, Mrs. Kahn told me to report to Herr Holland. She didn't explain the change in the routine. So I took a deep breath as Mrs. Kahn knocked on Herr Holland's door.

Herr Holland, the Gestapo's representative at the Community office, was no stranger to me, though I never had any direct dealings with him before.

I knew him from his many visits to the Anlernwerkstatt, remembering his occasional friendliness toward the boys and especially toward the master, and his more usual arrogant behavior that made it clear that the shops depended on his good will; and I had seen him at the Grossmarkthalle during the transports when he morosely watched from the sidelines as the SS contemptuously pushed him aside, taking charge of "his boys" from the Anlernwerkstatt. More recently I had seen him strutting around the Community Office being the "Big Boss."

Like many of the boys of the Anlernwerkstatt, I felt somewhat contemptuous toward him. But now I had to face him, and that was different. While we waited for Herr Holland's permission to enter his office, Mrs. Kahn gave me instructions on how to correctly approach a Gestapo official.

"Walk up to his desk. Stand quietly and don't move. Don't fidget and don't slouch! Stand straight. Wait until Herr Holland gives you permission to speak."

Mrs. Kahn entered the office with me but remained standing near the door, as protocol required. Herr Holland, wearing his black SS uniform, sat imposingly behind a large desk looking at some papers.

A little push from Mrs. Kahn and I walked reluctantly up to his desk.

I stood there facing him, nervously wondering what this was all about. Herr Holland continued busying himself with his papers. An eternity of silence elapsed, a minute or so, before he looked up. Staring at me with an irritated frown he told me I stood too close to the desk. I took a step back. More silence, more paper shuffling.

"Your prayer, I want to hear your prayer." This time he did not even look up from his papers.

Prayer, what prayer? I was puzzled. Of course I did not dare to ask him what prayer he wanted to hear, nor did I dare to look at Mrs. Kahn to signal for help. Either she had failed to instruct me properly concerning this requirement for a "prayer" or, more likely, I had been too nervous to pay proper attention to what she said. Realizing that something wasn't going right, she stepped forward. In a low voice she asked me what the problem was.

"He wants to hear my prayer," I whispered.

She gave me the proper instructions and quickly returned to her post near the door. All the while Herr Holland continued studying his papers.

Herr Holland looked up: "Speak!"

Confused and intimidated I stumbled through the required formula:

"I am the Jew Hans Israel Marx, Kennummer (identity number) A12270."

(A regulation enacted on 17 August 1938 and coming into force on the first of January 1939 required Jews to have an authorized "Jewish" name. If one did not have one, the name "Israel" was given to men, "Sarah" to women. One always had to use one's "Jewish" name when dealing with a German official. My Jewish name Benjamin wasn't Jewish enough for the Nazis, so my birth certificate was amended to include "Israel.")

"Louder!" This time Herr Holland shouted.

I started over, even more flustered. I tried hard to sound loud and steady, but I was aware that my voice was terribly shaky and squeaky. Another pause only increased my nervousness. His next words sounded to me like a sneer:

"So you are sorry you are a Jew."

Was this a question or an assertion? I wasn't sure, but I didn't really care what it was. With this statement, or question, or whatever, my nervousness, my near panic, evaporated. I answered, or rather shot back at him, and this time with a voice that was loud and clear:

"No! No, I am not sorry to be Jewish! I'm proud to be a Jew!"

Silence filled the room.

Then came the explosion. Herr Holland's normally ruddy face turned even redder, nearly purple. His fists came crashing down on his desk.

"Out! Out!"

If he shouted anything else, I didn't hear it. Mrs. Kahn, having recovered from her shock, rushed forward, grabbed me firmly by my arm and dragged me out of his presence.

In the community office everyone was standing. Apparently all had jumped out of their seats when they heard Herr Holland's bellow. They stood there, their faces showing shock, fear, and resentment. The resentment, I realized, was directed against me. By upsetting the routine I had endangered everyone's position, especially Mrs. Kahn's. No one spoke a word, not to me, not to each other. We stood in silence, waiting.

After a few tense moments, Herr Holland's voice came through the closed door ordering Mrs. Kahn into his office. I felt guilty. Now she had to deal with his rage and with the consequences of my foolish loss of temper. After only a few minutes, she re-emerged. In an accusing tone she ordered me to go home and tell my mother to report to Herr Holland at once. Then she pushed me out the door.

I ran home, I ran all the way. Briefly I told my mother what had happened. Quickly she informed Schwester Oberin of the emergency then rushed to the community office.

I stayed behind, feeling fearful, helpless, resentful; resentful at myself, at Mrs. Kahn, at Herr Holland, the Germans, at the world. All kinds of nightmarish thoughts entered my mind. Would my mother be arrested? Would Herr Holland send us to jail or a concentration camp?

Upon her return from Herr Holland's office, my mother went directly to the office of Schwester Oberin. There the two women talked for a while. I waited outside the closed door, my imagination continuing to run wild.

At the community office my mother had been told to go directly to Herr Holland; he was waiting for her impatiently.

Herr Holland seemed far from being agitated. He opened the conversation, if what took place could be called a conversation, by telling my mother of the discovery he had made: He and my mother had been born on the very same day.

Looking at their lives, which had started practically at the same moment, it was clear to him who had made the right choices. He reminded her that both she and the Jewish Community were in violation of the law. No "Aryan" (legally my mother was an "Aryan" despite her conversion) was permitted to work for Jews. He would overlook the violation, but she must leave her job at once. He referred her to a company authorized to employ foreigners, various second-class citizens, and other lower orders, but no Jews. He did not elucidate to which category my mother belonged. Then the audience was over. My behavior in his office never came up.

Years later the thought occurred to me that there was something not quite right with the story. Letting my mother and the community leaders off the hook when there was a clear violation of the segregation law did not readily fit the patterns of Gestapo behavior. And I found it difficult to believe that Herr Holland, or the Gestapo, had been unaware that my mother was a convert; no one had ever made it a secret. But more than that, the affair of the cook had taken place only a few months before. Yet all this time no one, not Herr Holland nor anyone else from the Gestapo, had raised objections to my mother working at the Jewish old age home. So the question, what game was being played?

Whatever the reason for this charade may have been, our stay at the home on the Sandweg came to an end. We gathered our belongings and moved into an apartment, sharing it with another family. In August '42 my mother went to work in a factory and I was sent to a job without having to see Herr Holland.

For us a new chapter began.

As the summer of 1942 faded into fall, most of the inhabitants of the old age home and much of the remaining staff had been shipped to death camps. The home was closed. A smaller and rather decrepit facility was set up to house the shrunken community office and the few old and sick people not yet deported. The best room in the building was set aside for Herr Holland's office. My sister and a couple of other young girls continued to work for the community.

* * * *

Eventually Herr Holland's position was eliminated. The Gestapo handled the few Jews remaining in the city without intermediary. Herr Holland was drafted into a citizens' militia of boys and older men organized for a last ditch defense of the crumbling Third Reich. He was killed in the defense of Berlin.

In 1933 the Jews of Frankfurt had numbered about 30,000. When, in 1939, the doors of the world were shut to Germany's Jews, several thousand found themselves trapped in the City. By 1943, following the major transports, the number of Jews had been reduced that to a mere 600. When in late March 1945 American troops entered Frankfurt they found fewer than 300.

Of those that had been deported, only a small handful survived.

PART IV

A GHETTO WITHOUT WALLS (1943 – 1944)

CHAPTER 12

AMONG THE REMNANTS

The House on Weiherstrasse

With mixed feelings I said good-bye to the small attic room at number seven Sandweg, my abode for the past two years. Giving up the room also meant giving up some of my independence. I had become quite used to being alone, daydreams filling much of my time. Wandering through the lush and peaceful world of my fantasies had provided an escape from the harsh and terrible realities of the present: The transports, Gestapo actions, and not least, hunger.

Yet, contrary to these negative feelings, I welcomed the move; I felt I was returning home, back to the family. Once again to be together with my mother and sister in a real home, no matter how cramped, restored my confidence that I was not alone in this hostile world.

Perhaps it is ironic, but thanks to the Gestapo's decision that my mother, though converted to Judaism, was racially "Aryan" and therefore could not work for Jews, we were now much more part of the Jewish community. At the home my mother, busy from early morning to late at night, had had little time for her friends and neighbors, and her children, or for getting involved in the affairs of the community.

Now with a regular job, working regular hours, she no longer had to be on call twenty-four hours a day seven days a week. Once again she took care of our home rather than of a home for schoolgirls or old people. And once again the burden of making a home for my sister and me was on her shoulders; I felt I had been set free.

Frankfurt's shrunken, and shrinking, Jewish community was made up of families of mixed marriage, including some who were barely willing to acknowledge their Jewish connections, and a few old and sick people the Nazis did not think worth the effort to be send to the death camps; they weren't expected to live much longer.

Although walls did not surround us, ghetto life was the reality. As in medieval times laws prescribed where Jews could live, where they could shop, where they could work and what work they were permitted to do. Contact with non-Jews was limited: At the workplace with supervisors and a few German workers, and at the non-Jewish "Jew" store to rather unfriendly store clerks.

The "Aryan" partners of mixed marriages had a bit more freedom than the wearer of the Jewish Star, and hence had a bit more exposure to the outside world; but even they spent much of their time inside this wall-less ghetto. Social contacts outside our confined world were practically non-existent.

For the community of remnants, the complexities of the racial definitions and the rules of segregation that evolved from the "Nurnberg Laws" of 1935 were not merely theoretical legal matters, they had real everyday consequences. Who was Jewish and the degree of "Jewishness," that is, how much "Jewish blood" coursed in the veins, couldn't be dismissed as nonsense. The consequences were deadly serious; they determined one's fate.

The Nazis had not kept their plans secret. Once all "Volljuden" (both parents were Jewish by birth) who did not have an "Aryan" spouse were deported, the turn would come for the "Geltungsjuden" (offspring of a mixed marriage brought up Jewish) and for Jewish partners of mixed marriage without children, or with no children under the age of eighteen. Even though the implementation of the "Final Solution to the Jewish Question" was not always consistent or uniform throughout the Reich, it was quite clear that if the Nazis remained in power long enough, even some categories of "Mischlinge" (those of "mixed" blood not brought up Jewish) would also find themselves on deportation trains.

Like a Sword of Damocles, the threat of deportation hung over our heads, a constant backdrop to all that we were doing. We, the remaining "Volljuden" and "Geltungsjuden," knew that we were living on borrowed time and time was running out. The protection against deportation provided by the "Aryan" spouse or parent would not last much longer. Though expecting the summons to report for deportation, we prayed it would never come. Selfishly each one hoped that someone else would be filling the next transport's quota.

When the City of Frankfurt expanded beyond the confines of its medieval walls, the walls came down and the inner city became enclosed by a chain of pleasant parks. The first to move out of the inner city, even before the walls were all gone, were, of course, the well to do. With the city's continuous expansion, the middle class followed the rich. Soon industry, needing space to grow, invaded the area beyond the former wall, especially areas adjacent to the river. On the city's east side a river port and rail facilities were developed, attracting more factories and warehouses. With their arrival upper and middle class residents moved out and the East End turned into a working class neighborhood. With the working class came the Jews: Small shopkeepers, artisans, and simple working people.

In time an area in the East End became known as the "Jewish East End." East End Jews were generally more orthodox, less assimilated, and not as prosperous as those living in the city's other "Jewish" neighborhood, the fashionable West End.

The difference between the prosperous, liberal, and more assimilated "West End Jews" and the less wealthy, more traditional and less integrated "East End Jews" was exemplified by the two large synagogues that dominated each area: The West End's "Liberal" Temple and the city's Main Orthodox Synagogue located in the East End.

Following the November 1938 pogrom, the Jews of Frankfurt were gradually forced out of the city's more desirable neighborhoods, which became "Judenrein." By early 1941 the city's Jews found themselves concentrated in a few East End "Judenhauser" (Jew houses).

Buildings with a majority of Jewish tenants were designated "Jewish" and, like their inhabitants, were marked with the Jewish Star. The Star had to be affixed to the building's entrances and at each apartment door.

When Jewish tenants became the minority, mostly due to the deportations, the Star was removed from the building and the remaining Jewish families forced out. If a "Jewish" house was damaged in air raids, assistance or materials for making repairs were not provided; and when a

"Jewish" house was destroyed or made unlivable, there was no replacement. Gradually Frankfurt's Jews became ever more crowded together in what remained of "Jewish" apartment houses.

Our apartment was on the second floor of a "Judenhaus," not far from the former orthodox Main Synagogue. Like most of the buildings in the neighborhood it had seen better days. How old it was I do not know, though most likely well over a hundred years. It stood at the corner of a small street of four buildings, three on one side one on the other. Number two, at the opposite end of the street faced a park with a small pond (Weiher), which had given the street its name.

Unlike most other apartment houses around us, ours had once been a mansion put up by a rich burger trying to escape from the crowded city. The second floor balcony, the only balcony on the house, with its sculptured stone balustrade and two heavy stone column supports, hinted at past bourgeois solidity. But with the columns crumbling, the now unsafe balcony symbolized the decay of the building and the decline of the neighborhood.

The stucco on the outside walls of the building was cracked, and in many places patches had fallen off exposing bare bricks and stones. The wooden window shutters, once painted green, now exhibited a nondescript color, the product of time and uncaring.

In its prosperous past, the building had two entrances: A main entrance on Weiherstrasse and, in the back, a door for servants and tradesmen. The main entrance had been bricked over to create additional living space on the ground floor, leaving the backdoor as the building's only entrance.

At one time the building's large yard must have included a lovely garden, or so I imagined. Now the yard was barren, its soil trampled hard by the feet of children playing and the feet of housewives hanging out laundry. Even weeds no longer grew in its soil though here and there, having found refuge in a protected corner, some struggled to survive. A few marvelous old trees, having withstood the changes of time, hinted at what must have been.

The five-room apartment, now divided into two apartments, must have been luxurious at one time: Large glass paneled double doors led into an imposing entrance hall. To the left, and somewhat separated from the rooms, were the facilities requiring plumbing: the kitchen, the bathroom, and the toilet.

Our part of the apartment was made up of two large rooms, the large kitchen, and the apartment's only bathroom. Obviously, we let the apartment's other family use the bathtub if they so wished. But the lack of hot water (quite frequently we had no water at all) made our gesture a mere token of good will. The apartment's one toilet, not part of the bathroom, was shared.

The kitchen was equipped with a gas range and a small, and very useful, auxiliary coal (or wood) burning stove. During air raids, gas was usually cut off and frequently remained cut off for a day or more, so my mother did her cooking on a coal or wood fire. The stove helped to keep the kitchen warm, and on very cold days we kept a fire burning, if we had something to burn, even if gas had been restored.

Coal was rationed and even with an "Aryan" in the household Jewish homes did not receive coal allocations. Scrounging around for coal, firewood, or anything else that could be burned was a constant effort. The living room had a good coal stove, but it too had to remain cold much of the time.

Our living room's large window looked out on a large old tree. When in leaf, its branches hid from our view the neglect of our neighborhood, creating the illusion that we lived on a rather pleasant and peaceful street. Many a free Sunday afternoon I sat by the window with my sketchpad trying to capture the magic of the tree.

Using furniture we divided the large bedroom into two. The larger part was for my mother and sister, while a small corner area was for me. My "bedroom" was simple: a bed, a chest of drawers, a chair. Hidden behind a massive floor-to-ceiling stove of glazed Dutch tiles and blocked off from the other part of the room by a large wardrobe, I did indeed enjoy my privacy. Here, with a stack of books, I could withdraw from the world, leaving the tensions and the horrors of the present outside.

The old-fashioned tile stove, decorated with a hunting scene in bas-relief, fascinated me both in its appearance and in the way it functioned. This type of tile stove had a small firebox and an extensive and complex draft system made of heat-absorbing bricks. The bricks, once heated by a strong fire, retained heat for a long time, requiring only a small fire to keep them hot. Thus the stove, giving up heat slowly, could keep the large room warm with only a small expenditure of fuel. But this was all theory. During an air raid a nearby bomb explosion rattled the old stove, collapsing the ingenious system of drafts. The room remained unheated.

Why the need to go into details about the house on the Weiherstrasse? Certainly I have no sentimental attachment to it. However, recalling the house stimulated many memories.

Number Six Weiherstrasse provided the background for many of the stories that follow: It was the house we defended against fire when bombs rained down on the city; it was the home from which I departed to Theresienstadt during the Nazis' last frantic effort to fulfill their aim to rid Germany of all Jews, and to which I returned after their final defeat.

After the war's end, our apartment had to fulfill one more function: It became a shelter for members of the Jewish Brigade on their illegal mission to find survivors of the Holocaust and smuggle them into Eretz Israel.

And from this apartment my mother, my sister and I departed for America to begin life anew.

Friends and Neighbors

Obviously we were somewhat apprehensive having to live in close quarters with three adults and sharing with them the apartment's only toilet. The O's were a retired elderly couple of mixed marriage; he was the Jewish partner. With them lived their daughter Mrs. F, who, like my sister and me, was a "Geltungsjude."

The three of us left for work early in the morning and it was late in the afternoon before we returned home. By the time our daily chores were done and we had had our dinner, we thought there wasn't much time left for socializing, nor did we think that anyone would be in the mood for it. Hence we didn't expect to see much of the O's and Mrs. F.

Yet we did have a social relationship, and not only with our direct neighbors. Three factors provided the impetus: Mrs. O's infectious optimism, the increasing intensity of the Anglo-American air war against Germany forcing the remnant community closer together, and our collection of books, which became known as the "Marx library."

After my mother had been forced out of the girls' home, she worked briefly as a short-order cook in a department store. There, just as Herr Holland had ordered, she did not work with Jews. The job didn't last very long, about a month at most.

My mother's next employment was in a chemical factory, filling bottles with some chemical fluid used for making dentures. Not very interesting work, but it was certainly better than standing in a hot kitchen all day. Her new job had another advantage: The factory was only a few blocks from our apartment.

Most of the factory workers were people at the margin of German society: Foreigners, mentally handicapped, petty offenders, including prostitutes, and in contradiction to Herr Holland's orders, Jews. We weren't sure how my mother was categorized.

The job provided another, and unexpected, bonus. One of her co-workers was a young Frenchman brought to Germany to alleviate the manpower shortage. Many of these "Fremdarbeiter" (foreign workers) lived in dormitories. One of the Frenchman's roommates was employed in a food factory. Among the factory's products was a dry baby cereal. The workers had the right to take boxes of cereal that had been damaged during the production process. Once a week the young Frenchman brought my mother a "damaged" box of cereal. The baby cereal was a welcome addition to our diet of mostly beets.

Mrs. O's high spirits and irrepressible optimism contributed much to counteract feelings of depression, feelings that so easily invaded our moods. She kept us informed of the latest neighborhood gossip and the newest anti-Nazi jokes and anecdotes, and she enjoyed relating to us any hilarious goings on that she had uncovered during her forays into the community.

As the Allied air offensive gained in momentum, a new problem intruded into our lives: lack of sleep. Although most night alerts turned out to be false alarms, they did interrupt sleep. But the raids on German cities were real enough for us not to ignore the blast of the sirens. I often protested against having to get out of bed, arguing that it was surely a false alarm. I rarely won the argument with my mother.

The "all clear" did not always ease the tension alerts produced, keeping sleep from returning quickly. If that happened, my mother made a cup of "ersatz" coffee or a cup of (herb) tea (real tea was not available), and we sat or stood around talking until the tension eased and we were ready to go back to sleep.

Having returned once again from the basement after a brief bombing raid, we stood in the dark hallway, electricity having been knocked out, debating whether to have coffee or tea, that is, if we had gas. The only illumination came from a couple of candles.

Mrs. O began to giggle. She had noticed, she explained, that the flickering light of her candle produced flickering shadows on the wall. Now with skillful hands and fingers she produced shadow figures that seemed to be dancing in the unsteady candlelight. Soon we all tried our hands at producing dancing figures, though not always with success. Within minutes the foyer was filled with laughter, the feeling of misery and depression banished for the moment.

In contrast to his vivacious spouse, Mr. O was a quiet man. He was retired, but I can't recall from what, and because of his age (he was in his mid-seventies) was not forced to work. He seldom left the apartment, preferring to sit in his armchair and read or dream about the past and about what he thought had been the good days.

The O's daughter, Mrs. F was, like Claire and me, a "Geltungsjude," that is, she had to wear the Jewish Star. But the reason she was classified "Geltungsjude" was different: she had married a "Volljude." Her husband had fled the country and lived in England, and although the couple had no children, she had not divorced him. If she had, she most likely would have been freed from wearing the Star.

The reason that Mrs. F had not yet been shipped off to the camps was that she had a daughter: a "Mischling of the second degree," that is, she was only "one quarter" Jewish. In her late teens Mrs. F had had given birth to a daughter whose father was not Jewish, hence her daughter's racial classification and her own temporary safety. (Germany's racial laws were complicated and often rather absurd. However, they were deadly serious.)

Mrs. F – she was in her late thirties or at most in her early forties – loved to reminisce about giving or attending social events and how much she enjoyed dancing. She even tried to teach me to dance the waltz. I found dancing around with her embarrassing though rather pleasant. She chafed under the restrictions the persecution of the Jews and the war had imposed upon her life. Frequently she mused about a revived social life once the Nazis had been deposed. Yet, like her mother, she was not given to brooding. She remained cheerful and full of optimism.

An attractive woman, Mrs. F liked the company of men, and she had found herself a boyfriend. Of course, this was nobody's business, and certainly none of mine. Yet I felt a slight sense of betrayal: While she was enjoying the company of another man, I pictured her husband in England spending all his time worrying about his wife's welfare.

Being only "one-quarter" Jewish, Mrs. F's daughter Otti had to serve in the German army. One day she showed up at the O's apartment in her army uniform. She was pregnant and had to leave the service. With not one of her soldier friends accepting responsibility for the baby, she had no other choice but to go to her Jewish Star wearing mother. Within a few short months, the family O had grown to five: four adults and one little baby.

Despite our wanderings following the eviction from our suburban home, we had held on to many of our books, and even added a few, though most had remained packed in boxes. Now, once again living in a real apartment furnished with our own furniture, the books came out of the boxes to find their rightful place on shelves and in cabinets to be seen and, more importantly, to be read.

Soon a circle of friends developed around this "library." Once again Sunday afternoons became a distraction from the drabness of the working week. Friends and other members of the community would stop by to borrow a book or two, or return borrowed books and stay for a while to chat and exchange with us war news, the latest rumors and community gossip.

Among our more frequent visitors and a heavy user of our "library" was the head of the Jewish community, Mr. Levy.

During the winter of 1938/39 Mr. Levy had been in a concentration camp. (I think it was Buchenwald.) Inadequate clothing, unheated barracks, and standing for hours in snow, for the winter had been very cold, had exerted its price: Mr. Levy walked with an awkward gait; he had lost several toes to frostbites.

But Mr. Levy was a tough man. Though he had experienced the inside of a concentration camp, he was not afraid to stand up to the Gestapo, especially when the issue concerned the few young people still left in the community. He did his utmost to protect the young from Gestapo abuse.

But he could do nothing for himself. When the leaders of the community were sent to the camps, Mr. Levy and his wife were among them. They didn't come back.

Another couple that made extensive use of our books was the Schnierers. Mr. and Mrs. Schnierer were from Romania. As Romanian citizens they enjoyed, at least for a while, the protection of their Government, an ally of Germany. The Gestapo kept its hands off them. Many Sunday afternoons Mr. Schnierer visited us to chat, but mostly to borrow a book or two or return some. He always had interesting war information he received from friends in Romania via the Romanian consulate.

Russian advances on the battlefront brought an end to Mr. Schnierer's visits. After Russian forces penetrated into Romania, Hitler placed that country under German "protection" and Romania lost what little independence she had; and with that the Schnierers lost their protection. When in an air raid the building in which they lived was destroyed, they disappeared.

After the war an unconfirmed report placed Mrs. Schnierer in one of the concentration camps where she may have survived. Of Mr. Schnierer there was no trace at all.

Four Portraits

Frankfurt's community of remnants was a Jewish community only because Nazi law had so decreed. What all families had in common was this: Each had at least one member who was Jewish in accordance with the Nurnberg Racial Laws, and had at least one "Aryan" member also as defined by "Nurnberg."

Those among the remnants who saw themselves as Jews, be it by religion, by national identity, or by loyalty to family and the past, knew where they belonged; but those who were "Jewish" only because the authorities had so determined had to face serious issues:

The considered themselves Germans and took it as an insult to suggest otherwise. Believing to have fully assimilated into German society, they had some time ago separated themselves from the Jewish community and from their Jewish past. The new laws had forced them back into the community they had left, compelling them to come to terms with their identity, their loyalties, and their memories.

Converts to Christianity, or those who had not converted but had agreed to have their non-Jewish spouses bring up their children as Christians, now had to pay for their decisions. The world into which they had so readily, even eagerly, entered had been closed to them. Cast out by the people to whom they had thought they belonged, they had become strangers to the people of their ancestry.

Thanks to my mother's decisions, my sister Claire and I were not beset by doubts: We were Jewish. But to many of the people among whom we lived, and with whom I worked, the issue was not quite so clear: They tried to find their place between two chairs, but between two chairs there seldom is a comfortable seat. Some handled their situation well, others with difficulty; and there were a few who had become hostile, not toward their oppressors, but toward the Jews around them.

Gossip claimed that there was an informer among us, someone who was willing to trade information about his fellow Jews, not for money, but for his own safety. I don't know if this was true, but at least among the people that I knew not one would have stooped that low.

Mr. Wolf, an officer in the former Imperial German Army, and his wife had an apartment on the ground floor of Six Weiherstrasse. In World War I he had gained many honors and high decorations, and had lost both his legs. At the end of the war he married the non-Jewish nurse who had taken care of him in the Army hospital.

During the period of optimism in the mid-1920s, Mr. Wolf's tobacco business prospered. When the Nazis came to power, he was forced to give up what he had built. He retired with his military pension, which he continued to receive, and with whatever money he had been able to realize from the sale of his business. His wife remained with him.

Contemptuous of the Nazis, he had remained loyal to Germany and the Jews. A courageous man in the Great War, courage had not deserted him. With Jews stripped of access to radio and newspaper, Mr. Wolf became our community's eyes and ears. Confined to a wheelchair, wearing his Jewish Star alongside his war decorations, he frequently ventured forth into the streets, often without his wife, to gather news. I don't know how and where he obtained his information, but what he brought back from his forays was usually quite accurate.

Because of our Jewish Star we were reluctant, following an air raid, to go much further than a block or so from our house, fearing possible violence against us.

Not so Mr. Wolf. He went scouting around riding his wheelchair, checked up on Jewish families and reported back to us on the raids' local impact.

When American troops entered Frankfurt and everyone stayed indoors during the street fighting, both for fear of bullets and possible attacks on Jews by the retreating Nazis, Mr. Wolf scouted the streets to keep the community abreast of the battle's progress. He was the first to greet American soldiers in the name of the Jewish remnant.

A "Volljude," Mr. L nevertheless enjoyed a number of privileges. He did have to wear the Jewish Star and had been forced to sell his men's clothing store, though he did not have to move into a "Judenhaus." But most of all, his name never appeared on any of the dreaded deportation lists.

During the chaotic period that followed the collapse of the German monarchy at the end of World War I, a group of right wing officers and unemployed soldiers of the defeated Army organized fighting units known as the "Frei Corps." The ultra-nationalist and anti-democratic corps' self-defined mission: To defend the Fatherland while the regular Army was in disarray. These guerilla bands operated in East Prussia to "prevent the Bolshevik revolution from spilling over into Germany."

When the German government failed to meet the reparation payments imposed by the Versailles treaty, claiming bankruptcy, French troops seized the coal mines and heavy industry of Ruhr Valley. Although the ultra-nationalist and anti-democratic Frei Corps had considered its main mission to fight Bolsheviks in the East, they didn't hesitate to take on the French Army in the West. France responded by hunting down the leaders of the Frei Corps, executing many of its leaders by firing squad. The executed leaders became heroes and martyrs in the Nazi mythology.

Once the German Republic achieved a degree of stability, and as a member of the League of Nations had acquired the right to protect its borders, the Frei Corps dissolved. Many of its members joined Hitler's Storm Troopers.

A Frei Corps volunteer, Mr. L had shown much bravery and eventually attained the rank of sub-lieutenant. When the corps was dissolved, Mr. L could of course not join the Nazi gang. But the Nazis had not forgotten the contributions he had made and they showed their appreciation. He was designated a "privileged Jew."

It had bothered me that a Jew would join a German ultra-nationalist group.

I suspected that he lived a rather isolated life. Though he never denied being Jewish, even in his Frei Corps days, few in the Jewish community were willing to trust him, and his Jewish Star was surely not all too welcome where he lived.

Mr. N was a short roly-poly man. Even his head, nearly completely bald, was round like a bowling ball. Cheerful, hardworking, eager to please, he was always ready to cheer up the other Jewish members of our work crew. Apparently feeling secure in his non-Jewish family, he wore his Jewish Star with indifference, neither embarrassed by it nor identifying with it. To him all this was temporary, something that did not affect what was most dear to him, the love of his family.

Was he worried about his future? I could not tell from his demeanor. Always friendly to me, he treated me like the teenager I really was (I was approaching seventeen) and not as an adult the way my Jewish and non-Jewish coworkers looked at me. At first I did resent his attitude, but soon realized that he did not wish to be condescending, but helpful. Frequently acting as a lubricant, he managed to prevent excessive friction between our foreman and us.

Not that our foreman was a bad guy, he was rather simple minded. He mouthed the Nazi slogans, their anti-Semitic propaganda, and the official anti-democratic pronouncements without apparent malice and without much understanding or conviction. He treated the Jewish workers in full compliance with the rules, doing so as a law-abiding citizen, again without any sign of hatred. Nor did he understand the resentment we felt toward our position. The world was the way the world was; we all had to accept our role.

I regret not knowing what happened to Mr. N. I lost track of him after

I received a new job assignment. I hope he survived the war and was able to continue to enjoy his family, and under better conditions.

Mr. Friedman was a tall and handsome man. I assumed that at one time he had occupied an important position in business. Now a common laborer, he still insisted on being well dressed, even wearing a tie when sweeping streets. He bitterly resented having to wear the Jewish Star and having to work with Jews; he would have much preferred to serve in the German Army; not as a common soldier, of course. He assured us he would have made a good officer.

He and I constantly feuded. I'm no longer sure what our quarrels were about, and much of our quarrelling was probably my fault. Feeling challenged by his hostile attitude toward Jews and his German patriotism, I made no secret of my feelings that it was much better to be Jewish than German. I could accept that Germans were anti-Semitic, Germans simply didn't know better; but anti-Semitism from a Jew – that I wasn't willing to tolerate. Angrily I called him a Jew-hater and probably worse things. In response he told me that young people had no right to talk back to grownups. He warned me that I would find myself in deep trouble if I did not get rid of my "Jewish impertinence." I tried to stay out of his way, but as we had to work together this was not easily achieved.

Zitko's Story

He was a tall lanky boy. A year or so younger than I, he towered over me by at least a head. He lived with his mother in the apartment house across from our courtyard, one of the "Jewish" houses in the neighborhood. Though Zitko was the family name, everyone called him only by his last name. I can't recall much about the Zitkos. I doubt that I had met Zitko at any time before, certainly not at school, and definitely not in the Anlernwerkstatt. He wore the Jewish Star and he was assigned a job under the prevailing Gestapo rules, so he must have been Jewish, yet I had the feeling that he did not consider himself part of the Jewish community.

In December 1942 Zitko and I were told to report for work at the city-operated Holtzhof (wood yard) located in the far outskirts of Frankfurt. Living near each other, we went to work together.

Our workday began at seven o'clock in the morning. Jews were not permitted to use transportation, so we had to start out before five o'clock, before the end of the night curfew. Working a nine-hour shift, not including lunch break, we didn't return home until well after dark. And thus, during the long walks to and from work, I learned something about Zitko.

With permits in our pockets allowing us to be in the street before the end of the curfew, we walked through dark, blacked-out streets the several blocks that took us to the embankment of the Main River. Following the road along the river, we past the center of the city known as the "Altstadt," the part of the city dating from medieval times, to eventually reach the city's west side; there we crossed the river. Continuing to follow the river, we passed several of the city's suburbs. As we approached city limits, a footpath, veering away from the river, brought us to the City Forest and eventually to our destination.

When the weather was fine the two-hour plus walk from and to work wasn't bad, but the winter of 1942/43 was harsh. Several times we had to walk through deep snow.

Though the day was long, the work itself was not demanding. The Holzhof provided firewood for the city's mobile and stationary construction huts used by municipal crews doing outdoor work: park maintenance, sewer repair, streetcar track repair, etc.

The war had given the Holzhof an additional task. With the gasoline shortage, many trucks had been equipped with fuel converters, converting wood chips into methane gas. (The gas did not deliver much energy and the converters gave off a terrible odor. The weight of the converter further subtracted from the vehicle's carrying capacity). The Holzhof supplied the wood chips for the city's fleet.

Our job, Zitko's and mine, was to chop wood. Early in the morning, before we arrived, logs had already been delivered to the Holzhof. After these had been cut to length, Zitko and I went to work splitting wood using axes. We did not have to work very hard to fill the day's quotas: so much for firewood, so much for the converters. Usually by lunchtime we had split about all there was to be split. So, after a lengthy lunch, Zitko and I swept the yard and then stood by a fire waiting for quitting time.

Neither Zitko nor I were big talkers; I think he was even less of a talker than I. At first we said very little to each other during our long walks to and from work. We didn't talk about the war, about the situation of the Jews, or even about what we wanted to do once the war was over. These topics were much discussed in the community and certainly of concern to me, but they seemed to have no interest for Zitko. I'm sure that occasionally we did engage in some conversation, a bit of boy's talk, about girls perhaps, but I can't recall any of it.

One cold morning as we made our way to work, Zitko began to talk. At first I listened with only half an ear. Most likely my mind was occupied with my own thoughts, if by any thoughts at all. Who wanted to do any thinking that early on a cold morning?

Then he said something that did get my attention: Because he lived alone with his mother, no husband being in the home, he thought it was his obligation to protect his mother.

It was the peculiar way he put it: "no husband being in the home" that pulled me out of my half sleep. It came to me that Zitko had never mentioned his father. I mumbled that taking care of his mother seemed to be the right thing to do, thinking that perhaps his mother was not well.

Zitko realized that I hadn't understood what he was trying to tell me. Giving more details, he tried to explain, and justify, his relationship with his mother. He insisted that it was very important that he protected her, especially from men. Even at night, he stressed, he had to be on guard; and that is why he shared the bed with his mother. Now he had my full attention.

Feeling compelled to explain further, he continued after a short pause: The other day, having come home a bit earlier than usual, he had found a man in bed with his mother. Angered, he had pulled the man out of the bed. After beating him he dragged the naked man into the hallway and threw him down the stairs, tossing his clothing after him. (Zitko was a big fellow and physically quite capable of doing what he said he did.)

He didn't know if the man was hurt falling down the stairs, but he didn't care. What he wanted to know was, had he done right?

What was I to say? Was the story true? I didn't doubt that he had told the truth. I should have listened more carefully, I reprimanded myself, from the very beginning. Reluctantly I asked him to repeat some of what he had said, though I wasn't sure that I wished to hear it.

A grown boy sharing a bed with his mother, his mother in bed with a man not her husband; throwing a naked man down a flight of steps!

No, I really didn't want to deal with problems like that.

His story painted a strange picture of relationships; relationships of which I preferred to remain ignorant. Despite the many vulgarities and brutalities of the Nazis, despite war and the destruction of the Jewish community, and despite corruption all around us, I thought of the world as orderly; and this, certainly, it was not. I assured myself that in normal times what Zitko told could never have happened.

I can't recall how I answered Zitko's question, or if I answered at all. If I said anything it must have been vague and most certainly not very profound.

Zitko and I worked at the Holzhof for a little over two months. As the winter's snow began to melt, we were dismissed. I lost contact with Zitko. During a heavy air raid the building in which the Zitkos lived was destroyed. Mother and son disappeared. I do not know what happened to them.

The Girl in the Attic

She was a pretty girl, slim with long dark hair, a few years younger than I, perhaps fourteen or even a bit younger. She sat quietly on an old box or trunk, legs drawn up, seemingly staring into nothing. A few times I caught her looking at me furtively, and when caught thus she quickly looked away. If our eyes did meet, her face changed from its blank expression, becoming wistful, questioning, perhaps expectant; I wasn't sure. We never said a word to each other.

For quite some time Jews had found it difficult to buy clothing, shoes, furniture, things for the person or the home. Neighborhood shops, small stores in the city, even most department stores refused to serve Jews. With war the difficult became impossible. All stores were off limits to Jews. When ration cards for clothing and shoes were issued, there were none for us.

Clothing for growing children was not much of a problem in our community; few children were left. But clothing does wear out, for both adults and children, and the small number of children and young people not yet shipped to the ghettoes or the camps of death did outgrow what they had.

To meet the need for clothing the community set up a used clothing exchange, the "Kleider Kammer." Here people could bring still wearable clothes, exchanging them for what they needed. Or, with proof of need (the rules were vague and not strictly enforced) they could pay a small sum for what they want – if it was available.

The rules for work clothing and work shoes were different. If the Kleider Kammer was unable to satisfy the need, the Gestapo's representative, Herr Holland, could at his discretion approve the purchase of the item in a store that he specified. I once got a pair of work boots that way.

Not being able to buy furniture was not really a hardship. Who needed to buy furniture? Not even the general population had much opportunity to buy home furnishings. Everyone had to wait for the war's end.

The devastations the air war brought to Germany changed that: Furniture, clothing, and other household items were needed to replace, at least partially, what had been lost.

Jewish homes did not, of course, escape the bombs and fires, but Jewish victims did not receive government help; they had to rely on the meager resources of the remnant community. In response to this need, a furniture exchange, appropriately named the "Moebel Kammer," was added to the "Kleider Kammer."

Much of the inventory for the Moebel Kammer came from homes of people who had been deported, forcing them to abandon their household. Of course the Moebel Kammer could pick up only what the SS and Gestapo left behind after plundering the homes. Some furniture came from people who had been forced to move to smaller apartments; a few items were voluntary contributions.

I had volunteered to work at the Moebel Kammer. Much of the furniture received was in bad shape: some had been damaged in air raids, other pieces were broken either through use or neglect, and many items were ready for the dump heap. Using what little free time I had I tried to fix at least the better pieces.

The job was difficult and frustrating. I lacked about everything needed for making repairs: wood, glue, screws, nails, finishes, etc. These were not available to Jews, even with money, which few in the community had. So I learned to make do with used materials and parts taken from furniture not worth fixing. Much of my time was used up straightening old nails and retrieving screws.

The clothing and furniture operation had been set up in one of the neighborhood's "Jewish" houses. While inspecting the building for the needed space, a veritable treasure trove was discovered: the building's attic was full of old clothing, pots and pans, and other potentially still usable items, including even some furniture. Most likely these had been left behind by former tenants as useless junk, or by people who had been deported and simply left what was up under the roof.

The attic space had to be cleared out. An attic crammed full of junk presented a fire hazard, and with the increase in air attacks, the danger of fire had become greater. So far no one had bothered to inspect the building, but with the clothing and furniture exchanges in operation, Herr Holland, a Gestapo agent, or even a neighborhood air raid warden may well take an interest in the building and look around.

I was asked to clear out the attic, salvaging anything that could still be of use. A young boy about Bar Mitzvah age (I was 16) was asked to help me. We didn't look forward to the job, expecting the task to be dirty and boring. Reluctantly we went up to the attic to confront the mess.

After a few weekend or evening sessions my fellow worker deserted me and I found myself alone in the cramped and dirty space under the roof. I wasn't alone for very long.

Among the building's tenants were a woman and her two daughters. I surmised that the father, or perhaps fathers, of the two girls had not been Jewish and had deserted the woman and her children. The girls were Jewish, at least by the Nazis' definition.

The woman made a living by doing laundry for the neighborhood (for non-Jews; Jews couldn't afford to hire anybody). I clearly remember the smell of laundry being boiled; it penetrated the whole building, even reaching up into the attic. Combined with other stale odors that emanated from the various apartments in the building, the smell was most unpleasant.

The older daughter made her contribution to the family's income. After dark and after the start of curfew, the young woman would remove her Jewish Star to go out on business, returning home in the morning, after the end of curfew. This time, being daylight, her Jew badge was back on her coat.

Jews were not allowed to have a business and a Jewish girl being a prostitute, outside the Jewish community, certainly ran afoul of racial laws. Yet the Gestapo never bothered the enterprising mother and daughter. I was most curious about the three but couldn't find anyone in our community willing to talk about them.

The day or so after my helper deserted me the younger of the two girls showed up in the attic. Not saying a word, she perfunctorily blew some dust off an old wooden box and sat down. At first I thought she had come to help, though she made no move in that direction. I tried to ignore her; but it wasn't all that easy.

Her thin and badly worn red sweater, much more suitable for a hot summer's day than for the drafty attic during the cold days of winter, revealed what there was to be revealed.

I tried to work as if she wasn't there. Yet I felt attracted to her. I caught myself stealing furtive glances at the shapeliness of her young breasts, emphasized by the sweater's tightness. I kept working, not knowing which way to look, though my eyes kept wandering toward where she sat.

What did she want here? I feared (hoped?) that, following in her older sister's footsteps, she was trying to seduce me. Perhaps she had come upstairs out of boredom, or, more likely, to escape having to help her mother with washing laundry. Perhaps that was all there was to it.

Finally, after a couple of days, I had enough of the dusty attic, the nauseating smell, the girl in the tight threadbare red sweater. I left the work unfinished, though I wouldn't tell my mother all the reasons why. And apparently no one cared.

The used clothing and furniture stores came to a flaming end; the building in which they were housed and in which the woman with her two daughters had lived was destroyed in an air raid. What happened to the girl in the attic, I do not know.

A Deception

How Jewish was our remnant Jewish community?

In October of 1941 the deportation of Frankfurt's Jews got underway. Soon after the start of the "transports" the one remaining synagogue was closed, and in summer of 1942 the last Jewish school had to shut its door. Dedicated community leaders, Rabbis and teachers were deported to labor camps, concentration camps or ghettoes. Possessing Jewish prayer books and ritual objects was outlawed; Torahs, those not already destroyed, were seized by the Gestapo; and Shabbat? Saturday was an ordinary working day.

By late 1943 Frankfurt's Jewish community had become a community of mixed marriages whose Jewish identity was tenuous (only a minority showed interest in their Jewish heritage), of a small number of elderly Jewish couples, and an even smaller number of converts, husband or wife, and their Jewish children.

Our Gestapo-appointed leaders reflected the make-up of the majority of this leftover community: they too were only marginally Jewish. Dedicated to their own survival, they made little effort to lead, they just followed Gestapo orders. And if a little corruption and betrayal benefited their chances to survive, so be it.

Although the full brunt of the Allied air war against Germany had not yet hit the city, effects of air raids could already be seen and felt. Jewish residents had been forced out of their apartments to make room for their non-Jewish bombed-out neighbors.

The Jewish community office and the old age home were forced to move once again. The "new" facilities were in a severely bomb-damaged building. Only the rooms on the ground floor were usable.

Two bare rooms made up the "old age home." Plaster had fallen from walls and ceiling; the glass-less and even sash-less windows were covered with plastic sheets; floorboards were warped. Here a few elderly people, people no longer able to fend for themselves, and who the Gestapo considered not worthy shipping to a death camp, slept on straw sacks and were fed their meager meals while waiting for death.

My sister and another young girl employed by the community did their best to make these unfortunate people comfortable. It was a thankless job; there really wasn't much the two girls could do for them.

Acting as the community's handyman, in addition to my regular sixty-hour a week job, I was asked to do some needed fixing up at the "new" Jewish center.

The office of the Gestapo's representative, Herr Holland, had also been moved to the bomb-damaged building. Of course it was set up in the least damaged of the rooms and the only one where real repairs were made. Herr Holland had me released from my regular job for a few days to install window sashes, replace the door and fix damaged floorboards. The needed material I had to scrounge from abandoned bomb-damaged buildings nearby. That was against the law, but the Gestapo seldom worried about the law.

Of course I took advantage of what I had to do to obtain material for repairing bomb damage in our own home.

Herr Holland did not enjoy his office very long: He was called up to the defense forces recruited from older men and boys to stop the Russians at the German border. The Gestapo took direct control of the remnant community.

In their war against the Jews the Nazis' arsenal included deception and obfuscation. Keeping alive even the smallest glimmer of hope tended to make their victims more compliant. As their victims were being herded into cattle cars to be shipped to slave labor camps and death camps the Nazis preferred words like "evacuation" and "resettlement."

Despite the mistrust most in the community felt toward favorable pronouncements coming from the Gestapo, once in a while we did fall victim to their game. Perhaps these occasional lapses in our awareness can be attributed to most people's predilection to believe that authorities will act rationally and even decently, at least most of the time. More likely wishful thinking permitted our oppressors to lull us at times into believing that our situation was not as hopeless as it appeared.

(Wishful thinking does have a positive side. Without it the suicide rate among the remnants might have been much higher.)

It began as a rumor: If the Jews wanted a place where they could "pray to their god" the Gestapo would be indifferent. I dismissed this as a bad joke. But the rumor persisted and the Gestapo hinted that this was not just a rumor.

What could be the possible meaning of this indifference? The Gestapo was not known for generosity toward Jews. Speculations were rampant: With the war not going well for the Germans, did some local chieftain want to look good in the eyes of the potential victor? Or perhaps the remnant community was too insignificant to engage badly needed manpower. Optimists took it as a sign that the worst was behind us. Only a few saw in this unofficial permission a cruel hoax. But who wanted to listen to pessimists?

A decision had to be made: Act on or ignore the Gestapo's unofficial position. The community's heads weren't really interested in a "shul" and they didn't dare ask the Gestapo for clarification. The question: What consequences could we expect if we ignored the Gestapo's "unofficial" permission?

The argument that the Gestapo's generosity should not be ignored won. And so, with the reluctant approval and cooperation of the community's leaders, a few volunteers set the "synagogue" project in motion.

I was asked to help. My skills as a carpenter, I was told, were needed. We had to construct a reader's desk and an Aron HaKodesh (Arc of the Law), even though we didn't have a Torah. (How could one have a synagogue without an Aron HaKodesh?) Flattered I gave up a few evenings and even a rare free Sunday.

Our "synagogue" could not be in the community center. Space was too limited and the "synagogue" would look too official. But the Gestapo had shown little interest in what we did in the clothing and furniture exchange, so the decision was made to locate it there. The Moebel Kammer could provide chairs and other needed pieces of furniture.

The wife of one of the volunteers (I'm not sure she was Jewish) made a curtain for the Aron HaKodesh, embroidering it with a flower motif. She avoided using Jewish symbols, not wanting to test the Gestapo's good will too far.

To my incredulity many were in favor of having Shabbat services, even though only the elderly would be able to attend. And God willing, and with the Gestapo's approval, we may even have had High Holiday services in the fall.

With the "Aron HaKodesh" set up at the eastern wall, seats arranged in the traditional manner, men in front, women in the back, our "synagogue" was ready.

Shabbat arrived. As expected only a few elderly men who didn't have to go to work showed up for the "historic" opening service.

The Gestapo was waiting for them. The men who had come with so much faith to this first Shabbat service were arrested, charged with illegal assembly. The Gestapo reminded them that it was forbidden for Jews to assemble; no exception had been granted. And, since Jews were not permitted to have Hebrew books, the Siddurim that had surfaced with so much optimism were confiscated.

Despite my enthusiasm for our "shul" my mother had not permitted me to contribute any of our hidden Siddurim. She hadn't quite trusted the Gestapo.

The arrested men were let go. Did the Gestapo have a good laugh at the credulity of the Jews? Or wasn't it worth their while to jail them or ship them to a concentration camp? The next transport would take care of these men.

For a brief moment we had nourished the delusion that this insignificant remnant of Jews would be left alone, that we would be permitted to settle into a quieter life. To be sure most of us worked long hours, were hungry much of the time, had no medical care, and were nearly completely isolated from the world. But with the war's fortunes turning against Germany, these were mere "inconveniences."

Yet the Nazi's destruction of the community continued relentlessly. Even this only marginally Jewish remnant, small and impoverished, was not to be allowed to live.

When the bombing offensive against German cities targeted Frankfurt, to our fear of being killed by the Nazis was added the fear of being killed by the bombs of our would-be liberators. Our community's demise was clearly in sight.

CHAPTER 13

In Double Jeopardy

Fears

By the time the calendar flipped from 1942 to 1943, Germany had been driven onto the defensive. In November '42, the U. S. Army landed in North Africa. After eliminating Vichy French resistance in Morocco and Algeria, they advanced toward Tunisia. The British, following their victory over Rommel's Africa Corps in Egypt, pushed through Libya to join the Americans in attacking the trapped Axis forces. By May 1943, German and Italian resistance in North Africa ended.

On its eastern front, the Wehrmacht did not fare any better. After cutting off a German army corps in Stalingrad, Soviet forces advanced along the whole front, from the Black Sea to the Gulf of Finland. By the end of January the Germans trapped in Stalingrad surrendered.

Yet all the war's fighting was still beyond Germany's borders. Even the air war, brutally initiated by Germany, had barely touched the country. But as the war's fortunes began to turn against her, a devastating bombing campaign by the Air Forces of the Western Allies was bringing the war home.

Like storms and earthquakes, which do not differentiate between the God-fearing and the godless, so the bombs did not differentiate between Nazis and Jews. "Jewish" houses were as vulnerable as those of non-Jews. Yet despite the dangers the air raids brought us, we welcomed them; they were the most tangible sign that this war's initiative was no longer Germany's.

Apartment houses were ordered to have basement shelters. The shelter area had to have a reinforced ceiling, blast-proof doors and windows, and at least one alternative exit. Emergency equipment, including gas masks, had to be at readiness in the shelter. The cost of construction and equipment was partially paid for by local authorities.

None of this applied to the "Jewish" houses. We had to do the best we could on our own.

Our building's owner, not Jewish, had been somewhat helpful. He installed a ceiling support in one of the larger basement areas and permitted us to use it as our air raid shelter. An ax and a couple of shovels, contributed by tenants, were our rather useless emergency tools. And instead of battery powered emergency lights, we had candles.

While we made do with what we had, the building's caretaker (also not Jewish; he lived on the top floor) had a properly constructed, equipped, and subsidized shelter in the basement, just large enough for himself, his wife, and their teenage son.

In October 1943 we experienced our first major air raid. Frankfurt's East End, with its factories, warehouses and rail facilities – and its "Jewish" houses – was a prime target.

Although it had not come unexpectedly, when this first massed air raid hit us we had to acknowledge that we had been rather unprepared. The reality of sitting helplessly in a dark basement lit only by a couple of candles while outside the world exploded was well beyond what imagination had been able to foretell.

The barking of the heavy anti-aircraft guns, at first vaguely heard, grew louder and louder and more intense; it was joined by the nearly uninterrupted rat-tat-tat of lighter guns. As the gunfire appeared to reach a crescendo, the roar of hundreds of airplanes overwhelmed it.

But these assaults on the ears were quickly pushed aside: The almost simultaneous detonation of hundreds of bombs nearly burst the eardrums. And as the attack moved directly overhead, a new sound, even harder on the nerves, joined the cacophony: the whistling of bombs rushing down from the sky.

We sat in our improvised shelter, only dimly lit by the flickering candles, electricity having failed as soon as the first bombs fell, nearly paralyzed by the fury of the explosions. In dimness we couldn't see the dust loosened from ceiling and walls, nor the grit and smoke that penetrated into the basement. But we smelled the acid smoke from the exploding bombs, tasted it in our mouth and felt it in our burning eyes. And we felt the shaking of the building and the heaving of the floor.

I cannot say that I was afraid; that would be an understatement. What I experienced was far more primeval than mere fear; what I felt seemed to come from deep inside, pushing aside any rational thoughts. The mind appeared unable to comprehend the inferno which had been let loose. An animal helplessly caught in a trap must experience this kind of terror. Panic urges: run! But the body, frozen in terror, refuses to move. Knees trembled uncontrollably; the sense of doom increased with every blast.

Gradually two strong urges began to assert themselves: An urge to do something, to try to gain control by taking some action, no matter how trivial; and curiosity: What was going on outside?

A brief chuckle drew my attention: Hysteria?

A calm voice came out of the darkness: "I tried to get my mind off the bombs, to find some kind of a diversion. After all there is nothing I can do. Noticing the trembling of my knees I concentrated on controlling them. Mustering all my will power I ordered them to stop shaking; but to no avail, my legs no longer obeyed my brain." This helplessness, the man explained, had struck him as amusing.

His voice, his words, and his lengthy explanation acted like a balm on our nerves. Knees still trembled, but now this could be ignored; the feeling of panic had dissipated.

Nearly everyone was talking. Bombs still exploded, anti-aircraft guns still blasted away, and the building still shook, but only close-by hits could interrupt the streams of words. Someone, quite seriously, suggested counting time from the onset of a whistling sound to the detonation. Like trying to estimate the closeness of a lightning strike by counting the seconds between lightning and thunder, we could estimate the closeness of a hit. That produced a pearl of wisdom: the bomb you can hear is not the bomb that will kill you.

Gradually the uproar subsided. With fewer heavy bomb blasts, the sound of anti-aircraft fire became dominant once again. Then the gunfire too faded. Finally there was stillness.

For a moment we sat quietly, not quite ready to believe that it was over.

A few additional candles were lit making the shelter just a bit brighter, improving the mood further. Cautiously one of the men went to the cellar stairs looking up into the dark. No debris covered the stairs, so we could assume the building still stood. Carefully, and a bit hesitantly, he went up the stairs. Others followed.

I stepped out into the yard. Fires lit the night; the air was thick with smoke and dust. Distant "all clears" mixed with the sounds of sirens from fire engines and the rushing sounds of the inferno. Yet an eerie silence seemed to prevail.

Walking on shattered glass and pieces of fallen plaster, my mother, Claire and I went to inspect our apartment. Happily, we found only minor damage. My mother suggested one quick look at the neighborhood and then, after a bit of cleanup, to bed for a few hours' sleep. Not much was left of the night. Still unaware of the extent of the destruction, we expected to go to work in the morning.

Only when we went to check on the nearby Jewish houses (none had been hit) did we realize the magnitude of the devastation: Buildings were burning while others had been blasted into piles of rubble. Bomb-craters and debris from collapsed buildings made walking difficult.

Driven by curiosity I went up to the roof of our building to watch the spectacle: a city on fire. What I saw gave me a shock: The factory where my mother worked was a flaming torch: The chemicals for making dentures burned well.

What now? I thought. That my mother had been working near our home had been comforting: The last to leave for work in the morning, she was the first to return in the evening. Shopping and household chores had been all hers to do.

Any change in our life, I was convinced, could only be for the worse. Only the final change, the defeat of the Nazis, would make things better. Then everything would be all right again; overnight, so to speak.

In response to the intensified air war, many factories and businesses had begun to relocate in rural areas. The factory where my mother worked too had made preparations, so it did not take long before work could resume. But instead of just walking around the corner to her job, my mother had to travel for two hours: First by streetcar to Frankfurt's main station, then by train to a small town, and finally, for about half an hour on foot along a country road to the factory. With my mother the first to leave for work and the last to return home, most shopping and household chores fell on my sister and me.

Nothing in life seems to be wholly negative, and my mother's long journeys too had a positive side. The rural road from the railroad station to the plant passed along an apple orchard. At day's end, on their way to the station, the workers stuffed their bags and pockets with apples that had fallen to the ground, though I suspected that not a few had "fallen" directly into their hands. Most weren't quite ripe, many were bruised, a few partially rotten; but we were not choosy. The few good apples we ate fresh; from the others my mother made applesauce (without sugar, of course), a welcome addition to our meager and monotonous diet.

We quickly settled into our new routine. But the war didn't permit routines to last for very long.

Following the landing in Normandy in June 1944, the Western Allies began to attack the German transport system, especially the railroad. Almost daily fighter-bombers were in the sky hunting for engines and rolling stock. My mother's train came under attack a number of times, forcing her to take cover in a slit trench (trenches had been dug along railway tracks and highways) while machine gun bullets whizzed around her. And after Germany launched her rocket weapons (the V2-rocket) against England, this danger became even greater: A launch-site was near the village where my mother worked.

What would happen to my sister and me if my mother was killed or hurt? The possibility that one day she might not return home had become real. The loss of my mother would surely place my sister and me into double jeopardy: We would be without parents and we would lose our "Aryan" protection. Deportation to a ghetto or a death camp would be a certainty. And if she were "only" seriously hurt, what hospital would take her?

Fortunately, these questions never had to be answered.

On Our Own

Like storms and earthquakes, bombs did not differentiate between rich and poor, friends and foes, God-fearing and godless, and not between non-Jews and Jews; all were vulnerable – though Jews only more so.

The dangers brought by the air raids – death and injuries and the loss of home and possessions – we shared with the general population. For us, however, there was no help from the authorities: No fire engine, no rescue team, no ambulance would come to a "Jewish" house; and we had no doctors or medical facilities to care for the injured. Isolated, with barely any resources, we had to deal with the air raids on our own. And there was one threat that was ours alone: A backlash against the Jews by the frightened population.

With two heavy raids behind us, and several less severe ones that we considered mere nuisances, my mother had adopted a post-raid routine: After making sure that our apartment was all right, the three of us checked on the neighborhood's "Jewish" houses to see if any help was needed.

Though the Angel of Death skipped over the houses marked with a Jewish Star, the protective hand didn't save us from injuries, mostly eye injuries and smoke poisoning. These we treated the best we could, falling back on home remedies. Occasionally the non-Jewish marriage partner was able to obtain non-prescription drugs from a sympathetic druggist together with a bit of advice.

Some injuries did cause permanent damage, but at the time this was of little concern. One of our neighbors, unaware of an unexploded bomb buried near the entrance to their house was injured when the bomb detonated: he lost an eye. Otherwise unhurt, he was considered lucky. Mere bumps, scratches and even simple burns, however, we ignored.

The air raids accelerated the process of making city neighborhoods, with the exception of the East End, "Judenrein." Jews had to surrender their apartments to victims of air attacks and find homes in the East End's few "Jewish" apartment houses. Jewish living space became ever more crowded.

A two-room apartment with a kitchen was considered too "luxurious" for three people, so my mother gave up one of our rooms. Once more we packed our many books into boxes and moved into the bedroom, the larger of the rooms. The living room and most of its furniture we turned over to a bombed-out couple, the K's. They had lost everything.

Mr. K was from Vienna, Austria, his wife from Cologne, Germany. What had brought the Jewish salesman together with a Christian woman from Northwest Germany was their love for partying and ballroom dancing. When the Nazis came to power, partying came to an end, at least for the Jewish partner. After that not much was left of their marriage except their one daughter. And when she married and went to Australia, their last common bond was gone.

The Ks made little secret of their discord, their boredom with each other, and their desire to get divorced as soon as the Nazis were out of power. They never fought openly, at least not much, yet they kept us informed about their discords.

Mr. K complained that his wife was frigid, which she readily admitted, saying she couldn't stand his touch. Mr. K got himself a girlfriend.

His friend, the Jewish partner of a mixed and also discordant marriage, was a pretty petite woman. Her husband, a tall quiet man, seemed resigned to his wife's affair. Perhaps he was even a bit relieved, at least that was the impression he gave. Mr. K lamented that his woman friend had an excessive sexual appetite that he wasn't always able to satisfy. He blamed that on our starvation diet.

"She squeezes me out like a lemon," was his lament, complaining even to his wife.

The Ks were really nice people. Though we had to live in very close quarters we got along well. Mrs. K possessed an indomitable spirit, which helped to keep depression away.

The Ks were not the only couple among the remnants with marriage problems. For a number of mixed couples the end of the war also spelled the end of their marriage. An uncertain future, cold-shoulder treatment, or pressure from relatives and friends of the "Aryan" spouse, or the re-discovery of "Jewishness" by the Jewish partner had been too much to keep their marriages intact.

Yet despite the temptations of an easier life and freedom from Gestapo harassment, the non-Jewish spouses remained loyal to their marriage partners, providing a few of the positive stories coming out of the Holocaust.

Not surprisingly, the death and destruction raining down and the many sleepless nights due to alerts caused anger among the German people. For us, the question was against whom the anger was directed. The few remaining Jews would make an easy target for Nazi propaganda.

To divert the people's attention from the fact that the American and British Air Forces dominated the sky over Germany, Nazi propaganda went into high gear.

Exaggerated claims of British and American losses, stories of heroic deeds by German fighter pilots, and an occasional "revenge" raid on cities in England dominated the news.

For the Minister of Propaganda, Goebbels, this wasn't enough; someone has to be blamed and again "the Jews" were the target: Jews who had left Germany and were familiar with the country were directing these barbaric attacks against civilians and hospitals. Instead of having permitted these criminals to leave the country, Goebbels raged, Germany should have hanged them.

To our relief the people's anger did not turn against us, though it did also not turn against their government; hate was directed against America and England. A few unpleasant incidents did occur, and for the first couple of days after a major air raid we tried not to be seen in the street.

We seemed to have taken these dangers rather calmly, or perhaps fatalistically. Our fear of the "transports" was greater than that of bombs. Aware that we could influence neither the transports nor the bombs, we tried to keep our sanity and not succumb to despair by not thinking about what might be in store for us.

Good Neighbors

In the modern Western World we take the delivery of mail for granted; even in Nazi Germany Jews still got their mail delivered, though sometimes only after the Gestapo had a look at it. Following the outbreak of the war, our mail dwindled to an occasional Red Cross letter from my father, and even less frequently a letter from my mother's family (no return address shown). After the Anglo-American invasion of Italy all that stopped. Finding a letter or a small package in our mailbox had become a most unusual event.

Another major air raid occurred, the third on the city within a short period of time, and again our part of town was hit hard.

As soon as we were sure the raid was over, my mother, Claire and I made our rounds of the neighborhood's Jewish houses. After ascertaining that all had come through with only minor damages and none needed help, we began to make our way home. A young man with a pronounced limp, who did not wear the Jewish Star, stopped us. The building where he lived, he said, was on fire. The residents had tried to put out the flames but had failed. Now they wanted to save as many of their possessions as they could. With all their immediate neighbors busy with their own problems, they were looking for help. He begged us to give them a hand. My mother said yes.

When we arrived at the endangered building, the tenants stood in a cluster in the front yard watching irresolutely as heavy smoke billowed from the roof and the top floor windows.

Perhaps the arrival of reinforcements, or the return of the young man with the limp, or flames along the eaves, finally galvanized the watchers into action.

But what were we to do? How much time did they have to empty the building? Clearing the upper floors by carrying everything down the stairway would take too long. The man with the bad leg suggested using a rope to lower furniture into the yard. A rope was procured.

Action became urgent: Flames showing at the roof's edge appeared to be increasing in intensity; smoking debris, roof shingles, and loosened bricks were falling into the yard. The men rushed upstairs to lower furniture and other items through one of the windows. The women's job was to move the items to a safe spot in the yard. That left one task open: To receive what was being lowered and untie it from the rope; I took the assignment.

The operation progressed rather well. A substantial amount of household goods were brought to safety. But time was running out: Flames were shooting out of some of the upper windows and the roof was burning more fiercely. More and more debris was falling into the yard, much of it hitting near where I stood. When thick smoke began to come out of lower floor, windows a halt was called.

The last item lowered was a sewing machine stand. As I received the stand, a small part of wall from below the roof collapsed. Bricks, roof shingles, and pieces of burning wood rained down into the yard. Luckily, I had my head under the stand's tabletop while untying the rope, so only the stand and my back, well protected by layers of clothing, were hit. (When going to the air raid shelter we always wore as much clothing as possible.) After a few words of thanks from the building's residents, the three of us left for home.

A few days had passed when I found a small package in our mailbox, addressed to me. No postage stamps were on the package and no return address. No note was inside. In the package were ten cigarettes.

Today it is difficult to understand what this meant. No one had yet thought that smoking was harmful. Cigarettes were rationed, and by many were valued more than money. For dealing in cigarettes on the black market the penalty was hanging. Jews did not receive tobacco rations, and giving cigarettes to a Jew was a criminal offense.

I was sure that I knew who had placed the cigarettes into our mailbox: The man with the limp, the man who had asked us for help, was the local mailman.

A Most Precious Possession

If I were a poet I would compose an ode to the bed. The bed had become one of our most precious possessions. At the end of a long day, still somewhat hungry after the evening meal, it felt good to crawl into bed, pull the comforter all the way up to just under my chin, and soon feeling cozy, let my mind roam freely for a brief moment. Wandering away from the realities of the day, it created pleasant fantasies about plentiful food, about good friends with whom to explore woods and fields, about walking the streets without fear. Eventually, as I became overcome by sleep, fantasies faded into dreams. Perhaps it was this feeling about the bed that made me risk my life for a bed, and not even my own.

The "all clear" had brought us out of the basement, somewhat shaken by the heavy bombardment. After a quick check of our apartment for fire or serious damage, we found no major problems, so I went with a few other tenants to check the upper floors and attic. Having once again escaped practically untouched, I joined my mother and sister to see how the neighborhood had fared.

The "Jewish" house across the street was burning fiercely; flames were shooting out from many windows. Only the two lower floors didn't show smoke or flames. The building's residents stood in our yard, their eyes fixed on the flaming torch that had been their home. They made no attempts to save any of their belongings.

An elderly couple, who stood a little away from the others, also stared at the burning building. I asked if they had been able to save anything at all. They did not respond to my question; the woman just kept moaning something, which at first I had trouble understanding.

"My bed, my bed" she repeated over and over again. I asked which apartment was theirs. The old man pointed to the second floor.

I ran into our apartment. Taking two thick scarves, I soaked them in water and wrapped them around my head, covering hair, nose and mouth; only my eyes looked out. Thus protected, I dashed into the burning building.

Passing through the large double doors, I went into the smoke-filled tunnel-like carriageway. After pausing for a brief moment to orient myself, I entered the stairway, where I was greeted by the most eerie sounds: Sounds of a rushing wind and sounds of moaning as if the building were in pain; now and again sharp, explosive cracks, like a warning of coming disaster, made my heart skip a beat.

Undeterred, I darted up the stairs to the second floor. There I tried to guess which of the apartments belonged to the old couple. One apartment door stood open. Assuming that it was the right one I entered. A few steps down a narrow hallway and I saw a room with two beds.

For a second or so I stood in the door staring at an inferno: A curtain of flames, reaching from floor to ceiling and nearly smokeless, appeared to be advancing across the room. The beds, still untouched by the flames, stood between the fire and me. Grabbing the mattresses, I stacked them on top of each other. Then with the stack on my back, I ran.

How I managed to put the mattresses on my back and run with them through the narrow hallway and down two flights of stairs I don't recall. In retrospect this seems rather impossible; yet somehow I got my load down into the smoke-filled carriageway. (I did have experience running with mattresses on my back, gained during the Markthalle deportation operation.)

After readjusting the mattresses on my back, I was ready to dash through the carriageway into the open when the world crashed down on me.

What happened I'm unable to recall. What I do remember is that I found myself standing on the sidewalk at the end of the driveway with bricks, pieces of wall, burning timbers, and what not all around me; and behind me a pile of smoking rubble. The building was gone. The mattresses were still on my back.

Several things must have happened: The carriageway didn't cave in right away but came down only after I had passed through; the building collapsed inward, and the mattresses, rewarding one good turn with another, had protected me against the fiery rain of debris.

I crossed the street to our yard and dropped the mattresses in front of the elderly couple. "Your bed," I said, starting to walk away. The old man grabbed my arm to hold me back. His wife, groping in her pocket book, came up with a ten-mark note and tried to hand it to me. I tore away, feeling insulted.

"Ten marks for my life," I fumed.

I hadn't done this for money. My mother tried to calm me. The woman just wanted to say thank you and didn't quite know how to say it.

"'Thank you' would have been enough," I mumbled.

I sat down on the low wall surrounding our yard, staring at the smoking rubble across the street that only a few moments ago had been a building. My legs were no longer willing to carry me.

I had risked my life for a set of mattresses! I felt a fool. Had this grandstanding really been necessary? I wanted to forget the whole derring-do, erase it from my mind.

I must have caused my mother considerable anguish. Perhaps she too wanted to forget the episode; she never mentioned it.

Seventy-Two Hours

Although the city had received its fair share of air raids – some rather heavy – talk persisted that Frankfurt had so far been spared the devastations the Allied Air Forces were inflicting on other major cities. "The Jews," the talk said, were protecting the city: Once the war was over they would want to return to the birthplace of the Rothschilds. Others, local patriots, gave the credit to "International Big Business:" The city was to be the capital of a post Prussian-dominated Germany, a Germany oriented toward world trade.

To me the talk sounded like so much amusing nonsense not to be believed. And the onslaught did come, lasting three nights and three days. When it was over, whole areas in the city were in total ruin. On my way to work, I remember passing through streets in which not a single house remained standing.

Still, certain facts couldn't be denied: The suburban headquarters complex of IG Farben, the giant monopolistic chemical corporation, remained untouched. Its modern office buildings and apartment houses became General Eisenhower's headquarters. The mid-city offices of the Metal Gesellschaft, a mining, smelting, and manufacturing company of metals other than iron and steel with interests around the globe, also weren't touched by the bombs; the neighborhood, which included the Opera House, however, was destroyed. The office building became the seat of the Allied Military Government.

The First Twenty-Four Hours -- About midnight wailing sirens interrupted our sleep. We dressed without hurrying and took our time gathering the things we routinely took with us to the basement.

Usually after settling down in the shelter I tried to go to sleep, but not this time. A feeling of unease, shared by others, kept me from dozing off. The consensus was that this was not an ordinary alert, although no one could explain why. Something wasn't quite routine, but what? Most likely feelings of unease had been felt before, but with nothing unusual having occurred these were quickly forgotten.

After several unsuccessful attempts to snooze or to read, I begged my mother to let me go upstairs to stretch out on my bed. But before she could answer, the man sitting nearest the door demanded quiet. He was hearing sounds that could only come from a large number of aircraft. Soon others became aware of it too.

The approach of a large number of aircraft was usually announced by distant anti-aircraft fire gradually coming closer and increasing in intensity. Yet, this time, as the sound of aircraft became unmistakable, the guns remained silent.

As tension in the basement rose, curiosity overcame fear. I wanted to see what was going on. Unable to sit still and defying my mother's protests, I dashed upstairs into the yard. Others, just as curious, followed.

Cautiously we stepped into the open. The air was trembling from the churning of hundreds of propellers, or maybe thousands. Searchlights scanned the sky.

With fascination we watched as the searchlights picked out a single plane. The plane, which appeared to be directly overhead, released clusters of multi-colored flares, which slowly descended, illuminating our yard with an eerie light. Hypnotized, we watched the plane's maneuvers in trying to escape the searchlights.

Then the guns opened up. Furious anti-aircraft fire filled the air. The tracers racing toward the sky, the flashes from the firing guns, and the scanning searchlights produced, along with the multi-colored flares released by the plane, a light spectacle outdoing any fireworks I had ever seen. We made a mad dash for the basement.

As we reached the steps, the lights went out. Driven by the whistling of the falling bombs, I groped my way down the dark stairs. The nearly simultaneous detonations of hundreds of bombs nearly knocked me off my feet.

A deafening uproar, like the thundering of the Days of Damnation, filled the air. The building shook. The floor heaved under my feet as I groped for my seat.

We seemed to be at the very center of the fury that had been unleashed.

How long did this terror last? The dimensions of time seemed swallowed up by the chaos of the moment; perhaps the terror lasted a few minutes, perhaps an eternity.

As the sounds of destruction faded, curiosity regained the upper hand. I was eager to go outside to look around, to see if the world was still there.

Not quite having the courage to go alone, I waited for someone to come along; no one seemed inclined to do so.

I was still hesitating when the caretaker's son, a boy of about fifteen, came into our shelter carrying a big flashlight and two firemen's helmets. He asked for volunteers to check for fires. Maybe, he suggested importantly, we'll have to evacuate. I volunteered at once.

Placing the helmets on our heads, we ran upstairs. Checking the upper floors, the caretaker's garret apartment and finally the space under the roof, we found only the usual damage caused by nearby bomb explosions: broken glass and fallen plaster. (With every air raid the amount of broken glass decreased as window glass was replaced with plastic sheeting.) Quickly we returned to the ground floor shouting down to the basement that the house was all right. Then we set out into the yard.

The city was burning. The sky seemed aglow from many fires, while dense smoke filled the air competing with the acrid smell from explosives and gunfire. Though curious about what had happened to the neighborhood, we didn't dare to move far beyond our courtyard; searchlights were plying the sky.

With all apparently quiet, others came out of the basement. No one moved far from the door as curiosity and fear competed. Now and again brief bursts of anti-aircraft fire made us run toward the basement steps, only to return to the yard when the burst ended. With no planes overhead, we attributed the shooting to nervous gun crews.

The sound of approaching airplanes and the resumption of intense anti-aircraft fire made us hustle back into the basement.

Two more waves of bombers dropped their devastating loads before we finally heard the "all clear." We had come through unharmed.

In the morning we didn't go to work. Raging fires, collapsed buildings, and explosions of delayed bombs made many streets impassable or unsafe.

Shortly before noon, Allied bombers paid a return visit, continuing their work of destruction. It was the first heavy daylight attack on the City. Again, our building escaped serious damage.

The Second Twenty-Four Hours -- Another night of falling bombs and spreading fires. Though our neighborhood was hit again, our luck held: our small street with its four buildings again escaped destruction. Of course we had not remained completely untouched: Interior walls and ceilings showed cracks; furniture had been upended and damaged; dishes had been broken. But all this was of no importance; we still had a roof over our heads.

However, we began to show the effects of the raids: our eyes were bloodshot from lack of sleep and burned painfully from the acrid smoke; throats were sore and lungs hurt from breathing in smoke and building dust. The wet handkerchiefs we placed over mouths and noses were of little help.

We looked dirty, grimy, unwashed. What little water was available was for drinking. Even the toilet wasn't flushed. Food and drink tasted of smoke.

Late in the afternoon, after having escaped another daylight raid without serious damage, my mother decided somewhat optimistically to begin cleaning up and doing some straightening out, and even to start making repairs. We were tired of the wall plaster that was everywhere, including in our beds, and of stepping on broken glass. I fixed the kitchen window's blackout in the naïve hope that electricity would be back by nightfall and we could have our supper with real light. Eating by candlelight wasn't romantic anymore.

I lit a fire in the auxiliary stove. My mother prepared a hot meal, and using a portion of our precious water, made a pot of tea. To save candles – power had not been restored – we went to bed early. We badly needed a good night's sleep. Another night of bombing seemed unlikely.

The Third Twenty-Four Hours -- Wailing sirens woke us up. "False alarm" I insisted. My mother wasn't so sure.

Reluctantly I crawled out of bed and dressed rather slowly, hoping that before I was finished getting dressed, the "all clear" would sound. Heavy anti-aircraft fire made me move with alacrity. By the time we reached the basement, bombs were falling.

After the bombers had dropped their deadly cargo and faded away, the caretaker's son and I rushed upstairs to check for fires.

This night differed from the previous nights: We had been hit. The caretaker's apartment was in shambles: Furniture had been smashed, and an internal wall had collapsed. Several small fires were burning. Luckily, none of the fires had yet begun to spread. We quickly covered the burning incendiary bombs with sand. Then back into the shelter: another wave of bombers had arrived.

With neighborhood sirens knocked out, we didn't hear the "all clear." But with the raid apparently over we congratulated ourselves: once again we had come through a major attack relatively unscathed.

We had spoken too soon.

Of our street's four buildings, two had again escaped destruction: The "Jewish" house and the one across the street, a dormitory for foreign workers, young men from France, Belgium and other West European countries. But the other two buildings were burning: Flames were creeping along the roof's edge of the house next door, and smoke was coming out of upper floor windows; the building at the corner, facing the park, was engulfed in flames, from ground floor to roof.

The building's caretaker insisted that we keep checking the attic. With all the fires around us, he insisted, the roof could catch fire.

Back up into the attic.

Dense smoke greeted us. And, where our building abutted the one next-door, flames were creeping along floorboards and rafters. Quick action was called for.

We needed water; sand wouldn't do this time. But, with the water supply shut off, where could we get water? The nearby pond had plenty of water, so our problem became how to get the water from the pond to the attic. The answer: a bucket chain. Next problem: how to find enough people to man a chain reaching from the pond to the attic.

We couldn't expect help from our neighbors; they were far too busy with their own problems. Besides, would they aid Jews?

A group of the foreign workers living in the building across the street offered help. Though grateful for the offer, we still didn't have enough people to form a bucket line to the pond.

Puzzled about what to do, we found help from an unexpected source: the German Army.

Soldiers from barracks around the city had been ordered into the streets to help residents cope with the disaster. Looking for help, my mother encountered a group of soldiers looking for something to do. They were willing to come with my mother, but would they still be willing to help us when they saw our Jewish Star?

We had covered the star on our clothing. But the entrance to the building and each apartment door was also marked with the Star and we weren't sure what other telltale signs there might be revealing that this was a "Jewish" house. We thought it best to keep the soldiers away from the building.

Quickly we organized ourselves: inside the building and from the entrance to the corner of the street the bucket chain was made up of residents and foreign workers; from the corner to the pond it was manned by the soldiers.

The caretaker's son and I volunteered to handle the hoses and the two hand- pumps the caretaker had provided. In the confined space under the roof the two of us crawled as close as we could to the burning rafters and floorboards. Within a short time, with plenty of water available, we managed to extinguish the fire. Aided by the Nazi Wehrmacht, a "Jewish" house had been saved.

Our problem hadn't been fully solved: The fire next door was still burning and its intensity was increasing. Flames might once again leap across to our roof.

Our building's caretaker volunteered us to help our neighbors to control the fire, but they showed no willingness to fight the flames. Convinced that their building was lost, they concentrated on saving their belongings. But they gave us permission to go up into their attic to see what we could do. Perhaps we could prevent the fire from jumping roofs.

Led by the caretaker, a few of us went up to the space under the roof to inspect. The situation didn't look good: though few flames were visible, the intensity of the smoke hinted at a large fire.

With the soldiers and foreign workers having left, we decided not to fight the fire – that would have been too much for us – but to concentrate on keeping it away from our roof. I volunteered to handle both the hand pump and the hose.

Lying on my stomach, awkwardly pumping with one hand and aiming the hose with the other, I gained the impression that I was making progress: Flames could no longer be seen where the two buildings touched and the smoke seemed diminished, or at least so I thought. I felt sure we were winning the battle.

Having run out of water, I yelled for more.

What I received was more silence.

I yelled louder, but the silence persisted. I realized that I was alone in the burning attic; the smoke seemed to be increasing.

I had no flashlight and the flames dancing along the rafters provided no light. I groped my way to the stairs. Cautiously my foot searched for the first step. I was certain that I had reached the stairs, but where was the step?

It hit me with a shock: The top step was missing, or perhaps several steps were gone. I had been crawling over a lot of debris presumably coming from the roof, which, I feared, might be on the verge of collapsing. But this did not explain a missing step. I was sure that the step had been there when I came up, so why wasn't it there now?

Confused, tired, and with burning eyes, a new fear entered my mind: Perhaps a section of roof had collapsed and had taken the stairway down with it.

I couldn't concern myself with explanations; I had to figure a way down from the burning attic.

Think! Think! Don't panic!

I sat on the floor by the stairs, letting my legs dangle where the first step should have been to consider my choices: Wait until someone missed me and came looking – or take action. Yelling wouldn't help; no one would hear me.

Waiting for rescue had little appeal. It would take some time before anyone missed me and came looking, and I really didn't know how much time I had before the roof came down.

And I had an even stronger motivation: embarrassment. I didn't want anyone to know that I had let myself be trapped under a burning roof.

I concluded that I had only one choice: to go down the stairs. I decided to jump in the dark over the missing step or even steps.

I was still holding the hand pump with its attached hose. I estimated that the hose was about two meters long. Disconnecting it from the pump, I used it whip-like, trying to determine how many steps were missing. Gradually letting out lengths of hose, I soon hit what I thought was a step.

With one hand braced against the wall and the other holding on to the banister as far forward as I dared, I jumped.

Apparently I had guessed the distance correctly, my feet found a step and the step did not break. Or perhaps no steps had been missing? Had the smoke or insufficient oxygen impaired my judgment?

After regaining my balance and letting my heart quiet down, I cautiously descended the remainder of the stairway to the floor below.

On the lower floors, the residents were still moving their possessions out of the house to the safety of the nearby park. I offered my help. But we had to give up. The firestorm generated by the intense heat of the large fires raged hurricane- like through the streets, making walking difficult and carrying anything large impossible.

Exhausted, dirty, tired, with eyes tearing so badly that I could hardly see, I returned to our apartment. After brushing fallen plaster off my bed, I tried to get some sleep, but found it impossible. I couldn't decide what was more painful, keeping my eyes open or keeping them shut. My mother made a solution for washing out my eyes, and so I sat at the edge of my bed trying to sooth my burning eyes. As the sun struggled to come through the dense smoke hanging over the city, I fell asleep.

Eventually the roof of our neighbors' house collapsed. The fire burned itself out, ending the danger to us.

Late morning or early afternoon, I got off my bed. We had very little water left and weren't sure that we could find some soon. I washed up, using water sparingly.

Once more I rinsed my burning eyes; then I changed from dirty clothing, smelling from smoke, into clean clothing smelling from smoke. Everything smelled from smoke.

I went into the kitchen to see what there was to eat and to look for something to drink that could sooth my sore throat. Claire and my mother were already there. My mother had put some sort of breakfast/lunch together.

Curious about what was going on in the neighborhood, we ventured forth, this time not hesitating to hide our Jewish Star. First we made our usual rounds of Jewish houses. Our survey was shorter than usual: Several of the houses were beyond our help, having been completely destroyed.

And with the residents apparently having found shelter, there was nothing useful we could do. So we went searching for water.

We wandered around carrying an empty bucket, just like everyone else, and probably looking somewhat dazed, also just like everybody else. After a while we met a tanker truck dispensing potable water. And again like everyone else, we stood patiently in line for our turn to fill our bucket.

After returning home with our precious water, I lit a fire in the kitchen stove to heat a small portion, just enough for three cups of "ersatz." I had always liked to make a fire in the stove; but with the smell of fire everywhere, even the stove's fire appeared unfriendly.

A cup of "ersatz," a brief rest, and then to work: sweeping up dust and debris and once again starting to make repairs. But even a brief rest was not permitted. We had barely finished our cup of "coffee" when the sirens wailed (mobile sirens, this time), and if we questioned whether we had heard correctly, any doubt was quickly removed: anti-aircraft fire began blasting away and sounds of exploding bombs once more hurt the ears and shook the building and the nerves.

To our relief our part of the city was spared the brunt of the attack. A few bombs did fall in our immediate neighborhood, hitting mostly already destroyed and burning buildings. There wasn't much else to hit.

Tired of sitting in the basement, I went upstairs into the yard. Daytime raids were far less spectacular than those at night: No tracers rushed upwards, no colorful flares descended, no searchlights described ever-changing patterns in the sky, even the flashes from the heavy guns were far less pronounced. The sounds however were the same, and just as terrifying.

I stood in the doorway, somewhat protected against falling shrapnel, listening to the cacophony of anti-aircraft fire and the "music" made by the shell fragments returning to earth. The thousands of fragments cutting through the air produced a peculiar hum, different shapes and sizes producing different pitches that together had the effect of a pipe organ playing high notes only. But these musical pieces of metal were deadly.

Finally even distant explosions came to an end and the anti-aircraft fire faded out. But clearly, there was confusion. While an "all clear" signal came from one direction, a new alert could be heard from another; a nearby siren, still functioning or functioning again, sounded an alert only to reverse itself immediately. Sporadic anti-aircraft fire worsened the confusion.

My mother decided it was better for us not to venture forth, to go out only if we saw or heard a truck dispensing water nearby. We could have started to clean up, but there seemed little incentive for doing so. One question was on all of our minds: Will there be another attack in the coming night?

As he did after previous heavy raids, Mr. Wolf went out in his wheelchair to see how the neighborhood had fared. This time he didn't go very far; maneuvering through the destruction had been impossible. Whole blocks were afire; collapsed buildings and bomb craters made many streets impassable.

Distraught and disoriented people wandered the streets. On more passable streets and avenues anything with wheels was moving toward the city's exits trying to find a way out of the inferno. Panicked parents threw their children on passing vehicles, not asking where they were headed as long as they were heading out.

Intermittent wailing of sirens, occasional bursts of anti-aircraft fire and sounds of exploding delayed-action bombs sent people scurrying into shelters. As night came I didn't get undressed. Stretched out on my bed I fell asleep.

The night remained quiet: no alert, no anti-aircraft fire, no sounds of airplanes, no bombs. The city, the anti-aircraft gunners, and perhaps the bomber crews, all must have been exhausted.

The Day After -- As the smoky morning dawned the authorities were ready to stem the panic. Large trailer trucks, manned by soldiers, Nazi Party workers, and volunteers, rolled into the city. Parking at major intersections, they handed out food and drink, no questions asked: Sandwiches, red wine, and coffee (not "ersatz"). One could have as much as one could carry. Tanker trucks moved through passable streets, their loudspeakers announcing that drinking water was available. Out-of-town fire trucks and their crews arrived, reinforced by soldiers and prisoners of war, to begin fighting the many fires in a more systematic way. Other teams started to clear major streets and intersections, making it easier for emergency vehicles to move around. Some streets were roped off as structures in danger of collapsing were being blown up.

As evening approached the panic subsided. Parents looked for their children, families searched for missing members.

After two days the food trucks withdrew. Police and uniformed Nazi party members patrolled the streets. Trucks mounting loudspeakers crisscrossed the city urging calm and warning that looters would be shot on sight. We put our Jewish Star back on and returned to our jobs.

But for two days we had feasted. Our plates had been heaped with food, our cups filled with real coffee, our glasses with wine.

CHAPTER 14

ADVENTURES OF A STREET SWEEPER

Ordinary People

Being out of work, I can't recall why, I went to our community office to "request" a job, as Gestapo regulations required. My hope to remain unemployed for a while was quickly disappointed: A job was waiting for me.

The following morning I reported for work at the Department of Sanitation's depot in the Old City. And so, a few weeks before turning sixteen, I became a municipal street sweeper, a "career" that lasted until I received another slip of paper telling me that the Gestapo had ordered me to report for deportation.

The Department of Sanitation was responsible for garbage collection and the cleaning of streets and sewers. The war's demand on the country's manpower had forced the department to give up many of its workers. To compensate for the loss, it had received Gestapo permission to hire Jews. Soon it was not unusual to see men wearing the Jewish Star manning municipal garbage trucks.

But not for long: the deportations took away most of the younger and stronger Jewish men. Jews still with the department, mostly older men, were shifted to street cleaning. A few Jewish boys were hired to augment the Jewish street cleaners.

When my "career" with the municipality began, the heavy air raids on the city were still in the future. The city's historic "Altstadt" (Old City) had not yet been destroyed. Its half-timbered houses, dating back to the Middle Ages, still lined the narrow, picturesque cobble-stoned lanes.

The depot, located on one of these old narrow lanes, the Elephantengasse –Elephant Lane – appeared to be part of this historic environment: The facilities and the equipment looked like leftovers from an earlier age. Even the workers seemed a bit out of date; most were older men called back from retirement.

The Jews, all from mixed marriages with only slight ties to the Jewish community, were well integrated. As a young boy, and not at all embarrassed to wear the Jewish Star, I was definitely not welcome. During the few weeks I spent at the Elephantengasse I was ignored. Most of the time I sat around in the depot feeling bored. Eventually I was reassigned to the Department's main depot.

This depot, a complex of garages, workshops, stores and offices dated from the 1920s, reflected the progressive architectural and social thinking of the post-World War I, pre-1933, period. It was certainly more attractive than the dingy and cramped quarters in the old city. Here, in a large and pleasant day room, the workers could take their breaks and eat their lunch in comfort while listening to music and to the perhaps not always so pleasant news.

Jews were not permitted to have lunch together with their non-Jewish co-workers and were forbidden to listen to the radio. To solve this problem, a small room furnished with a table and a few chairs had been made available to the group of five Jewish street sweepers.

Our room lacked the amenities provided for our "Aryan" colleagues - hot plates for warming lunch and hot water for tea or coffee. But it was comfortable and clean and, most importantly, warm during winter.

I preferred the segregation. I didn't like to be among Germans, to have to listen to their bragging about the superiority of the German soldier over his adversary, and their condemnation of those fighting against the Third Reich as criminals. Nor did I wish to hear the incessant propaganda celebrating real or imagined victories on the battlefield. And I certainly didn't want to hear the daily "news analysis," which consisted mostly of vulgar denunciations of Jews.

The walk from home to the depot was long, over an hour. In the morning I didn't mind the walk; it provided an opportunity for musings and daydreaming. With few people in the street, there were fewer chances of being harassed. But walking home in the evening after a long day's work was awful.

The wartime personnel shortages forced the department to change its street-cleaning practices: The individual career street sweepers, responsible for a number of city streets, were replaced by teams of ten or more workers taking care of large city areas; and instead of sweeping all streets at least once a day, main streets were swept once a week with side streets only occasionally.

Our team of eleven was made up of the five Jewish men, four German women and two career city employees: one acting as the team's foreman, the other as his assistant. The arrangement was a clear violation of Gestapo regulations: Jews had to work as a segregated unit. Yet no one complained, not even the Gestapo.

But the not quite proper team arrangement wasn't my concern; my concern was whether I could work alongside Germans without being subjected to hate harangues and to harassments. To my astonishment the arrangement worked quite well, at least most of the time.

Many of the department's career workers had served in the military, and most were members of the Nazi Party. Civil servants were "urged" to join the party; that is, they paid dues and appeared at gatherings and demonstrations when ordered to do so. Both our foreman and his assistant were Party members, though only the assistant was an active member.

Herr Beck, the street cleaning boss, a former master sergeant in the pre-1918 Imperial German Army, was a somewhat remote fatherly figure. He expected everyone to follow his orders without question. In return he treated everyone as fairly as he could, and that included the Jews. Herr Beck set the tone among the depot's supervisors and foremen.

We saw little of our supervisor, Herr Schuhmacher. Responsible for several cleaning teams, he didn't pay much attention to us. At the start of the day, before dispatching his crews, he gave his instructions that, as time went on, had less and less to do with street cleaning. With the increase in air raids and the resulting destruction, keeping the streets swept often had to yield to other tasks: clearing intersections of all kinds of debris and opening sewer inlets.

During the day Herr Schuhmacher came by a few times to assure himself that everything was going smoothly, chit-chat with the foreman, or revise instructions. As the frequency of daylight air alerts increased, his visits became fewer and shorter; he preferred to remain at the depot, which had a good air raid shelter.

The foreman was an easy going fellow who subscribed to a simple motto: We have a job to do, so let's do it and leave politics out of it. That suited the other Jewish workers and me just fine. Of course he mouthed politically correct opinions concerning the war and the Jews, but his anti-Semitic remarks were a matter of routine, said without malice. Following his boss's lead, he didn't differentiate between his Jewish and non-Jewish workers.

Being part of the mixed crew – career workers, German women, and Jews – was a new experience for me. True, when I worked for the landscape company, I had worked alongside Germans, but those had been social outcasts. But these were ordinary people with steady jobs; several had civil service careers with good pensions; and most had families with children and grandchildren.

The arrangement gave me an opportunity to hear how the common people perceived the Nazi regime and the war. Of course, these were no longer the high days of German military successes: Allied air strikes pounded the cities, the Wehrmacht was bogged down in Russia, and General Rommel was no longer undefeatable in North Africa.

The German workers – the foreman and his assistant, the women of our crew, truck drivers, the storekeeper, and others – were patriotic citizens who supported the war and to some degree the ideology of a "Greater Germany." The regime's corruption and brutal suppression of any opposition were rationalized: Excesses by the government and the Nazi party were due to the war that had been forced on Germany. When we lost Jewish workers due to the deportations, our supervisor showed some sympathy. Germans, he commented, had to go to the war front, Jews to labor camps. Neither, he felt certain, were pleasant experiences.

Aware of the possibility of informers, the workers watched what they were saying. Informers, they knew, were quite willing to denounce dissenters to the Party or worse, to the Secret Police. But again they rationalized: The repressive atmosphere was due to the necessity of fighting

International Communism, which was trying to undermine the will of the German People.

Of my female German co-workers I remember two. Both were in their fifties.

Mary was a short woman, always friendly to everyone and close to no one. She wasn't married and lived alone in a garret apartment. She followed the rules and never talked about the war or politics when a Jewish worker was within earshot. I never heard her make anti-Semitic remarks.

When her apartment was bomb damaged, our foreman asked me to help her with the cleaning up. This was a violation of the rules, of course, but that was all right with me. Removing debris, pieces of a fallen ceiling, portions of a collapsed interior wall, much glass, seemed to me no better or worse than sweeping the street. The only words she spoke to me while cleaning up were those necessary to do the work. Even away from everyone else, she followed the rule of no conversations with a Jew. Or, perhaps, she had nothing to say.

The other woman, Gretchen, was very tall, towering over everyone else; and she thought of herself as towering above everybody, and not only in height.

Gretchen did not always deign to follow rules. She liked to talk to me and especially about politics, taking pride in her non-conformist opinions, though consistency was not one of her strong points. Only when it came to the Fuhrer was she constant. Once she whispered to me that she was in love with Adolph Hitler; she would do anything for him.

Another time she assured me, this time in a voice loud enough for others to hear, that the Nazis were a corrupt and evil bunch and once the war was over, Hitler would deal with them appropriately. A few days later, she reversed her opinion, calling the Nazis the saviors of the German Nation. She was proud, she announced, also in a loud voice, to be called a National Socialist. To stress her point, she painted swastikas on her broom, only to erase them a few days later when something had irritated her. I must confess that I rather liked Gretchen.

The assistant foreman was the fly in the ointment. A mean spirited Nazi, he was disliked by everyone, not only by the Jews. Before '33, Gretchen told me in confidence, this ardent Nazi had been just as ardent a Communist.

He intimidated his fellow civil servants by threatening to denounce them to the Party for not showing a proper Nazi spirit and for lacking enthusiasm for the war against the Bolsheviks. He berated the foreman and the women for being too friendly with us. To us he didn't speak at all, except to give orders. Then his tone was rude. No one dared to talk back to him, not even the German workers. Yet once I did.

Following an air raid, our team was dispatched to remove debris from an important street intersection outside our normal area of work. As it was some distance away, we traveled to the site on the back of a truck. On the way, while passing through a heavily bomb-damaged area, our little Nazi kept up a steady tirade against the enemy, especially the Jew-dominated Americans.

Nothing was unusual about that and, although I felt somewhat uncomfortable, I paid little attention to his hateful diatribe. When we passed a burned out church, his attack became more personal.

"See what your friends have done," he shouted, pointing a finger at me. "You Jews are the destroyers of Christian churches." For whatever reason, for once I didn't remain quiet.

"My friends?" I shouted back, "who made them into my friends? Did you give me any choice? Have I ever harmed you? What have I done to you to make me into your enemy?"

On the back of the truck there was shocked silence. The Germans pretended being interested in something we were just passing; the Jews looked worried. And the little Nazi? He just stood there, having forgotten to close his mouth.

My outburst had not been very prudent, and on reflection I thought it had sounded too defensive. For a few brief seconds talking back had felt good. Feeling uneasy, I reprimanded myself for having lost my temper. Would he denounce me to the Gestapo?

After a few days had passed without anything untoward having happened, I relaxed. Within a few days the incident was forgotten.

A Military Dilemma

One month after my seventeenth birthday, I received notice to report to the local military district command for pre-induction processing. Boys born in 1927 were being called up for service in the Wehrmacht.

This could only be in error; Jews had been denied the "honor" of becoming soldiers since the Nazis had come to power. A check with the community office elicited the opinion that I had no choice but to report as ordered.

At work I showed the order to my foreman. He gave me the day off without making a comment, although it must have puzzled him. My Jewish co-workers thought it was funny; I failed to see the humor.

On a cold morning in February 1944, I set out on my long walk to the district command headquarters in one of Frankfurt's suburbs.

The headquarters occupied an attractive white building in the International Style of the 1920s, a style the Nazis had denounced as an example of "Jewish decadence." I don't know the original function of the building, but this example of "Jewish decadence" seemed quite suitable for its use by the Wehrmacht.

With my "Order to Report" in hand and my Jewish Star properly displayed on my coat, I reported to an elderly man in a soldier's uniform who appeared to be a receptionist. Without batting an eyelash at my Jewish Star, he checked my name against a list. Finding the name, he told me with a wave of his hand, to join a group of boys, all about my age, already lining up.

I did not relish joining a group of German boys. I expected at least verbal, if not some physical, abuse. To my astonishment and great relief, the boys were rather oblivious to my presence. They were far too excited about their forthcoming military service to pay much attention to me. There were a few stares, for they must have been puzzled to see a Jewish Star in the line, but they quickly returned to their lively discussions.

Germany's military situation was deteriorating. Soviet forces were at the border of German-occupied Poland. Following the Anglo-American landing in Italy, Italy's dictator Mussolini had been forced to resign. The new Italian Republic was ready to ask for peace. Yugoslavia's partisan army, having seized much of the territory abandoned by Italian troops, was endangering the German forces in the Balkans. American and British Air Forces rained destruction on Germany's cities by day and by night.

Yet from what I could overhear, the thought of losing the war had not entered the minds of these young Germans ready to join the Nazi Army. For them, war was still a great and exciting adventure. Some showed off their familiarity with military lingo, picked up from a father, an older brother, or a friend. Speculating about the service branch to which they would be assigned, they argued about the merits of the various services, defending with enthusiasm their preferred choices. In the same vein, they speculated about the country in which they would most likely be stationed. Showing little apprehension, they wondered at which front they would see action. And, of course, they talked about girls.

As we slowly proceeded along the corridor, neither the soldier who guided us nor passing military personnel paid the slightest attention to my presence. German officials were usually rude, hostile, and often threatening toward Jews. I hadn't expected anything different, yet officers, non-commissioned officers and even lower ranks treated me in no special way. In the tradition of the military, they barked at everyone.

After checking names once more, the non-commissioned officer in charge of the group I was in divided us into smaller groups for medical examination. Again, no exception was made for me. And again we stood and waited. (Standing around waiting seems to be common to all armies.)

I worried that the process would last past the curfew time for Jews. With nothing else to do, I kept my mind busy speculating about lunch. The Army would certainly feed the potential recruits, but would I be fed too, separately of course as the law required? I figured that most likely, I would simply be ignored.

Finally our group was marched to the medical station. There our names were verified once more. My name was still on the list. Each of the young men was handed a medical form to fill out, but this time I was excluded. After the filled out forms had been handed back, medical officers questioned each potential recruit separately. Although my name was called out, and I answered with my full name, including the mandatory "Israel," I was not questioned. Then we were ordered to strip. Would I have to strip too before being ignored?

Due to the intervention by the Allied Air Forces, the questions of stripping and lunch had to remain unanswered.

Wailing sirens brought the medical examination to a halt. Orders were given to evacuate the building and proceed to the nearby air raid shelter, one of those multi-storied, windowless reinforced concrete structures known as bunkers that had sprung up all over the city. The bunker was located a short distance away, just across a soccer field that had once belonged to the Maccabi Sports Club.

Jews were not permitted to enter bunkers. So what to do? I couldn't remain in the building, I could not go to the bunker, and I couldn't be out in the open; this too was prohibited. (This prohibition applied to everyone, not just to Jews.) A couple of officers seemed to understand the problem. While I waited to be given orders, they stood there staring at me, apparently also wondering what to do.

Minutes ticked off. The officers became increasingly nervous as they listened anxiously for the first indication of an air raid: the firing of anti-aircraft guns, the sound of airplanes, or the explosion of bombs. Most likely they were praying for the "all clear."

The officers came to a decision. I was ordered to come along with them. So we, a Jew wearing his Yellow Star and two German Army officers, sprinted across the soccer field toward the bunker. I don't know what made the officers more uneasy, the fear of bombs or of being seen with a Jew.

We entered the bunker a few brief minutes before the "all clear." On the return to the district command I walked unescorted.

The Army had learned its lesson. I was instructed not to rejoin my group. An elderly soldier escorted me to another part of the building. There, after verifying who I was, a clerk handed me an already prepared exclusion certificate. The reason for exclusion from military service was stated in one word: "Jude" (Jew). I signed my name, and for me the pre-induction process was over.

I started on my long way home, puzzled by the stupidity of the whole process and hoping that I could reach home before the sounding of another alert.

The Baker's Daughter

"And he [Abraham] said: 'Let the Lord not be angry and I will speak but once: Perhaps ten righteous men shall be found there.' And HE said: 'I will not destroy it for the sake of ten' " (*Bereshit* (Genesis) 18:32).

As destruction rained down on the German people, as armies converged on the country from all sides, and as boys and old men were being sacrificed in the defense of a madman's fantasies, the story of Sodom and Gomorrah came to mind. Why did so many so willingly participate in the criminal deeds of a criminal regime? How many righteous were in the Land of the Nazis?

The war's manpower demands were taking their toll: Men once exempt from military duty because of age or physical handicap were called up for military service, while the war industry absorbed more and more women. Prisoners of war, once available to fill in for the men called up, were busy repairing roads and railroad tracks damaged by the relentless air war. Manpower available to street cleaning was reduced to a few men too crippled or too old to serve in the hastily formed citizen militia and to a few leftover Jews. And as deportations to the camps continued, this small number of Jews became ever smaller.

Large areas of the city were in ruin. Many streets were but narrow lanes, as debris from collapsed buildings covered sidewalks and much of the roadway. Frequent air raids added to the destruction, making the sweeping of streets more and more absurd; the reduction in available manpower made it nearly impossible.

The Sanitation Department abolished the street sweeping teams and reverted to the pre-war operation of individual sweepers. Each sweeper was given a large area, not to sweep but to keep sewer inlets free of dirt and rubble and to remove dog droppings, horse manure, and household waste. Garbage collection had become rather spotty; more and more garbage ended up in the streets.

Violating the Gestapo rule that Jews had to work in supervised groups, I was given a street cleaner's cart and assigned a city area. I worked alone, with my supervisor checking up on me no more than two or three times during the long working day.

There was a women I called "the baker's daughter." She was a young woman, rather the Wagnerian Brunhilde type, long blond braids hanging down past her shoulders. I noticed her one morning pedaling past on her bicycle, a basket strapped to the handlebar, apparently delivering bread and rolls in time for the noontime dinner. A normal activity in normal times, but these times could hardly be called normal. The terrible realities of the war the Germans had entered so triumphantly were knocking at their doors. It was this "normalcy" that had attracted my attention.

I thought that surely she hadn't noticed me, a Jewish boy sweeping streets, the Yellow Star properly sewn to the left breast pocket, clearly visible as the law demanded.

Not being noticed was not at all unusual. I rather preferred it that way. Occasionally someone did notice me and directed curses at me, or made some routine anti-Jewish remark; but mostly people were far too busy coping with the problems the war had brought them to pay attention to a street sweeper. Their gray faces and tired eyes showed the effect of the many sleepless hours spent in air raid shelters. They hurried to work, hurriedly did their shopping after work and then hurried home anxious to get there before the sirens wailed.

The mode of operation I had adopted was to leave my cart at a convenient street corner. Then, armed with broom and shovel, I worked the adjacent streets, leaving the collected dirt in piles to be picked up when I moved my cart to the next convenient corner. The work wasn't hard, and being mostly unsupervised, I worked at a leisurely pace.

One morning, returning to my cart, I found that a brown paper bag had been placed on top of it. Once in a while a neat citizen would dispose of some trash by opening the cart's dirt hopper and throwing the trash into it. Perhaps one of these neat citizens had been reluctant to open the hopper or had been too much in a rush and just left it on top. But this bag did not look like trash. With the existing shortages, who would throw anything away still of some use? Even paper bags were saved.

Curious, I opened the bag. In the bag were two large sandwiches, neatly wrapped in wax paper, also an item hard to get.

What to do with this package? Was this spoiled food someone had wanted to throw away, or had it been placed on my cart for me to find? I looked around to see if anyone was paying attention to me. No one was. I decided to take the package home.

I showed my find to my mother. We looked the package over, and since the wrapping was clean and both the bread and the content looked and smelled fresh, we concluded that a kind person had left it. We ate the sandwiches together with our usual fare available to Jews, beets or sauerkraut, and our inevitable cup of "ersatz." This evening's meal was certainly different from the routine. About a week later, when my cart stood at the same spot where I had found the bag with the sandwiches, another paper bag with sandwiches appeared.

Naturally, I had become curious about this benefactor. It occurred to me that the package had shown up on the days I had seen the "baker's daughter" making deliveries.

The following week I purposely left my cart at the corner where the young woman usually passed. Working slowly, I kept an eye on my cart, making sure, however, that I was sufficiently far away not to make it obvious that I was watching. Sure enough, at about the usual time I saw her peddling by with her basket strapped to the bike's handlebar. As she reached my cart she paused for a moment, and when she peddled on the now familiar brown paper bag was there. I could think of no way for me to thank her.

After several weeks the sandwich episodes came to an end. I no longer saw her making her deliveries, not very surprising in the deteriorating war situation. I hoped that she had not gotten herself into trouble for her good deeds.

The Boy From Smolensk And Other Allies

Often alliances are formed not because of shared ideologies but because of common enemies. We, or, perhaps better I, looked at the grand alliance against Germany as our friend. Yet I really knew better. The abandonment of the Jews had been all too obvious. Again and again attempts to escape from Nazi Germany had been frustrated by bureaucratic obstacles, official indifference, or hostility toward Jews. But these were subjects we rarely talked about. An Allied victory was our only chance for survival.

Our faith in the Great Alliance was not uniform. The Hitler-Stalin pact had generated misgivings about the Soviet's intentions; few trusted the

Russians. (Revelations of Stalin's anti-Semitism were still in the future.) We happily cheered the Red Army's victories, but what we really cheered were the defeats suffered by the once mighty Wehrmacht.

Attitudes toward France were more positive, though we were rather wary. Even admirers of French intellectualism and French culture harbored doubts about France's commitment in the battle against fascism. Her inability or unwillingness to seriously confront Germany while German forces were engaged in Poland had made France a dubious friend at best. Her subsequent quick defeat reinforced these doubts. A French prisoner of war with whom I worked assured me that the common soldier had been willing to fight, but the nation had been betrayed by officers, many of who had been flirting with fascism.

Our greatest admiration was for the British. Their stubborn refusal to give up when they had to confront the Nazis alone had boosted our morale; our real hope, however, was America.

With the war dragging on, Germany made increasing use of workers from German occupied lands and prisoners-of-war. After Italy's surrender to the Allies, Italian prisoners, soldiers and civilian anti-fascists were added to this kaleidoscope of peoples forced to work for the Third Reich.

I was most curious about people from the Soviet Union. All I knew of Soviet Russia was tainted by propaganda, either anti-communist or pro. With large numbers of Russians working in Germany, I had hoped to gain some insight into the Soviet enigma. Yet it appeared impossible to get to know any Russians. I had watched them working alongside us, clearing rubble after an air raid, wondering about their thoughts, their attitudes. But the supervisors, theirs and ours, had kept us apart. Working alone as a street sweeper, I saw little chance for meeting a Russian.

With the strains of the war eroding many rules, I finally had an opportunity to get to know a Russian. With my workload increasing, I was given a helper: A Russian boy, or young man, about my age. Surely a sign of the deterioration of the Reich: A non-Jew – even if "only" a Russian – was being supervised by a Jew!

The young Russian was from Smolensk. This major city, about four hundred kilometers west by southwest of Moscow, had been captured by the Germans in the summer of 1941. Many of its citizens, among them the boy, were brought to Germany as laborers. While working on a farm the young Russian had learned to speak some German. Why he had to leave the farm for other work I don't know.

I was most curious about his reaction to my Jewish Star. But he seemed not to have noticed it. Even when I pointed it out to him he made no comments nor did he ask questions. I told him about the persecution of the Jews, the destruction of synagogues, the shipping of children, women, and men to concentration camps and Ghettoes. Again, he showed no signs of interest. I attributed his lack of responses to homesickness. And, as I was more interested in finding out about the Soviet Union, I changed the subject.

When I turned to questions about his hometown I finally got a response: His voice perked up, his sagging shoulders straightened. He glorified his hometown. He compared the devastated city of Frankfurt to the Smolensk he remembered, before the Luftwaffe, the German artillery and the street fighting had reduced it to rubble.

In Smolensk, he asserted, electricity – apparently to him an important sign of progress – never failed. I felt no need to defend Germany by explaining the reasons for the power failures. The frequent air attacks and shortages of supplies and manpower were causing many problems, electric outages being just one.

(He was not alone in his belief that electricity was a sign of superiority. A German woman once asked me if other countries had electric light like Germany.)

His greatest pride was reserved for Moscow. He was sure that there was no city in world that could compare favorably with the Russian capital, not even his beloved Smolensk: The monumental buildings, the Kremlin, the extensive public parks, the broad boulevards. What had impressed him most in that city were the large department store and the system of public transportation.

To my regret, the time we worked together was far too short to get to know him better and learn more about Soviet Russia. After about two weeks he did not show up for work. My foreman gave no explanation, nor was he willing to answer my questions about the young Russian.

Hardly a night or a day went by without an air attack, or at least an alert. Forays by swift fighter-bombers swooping down from the sky, a rarity only a few months before, had become a major disruption. But attacks on bridges, road and rail junctions, and other "choke" points were not the only damage they caused: The frequent alerts slowed production, interrupted essential services, and robbed people of their sleep.

To reduce the loss in production, a pre-alert was introduced and the time from the first sounding of an alert to the expected arrival of the planes was drastically shortened. The pre-alert was sounded when a small number of planes had been detected, or a larger fleet appeared to be only passing over. During pre-alerts work was not to be interrupted. Air wardens were supposed to listen for anti-aircraft fire, distant bomb blasts or other signs of an impending attack.

With Allied forces in France the approach time to targets in Germany had become relatively short and the new alert procedure did not prove very effective. It did, however, achieve lots of confusion.

As welcome as the stepped-up air war against Germany was to us – another sign that Germany was headed for defeat – the activities by our "Allies" had created a serious problem for me: Where to find shelter when bombs were falling, bullets from machine guns zipped through the air, and shrapnel rained down? Though working for the city, I still couldn't use public shelters. Remaining in the street was dangerous and against the law; and for a Jew, ignoring any law could be as deadly as the menace from the sky.

With no "Jewish" house in the area where I worked, the nearest shelter I could use was that of the so-called Jewish Community Center, housed in a heavily bomb-damaged building. Only the ground floor was fit to be occupied. I had sacrificed several of my rare free Sundays to fix up some of the rooms, including two rooms pretentiously called "Juedisches Wohnheim" (Jewish Living Quarters). Here a few elderly couples, no longer capable of taking care of themselves, slept on mattresses on the floor, and were fed their meager rations and generally taken care of by two young girls, my sister and another "Geltungsjude."

The Center had no shelter of its own but had the Gestapo's permission to go to the still usable basement shelter of a nearby burned-out school.

Taking advantage of an apparent "schedule," raids occurred at about the same time each day I managed to be at a point closest to the Community Center's shelter, though this was still a considerable distance away. Most days this worked out all right, but not always.

The alert had sounded earlier than I had expected. Too far away from the "Jewish" shelter, I considered what to do when anti-aircraft guns began firing. Looking around for protection against the falling shrapnel, I noticed a group of French prisoners of war, also caught in the open, motioning for me to join them. With the Frenchmen, all rather tall fellows, surrounding me so that my Jewish Star could not readily be seen, we ran to a public shelter as bombs began to fall.

With the Allied air activity steadily increasing, the air raid "schedule" became less and less reliable. I was on the way to the sanitation department depot at the end of the day, usually a quiet time between attacks from fighter-bombers and raids by heavy bombers, when an alert sounded. I began to walk faster, trying to reach the depot's shelter, which I was permitted to use.

I was maybe still a hundred yards from the depot, passing an open field where anti-aircraft guns where positioned, when I heard the sound of heavy bombers. With the anti-aircraft guns firing, I made a mad dash for the depot's entrance.

Bombs began to fall. Still too far from the shelter, I crouched low against the wall near the depot's gate. A tremendous blast swallowed me up. Realizing that I was still alive and apparently unhurt, I slowly got up in the silence that surrounded me. As my hearing slowly returned, I noted that the attack had moved on; the sounds of aircraft and bomb blasts were fading; anti-aircraft fire had ceased.

The wall against which I had thrown myself was pockmarked from the impact of bomb fragments, yet for about two or three feet off the ground, the wall was unmarred. The large garage next to the gate was no longer there; and the field near the depot with its anti-aircraft equipment looked like a moonscape.

Many times, as I passed on my way to the depot, the young women manning the position had lined up to harass me. I didn't know what happened to them, nor did I care.

Endgame

In August 1944 Romania surrendered to the Russians. By October Russian troops reached the Hungarian capital, Budapest, and, penetrating deep into Poland, were approaching her capital, Warsaw. Mid-September American forces crossed into Germany. Allied heavy bombers pounded the country, while swift fighter-bombers attacked anything that moved on rails or highways. For the Germans not many options were left. As fall turned toward winter, the war seemed almost over.

Neither the intense air campaign against the homeland nor the setbacks on the ground deterred the Nazi regime from proceeding with the extermination of the Jews. Should Germany go down in defeat, the Minister of Propaganda Goebbels screamed, repeating words from Hitler's Reichstag speech of January 1939, Jews will not celebrate victory, for the Jewish race will have been eliminated from Europe.

In a desperate move to rally German resistance, Hitler added control over the military to the bureaucratic empire of Gestapo chief Heinrich Himmler, already the boss of both the SS and the police. But Himmler, obsessed with his mission against the Jews, was ready to fulfill Goebbels' words, using what shrinking resources were left to him, to murder the remnant of Europe's Jews before the final curtain came down on the "Thousand Year Reich."

"Transports," sending Jews to ghettoes, camps and death, continued. For our remnant community the war's final days – we thought of them as final days – had become a race between advancing Allied Armies and the German efforts to implement the "Final Solution to the Jewish Question."

Following the fourth and last of the large "Transports" at the Markthalle, smaller operations took place periodically, shrinking our community to an ever smaller remnant. Fortunately I had been spared assisting in the operations. My sister, working for the community, however, had not escaped the unpleasant duty.

With fewer and fewer young Jews available, I was once again called upon to be a helper. The Gestapo ordered the city's sanitation department to release me temporarily from sweeping streets. So for one day I gave up my broom and shovel and together with my sister and a few other young people reported to the Gestapo to assist shipping Jews to camps.

The deportees were being assembled on the ground floor of a bomb-damaged building. Most of the people had come on foot carrying their small suitcases; a small number, coming from further away, had arrived in a moving van.

We didn't have much to do. With the amount of luggage the deportees were allowed to bring with them, they didn't need much help. Hence, most of the time we stood around wondering why we had been called.

As these things go, one of the fellows had to go to the bathroom. As he opened the bathroom door he received a shock: a woman was hanging from one of the overhead pipes, a rope around her neck. A turned-over chair was lying not far from her dangling feet.

In one respect this transport did not differ from those I had experienced before: SS men stood around laughing and joking, apparently with no care in the world. The young man who had stumbled upon the suicide called one of the troopers, who simply cut the rope. One of the helpers caught the woman before she hit the bathroom floor. He gently put her down.

The news of the suicide got around quickly, and within minutes people had gathered at the bathroom door, pushing and shoving, trying to have a look at the apparently lifeless body. No one seemed to know what to do.

Finally the SS officer in charge pushed his way into the bathroom bringing the gawking to an end. With disgust he looked down at the body.

Then the woman screamed. It was a piercing scream, a scream without pause, that sent shivers through me. The scream was not a human scream, not even the scream of an animal. It was the most horrifying scream I ever heard; it appeared to come from beyond this world. The woman lying on the cold hard bathroom floor responded to neither words nor touch.

"Out with her!" The officer in charge shouted his order, annoyance in his voice. "Lock her in the van."

Two men picked up the screaming body and carried it out to the moving van, the officer and a few of the curious following behind. With the woman in the van, the officer closed and locked the doors. Her screams could still be heard, though muffled by the van's padding.

With darkness, the operation was complete. The deportees were locked into their cattle cars waiting for morning and departure. The moving van, now quiet, also was waiting for morning when it would take the dead body to the cemetery.

We berated the fellow who had found the woman for reporting the attempted suicide to the SS. He should have quietly closed the bathroom door and looked for some other place to satisfy his need, warning others to stay away from the bathroom. She should have been permitted to die without that much pain.

Next morning I returned to work at the Sanitation Department depot. My German fellow workers didn't ask why I hadn't been at work.

Air raids by day and night, spreading destruction, and manpower shortages forced the city to suspend street sweeping. To sweep streets in which only a few buildings remained standing made little sense.

I was assigned to a truck cruising through the city looking for trouble spots: clogged sewer inlets (there were lots of those), and since it was winter, icy intersections. Our job, the driver's and mine, was to free the sewer inlets and adjacent gutters as best we could and to make icy intersections more passable by spreading cinders that we carried in the back of the truck.

The truck driver, Herr Schafer, had been a city employee for many years. As was common among city workers, he owned a small plot of land on the city's outskirts. His dream had been to spend his retirement years tending his garden.

Sitting in the cab of the truck next to him – a violation of the rule, I was supposed to ride in the back of the truck – I had to listen to his angry outbursts.

Full of resentment for having to work past retirement age, he surprised me by not blaming Jews, Communists, or degenerate Americans, but by cursing the Nazis for taking Germany into a war she could not possibly win. Instead of the promised victory, he moaned, the government had brought ruin.

I guess he felt quite safe talking to me; he didn't have to worry that I would denounce him to the Party. Of course I didn't know what his attitude had been before the war had turned him sour on the Germans.

At the moment his greatest concern was to survive this war, and his greatest fear was that a fighter plane would spot his truck and strafe it. He was convinced that if we kept moving, sooner or later we would come under attack. At the slightest sign that an enemy plane might be in the area, he went for cover, parking the truck under a stand of trees. A good part of our working day we sat in the parked truck waiting for the danger, real or imagined, to pass.

A number of times, depending on the weather, we were dispatched to the large power station at the riverfront to pick up ashes and cinders for spreading on icy intersections. The coal burning station, though heavily bombed, had managed to continue operation, though not at full capacity and with many interruptions.

Huge mountains of coal were stored at the station. Incendiary bombs had caused these coal mountains to burn. To keep the fire, impossible to put out, from intensifying, workers kept wetting the coal with streams of water, filling the air with acid smoke and steam.

One relatively quiet day, after taking on a load of ashes and cinders, Herr Schafer, instead of driving away, went to a smoldering coal mountain, apparently fascinated by the clouds of smoke and steam rising from it. When the workers dousing the coal took a break and walked away, Herr Schafer signaled me to join him.

"Let's pick up some coal," he urged. We loaded a few large chunks, hiding the coal under our load of cinders. Noticing my reluctance to pick coal for myself, Herr Schafer said not to worry. Before returning to the depot we made a quick detour so I could drop off my coal at home.

Back at the depot, after helping Her Schafer clean off his vehicle, I was ready to leave for home when a pre-alert stopped me. Though pre-alerts had become so frequent that they were mostly ignored, I thought it better to wait for the all clear. I had a long walk home.

I was standing in the depot yard together with other workers when we noticed two planes high above us engaged in a dogfight. We watched with fascination.

Dogfights had become rather rare; German planes, short on fuel, seldom rose to challenge American or British fighters. As we watched, we saw one of the planes, trailing smoke, spinning toward the ground. From where we stood we couldn't see the markings of the crashing plane. Assuming that victory belonged to the German fighter the Germans cheered enthusiastically.

Moments later their cheers were silenced. A man came into the yard telling us that he had seen the plane crash. The swastika on its tail had been clearly visible.

Now it was my turn to cheer, but I thought better of it. But defeat was clearly written on the faces of the German workers as they silently turned away. With the "all clear" I made my way home.

* * * *

But the endgame wasn't quite complete. The Battle of the Bulge, around Christmas of 1944, halting the British and American advance through the Netherlands and Belgium, had given the Germans a chance to kill more Jews. Even though we believed that German news reports of great victories on the battlefield were exaggerations, it had become obvious that the war would not be over quite as quickly as we had believed.

German success on the ground coincided with a reduction of Allied air activities. Though this was mostly due to the weather, the lull further boosted the morale of the Germans, depressing ours. Once again my German co-workers walked with pride, glorying in the bravery of the German soldier and the Fuehrer's superior generalship.

My hopeful fantasies, and my fears, about the future had to be shoved back into the recesses of the mind. For us survival was the only concern.

PART V

SURVIVAL (1945)

CHAPTER 15

A TRAIN RIDE TO NOWHERE

A Long Journey's Beginning

With my eighteenth birthday, I lost the protection of my "Aryan" mother and in due course received my deportation order. (My sister, a year older than I, was on the small staff that the Gestapo permitted to work at the Jewish Community Center. This protected her, at least for the moment, against deportation.)

Mid-January, following the Christmas setback of the Battle of the Bulge, Allied forces resumed the offensive and rapidly regained their momentum. Warsaw finally fell to the Russians, and soon thereafter Russian troops smashed across the border into Germany. In February, American and British forces reached the Ruhr Valley, one of Germany's most important industrial areas.

Yet the Nazis' war against the Jews continued. Why local authorities still cooperated with the SS and the Gestapo in implementing the "Final Solution" is difficult to comprehend. With air attacks occurring virtually around the clock, with German resistance on the verge of crumbling, with chaos spreading through the land, and with Hitler's "wonder weapons" failing to slow the advances of the Allies, politicians and top bureaucrats must have sensed that the end was coming. And it must have been obvious even to a dedicated Nazi that the deportation of the small remnants of Jews contributed nothing to the defense of their country. To the contrary, the trains taking Jews to the camps and ghettos were diverting sorely needed resources. Local authorities surely would not have found it difficult to ignore orders or find arguments for non-cooperation.

Early in the morning on the appointed day, February 14, 1945, accompanied by my mother and sister, I dutifully went to the city's Ostbahnhof (East Railroad Station) where the latest, but not the last, "Transport" was being assembled.

The scene at the station was surrealistic, or, more appropriately, Wagnerian. In Wagner's version of the Germanic legends the old world, the world of the gods of Valhalla, went up in flames, for the gods had broken the moral laws: coveting power rather than love, gold rather than truth. As in the old German legend, the modern German tyrants and their Valhalla were reaching the end of their rule.

Rumblings of distant artillery fire signaled the coming of the end. American and British fighter planes screamed overhead unchallenged by the Luftwaffe, the once mighty sword of the German demigods. Bursts of fire from the attackers' aerial canons were answered by the defenders' desperate, mostly futile, bursts of fire from the ground. The resulting cacophony provided the overture to the drama "The Demise of the Thousand Year Reich." Occasional earsplitting detonations of aerial bombs brought this "overture" to thundering crescendos.

On one of the few still undamaged tracks stood the train of cattle cars so familiar to me. And at its tail end was the also familiar old passenger car for the SS escort. It was not a long train, perhaps a dozen cars.

Loading the few Jews onto the waiting train proceeded rather slowly and with far less shouting and cursing than I recalled from the large "transports" at the Markthalle. Every once in a while we had to seek cover, as shell fragments from bursts of anti-aircraft fire rained down, or a diving fighter plane strafed the rail facilities. Occasionally a bomb exploding nearby shook the ground. While the deportees and members of their families and friends who had come to say good-bye nervously listened to the sounds of war, the SS troopers strutted around as if bombs, machine gun bullets, or falling shrapnel were none of their concern. Perhaps they were demonstrating, mostly to themselves, the "macho" image the SS had created for itself, or perhaps they no longer cared whether they lived or died.

With darkness approaching, the officers began to display signs of impatience. Reverting to their routine performance of cursing Jews, they tried to hurry things up. The twilight lull in air activities would not last very long; the train had to be on its way before the "night shift" resumed the attacks. Commands, punctuated with vulgarities, ordered the deportees to climb into their assigned cars.

I said goodbye to my mother and sister. It wasn't much of a goodbye. What was there to say? I promised I would return. A final hug and slowly, reluctantly, I walked toward the train.

As I climbed into my assigned car a police officer, whom I had met at a previous transport and who remembered me too, whispered to me: "Today I am ashamed to be a German."

Why only today? And why was he still doing "his duty"? I felt little sympathy for him.

For a moment I remained standing in the door of the car to wave one more good-bye. I heard an officer shout something. Looking around to see what the shouting was about, I realized that the shouts were meant for me. The train commander motioned to me to jump down. Back on the platform, for a brief moment, the hope hit me that I may not have to go.

"You are responsible for your car. See to it that no one is missing when you arrive." With that command, the commander ordered me back into the car, cursing me for delaying the train's departure. The door was rolled shut; I heard the padlock being put in place.

I didn't take the order very seriously. How could anyone escape from a locked cattle car? If anyone really tried to get away, I wouldn't want to stop him or her and probably couldn't. I didn't think it was very likely that anyone in this car would attempt an escape. I promptly forgot the officer's order.

In February evenings darkness comes early. With the door shut and with blackout in force, and with much of the station's lighting having been knocked out by the bombing and strafing, little light penetrated the car. With difficulty I surveyed the car and its occupants.

At the car's forward end, maybe a foot below the roof, was a small rectangular window covered with barbed wire. If I stretched myself, I could manage to look out of this opening to the outside world. I groped my way toward it, hoping to see my mother once more. But I couldn't see her or Claire. Perhaps they had left, wanting to be home before the night bombers arrived. It surely made no sense for them to remain at the station.

I picked a place near the door and settled down. A strong odor, obviously from its previous occupants traveling toward their destiny, pervaded the car. In the darkness I couldn't see if they had left anything behind. I could feel some straw on the floor but had no desire to investigate further.

Barely ten hours had passed since I had walked out of our apartment, yet already No. 6 Weiherstrasse seemed to belong to the foggy past. With the car's door rolled shut, a barrier had moved between the present and what had been.

Ever since we were forced out of our home in the Romerstadt I had the feeling that I was moving away from the family, or rather being slowly pushed away. I had not fitted well into the life my mother had managed to make for us in those desperate days after my father's departure. I never had a proper place, certainly not at the home for girls and not at the home for the aged.

With my father far away, with all my friends swallowed up by the Moloch (devil) of the Nazi death machine, the separation from my mother and sister appeared to be the final step. What was perhaps my life's concluding episode I had to face alone.

Not that I really thought I would die, but once embarked on this journey, how could I know where and how it would end? I had promised my mother I would return; yet as the train was ready to leave the station, the promise did not seem to have much meaning.

The silence inside the dark cattle car contributed to the darkness of my mood. No one had made introductions. A few seemed to know each other, but mostly we were strangers to each another. Perhaps this was not the right environment for formal introductions. The thought came to me that a little social formality might have lifted the spirit. But even those who did know each other sat in silence; all seemed occupied with their private thoughts.

I wondered whether in the other cars a similar mood prevailed, an apparent desire to remain strangers. This mood persisted throughout our journey, broken only on a few occasions. No "camaraderie of shared fate" developed in our jail on wheels. Perhaps most of the car's occupants didn't identify with the Jewish People; yet fate had decreed that they share this people's misfortune.

I opened my satchel, groping for something to eat. Perhaps food would lighten the darkness of my thoughts. But I could not eat. I repacked my satchel just as the train gave a lurch and slowly began to move.

I joined the silence of the car.

The Train

Gradually light began to filter into our rolling prison, signaling that the journey's first night was behind us. The light crept in along the edges of the door and through cracks between the ill-fitting wooden slats of the body of the cattle car. The window near the roof became a gray rectangle on the blackness of the wall. The wheels pounded a steady beat on the rails, the car rocked rhythmically from side to side.

I hadn't slept much, hardly at all. The floor, made for cattle to stand on, was not very comfortable for humans to sit or sleep on. At first I tried to stretch out – the car wasn't crowded and I had plenty of space – using my backpack as a pillow for my head. But this was no more comfortable than sitting, leaning against the wall.

With morning advancing, more light entered, permitting me to make out the shadowy figures of my fellow passengers, and shadowy figures they have remained in my memory.

I stood up and stretched a bit while trying to keep my balance in the rocking car. Moving carefully so not to trip over any of the sleepers, I went to our only window to the outside world. I thought I heard a few muffled "good mornings," though I doubted that any one considered this a good morning. Daylight seemed reluctant to become brighter. Perhaps the day was cloudy, with rain or even snow on the way.

Looking through the barbed wire stretched over the window, I hoped to see a familiar name among the towns and villages rushing by to get an idea of how far we had come during the night. I was unable to make out any of the signs.

Disappointed, I returned to my place. After finishing an uninspiring breakfast – again I didn't have much of an appetite – I washed the food down with a few gulps of water, careful not to spill any. Who knew how long this trip would last and when we could get fresh water? I put the remaining food away, carefully closing my satchel, worried about vermin that might be crawling around on the car's unswept floor.

Twenty-four hours had passed since the train left the station in Frankfurt. With each passing minute, with each beat of the wheels on the rails, the outside became less and less real; reality was this confining box, my present and only world. But the outside did reassert itself, coming in the form of air attacks. The walls of our prison did not prevent the sounds of war from intruding.

With full daylight the air attacks against the German railroad resumed, and with that, on us. Bursts of gunfire disrupted the "peace" inside the cattle car. We were in real danger, a danger that did not come from our enemy the Nazis, but from our enemy's enemy. This train did not reveal to the airmen its cargo of hapless Jews on their way to a concentration camp.

Taking advantage of a stretch of good weather, a rarity in February, Allied Air Forces stepped up their offensive against the German transport system. Fate seemed to have determined that I would be on a train just as the air campaign went into high gear.

The train had been traveling at a steady pace when suddenly the car's rhythm was disturbed: It began to shake violently from side to side as the train rapidly accelerated. Caught off guard, those who had been standing, tired of sitting on the dirty floor, returned somewhat ungracefully to the sitting position. Regaining my balance, I rushed to my window hoping to catch a glimpse of what was happening, only to be disappointed once again.

Despite the racket made by the speeding train, the screaming of the diving plane could clearly be heard. Bursts of machine-gun fire further rattled our already tense nerves.

Which disaster would strike first: the train being hit by machine-gun bullets, the train going off the rails due to excessive speed, or a bomb wrecking tracks and train? Or perhaps all three would strike as one? Instinctively, as if attempting to make as small a target as possible, the car's inmates crouched on the shaking floor. Some covered their heads with their arms as if trying to ward off bullets and bombs.

With the same suddenness with which the train had speeded up, it slowed down, once more catching us by surprise. With a lurch, squealing brakes, and loud clanking of couplings, it came to a halt. I speculated that we reached a spot where the engineer found some protection for his engine: a tunnel, an underpass, a deep cut, or the like. Protecting the precious engine had priority; the loss of a few cattle cars was not as serious as the loss of an engine. And as for the train's passengers? They were only Jews.

Fortunately, the wild ride had caused no injuries and machine-gun bullets did not penetrate the car's thin walls. Viciously I hoped that our escort had received a good dose of bullets.

I went to my lookout, hoping to be able to make out a few details. The train stood along an open field. I could see our guards crouching in a slit trench alongside the railroad track. Their weapons were pointed toward us.

After a few moments of quiet the train began to move, taking us closer to our unwanted destination.

A Brief Intermission

Another night, another morning – the second day.

The night had been quiet; uninterrupted by air attacks, the train had made steady progress. Again I hadn't slept much, listening to the steady beat of the wheels on the rails, which were like the relentless ticking of a clock,

With daylight interruptions came, though air attacks were not their only reasons. Whatever their causes, to me the interruptions were not unwelcome. They provided relief from the car's constant rocking and shaking, but most of all, no matter how short the pauses, they delayed our arrival at our destination. I hoped and prayed that the war was moving faster toward its end than the train was moving toward ours.

I decided it was time to "mail" two of the five postcards I had brought with me. Mailing meant tossing them out of the window as the train passed through a station, hoping that some kind person would pick them up and put them into a mailbox.

Of course nothing important could be said, but then there wasn't really anything to report. But the postcards did say that on that date I was still alive and the post office's name on the cancellation would reveal how far the train had come, and the direction it was traveling. Of the postcards I "mailed" during the journey, two did reach my mother.

The third morning dawned a little brighter than the previous day.

I woke from an uneasy sleep. The rhythmic beat of the wheels had become irregular, indicating that we were passing over turnouts. I rushed to my window but before I could reach it, the screeching of brakes indicated that the train was coming to a stop.

The door was rolled back. An SS officer shouted a brief command: "Out!"

Blinking from the sudden exposure to full daylight, I climbed down to stand on real ground and not on shaking floorboards. We were ordered to form a line. An officer made a quick count. None of the passengers had gotten off early.

The train commander shouted his instructions: "You have fifteen minutes! You will be back in fifteen minutes! Not one minute longer!" And, adding in a quieter tone: "Don't forget to empty your buckets and get fresh water."

We had been locked in our cattle car for three days without a chance to step outside to do what was necessary. A bucket, partially filled with water, had been our wholly inadequate toilet. It gave off a most unpleasant odor strong enough to successfully compete with the car's cattle smell.

One of the men emptied the bucket and looked for a working faucet. I found myself a corner and did what I needed to do for some time. Done, I went to the faucet to wash up a bit. Assuming the water was not contaminated, I satisfied my thirst. With a little time remaining, I wandered around; perhaps I could figure out where this rail yard was.

The yard, nearly completely destroyed, appeared deserted. Not one building was whole; many were burned out shells, others had been blasted into rubble. Bomb craters, some rather large, dotted the area. Damaged equipment was scattered around, rusting. Apparently efforts had been made to clean up, but had been abandoned. Some of the ruins had been cleared of rubble, and here and there railroad parts and materials – couplings, wheels and axles, and other equipment I failed to identify – were neatly arranged. I was sure much of the equipment lying about was desperately needed to keep the railroad rolling. The yard was another sign that the war's end was approaching.

Having stretched my legs a bit, I returned to the train disappointed that I had not been able to determine the yard's location. I climbed into my cattle car to settle down. With resignation I waited for the next phase of the trip. Several of my fellow car mates had already returned; others quickly followed.

An SS trooper looked in and counted the number of people. He counted once, consulted the sheet he was holding and counted again. Then he motioned to the train commander. The two exchanged a few words. Something was wrong. The commander gave a quick look into the car.

"You" he shouted, pointing at me. "Out!"

I climbed down.

"You are one short! Find her and bring her back, or you are in trouble. Five minutes!" Now I recalled that I had been given responsibility for this car, to make sure no one would escape.

I returned to the ruins of the railroad workshops.

Out of the sight of the guards, I paused. What should I do? Look for the missing woman among these ruins? And if I found her, what would I do then? Take her back to the train? I couldn't force her nor would I want to. Just report where I found her? Or tell the officer that she was nowhere to be seen?

Or run away? Where to? We were in Germany, enemy country.

I walked around for a while, aimlessly. I did not feel particularly worried.

The sense of unreality, a dreamlike state that had dominated me since the start of the journey, became ever stronger. The only sound I could hear was the rhythmic chucking of the idling engine, otherwise the world was silent. I wasn't sure who it was that aimlessly roamed through these deserted ruins looking into empty windows and behind smoke-blackened walls. Was it I, or was it someone I was observing? Or perhaps I was imagining the scene?

I found her relieving herself inside a destroyed building with only the four outer walls still standing. Embarrassed, I stepped behind a shrapnel-scarred wall.

"I was ordered to find you and bring you back," I explained. "The train is ready to leave. If you want to come back, fine; if not," I shrugged, "I'll tell them I couldn't find you."

I wasn't worried about consequences. In my near dreamlike state there were no consequences; event just followed event, one after the other, no matter what I did.

"I'll go back," she said. "What else can I do? Run? I'm too old to run; and where would I run to? The Nazis shoot people on site, or hang them from trees. I'll take my chances with the train. Now turn away, young man. I want to pull up my panties."

We walked back to the train. I helped her into the car. A trooper rolled the door shut behind us, locking it. A brief moment and we were on our way.

Stepping Into Darkness

I woke up with a start from a brief restless sleep; it was the journey's fifth night. The train was standing still. Had we arrived at our destination? I groped my way to my lookout. From what I was able to see and hear, I inferred that we were in a rather large railroad station. Pressing my face against the barbed wire covering the window, I increased my field of vision just enough to make out a station sign. Even though the station was barely lit, I was able to read enough of the letters to determine that we were in the central station of the city of Leipzig. I announced my conclusion to my fellow travelers.

Why was the train standing in the central station of a major city, one of the largest and most important cities in the country, and not in a yard or a siding on the outskirts? The train had been avoiding major terminals.

This perhaps unimportant fact produced a lively discussion, the first animated conversation since our departure from Frankfurt. Speculations, some I thought rather silly, were tossed about, relieving tension for a moment. With optimism someone suggested that the Germans, finally realizing that the war was lost, had decided to return us home. Perhaps, another argued, all tracks had been blocked by the bombings and the train could go no further. We had to remain in Leipzig and not go on to Theresienstadt or to a concentration camp.

A pessimist dismissed all these speculations, proposing his own "more realistic" interpretation: The train had been abandoned; locked in our cattle car we would slowly starve to death. A rather doubtful, though not impossible, nightmare: the Germans would surely not have abandoned us in a major railroad station.

Standing at my window, I tried to detect a clue to what was going on. Clouds of steam and acid smoke from the engine drifted past, at times obscuring my vision, at times blowing into my little window to the world, making my eyes water. I couldn't see our guards. Were they also in their car, waiting?

With my effort to detect anything of significance futile, I returned to my place on the floor to have a bite to eat while the car was not rocking back and forth.

And then all hell broke loose.

The car shook and rocked, the cracking thunder of explosions drowned words and thoughts. "Bombs!" someone shrieked; had I heard my own voice?

I had been through many, some rather severe, air raids, but this was by far the worst. Being locked inside this wooden box amplified the usual feeling of utter helplessness.

Recovering from the initial shock, I rushed back to my lookout to see what was happening. The effort was futile; darkness was total. The dim station lights were gone; the sharp flashes from exploding bombs didn't illuminate anything, they made the darkness seem even darker.

Before I could sit down again a powerful jolt nearly knocked me off my feet. Panic screams filled the car: "We have been hit!"

The train began to move.

What now? Had we been disconnected from the engine and with failed brakes were the train's cars were rolling to their destruction? Or perhaps only part of the train was moving, bombs having destroyed some of it? Or, and that was difficult to believe, the train was trying to escape from the station. Why would the Nazis want to save us?

As the train picked up speed, the sounds of explosions grew fainter. We began to relax. We had escaped a catastrophe; we had survived. Survived for what?

Silence had returned. My fellow travelers once again were lost in their state of apathy and resignation. What lay ahead seemed inevitable: As Hitler's Third Reich was going down to destruction, these hapless people in these rickety old railroad cars were going down with it: killed by the relentless assault of the Allied Air Forces or by the hateful fury of the defeated Nazis.

My mind whirled in confusion: The air attacks on the railroad were a deadly danger to us, yet they might bring the war to an end more quickly, improving my chances to survive. I had promised my mother to return; but if I were killed here on this train, had I not failed to keep my promise? But it would spare me the experience of a concentration camp, an experience still ahead of me. Wouldn't it be ironic if I were killed not by the Nazis but by bombs dropped by my potential liberators; and if I were killed now I would never know how this war ended.

The last thought shook me out my confused speculations. I must survive! How else could I ever learn what happened to Hitler?

With daylight, I returned to the little window. The train had resumed its normal speed and our car its rhythmic rocking. Again I tried to catch names of stations as we speeded through them and commit them to memory. Once home, I would want to reconstruct my Odyssey.

By evening the train entered the mountainous area of the Bohemian Forest that stretches along the border between Bohemia and Moravia and Germany, the area where the seeds of this war had been planted.

The densely forested mountains with its tall pine trees, their branches reaching out like arms through the enshrouding fog that the often covered these hills and valleys, had given rise to many folk tales, fairy tales and ghost stories.

As daylight was fading and the train began to make its way through the forest, this otherworldly atmosphere soon enveloped me.

Floating specters (white patches of snow and torn whiffs of fog rushing by) accompanied this train of the damned. Like the Flying Dutchman, condemned to go wherever the wind pushed the sails, this journey would continue along endless rails; a journey unbound by time, a journey without destination, a journey to nowhere. With only me left on board, surrounded by ghosts from the past, this train was rolling along with no one giving orders; just running, running, running, until the very end of time.

I woke up. The train was slowing. Couplings clanked noisily as the cars adjusted to the reduction in speed. Brakes squealed, steam hoses hissed, our car gave one final lurch and came to a halt.

Why did I think that this was our final stop? The train had halted many times before: blocked tracks, attacks by Allied warplanes, other reasons. Why was this different?

Perhaps it was the silence, a silence that was there despite the loud rhythmic throbbing of the idling engine, a silence that was felt rather than heard. I wished the door would never open.

The large sliding door rolled back; I stared into darkness. The night-air's cold dampness made me shiver.

How can I describe how I felt? What are words but mere fragments poorly expressing thoughts and feelings?

Apprehension is a cold word that fails to tell the turmoil inside me. Fear, then? If it was fear, it was a fear different from that I had experienced when bombs were exploding around me. How many types of fear are there? And wasn't there deep inside, nearly hidden, a desire to pray?

"Ah," said a voice in a mocking tone, "at the gates of hell, you, the free-thinker, the non-believer, you too are crying out to God."

A second voice responded. "Moments like these gave birth to the idea of God when the frightened soul, feeling lost and in despair, searched for consolation."

"But in moments like these" a third voice intruded "the idea of God also dies; for all that can be heard coming out of the darkness are the cursing voices of evil."

A few dim lights showed up. A gruff voice ordered us off the train. A brief moment's hesitation and I climbed down from the darkness inside the cattle car into the darkness outside.

The Destruction Of The Self

In the darkness I couldn't see them, yet the voices of the SS troopers were unmistakable; I heard the voices of the Markthalle.

"Move, move! Faster, faster!"

The helpers, Jews, prodded us along toward the gate leading into Ghetto Theresienstadt. I hung back as if every minute, or even second, outside this gate was precious. One of the helpers gave me a not so gentle push:

"Don't make him angry," she whispered. I wasn't sure who "he" was; I didn't ask.

With everyone from the transport through the gate, the gate was shut; the train, still standing out there, just a memory. We entered a large, well-lit hall. For a moment I felt blinded by the brightness.

We stood crowded together, silent, apprehensive. What will happen next? I looked around, more curious than scared. In the light I was able to have a better look at the inmates who had received us. Perhaps their appearance and their demeanor could provide a clue to what we could expect. I wasn't at all curious about the SS men standing around. SS troopers looked more or less alike to me.

Most of the helpers were girls, or young women. Some of the girls I thought were rather attractive. What struck me as weird, out of place, was that most of them were wearing lipstick. This seemed to be a small matter, yet it did not fit into my perception of the ghetto. For years I had not seen women wearing lipstick. Though not forbidden, Nazi ideology discouraged the use of cosmetics as not in tune with the true spirit of the German maiden. Of course, these young Jewish women were not "German maidens." I wondered how were these women able to obtain lipstick.

New orders interrupted my musings.

Our luggage was taken from us. I had to hand over my knapsack with all my clothing and my small satchel with some of my travel provisions still left in it. The luggage, one of the helpers explained, would be searched for cigarettes and other, unspecified contraband. Our things would be returned to us later.

(Only the contents were returned. Larger pieces of luggage, including knap sacks, were confiscated. My small satchel with food, however, was returned.)

An SS officer looked us over. As he walked among us he rhythmically hit his high, shining black riding boots with the riding crop he carried in his right hand.

The expression on his face was one big sneer. I realized whom I was not to make angry. Having completed his inspection, he gave the order to undress. After a brief hesitation we undressed to our underwear.

"I said undress!" the officer bellowed. "Strip, strip, all the way!"

We stripped, all the way. We stood there in our nakedness: old women, young women, old men, young men. Naked we stood waiting, while, under the watchful eyes of the SS, inmates went through our clothing.

The officer observing the searching of my bundle of clothing permitted himself a little fun. Pulling the belt out of the trouser loops, he snapped it like a whip.

"Leather belts make good whips," he said with a grin. "Should I demonstrate?"

I braced myself for a whipping. After a few threatening gestures he returned the belt to my pile of clothing. With a blank face the inmate who had gone through them, handed my clothing back to me.

"Don't get dressed yet," she told me.

With clothing inspection over we were formed into two lines: this time one for women and one for men.

The SS officer in charge moved slowly along our line, once more looking us over. Now and again he tapped a naked man playfully with his riding crop, not to inflict pain but to humiliate and intimidate. His gesture seemed to say I have complete power over you.

The two lines of naked people moved slowly past SS officers sitting behind small tables. We were asked numerous questions, which I can't recall. Next we were examined for things we may have hidden on our bodies: in the mouth or in the anus. What could be hidden there? Cigarettes, perhaps? The SS seemed obsessed with the smuggling of cigarettes.

During this procedure the officers taunted us, heaping verbal abuse on us, making fun of our appearances. They aimed their sexual comments especially on the older people, some of whom tried in vain to cover their nakedness. Everything these officers did was designed to humiliate; to be naked was not enough, we had to feel naked.

Once I had seen woodcuts illustrating Dante's "Inferno:" Naked figures being herded into Satan's domain. Little evil looking devils tortured the condemned as they descended into hell while a monstrous looking Satan lorded over it all. A thought entered to my mind: would the illustrator have dressed the evil devils in SS uniforms if he could have seen the future?

Is there a defense against these assaults at the sense of self? The answer: Not to be there. Physically, of course, I had no choice. But I forced my mind to wander away from the present. The naked people, those in front of me and those behind, these people were not there, I did not see them.

I hardly noticed the smirking faces of my SS interrogators, nor saw the expressionless faces of the inmate aides who stood behind them. When ordered to move, I moved, when questioned, a voice answered; but I was hardly aware that the voice that answered was my own.

Our humiliation was not yet over. Having passed one gauntlet, we had to pass another. Again standing in line, still naked, we had to wait. After some time, a stern looking woman, an inmate, addressed us. She explained that we had to be deloused. The ghetto was clean and free of vermin, she asserted; all precautions had to be taken to prevent the Ghetto being contaminated by new arrivals.

After the brief speech, delousing got under way: Men, inmates, deloused the naked women; female inmates deloused the naked men. We were dusted with a powder, first under the arms and then the genitals; women were also dusted under their breasts. Some more waiting and finally we were permitted to dress.

Dressed again, we lined up to receive our identification number. Next came barracks and room assignments. But a problem arose: The list of arrivals that the Ghetto commander held in his hand did not match the transport roster. The number of people our train had brought was greater than the number expected and for which the Judenrat, the administrative body of the "self-governing" ghetto, had been prepared.

The flustered, rather pretty young lady from the Judenrat tasked with assigning living quarters tried to reconcile the two lists, but without success. The SS man in charge summoned a member of the "Judenrat." While the Jewish "official" struggled to find the answer to the problem, he had to listen to the SS officer's stream of vulgarities, berating the Jews for their incompetence. Finally the man from the Judenrat suggested placing the excess arrivals into temporary quarters. He promised the problem would be straightened out the following day.

The SS officer shrugged his shoulders: "Your problem." Then he walked away.

By the time the assignment of quarters was completed, the night was nearly over. Having again hung back – what was the rush? Did it really matter to what room, what barracks I would be assigned? – I found myself among those without proper quarters.

After some more waiting, our small group of men was marched off to a large building and up a dimly lit flight of stairs. We entered a large room, bare except for about twenty double bunks. On each bunk was a thinly stuffed straw sack.

I did not know any of my roommates and none of them had been in my cattle car. There were no introductions, and no attempts to get to know one another. Perhaps all preferred to remain strangers.

However, I do remember one man, a rather unpleasant fellow. He claimed he was suffering from tuberculosis, though I had no way of knowing whether this was true. He annoyed us with his constant coughing, and even more with his complaining and nasty behavior. After each coughing attack he would spit on the floor, cursing loudly while assuring us that we would not have to put up with him for very long. "Only a few more days" was his constant refrain.

I choose an upper bunk, hoping there I would be less disturbed and perhaps could catch a few winks of sleep before the expected morning call. But I was not able to slip away into the oblivion of sleep, not even for a moment. It was not the coughing and cursing of the sick man that prevented sleep from coming.

As soon as I had settled on my straw sack and the light was turned off, bedbugs came crawling out of their hiding. Not a few bedbugs, no, they came like an army. Attracted by the warm bodies, they came out of the wooden bunk frames, out of cracks in the walls, they seemed to be raining down from the ceiling. They came and came and came, crawling all over us, biting, and sucking, and most likely spreading diseases. First we tried to kill them, but there seemed to be an unending stream. What made it worse, when squashed these bugs gave off an extremely unpleasant odor. Soon a nauseating stink saturated the room.

With daylight the bugs disappeared. I was glad that I did not have my luggage. I did not want any of these bugs to get into my clothing or my blanket.

We had been ordered not to leave the room without an official escort. For meals we were marched to the mess accompanied by the (Jewish) Ghetto police to receive our ration. The first two days ended without memorable incidents and without the promised room assignment. I learned to sleep despite the coughing and the bedbugs.

On the third night, shortly after midnight, a guard, an inmate, woke us. He told us to report at once to the administration building. He didn't say why, probably he didn't know. With trepidations, expecting new humiliations, we followed him.

We were ushered into a large room packed with people. Some I recognized from our transport. But there were more people than our transport had brought to the ghetto. I learned the others were also recent arrivals.

A clerk from the Judenrat checked identities against a list. This time no difficulties arose; all names were listed. After the names had been checked off, we stood around waiting and speculating. No one seemed to know why we had been summoned.

Finally a representative of the Judenrat appeared and asked for quiet. After apologizing for getting us out of bed in the middle of the night, he said he had good news. The commandant deeply regretted that we had been brought to this Ghetto. It had been a terrible mistake and he would do everything possible to get us home as soon as possible. He urged patience. We would receive further instructions.

After waiting for nearly two hours, another representative from the Judenrat appeared. He told us to return to our quarters.

The next day I moved into my "permanent" quarters, received my ration card, fifty Kronen of ghetto money, and my work assignment. My induction into Ghetto Theresienstadt was complete.

CHAPTER 16

STORIES FROM BEHIND THE WALL

Theresienstadt

Ghetto Theresienstadt, the Germans called it an "Autonomous Jewish Settlement," had been conceived as a propaganda showcase. In addition the ghetto provided a home for a small numbers of "privileged" Jews, Jews who, because of their worldwide prestige and connections, the Nazis were not quite ready to put into the gas chambers. It was better to let them die a more "natural" death.

Life in the ghetto was strange, a life robbed of meaning and hope. It was a stage set to fool the world. I found it difficult to determine what was real and what was deception.

As the days of the Third Reich were coming to an end, the farce that was the "Autonomous Jewish Settlement" also came to an end. Theresienstadt became a deathtrap into which tens of thousands of Jews were herded to die of starvation and disease. Perhaps the Nazis had planned to kill even more by other means but no longer had the time to implement their evil scheme.

Theresienstadt was the last of the ghettos and concentration camps to be liberated. Russian troops entered on the day of the armistice in Europe, May 8, 1945.

In the rugged mountainous area, known as the Erzgebirge and the Bohemian Forest that stretches along the border between the former Czechoslovakia and Germany, remnants of the Wehrmacht were gathering for a last stand.

Looking at a map, one can draw an almost straight line from Berlin via the German city of Dresden to Prague, the Czech capital, and from there to Vienna, once the capital of the Austro-Hungarian Empire. A highway, roughly following the Berlin to Vienna line, passes through a gap in the mountains as it leaves Germany to enter Bohemia. It then crosses the Elbe River near its confluence with the river Eger on its final lap to Prague. Near the river crossing stands the fortress-town of Theresienstadt (Tereczin), once intended to block Prussian armies from reaching Vienna.

(Many towns and cities in the area have two names, a Czech name and a German name, reflecting the once mixed population and the long domination of the region by Austria. Though today the Czech names of the towns and cities are preferred, I will be using the German names that were in common use at the time I was there. In some cases I will provide the equivalent Czech name.)

Being billeted in temporary quarters and not fully integrated into the Ghetto's mode of life had masked for me the reality of the present. But once I entered into the daily routine of ghetto life, any illusions I may have had were quickly destroyed. The message was one of finality: Settle in, there will be no other future for you.

Quickly the world became divided between "outside" and "inside." "Outside" the coming collapse of Nazi Germany may have been evident, but "inside" the Nazis still ruled supreme. Here it was still within the realm of the possible that the evil empire would prevail; here it was conceivable that I would have to spend the rest of my life, however long or short, behind these walls.

I tried to resist this "reality." The first few evenings I spent little time in my room. In the cattle car I had ignored my fellow travelers, and so again I wanted to ignore my roommates and preferred to be ignored by them. By ignoring them and by being ignored I tried to deny the reality of the present.

To be alone, I walked the streets until evening curfew forced me indoors. Like a tourist, an outsider, curious but uninvolved, I wandered through the narrow lanes of this former fortress and garrison town, walked the somewhat wider streets along the Kasernen (military barracks), and explored the full length of the main street that bisected the town.

The main street, a broad boulevard, went in a nearly straight line from the main gate to a gate on the opposite side of town. On the way it passed the park-like central square dominated by a gleaming white church, the Garrison Church. (The church was closed.) In my mind I saw the soldiers of Empress Maria-Theresa (the fortress-town bears her name) parading along the broad boulevard in their colorful uniforms. In the evening, officers would stroll through the central park with their ladies at their arms. On Sundays, from late spring to early fall, soldiers with their girls as well as the townspeople would come here to listen to the garrison band, and perhaps have a cup of coffee or a jug of beer.

The fortress-town was enclosed by high grass-covered ramparts or casemates. Deep inside the casemates were large chambers for gun emplacements, with narrow gun slots facing outward. I do not remember how many gates cut through the ramparts, but I do recall two: The one near the railroad tracks through which I entered, and the other, the main gate facing the Dresden to Prague highway, the gate through which I walked out after the war's end.

In the early 1940's young Jews and their families, mostly from Czechoslovakia, were brought to Theresienstadt to rehabilitate the emptied and neglected fortress-town: streets were paved, water and sewer lines constructed, and dilapidated buildings improved. A "Judenrat," which included several prominent Rabbis from Germany and Austria, was set up to govern the ghetto's internal affairs. "Privileged" Jews brought in from Germany and German dominated Europe were added to the population.

Ghetto money, the Theresienstadt Krone decorated with the Magen David and the Tablets of the Ten Commandments, was issued. With the establishment of a library and a symphony orchestra a cultural life was developed. A general store and a coffeehouse opened their doors. A smartly uniformed Jewish police force patrolled the streets. Significantly, Ghetto Theresienstadt had neither a school for its children or a synagogue.

In summer 1944 all was ready. The Germans invited the International Red Cross to inspect this "Autonomous Jewish Settlement." The Jews, the Nazis intended to demonstrate to the world, though isolated from the general population, were treated well. Talk of slave labor camps, concentration camps, and death camps was vicious propaganda created by the international Jewish conspiracy in the Jews' relentless war against the German Nation.

On the day of the visit by the Red Cross commission the "café" on the central square was opened. The children of Theresienstadt were ordered to sit in the café around small tables. As the commission approached the café, neatly dressed "waiters" and "waitresses" removed "used" dishes from the tables and stood by for further "orders" from the children. The commandant, who accompanied the Red Cross commission, greeted the children with a fatherly smile:

"Did you have enough to eat?" he asked.

"Oh yes, Uncle Commandant" the children replied in unison.

"Do you want some ice cream for dessert?"

"No!" came the children's reply. "Not ice cream again! We had so much cake we cannot eat anything anymore."

What the visitors from the Red Cross made of this performance, no one could tell me.

Sometime after the visit, the Nazis had enough of this game. The young people who had rebuilt Theresienstadt and who had provided a disciplined police unit were now looked upon as a danger. They were shipped off to Auschwitz and other camps. Only older men were permitted to staff the internal police.

And the children who had performed so well? They were sent directly into the gas chambers.

Can one ever forgive? These Jewish children who never had the chance to reach adulthood and have children of their own, they are now merely part of the ashes of Europe's Jews. But the children and grandchildren of their murderers, they are now part of the new and prosperous Germany.

Ghetto Life

The room in our "permanent" quarters was large. Sixteen single bunks stood in two rows of eight. We slept on straw sacks, which were not too uncomfortable. And to my relief we were free of bedbugs.

With the exception of Mr. Marx (no relation of mine), my roommates were young men in their late teens (having just turned eighteen I was the youngest in the room) or early twenties. All were "Geltungsjuden" like myself, or "Mischlinge of the First Degree." Mr. Marx, in his mid-fifties, the Jewish partner in a mixed marriage, was our only "Volljude." When his children, who had not been brought up Jewish, reached the age of maturity and no longer needed a father, at least not legally, he was deported.

Mr. Marx, being much older than the rest of us, assumed the role of unofficial room leader. A somewhat impatient man, he insisted that we obey all the rules of the Ghetto and not to be rebellious. Although we resented his bossiness (after all he was an inmate just like us), we had to admit that he tried to act like a father, doing his best to keep us from sinking into depression. He made us keep the room, and ourselves, clean and orderly, and urged us to manage our bread rations properly so we wouldn't have days without bread. He made sure we went to bed early and that the light was turned off, even before bed check.

Nearly everyone in the ghetto worked, although there were exemptions. A substantial number were employed in "public services" under the direction of the Judenrat. These services included the Ghetto police, garbage collection, water and sewer maintenance, medical services, the food services (kitchens and the bakery), and housing and the very busy burial service. In addition there was a special service, which assisted the SS in processing new arrivals.

Actually the dead were not buried but cremated. The crematorium worked day and night to keep up with the supply of bodies. The black smoke rising from its chimney reached high into the sky. It must have been like a marker, visible from quite a distance. We called the black smoke the souls of the departed.

The ghetto had a large medical staff, doctors and nurses, but little equipment, and even less of a supply of drugs or medication. Medications most frequently dispensed were charcoal pills against diarrhea and a not very effective salve against the ever-present skin infections. The supply of charcoal pills appeared to have been unlimited, and it was needed.

Also located in Theresienstadt was a German defense plant making electrical insulation from mica, a mineral mined in the area. The plant employed only a small number of women. Most of the other work performed by inmates we thought of as "make work," the work's main purpose being to keep everybody busy. Yet, as we came to suspect, some of the so-called "make work" may have been deadly serious.

Our daily routine was well regulated, simple and unexciting: We worked long hours, ate little, and slept as much as possible.

We received three "meals" a day: Breakfast, lunch, and dinner, very normal sounding. Meals were dispensed at a central mess and at a number of auxiliary locations. There was no mess hall. We picked up our food and either took it back to our room or ate it in the open. Usually we didn't have time to go to our room after receiving our portions, so we ate in a hurry out in the open, snow, rain, or shine.

Breakfast was of a cup of a hot black brew called "coffee," which we picked up at the mess, and bread from our ration. During my first days we also received a spoonful of jam with our breakfast "coffee," but this largesse was discontinued, an indication of things to come.

Inmates who had been in the Ghetto for some time, swore that the Nazis added a chemical to the black brew that made men impotent or reduced their sex drive. Certainly, and perhaps luckily, no babies were born in the ghetto, but if that was due to the "coffee" I do not know. What I do know is this: All the fellows in my group enjoyed the drink, especially on the many cold and wet days of late winter and early spring. No matter what it was made of or what it contained, it was hot.

Managing our bread ration proved most difficult. The temptation was to eat the whole ration at once, satisfying one's hunger once and then feel hungry the rest of the period; or spread the allotment equally over the week, feeling hungry all the time but perhaps not quite as much. Eating one's bread in one sitting had other advantages: It could not be stolen nor eaten by vermin. Rats and mice were plentiful.

Lunch, at about one o'clock, was the main meal of the day. The usual fare was a bowl of soup (if what was ladled out could be dignified by that word), a thin greenish colored liquid, more water than soup, with a few pieces of dehydrated vegetables floating around in it. But like the "coffee" it was hot, and that was appreciated. With the soup we received small servings of stewed beets of one sort or another, at times accompanied by a bit of potato, but more often by a form of gruel (I preferred the gruel, it usually amounted to more than the potato), and some more of the dehydrated vegetables, which, uncooked, pretended to be a "salad."

A few times the lunch routine was broken. The kitchen prepared a specialty of the local Czech area: balls of boiled noodle dough served with fruit sauce. Not only was this a welcome change from the normal fare, we were also permitted two servings.

For the evening "meal" we received a few slices of cold cuts, an undefinable greasy "wurst." These cold cuts also vanished from our menu and nothing took its place. In addition to the bread and our daily meals we received small weekly rations of sugar and margarine.

Settled in, once again books became my refuge. Though not large, the ghetto library had a nice collection of books, mostly by Jewish authors. To borrow a book I had to deposit my initial, and only, Ghetto allowance of fifty Theresienstadt Kronen. In the evening, before "lights out," for a few moments, I was able to escape into a better world.

Among the books I read was a collection of essays by Herzl, essays he wrote while a correspondent in Paris for a Vienna newspaper. Most of the essays dealt with Herzl's growing awareness of the "Jewish Question" and his move toward Zionism, which he saw as the only viable solution to the "Question." If I survive, I told myself, going to "Palestine" would be my only option.

Within a short time after my arrival, conditions in the Ghetto deteriorated. The skimpy food rations were reduced: The sugar and margarine rations came to an end together with the undefinable "wurst" and the special noodles. Bread rations were cut by half and distributed only once a week. The store and the coffee house were shut, the orchestra stopped playing, and the library closed. But by then I had little opportunity or even inclination to read or listen to music. Like everyone else in the Ghetto I struggled against spreading chaos, starvation and the fear of two ruthless killers: cholera and typhoid fever.

(I regret having returned Herzl's essays; I should have kept the book. I still have the fifty Kronen deposit, which was returned to me.) My "permanent" quarters turned out to be not quite so permanent. Several of my roommates and I were selected to form a new work group, and since work groups had to live together we moved into new "permanent" quarters.

The members of work group were all recent arrivals in their late teens to early twenties. (I was the youngest.) The group also reflected the fact that Nazi Germany was running out of "real" Jews.

The group was made up of "Mischlinge" of one type or another and a few "Geltungsjuden." Most of the "Mischlinge" did not consider themselves Jewish, having only the most tenuous connection to that part of their ancestral past. I had the impression that these young men were rather indifferent toward religion, feeling neither Jewish nor Christian, an attitude which, I supposed, reflected that of their parents. Two of the fellows' "Jewish" parents were Christian, more for convenience than religious feeling. But in the Ghetto this was meaningless. The Nazis had decided they were Jewish and so here they were.

With one exception, none of the young men showed any resentment towards their parents, not even their Jewish parent. Their deportation to Theresienstadt was the result of the irrational Nazi racial laws as interpreted by eager and stupid local bureaucrats, people who still tried to impress their Nazi Party bosses with their vigilance and devotion to the "cause." Indeed, one fellow had been on active duty with an anti-aircraft unit when he was summoned for deportation. He still wore parts of his uniform, the swastika on his jacket having been replaced with a Jewish Star.

They thought of themselves as good Germans but felt no hostility toward Jews.

The present was an aberration that would disappear with the disappearance of the Nazis. Then they could return to their homes and be again with their friends, Jewish or non-Jewish, it didn't matter. Once again they would be German and forget as quickly as possible the Nazi interlude.

I was the exception. I could see Germany only as an enemy country and wanted to leave as soon as it was possible to do so. I did not wish to live among a people who cheered with so much enthusiasm for the gang that was out to kill me. My country was Eretz Israel.

Yet despite these differences we got along well. We avoided discussions about being German, Jewish, or Christian. Religion or ethnicity, Jew versus Christian, or Jew versus German, or even being Jewish versus having no religion at all, these topics were not on our agenda. We had an unspoken understanding: the present was not conducive for debating issues of this kind. Having been brought here not by our own doing but by fate, or by the irrationality of Nazism, the only issue at hand was to survive; and not just survive, but to remain whole.

Our day began when it was still dark. After a quick "breakfast" we assembled for roll call conducted by our foreman, an elderly inmate. We were always punctual and reported even when feeling sick, which happened quite often. No one wanted to find out the consequences of showing up late or of not showing up at all.

After roll call we were marched to work. At the worksite our foreman made his report to the SS officer supervising the work and to receive instructions. Most days the SS officer was late, which meant that we stood around waiting. Work could not start without the officer's direct order. We didn't mind the waiting.

Mid-morning we were given a brief "coffee" break. A couple of women from the kitchen brought us hot "coffee." The hot liquid was very welcome, especially since we were working in the rather cold and damp casemates. This demonstration of human kindness certainly did not fit the usual pattern of the SS commander's, or rather his adjutant's, behavior. About one in the afternoon we were marched to the mess for the noon meal. We had to stand line for quite a while, leaving little time to rest.

I do not know the purpose of the work. Our supervisor didn't know, and the SS man in charge saw no need to explain what we were doing. Nevertheless, he did drop enough hints for us to gain an idea of the "official" story. Of course, we never believed official stories, and lacking any credible information concerning the work, rumors had to fill in.

Each morning, seven days a week, we went down into one of the casemates deep inside the ramparts. The task, the "official" purpose stated, was to convert one of the larger chambers into an air raid shelter. The chamber had to be closed off from the outside and from adjacent chambers, except for a single entrance and airshafts passing from the chamber to the surface of the rampart above. The shafts (there were to be two or three) were lined with wood and about a foot and a half in breadth and width. I don't know the length of the shafts, but guessing from the earthwork above ground, I estimated their length to about equal to the height of a two or three story building.

If what we were constructing was an air raid shelter, the question was a shelter for whom? Certainly not for the inmates of the Ghetto. Why should the Nazis construct an air raid shelter for people they wished to kill? The chamber could house at best a few hundred and in the ghetto there were thousands. For the Jewish elite? We doubted that the Nazis cared much about the Jewish elite; to use them, sure; to save them, surely not.

Perhaps the shelter was for the SS. After all Jews had been killed, one rumor said, the SS planned to use the old fortifications for a heroic last stand against the Communists, defending the honor of the SS and that of Germany. Many Nazis were convinced that the West would eventually recognize the danger coming from the East. When that happened, the remnants of the fighting SS would be ready to join the West in the fight against this international menace.

With the death of President Roosevelt on April 12, 1945, the story gained strength. Many Nazis believed that the tide had turned in their favor. With the "Jew" Roosevelt out of the way, the West, having no real quarrel with Germany, would end the war. Freed of that burden, Germany could fulfill her destiny: Saving Western Civilization by destroying the evil Soviet Empire.

We didn't think that the semi-official story of an air raid shelter made much sense, nor did any of the other stories, except perhaps one.

Among the rumors and speculations the most persistent, and the one making the most sense to us, if the word "sense" can be used in this context, was that the Nazis were building new gas chambers to replace those that were lost to the advancing Russians. Jews still under the control of the SS would be brought to Theresienstadt (this part of the rumor turned out to be true), where they would be exterminated before the final curtain rang down on Nazi Germany.

Did the rumor make sense? We were afraid it did. The chamber was to be air tight except for the shafts. The shafts would serve a double purpose: first, for dropping the gas capsules into the chamber, and then to help airing out the chamber after the gas had done its job. In the extermination camps, the Nazis used a gas heavier than air. Hence, once the capsules burst open inside the chamber, the released gas would not escape up the chimney-like shaft.

We didn't give this rumor much credence either; perhaps we didn't want to believe it, preferring to think of the project simply as "make work." However, we decided to slow progress by doing some sabotage, though being careful not to make it too obvious; we wanted to stay out of trouble. The war would be over soon, we hoped and believed, and even a minor slowdown should prevent the project from reaching completion. Besides, doing something against the SS made us feel better. We weren't just simply obeying orders. So at times a piece of a partially finished wall collapsed, a fresh batch of mortar spilled "accidentally," a freshly dug shaft mysteriously filled up with dirt.

For reasons not always clear, the size of the group varied from as few as six to as many as a dozen. However, a core group of five young fellows, of which I was part, remained together to the very end. We roomed, ate, or better hungered, and worked together through the Ghetto's most difficult days. I'm not suggesting we resembled the "Three Musketeers" – "One for all and all for one." Quite often each one of us went his own way. But overall, especially in a crisis, we stuck together. We helped each other and we shared. If one managed to obtain something extra to eat, no matter how little, it was divided among us.

With liberation the bond that has held us together began to loosen. I'm not sure what had given the group its coherence. Perhaps it was a feeling that in this indecent world, decent behavior toward others, and each other, was essential in maintaining self-respect. No real friendships developed during the months in the Ghetto. We were aware that once out of this hellhole, we would never see each other again, or even want to do so. But, having been part of this group counts as one of the few positive experiences I had during my months inside the Ghetto's walls.

Each of our well-regulated days was but a copy of the day before. Time and calendar meant nothing. Whether the workday began at six in the morning, or seven, or any other time; or whether it was Sunday or Saturday, or any other day, what did it matter? Time rolled on, from one miserable day to the next.

"Protekzia"

"Protekzia," a little corruption and a bit of privilege, pervaded life in the Ghetto.

The Jew as corrupt and as a corruptor is an image that goes way back in the history of Christian Europe. Picking up on that theme, the Nazis fostered a Ghetto environment in which corruption would thrive.

Not all inmates were equal: "Privileged Persons" had better quarters, were given easy office jobs, and a few were exempt from work. Among the "Privileged" were highly decorated soldiers from World War I (if they had served with the Germans), members of the Judenrat, persons well known internationally and persons married to well-known non-Jews.

Work assignment depended on whom you knew in the Ghetto's hierarchy. Knowing someone in the administration could mean an easier job, and if that person had influence, a job in the food services. Knowing someone of real importance, a member of the Judenrat for example, was even better; it provided entry into the clique that handed out favors for an appropriate return.

Handling food – managing the supply, preparing the meals, dishing out the servings – was among the most desirable jobs, providing opportunities for buying favors. We suspected that that some of the ingredients that were to go into the "green soup" did not make it into the pot, and that a few of the potatoes, when potatoes were on the menu, did not go into the common stew.

Of course, the vast majority of inmates were without any "Protekzia" and hence received less desirable jobs: construction work, street cleaning, or worst of all, taking the dead to the crematorium to be turned into ashes; and they had to make do with the official food rations.

Keeping Up Appearances – Two things were greatly desired by many of the Ghetto's young women: lipstick and sheer stockings. Both were, of course, not available on the inside, at least not openly. Some women were quite willing to offer part of their meager rations for these items, and if these were not sufficient, even themselves. Another greatly desired item was soap for washing these precious "sheers," the issued soap being far too harsh for this purpose. But the shaving soap men could get at the ghetto store, while it was still open, would do just fine. So what's a little virtue lost when one can have clean sheer stockings?

How lipstick and sheer stockings penetrated the Ghetto's wall and barbed wire I don't know. They were certainly not "issued" items, nor had they been available at the store. I suspected that the Czechoslovakian guards employed by the SS, or even the SS themselves, smuggled these items into the Ghetto; though what they got in return I can't imagine.

Some illicit trade with the outside world most probably did exist, though it was risky. Being caught bringing unauthorized items into the ghetto, or just being in possession of them, was severely punished. Using lipstick or wearing sheers was rather obvious and should have been high risk, yet I never heard anyone being punished for these offenses.

In time I learned not to judge these young women. Maintaining one's appearance was often the only available antidote against depression, which certainly was one of the potential killers stalking us.

A Privileged Person – Although I hardly remembered the Adornos, when I learned that Mrs. Adorno was in Theresienstadt I paid her a visit, motivated mostly by curiosity, knowledge that Mrs. Adorno was a "Privileged Person," and a vague sense of obligation.

The Adornos had been among my parents' acquaintances in the long ago pre-1938 days. Mr. Adorno, an art critic, and his wife lived in an elegant penthouse apartment a short walk from our house in Frankfurt's suburb of Romerstadt. I remember the apartment's large curved balcony that provided a panoramic view of the meandering stream and the broad meadows that separated the suburb from the city.

But what had fascinated me more than the curved balcony and the view was a small monkey in a cage and a real crossbow that hung on their living room wall. I had wanted to touch the crossbow but could never find the courage to ask for permission. All this came back to me as I sat uncomfortably across from Mrs. Adorno in her nicely furnished, private Ghetto room.

I hardly recognized the gray haired old lady sitting in a large armchair. She did not get up when I entered but extended her hand as she greeted me. She politely apologized for not being able to offer me something, as social graces demanded. Her apologies make me feel even more uncomfortable.

She asked about my father. I told her where my father was, and also about my mother and Claire. She remembered my father well, but had no questions about my mother or sister, or even me.

After I left, it occurred to me that she never mentioned her husband who was not Jewish – was he the reason for her being "privileged"? – nor did she ever make references to the past in suburban Romerstadt.

I didn't see her again. I don't know whether she survived the last few terrible weeks before liberation.

"Naivete" – Apparently the Germans did not want to offend the king of Denmark.

The King had demanded the right to send aid packages to his subjects "resettled" in Theresienstadt and the Germans had given their consent.

I don't know how often packages arrived, or how much food they provided, but even a small addition to the daily diet was most welcome. I'm sure that most of the Danes did not abuse the largesse they received from their King and even shared the food with friends and others. But in a situation of rampant starvation, extra food meant power, and a few were willing to use the King's gift to gain privileges or obtain favors. For a can of sardines, was an unkind saying, a man could get any girl he wanted. But not every man was interested in girls.

One day a young fellow approached me, claiming that he had known me on the outside. I couldn't recall ever having met him before, but he insisted, so I didn't argue. He was big, looking a bit better fed than many. He told me that he represented a man from Denmark who was interested in young people, especially boys. He intimated, without expressively saying so, that he had encouraged occasional get-togethers when members could talk things over and deal with their problems, including problems associated with growing up in this environment.

As an inducement to join the group, the "recruiter" (as I later thought of him) assured me that thanks to the Danish King there was always something to eat at the young Dane's place. The "recruiter" felt sure that I too could gain something from talking to the Dane.

I agreed to see him. The "recruiter" would not tell me where the Dane lived; instead he suggested that we meet again.

When we met as agreed, the "recruiter" assured me that his Danish friend was willing to meet me. The Dane, he explained, had a small room of his own.

As soon as I stepped into the room, two flights up in a small building, I was struck by a feeling that something was not right. The young Dane greeted me casually, inviting me to sit down. Then he ignored me. While the Dane and the "recruiter" engaged in a lengthy conversation to which I paid no attention, I surveyed the room.

In the corner opposite the entrance was a small "kitchen," a coal stove and a shelf holding a few pots and pans and some dishes. (I wondered if the Dane had to go to the mess to pick up his daily rations.) Nearby stood a table with a few chairs grouped around it. However, it was the large real bed, not a bunk, neatly covered with a red blanket, with a white bed sheet showing at the edges that dominated the room. A cabinet, probably for clothing, and a few smaller pieces completed the room's furnishings. Carpeting covered much of the floor.

What struck me as most strange, making me feel more and more ill at ease, was the way the room was decorated. The walls, including the one window, were covered from ceiling to floor with deep red drapes, giving the room a reddish hue.

After a while the conversation between the "recruiter" and the Dane came to an end. The "recruiter" set the table: plates, knives and forks, and glasses, all for two. The Dane placed sardines, bread, butter, and a few other things I hadn't seen in a long while on the table. Then the two sat down to eat.

I was still being ignored. Perhaps the Dane expected me to ask for something to eat, but by now I felt quite annoyed. Not wanting to watch them eat, nor did I want to beg for something, I left without a word.

A few days later I again ran into the "recruiter." But besides a curt "hello" we exchanged no words.

The young Dane's reputation was well known among young males in the Ghetto; only I, it seemed, hadn't heard of it. Finally it dawned on me what this charade had been about. I felt rather embarrassed about my naiveté.

But apparently I had not been his type, something that I didn't mind at all.

Potato Chips – Everyone was always on the lookout for something extra to eat, although rarely with success. From where should this "extra" come?

We looked with disdain on the dealmakers, equating their deals with food service personnel as the worst kind of corruption. But in truth, the fact was that we didn't think we had anything to offer toward making a deal.

One day, on the way back from work outside the Ghetto, one of the fellows found a potato half buried in snow. Perhaps fallen off a peasant's wagon, it became revealed only after the sun had melted away its cover of snow. He picked up the half frozen potato and put it in his pocket.

Winter does not completely disappear in this region of Europe until early April. On many evenings and nights temperature fell well below the freezing mark. Our barracks room was, of course, unheated, at least most of the time.

We had a small stove and a small allotment of coal. The stove was inadequate to heat the room, and the coal allotment, a low-grade soft coal yielding little heat, was barely adequate for a even an hour's fire a day. Saving what coal we had for especially cold days, we had lit our stove only a few times. Then we sat around the warm stove while heating some water. Then quickly drinking our cup of warm water, we crawled under our blankets for the night.

Sitting in our cold room we contemplated the lone potato. What shall we do with it? After a lengthy discussion, one of the guys came up with a brilliant idea: Let's make potato chips. But how?

The potato, we agreed, was sufficiently special to justify lighting our stove. One fellow produced a pocketknife (another mystery: how did the knife get past the incoming search?) and thinly sliced the now partially defrosted precious potato. He then placed the slices on the hot stove for just a brief moment, and presto, we had potato chips.

Our one potato yielded enough chips for everyone to have a taste. The potato chip tasted delicious. Now we had to find a way of obtaining more raw potatoes.

We could think of only one possible source: the kitchen, and of only two ways to get potatoes: Stealing or trading. Stealing was immoral and too risky, while trading, though also not quite right, was only a little immoral.

What did we have to trade? One of the fellows had an extra pair of trousers, which he kept neatly folded for the day when he could walk out of the Ghetto. Then he would dispose of all his dirty clothing and go home wearing clean trousers. He offered to sacrifice his pair of trousers for potato chips. After some talking around, we found a cook willing to "obtain" (steal) a few potatoes in exchange for the trousers.

Rationing our potatoes carefully, we enjoyed several evenings sitting by the warm stove munching "potato chips."

The Verdict – Not to become bitter, or worse, to surrender to the petty, or sometimes not so petty, corruption was a constant struggle. Being hungry all the time was quite a challenge to one's moral fiber; the temptation to compromise one's integrity just a little was not always easy to resist.

Our room was bare except for the bunks and the stove. With the right connections, it was not impossible to get some additional furniture: chairs or even a closet or shelves for clothing. Being recent arrivals without any "Protekzia," our room had remained bare. The few possessions we had we kept on the bed, even at night. We avoided placing anything on the floor, being worried about vermin.

I kept my bread in my satchel, which I could close but not lock. The room and everything in it had to be accessible. Room inspections by the Ghetto police took place while we were at work.

Of all things in our possession, that which was most precious was our bread. Carrying the bread with us when going to work was not feasible. My satchel protected my bread against rats and mice but not against human hands. I had to trust my roommates, just as they had to trust me; and we had to trust the Ghetto police when they made their rounds inspecting rooms.

For a while we had no problem. Then one day one of the fellows claimed that some of his bread had been taken. We all checked, but since nothing seemed to be missing we dismissed his complaint. We tried to convince him that perhaps he had eaten more than he remembered, or was willing to admit to himself.

A day or two later another of my roommates reported that bread had been cut from his loaf; we believed him. Our suspicion fell on a fellow who often excluded himself from the group. Frequently he remained in the room when the rest of us went for a walk to relieve our depression. Confronted, he admitted his guilt. He promised never to steal again. We agreed to forget the episode. And for several days all went well. But then once again bread disappeared.

Confronted once more, the culprit again freely admitted his guilt and again promised not to steal from us. But we no longer trusted his promises.

What could we do or what should we do? Giving the thief a beating was rejected. Violence was a Nazi thing, we argued; we didn't want to copy them. The enemy to fight was on the outside, not within the Ghetto. Actually not one among us had the stomach for beating a fellow inmate.

Yet something had to be done, we couldn't let the thief get away with it. Our bread ration was simply too important. Finally we decided to present our problem to the Judenrat. We felt reasonable sure that the Judenrat would not turn the culprit over to the SS and we hoped that at least the Rabbis could find a solution. Surely, our experience could not have been unique. We decided not to reveal the culprit's name until we knew what action the Judenrat was willing to take.

After listening to our complaint, the Judenrat's representative explained the Ghetto's "criminal code:"

The Ghetto, she said, recognizes two types of violations: "Ordinary crimes," that is crimes committed against inmates – stealing, murder, acts like that – these were within the Judenrat's jurisdiction. However, the Judenrat could not punish offenders; persons to be punished had to be reported to the SS, and that the Judenrat was reluctant to do. Most crimes, therefore, went unpunished.

Violations of Ghetto rules – smoking or even being in possession of a cigarette, not bowing down to an SS officer and wishing him a "good day," walking on the sidewalk in front of headquarters – these were "major crimes" and fell under the jurisdiction of the Commandant. Punishment was incarceration in the "Kleine Festung" or by hanging.

The "Kleine Festung," meaning Small Fort, was a fort once guarding the nearby Elbe River crossing. There conditions were brutal: beatings, torture and depriving prisoners of food were routine. Few prisoners remained at the "Kleine Festung" for very long. If not returned to the Ghetto within a short time, and very few were, the chance of survival was small.

After completing her exposition on the "criminal code," the emissary promised that our case would be handled by the Judenrat and would not be passed on to the SS. Reassured, we told her about our vanishing bread.

Our expectations were not disappointed; the Judenrat acted without delay. After a brief hearing during which the culprit again readily admitted his guilt, the judge made his ruling. The young man, the judge said, must have been hungry and therefore stealing bread, even from his roommates, although reprehensible, was understandable. To prevent him from stealing bread again, the judge ordered that the offender be removed from our room and assigned to do kitchen work.

Within a day the fellow was out of our room. He also left our work team. He was not replaced, which made us one man short. No one, not our foreman nor our SS supervisor, seemed to care.

We were satisfied with the verdict. And the culprit? He too was happy. And when he was on food serving duty, we too had a little "Protekzia:" the portions we received were just a little larger.

THE ADJUTANT

We had few direct encounters with the SS. Only a small SS detachment was stationed at the Ghetto. The Ghetto guard was provided by the gendarmerie of the German Protectorate of Bohemia and Moravia, the Czech part of the former Czechoslovak Republic. They manned the gates and patrolled the periphery. During the day we could see them high on the ramparts of the fortress walking their posts with their dogs. They were among the many Europeans who willingly cooperated with the Germans in destroying the Jews in their midst.

At work we were guarded by a couple of gendarmes who showed little interest in what we did, neither did they care whether we worked at all. Our foreman kept us working, insisting that we had to show some progress, or we would all be in trouble. Although he refused to participate in our petty "sabotage," he did not prevent us from doing what we did,

Only when the SS officer known as the Adjutant came to inspect did we have to be careful. Always dissatisfied with progress, he threatened us with having to work more hours to speed up the work or to repair damage he accused us of having caused.

His rages failed to impress us; they never lasted very long and most of the time he left the site before making sure that we were following his orders. A few times he did make us work into the night. That was severe punishment: We missed our evening meal.

The Adjutant was the Ghetto's deputy commandant. While the commandant, an SS officer by the name of Rahm, was seldom seen, the Adjutant was difficult to miss. Frequently he could be seen walking ("strutting" would be a better word) through the streets, unaccompanied, arrogantly sure that no one would dare harm him. When encountering him inmates had to bow low and say in a loud voice: "Good morning, Herr Adjutant" (or "good afternoon" or "good evening"). At times he rode through the ghetto on horseback and then one had to get out of the way quickly not to be trampled under the horse's hoofs.

One had to be especially alert when he rode his bicycle. The bicycle did not announce his coming, as did the horse's hoofs pounding the cobblestones. And if one did not step quickly out of the way and give the appropriate greeting, punishment was surely in the offing. Occasionally he came through the Ghetto by car. Sitting in the back of his Mercedes, driven by an SS chauffeur, he now and again acknowledged the required greeting with a royal nod or wave of his hand.

Work had come to a halt: We had run out of bricks needed for closing off the "air raid shelter." Though having nothing to do, we had to remain in the casemate waiting for the Adjutant to give new orders. He didn't show up that day.

Next morning when we returned to work, he was waiting for us. After looking over the work that had been done so far and complaining of insufficient progress, he selected four of us to go and get the needed bricks.

With a wheelbarrow, shovels and a pick, and guarded by two gendarmes, we marched out of the Ghetto down the highway toward the river. After an hour's march we arrived at a broken down farmhouse. Our job: tear down the building and save the bricks.

The highway along which we had marched was lined with trees. Although the first leaves were not yet in evidence, the buds were swelling, signaling winter had come to an end. The weather was mild, a gentle breeze announcing the coming of spring. It felt good being outside the walls; here birds were singing.

The roof of the old farmhouse had collapsed. Most of the timbers had been carried away. Not having to worry about the roof crashing down on us made our work easier and safer. All we had to do was to remove some of the debris, knock down the walls, extract reusable bricks, clean off the brittle mortar, and stack the cleaned bricks into neat piles to be picked up. Though the work was hard and dusty, I preferred to work under a warm sun than inside damp casemates.

At noon our guards marched us back to the Ghetto for our meal. We had to eat in a hurry, not too difficult with the little food we received; two new guards were already waiting to take us back to the old farmhouse. In the evening we had to return our tools to the casemates before being dismissed for the day. Again we had to hurry not to miss the evening meal.

On the second evening, returning from the broken down farmhouse, we saw the Adjutant standing by the gatehouse, chatting with a couple of his SS officers. I don't know what inspired us, but instead of slouching, looking tired, as we walked, we squared our shoulders, fell into step and broke out into a hiking song. Singing at the tops of our lungs, we marched past the Adjutant and his cronies. The hard work, the ghetto conditions, we seemed to demonstrate, had failed to dampen our spirit. Or, perhaps we were mocking the Nazis who took pride in marching in step.

The Adjutant reacted with fury. Shouting at our guards, he ordered them to march us into the courtyard of the gatehouse. There we had to stand at attention.

Facing us, he stared at each one of us in turn, not saying a word. I wondered what punishment he was contemplating. All stood in silence: the Adjutant, his cronies, our Czech escort, and the four of us.

I tried to look calm and unconcerned. I don't know how well I succeeded. The other three young men made a similar effort. We kept our eyes straight forward, not daring to look at each other. Time passed and I began to worry that we would miss the evening meal. Finally the Adjutant spoke:

He was sure, he began, that while working outside the ghetto we had stolen food and were bringing it back into the ghetto, against regulations. He reminded us that this was a serious offense and we would have to be punished. He did not say how we obtained the food, nor did he say what punishment he had in mind. Then, ignoring our Czech guards, he ordered one of his SS troopers to search us. Of course he did not find anything; there had been nothing to find.

We continued to stand at attention. Finally, with no further word and without giving out punishment, he walked away. Our two gendarmes, who had been waiting nearby looking bored, took us back into the ghetto. The episode was over.

I don't recall whether we made it in time for the evening meal. But once safely in our room, we had a good laugh, more out of relief than out of amusement.

Two days later, while we were still collecting bricks at the old farmhouse, the Adjutant came by on his horse. For a while he watched us in silence before riding off in the direction opposite from which he had come. Soon the Adjutant and his horse were out of sight.

One of the Czech gendarmes approached us. Our guards had never said a word to us before except for the few commands necessary to march us back and forth between the Ghetto and the work site.

"If you want to relax," the guard said, "my comrade and I will keep an eye out for the SS chief." The two gendarmes disappeared behind a small stand of trees.

We were delighted, though rather skeptical. Could we trust the Czechs? After a moment's hesitation we laid down our tools. Sitting on piles of bricks, or whatever else was convenient, we relaxed.

I sat on the low remnant of one of the walls, my feet propped up on the wheelbarrow loaded with bricks, facing the path on which the Adjutant and his horse had disappeared. The three other youths were further back, behind one of the old farmhouse walls still standing, where I could not see them. The sun was bright, the air warm; I dozed off.

Something must have disturbed me. Looking up with a start, I found myself staring at the Adjutant standing in front of me. He had come back not on his horse, but quietly riding a bicycle. The two gendarmes were nowhere to be seen.

I jumped up. The Adjutant began to shout and curse.

Apparently having tired of his tirade, he lowered his voice. His new tone, I thought, was much more ominous than his shouting.

He had made a mistake in trusting Jews, he began in a cold voice; he should have known better than letting us work outside the confines of the ghetto. Now that we had violated ghetto rules (he was not specific about the rules we had violated) he had no other choice but to shoot us. His hand went to the gun in his holster.

I was standing in front of him, so I figured I would be the first to be shot.

I had to do something. Heroic action, trying to wrestle the gun out of his hand, never occurred to me, not even for a fraction of a second. Neither did it occur to me to make excuses for having been idle.

Turning my back to the SS man, I grabbed the handlebars of the wheelbarrow and walked away. It was an odd sensation thinking that a gun was pointed at my back.

Instinct urged: "run!" But common sense said: "don't, just walk normally." It took a considerable mental effort to keep walking steadily yet quickly, pushing the heavy wheelbarrow in front of me.

The Adjutant had stopped talking. In the silence I expected the sound of a gun discharging. I wondered, would the bullet hit me before the sound reached my ear?

Walking past my fellow workers, who had resumed working, I reached the stack of bricks. While unloading the wheelbarrow adding the bricks to the stack, I dared to look back. The Adjutant hadn't moved; he stood with his legs spread apart, his left hand holding his bike, the right hand still (or again?) at his holster.

With an abrupt movement, the Adjutant mounted his bike and rode off. The two Czech guards reappeared. We worked in silence for the remainder of the day.

Evening had come on our final day of working outside the Ghetto at the old farmhouse. Tired and hungry we went back to the Ghetto, walking slowly in the middle of the road with our guards following some distance behind. Suddenly we heard the sound of hoof beats rapidly coming up behind us. Turning around, we saw a troop of Ukrainian SS on horseback coming in a fast trot. The two Czech guards, who had stepped aside to let them pass, hadn't given us any warning, not even a single shout.

As the horsemen closed in us, they whipped their horses into a wild gallop and, swinging their horsewhips, tried to ride us down or at least hit us with their whips, all the while laughing and shouting. Fortunately not one of us was hurt. I have no explanation for the strange behavior of the Czech gendarmes.

With the war approaching its end, the Swedish Government arranged a deal with the Germans, exchanging the Danish Jews in Theresienstadt for German soldiers interned in Sweden. These soldiers, fleeing from the advancing Russians, had crossed into Swedish territory.

Sometime late in March a column of trucks and ambulances marked with the Red Cross and flying the flag of Sweden showed up at the Ghetto. Manned by unarmed Swedish soldiers, they were to pick up the Danish inmates (including the young man who liked boys). The appearance of the Swedes created much excitement. For many it was their very first contact in a number of years with the world outside the Nazi rule. It was not much of a contact, the SS made sure that no inmate talked to the Swedish soldiers.

Except for some pessimists, we took the Swedes' arrival as a sign that the war's end, and our liberation, were close at hand. (Our optimism proved to be a bit premature. Terrible weeks were still ahead.)

The Adjutant, as could be expected, supervised the loading of the Danish Jews into the Swedish vehicles. There was nothing the Swedes could do about that. But when the Adjutant tried to climb into one of the trucks a Swedish soldier stopped him:

"Out!" the Swedish soldier was quoted as saying, "this is Swedish territory. You have no right to go into this truck."

I cannot vouch for the truth of the incident; but it was told and retold with great relish.

After liberation a story made the rounds that all had not gone well with the Swedish Red Cross convoy: The convoy, making its way to Sweden, had to pass through shifting battle lines. A number of times it came under fire, either caught in cross fire between Russian and German troops, or the story said, by advancing Russians. With the Soviet Union not a signatory to the Geneva Convention, Russian troops fired on anything that moved, even if marked with the Red Cross.

I do not know what happened to the Adjutant. Some said he was killed in action during the final days of fighting; others said he escaped to Argentina. His superior, the commandant of Theresienstadt, was tried for war crimes in Vienna.

CHAPTER 17

DISINTEGRATION

Death Trains

They came by train, they came on foot; they came by the thousands. They were the remnants from labor camps, concentrations camps, death camps. Their numbers and their condition overwhelmed the Ghetto.

The Nazis were emptying the camps of Jews ahead of the advancing armies of the Western Alliance and those of the Soviet Union. Were they trying to hide their terrible crime from the eyes of the world, or were they hoping that the decimated Wehrmacht could hold out long enough for the SS to kill Jews still in their hands?

The human cargo that arrived in Theresienstadt during March and April 1945 had been in transit for days, some for weeks. Those from Auschwitz had been on the move since January, when Russian troops approached. Shunted from place to place, they had seldom stepped out of their crowded freight or cattle cars. They were given little to drink and less to eat; they had no facilities for human needs. For many, the only clothing they had to wear was their striped concentration camp suit, thin and worn, wholly inadequate for the cold winter days and nights.

Some arrived by foot. They had been walking for days with little rest, with barely any shelter against the cold of the late winter and early spring. As the prisoners were being marched along the highways, their numbers kept dwindling. Those who succumbed on the way were left dead or dying on the side of the road; others, too sick or too weak to continue, were shot by their guards. Many of those who survived the trains and the marches arrived half insane.

I have no words to describe the scenes that unfolded as the survivors arrived at the Ghetto's gate. I doubt that the hand of the illustrators of Dante's "Inferno" would have been able to describe what we saw. Man's imagination could never reach this terrible depth.

As the unloading proceeded, many of the still alive refused to leave the cars in which they had come, defending with inhuman shrieks the place they had secured for themselves, perhaps even had fought over. They feared that this latest stop on their journey was only a prelude for more horrors.

The worst off was a large group of men, perhaps several hundred, who had been transported in open coal cars. Unprotected from the elements, they had been traveling for about two weeks. The men had simply been piled into the cars, body on top of body. Those with some strength left had used the bodies of the weaker and the dead as covers. The bodies of the barely alive did not even generate enough warmth to melt the night frost that had settled on top of them.

Work in the casemates and the mica factory had come to a halt. The Adjutant had stopped strutting through the streets, though the headquarters building at the main square and a few other buildings on the Ghetto's periphery were still occupied by the SS. High on the ramparts Czechoslovakian gendarmes still patrolled faithfully.

Cut off from the world but free of direct German interference, the Judenrat ran the Ghetto. Faced with thousands of sick and starving people, the leaders had to mobilize all the meager resources available inside the walls to absorb them, feed them, and even try to heal them: an impossible task.

Yet the attempt was made. All the petty corruption, all the pilfering of food, all the arrogance of the leaders disappeared as the Ghetto pulled together to help these miserable creatures that the Germans had dumped on us.

Our group of young men had not been called upon to help in unloading the trains of the dead and half-dead. I'm not sure if this had been done on purpose. Rumors said (in the ghetto information usually got around in the form of rumors) that the elders of the Judenrat had wanted to protect the boys – we were once again "boys" – from being exposed to this unimaginable horror. Difficult to believe, but in this crazy world it may well have been the truth.

We could have volunteered, but didn't. We felt rather ambivalent. Yes, we did want to be of help, but we also wanted to isolate ourselves from the horror and the sickness. We had just one desire, to survive, to get out of the Ghetto alive. We did not want to expose ourselves to the diseases that were being brought in (a naive attitude). And we felt revulsion toward these filthy, nearly insane beings, who once had been human; we did not want to see how low humans could sink.

Yet we did watch the unloading of the dead, the near dead, the walking skeletons. Many of the bodies being removed from the railcars were covered with excrement and vomit; some showed marks of cannibalism. The presence of death was overwhelming; being among the living seemed almost sinful.

After a while, we did take on some tasks: handing out bread and warm drinks to the arrivals. Many mistakes were made in handling and feeding them. Who had any experience in this?

As the healthier of the survivors climbed down from their railcars, they were given bread and hot "coffee." The result was chaos. Some grabbed the offered bread with both hands, trying to stuff it into their mouth all at once; others made futile attempts to hide the bread under the rags they were wearing, demanding more; many tried to grab bread away from others. Skeletons covered with sores used their last remaining strength to beat and choke each other over a crust of bread. The experience was not edifying.

Other scenes were rather difficult to comprehend. A group of women, about a hundred, had been walking to Theresienstadt. I don't know where they came from or for how long they had been on the road during these still frosty and snowy days of early spring, herded along by female SS guards. I also don't know how many had started out on this march; probably many had died on the way. As the survivors reached the gate of the Ghetto, I found it difficult to believe what my eyes told me: Many of the women hugged and kissed their SS guards as they said good-bye.

Vomit and excrement marked the path from the railroad track to the buildings in which the arrivals were being housed. Soon the building's stairways and corridors too were covered. Chlorine powder was spread along the path. The reek of chlorine together with the other sickening odors created a nearly unbearable stench.

The bodies of the dead were taken directly to the crematorium. The quick incineration of the corpses, it was hoped, would prevent the spreading of the deadly diseases that had come with the trains. The black smoke rising from the crematorium reached high, polluting heaven for all eternity.

Probably no exact count exists of how many people were brought from the camps to Theresienstadt. One estimate spoke of about 30,000 that had to be absorbed. The epidemics they brought with them – cholera, typhoid fever, lung diseases – rapidly reduced that number and the number of the other Ghetto residents.

Between 130,000 and 140,000 Jews passed through Ghetto Theresienstadt since its inception. An estimated 90,000 were killed or died of hunger or diseases.

Housing and feeding the enlarged Ghetto population presented a formidable task. With the Ghetto cut off from the world, all the Judenrat could do was to make the small daily rations even smaller. For helping the sick there was no answer, the already inadequate medical supplies on hand ran out quickly.

But one problem the Judenrat was able to solve: housing. Means were at hand to relieve the overcrowding in the barracks and the houses. To accommodate the new arrivals, temporary prefabricated wooden barracks, stored in the Ghetto (for what purpose had they been stored?) were erected.

Finally our gang could volunteer for a job we could do and preferred to do. Erecting barracks was better, and we felt more constructive, then handing out bits of bread and cups of "coffee" to half dead people.

Soon after the new barracks had been erected and had been made livable, we had to evacuate our quarters in one of the Kasernen. The Judenrat had decided that the new arrivals would be better off in the solid buildings of the Kasernen than in the flimsier temporary buildings. We did not protest; we much preferred the new wooden barracks. They were not yet infested with vermin and were much easier to keep warm than the large drafty rooms in the old Kasernen.

Hard work and many sacrifices made by Ghetto's inmates, not always done willingly, succeeded in integrating the new arrivals. Miraculously, the almost dead showed signs of recovery. Even among the near insane, recovery became evident.

Evidence

Early in April the SS withdrew from inside the Ghetto, though they remained in control of the periphery. Czech gendarmes and their dogs could still be seen patrolling on top of the ramparts.

One of the buildings being evacuated was the Sudeten Kaserne, a late addition to the Theresienstadt military barracks. Surrounded by barbed wire it was guarded by SS troops. All anyone seemed to know was that the building was used to store SS records.

With the Russians and the Americans approaching rapidly, the Nazis didn't have much time left to destroy the archive. The archivists asked for volunteers from the Ghetto to help. (Conditions surely had changed: now they asked us for help.) I, and a few others from our gang, volunteered for the task.

Why we decided to volunteer is difficult to explain. I could claim great motives to our action, but that would be a lie. Most likely we were bored and burning some archival papers seemed like a harmless diversion. Mostly we hoped that the people at the archive would feed us while we worked there. Possibly it was also curiosity: What was it that the SS wanted to destroy?

The Nazis had been thorough record keepers. The archive was filled with stacks upon stacks of records, all in identical format. When we somewhat surreptitiously examined a few of the record sheets, we nearly went into shock. What had been a rumor, but feared to be the truth, appeared to have been confirmed: the extermination of Europe's Jews. The evidence was printed in neat rows and columns.

The records consisted of lists of names, names of thousands, tens of thousands, or perhaps hundreds of thousands, or even more, of Jews fed into the Nazi death machine. Here were the names of the victims, their places and dates of birth, places and dates from where deported, last camp or ghetto, and in the last column their "final dispositions." Here in cold print was the fate of Europe's Jews.

The entries under "final disposition" were terse:

"Shot while attempting to escape"

"Died of disease"

"Liquidated"

"Liquidated" was the most common entry. Here and there were other short comments such as "shipped out to a labor camp" and a very, very few "escaped" or disposition unknown. I can't recall having seen a single entry "released."

We tried to save some records, hiding them under loose floorboards, in piles of trash, and whatever means we could think of at the spur of the moment. What we managed to hide was a tiny fraction of the total, but even these few sheets could have been valuable in documenting the horrendous crime committed in the name of the German nation. Collecting evidence of Nazi crimes had not entered our minds. "War crimes" was not yet a common notion. We had hoped the few records that we tried to save could be of help in tracing missing persons.

I never learned what happened to the records we managed to hide. After the final withdrawal of Germans, we informed the International Red Cross of the existence of the records and where to look for those we had hidden. Whether the Red Cross ever did anything about it, or whether the Russians after they entered the Ghetto found them, remains a question mark.

In No Man's Land

Spring, the season of life's renewal, in Theresienstadt had become the season of death. Recent arrivals from the camps were the first to die in large numbers; then more and more of the old among the inmates succumbed to hunger and diseases; soon the not so old followed. The dead exceeded the crematorium's capacity to turn corpses into ashes. In the courtyards of the larger Kasernen the dead, mere skin and bones barely covered with torn rags, lay in long rows.

The smell of decaying corpses, the stink from the no longer functioning toilets and latrines, the nauseating odor of vomit and excrement, combined into a stench that saturated the air. This stench of hell spread far beyond the Ghetto. People in neighboring villages covered mouth and nose against this air of death; inside we were no longer aware of it.

Idleness too had become an enemy contributing to the deterioration of the spirit. Sitting in our barracks thinking about nothing else but just one more slice of bread or telling stories, or lying on our bunks trying to sleep, all had become depressing.

Attempting to get away from the barracks' gloomy atmosphere, our gang of six had taken to wandering the streets of the Ghetto. But these aimless walks brought no relief; being in the street wasn't much different from hanging around in the barrack room: The same smell, the same hunger.

We decided to look for a place that in some way would be different from the dismal atmosphere around us, a place where we could feel the warmth of the spring sun. Perhaps we could escape for a moment the poisonous air; and if not in reality, at least in our minds.

Miraculously we found a place. In a far corner of the Ghetto, abutting the ramparts, we discovered a deserted grassy plot. We had never been there before, and for some reason the area was being avoided by most people. The grass looked young and fresh after a frosty night.

We were ready to sit down and rest when a short, wiry, and rather bald man joined us. He greeted us cheerfully.

"Don't sit down," he admonished. "You will be sitting on your food. Look around, there must be dandelions."

Finding a small plant jutting out between two rocks, he ripped off a couple of leaves and put them in his mouth.

"Dandelion leaves make an excellent salad," he informed us, "they are rich in iron and vitamins, just what you fellows need right now. Get busy: Find them, pick them, eat them!"

So, instead of sitting in the warming sun, we crawled around searching for just emerging dandelions. It was really too early in the spring for dandelions, but here and there a few had been eager to greet the sun. After some searching, we all were chewing on dandelion leaves (unwashed, of course.) One of the fellows, frustrated that he could not find any more, pulled out some grass and began to chew on that.

"If dandelion leaves are good for you," he proclaimed, "then blades of grass must also." We didn't agree with him.

After returning to our barracks, we learned that the field with the dandelions had once been used for spreading the ashes from the crematorium. I preferred not to believe what I heard.

With the enemy out of sight – the SS could no longer be seen inside the Ghetto – hatred had turned inward; and a lot of hatred was stored up inside the Ghetto. Hate became directed against all who were perceived as being different: The religious blamed the secular for the disaster that had befallen the Jewish people; the secular blamed the religious for anti-Semitism by hanging on to "primitive and outdated" ways of life; Czechoslovak citizens accused Jews from Poland and Hungary of having cooperated with the Nazis. (When Nazi Germany dismembered the Republic of Czechoslovakia, both Poland and Hungary received a slice of land. But what did this have to do with the Jews?) Jews from Germany were blamed for bringing Nazi rule to Germany. "All of you voted for Hitler," a fellow inmate from Prague told me.

Nastiness had become the dominant tone. Recent arrivals from the camps took their anger out on the Ghetto's longtime residents, accusing them of having been "pampered" by the Germans; in turn the new arrivals were accused of having cooperated with the Germans: how else could they have stayed out of the gas chambers?

The Judenrat had allotted extra bread rations to survivors of the death trains and death marches. Whether the small supplement was of any real help to them is questionable; that it contributed to a more rapid decline of the Ghetto's supply of flour would be difficult to dispute; that it created antagonism between those who received the supplement and those who didn't was beyond doubt.

The ill feeling between longtime Ghetto inmates and the more recent arrivals (dubbed "KZs" from the German "Konzentrationslager") was not the only cause of disturbances. Survivors from one camp claimed that they had suffered more than those from other camps and therefore deserved more privileges. At times the arguments about who had suffered more ended in violence and even bloodshed.

What shocked me was the appearance of European nationalism. While the Adjutant was strutting the streets of Theresienstadt we had been Jews, but with the Nazis out of sight inmates began to identify with the country from which they had come. Ignoring the culprit, Germany, they blamed one another for the calamity that had befallen the Jews.

Friction between Jews from Hungary and those from Poland was especially intense. The Hungarians blamed Poland for the Second World War. (When Hitler dismembered Czechoslovakia, Poland had received a small slice of territory.)

They refused to exempt the Polish Jews from this blame. Polish Jews, accusing Hungary of cooperating with Nazi Germany, included the Hungarian Jews in their accusations.

A vocal group of young men from Czechoslovakia carried their nationalistic fervor a bit further. Theresienstadt, they argued, was within the borders of the Czechoslovakian Republic. No longer a Nazi prison for Jews, the town, they said, should be called by its proper Czech name: Tereczin; and the official language Czech.

The Ghetto was a poly-clod society. I don't know how many of its "residents" were from Czechoslovakia, but Jews from Poland, Hungary, Germany/Austria, the Netherlands and other European countries made up the majority, and few of them spoke Czech. In the days of the Austro-Hungarian Empire, German had been the "lingua franca" in much of Eastern Europe and the Balkans, and many European Jews understood at least some German.

Few in the Ghetto paid attention to the exhortations of the Czech patriots, and German remained the Ghetto's common language. (I thought Yiddish would have been more appropriate.) When Russian troops finally entered Theresienstadt, German-speaking officers and non-commissioned officers provided the liaison with the liberated inmates. And that settled the issue.

Among the concentration camp survivors the trains had dumped into the Ghetto was a small group of criminals. With their arrival crime became part of our daily life.

The criminals were easily recognizable: They didn't wear the Jewish Star – with the SS no longer inside the Ghetto wearing the Star was not enforced, but few had removed it – and they looked healthier. As on the outside, inside the camps Jews had received smaller rations then "Aryan" prisoners. How these non-Jews got mixed in with Jews I don't know.

With people starving the criminals had little trouble in recruiting members for gangs that soon roamed the Ghetto looking for food, especially bread. These gangs did not hesitate to use force, even murder, to get what they wanted. When the SS and the Czechoslovakian gendarmes disappeared even from the Ghetto's periphery, the Judenrat lost what little authority it still possessed and the Ghetto police disintegrated. (Members of the Judenrat were mostly from Germany or Austria and had been looked upon as mere lackeys of the Nazis.)

In a spontaneous response "self-defense units" were formed. Armed with sticks – hence "stick brigades" was a more popular designation – they patrolled the streets during daytime and guarded the barracks at night. Our group had taken the night watch at our barracks. Whether due to our vigilance or good luck, our quarters were never raided.

But even "stick brigades" had their darker side: Some turned into vigilantes who aggressively sought out criminals. They attacked, often violently, anyone who fitted their conception of a thug.

Situated between American forces to the west and Soviet forces to the east, the Ghetto was virtually isolated from the world. We were truly in a no-man's land. The sick and starving remnant of Europe's Jews, having little knowledge of the war's progress, felt abandoned.

The Ghetto sank ever deeper into chaos.

With Theresienstadt no longer part of German-occupied Czechoslovakia, a group of young men from Czechoslovakia asserted that as citizens of their country they were free to leave. With no one to stop them they set off to the nearby town of Leitmeritz – again the town of Litomeric – looking for food and perhaps plunder and revenge.

The group returned quickly. With various trigger happy bands – Czech underground fighters, retreating Germans, leaderless Ukrainian soldiers who had sided with the Nazis, SS bands, marauders of all kinds, and advanced Russian patrols – roaming in the area it was safer inside the protective ramparts of the old fortress. They had come under fire even before they had reached the town and they were not sure who had been firing on them.

Their brief foray had been mostly unsuccessful; they had come too late. The area had been thoroughly ransacked, and they had missed any opportunity for exercising revenge. The Sudeten Germans had fled together with the German troops. The few non-German who had remained on their farms had barricaded themselves in their homes, shooting at anyone who approached too closely.

However, the adventurers did not return completely empty handed. A few of the younger fellows had found new or almost new bicycles. Riding around in the streets of Tereczin, they proudly showed off their new possessions.

Rumbling cannon fire had become a steady background noise – and hope. An occasional fighter plane, American or British – German planes hadn't been seen for some time – swooped low overhead with guns blasting at some target we couldn't see. Could the pilot see our misery down below?

Mid to late April, I don't recall the date, a white Mercedes marked with the Red Cross and flying a Swiss flag drove through the unguarded gate of Tereczin. An agreement between retreating Germans and advancing Americans placed Theresienstadt into the hands of the International Red Cross. A large Red Cross flag was hoisted over the former SS headquarters building and Red Cross emblems marked the roofs of the larger Kasernen.

Cut off from the outside world, the lone Swiss doctor who represented the Red Cross could do little to improve, or even just stem, the rapidly deteriorating health situation. Appeals to German and Allied Forces to let Red Cross aid pass through the frontlines remained unanswered.

Aided by former members of the Judenrat and a few civic spirited inmates, men and women, the energetic Swiss doctor succeeded in re-establishing some order. He organized a police force and in deference to the re-established Republic of Czechoslovakia appointed a former Czech army officer as its head.

Lawlessness eased and corruption became more restrained. Though much credit belongs to the new police, other factors contributed to the decline of crime and disorder. Most residents, grown tired of the prevailing chaos, cooperated with the new administration and police. Corruption was reduced and a little of the filth cleaned up. Curiously enough even the criminals seemed to have grown tired of the disorder and cooperated with the new authorities. Or, perhaps, they found nothing worth stealing. When the known criminals were rounded up to be jailed, none resisted.

But there was a problem: What to do with them; Ghetto Theresienstadt didn't have a jail.

A small rundown building was selected to serve as a jailhouse. After some crude repairs to the building, the inside was divided into small cells. Window bars and door locks, stripped from the former SS headquarters, were installed. Bricks and cement came from the defunct casemate projects.

Having volunteered to work on building the jail, I had the opportunity to meet one of the criminals. He was a big fellow who seemed rather bemused by all this activity around him. A chair had been placed in the middle of his not quite ready cell. There he sat, a half-smile on his face, watching as we installed iron bars on the window and a lock on the door. He could have easily walked out, but made no move to do so.

Tereczin did not remain untouched by the final fighting of the war. Bands of SS, cut off from their units; local Nazi militia; and members of disbanded Ukrainian forces, ignoring the Red Cross markings, expressed their hatred for the Jews by firing mortar shells and bursts of machine gun bullets into the Ghetto.

The thick walls of the Kasernen gave protection against bullets, but the thin wooden walls of the temporary barracks were easily penetrated. Against mortar shells we had little protection. Exploding mortar shells killed a few people, but with hundreds dying every day of hunger and diseases, hardly anyone paid attention to these casualties. Occasionally, when the gun and mortar fire became too intense, the Swiss doctor raced in his white Mercedes, flying the Red Cross flag, toward the source of the firing to demand an end to the shooting. Usually the firing stopped, only to be resumed a short time later.

And so we waited. We waited for the Allies, preferably the Americans, to come to our rescue before starvation, diseases and Nazi bullets made any effort to save us unnecessary.

Keeping A Promise

On May 1, 1945 Adolph Hitler killed himself in his Berlin bunker. The news of his death traveled quickly through the Ghetto. For the first time in a long while I saw people not just smiling, they actually laughed. Nazi Germany's end had come. If I could hang on just a bit longer, I had a chance to survive.

The situation in the Ghetto had grown ever more desperate. The water system produced a mere trickle of potable water, while water available from local wells had become polluted. The sewer system had broken down, trash remained uncollected, and filth overwhelmed us. We suffered from fleas and lice; huge rats roamed brazenly through streets, alleyways, and courtyards. As we became ever more emaciated, the vermin grew big and fat.

Perhaps the world had forgotten us, or no one cared what happened to the few thousand Jews that had survived the Nazi atrocities. Or perhaps aid was on its way but could not pass through the battle lines. For whatever the reason help failed to reach us; for us time was running out. The Red Cross representative was as helpless as we were.

No, I did not want to die. Death was ugly. Death was these stinking corpses that lay in long grim rows in the courtyards of the Kasernen. Death was these horrible things of skin and bone, the skin covered with sores, which once had been human beings. No, I did not want to be part of that. But I wanted to sleep, wanted to close my eyes so as not to see the decay. I wanted to sleep, just sleep.

Like many in the Ghetto, I had developed a low-grade fever. The fever did not bother me very much. And again like many in the ghetto, I was suffering from a sore throat, from constant coughing, from skin rashes, from dysentery. And like nearly everyone in the Ghetto I was constantly chewing on charcoal pills. It was strange, but there was no shortage of charcoal pills.

Suddenly my fever jumped. Vomiting made it impossible for me to eat or sleep. Even charcoal pills or a sip of water brought on an attack. I turned my meager rations over to my roommates. There was no sense in wasting it. I felt no longer hungry; the very thought of food brought on a feeling of nausea. After not eating for a couple of days, there was no further diarrhea and the vomiting too stopped. The fever remained high.

My friends urged me to see a doctor. At first I refused. With the Ghetto overcrowded with sick and dying people, what could the medical people do? But with my friends insisting, I gave in and went to the clinic, though still convinced that it was a waste of time. But then, I thought, I had time to waste.

The clinic was crowded, the doctors and nurses rather short tempered.

With no medicine to dispense, they blamed the sick for not taking care of themselves, which may have been true, at least to some degree.

After several hours of waiting, and feeling confirmed that visiting the clinic was useless, one of the doctors was ready (or willing) to see me. After a cursory examination, I received my "prescription," a lecture on keeping clean. True, by then we were all rather filthy. Our clothing had not been washed for some time, and even keeping ourselves clean was not easy. We had run out of soap and the water, when it ran at all, was dirty and polluted. Nevertheless, taking the "prescription" seriously, I went to our not-so-clean washroom (no one was cleaning it any longer) and despite the high fever, stripped and washed myself as best I could with a trickle of polluted water and no soap. Then back to the clinic.

The waiting room was still, or again, filled with coughing, spitting, and vomiting people. I waited, but the doctor's office remained closed. After a while, one of the patients lost his temper and pushed open the door to the office. The picture revealed by the open door made the people in the waiting room forget their sickness for a moment: The doctor and two nurses, partially clad, were engaged in some sex game.

I returned to my room feeling disgusted and angry, and justified in my belief that medical aid was not available.

Yet anger can be a powerful stimulant. Angry with everybody, but mostly angry with myself, I had to find some way to overcome this sickness.

I had heard of a much-admired doctor of whom it was said that he had been able to help people. Obviously he too had no medicine to dispense, but there must have been something he was able to do. He was not part of the clinic but had his own office. How he had been able to do this is another one of the many unexplainable things that happened in the Ghetto. Though skeptical, I went to see this "wonder" doctor.

Just as at the clinic, the waiting room was crowded. But as soon as I walked in I noticed a different atmosphere: No impatient pushing and shoving, no cursing of the callousness of doctors; the sick even tried to restrain their coughing.

The office of Doctor Elsas was large, neat and clean and dominated by a large and uncluttered desk. The doctor was a short man, a small beard hiding his chin. He too must have been suffering from lack of food and from the awful conditions that prevailed in the Ghetto. But his demeanor showed nothing of that. He stood up when I entered to greet me.

During the slow, and I assumed thorough examination he didn't say much. When finished, he went back behind his desk where he sat quietly waiting for me to finish dressing. After a moment he announced his verdict:

"You are not going to die, not today, not tomorrow, and probably not during the next few days. After that, I don't know. But I can assure you, if you get a proper diet, you will recover quickly and probably completely. Don't give up. The Russians will be here soon."

He said a few more things, saying them more to himself than to me. I heard something like possible damage to the lungs, but I was no longer listening. I had heard what I wanted to hear: I would be all right.

I went back to my room to get some sleep. I still did not feel hungry, and the fever continued unabated, but I slept better than I had slept in a while.

(After liberation, special efforts were made to get Dr. Elsas home to Holland as quickly as possible.)

I woke up with a start. Bursts of machine gun fire filled the air. I could feel the walls vibrate from the impact of bullets. My roommates had apparently fled to find better protection in a more solid building. As I listened to the firing, sleep overcame me once more.

I don't know how long I slept when again something pulled me out of my sleep: not the sounds of machine guns, but of silence. An eerie quiet seemed to have invaded the Ghetto: I heard no shooting, no people talking, I heard only complete silence. Looking around, I saw no one. Perhaps, I thought, the fellows had not yet returned from their shelter. I strained my ears, listening to the stillness, but all I could hear was the rushing sound in my ears caused by the unabated fever. I turned toward the window. A bit of sunlight broke through grimy glass.

The sun! The sun's warmth will heal me! The idea leaped with suddenness into my mind, like a revelation. I had to find a place exposed to the sun all day long, unhindered by buildings or by trees. I knew just such a place: on the ramparts.

Getting down from my smelly bunk, I rolled up my blanket and went into the street. It did not puzzle me that the street appeared deserted. I kept walking toward my goal, happy that I was alone, that I did not have to answer questions.

The ramparts rose steeply in front of me; I do not recall how I managed to climb to the top. From the height of the rampart I could see nearly the whole of Tereczin spread silently in front of me. Looking in the opposite direction, I could see the empty main road coming from a far distance, curving its way around fortress Tereczin only to disappear again at the horizon. Spreading my blanket on the fresh grass of spring, I stretched out on it. Absorbing the sun's warmth, I slept until the coolness of the evening woke me.

Next morning I was up with the sun and returned to my place on the ramparts. On the evening of the third day I asked my roommates for my ration card. They gladly gave it back to me. The following morning before returning once more to the ramparts, I ate what little food there was, drank the hot black "coffee" and felt good.

Something had disturbed my sleep. As I looked down toward the highway I saw a tank with Russian markings slowly moving toward the main gate of Tereczin.

I was alive!

I had kept the promise I had made to my mother to survive.

CHAPTER 18

LIBERATION

The Russians

Liberation should have been a joyous occasion: The Ghetto's inmates should have been lining the streets welcoming the men of the Red Army. Yet what happened was nothing like that.

We were impatient, confused, and most likely rather naïve. Of course we didn't know what was happening in Europe, how the conquest of Nazi Germany was progressing; all we could see what was being played out in front of our eyes, and there wasn't much for us to see. And what we heard were mostly rumors.

On May 8, 1945, the day of the ceasefire in Europe, the Red Army finally arrived at the gates of Tereczin, and there they waited while we starved. Not a signatory to the Geneva Convention, the USSR looked with suspicion on the Ghetto being under the protection of the International Red Cross; and, as Switzerland did not have good relations with the Soviet Union and was not part of the great anti-fascist alliance, her representative at Tereczin had, in the eyes of the Russian commander, no legitimacy being in charge of the "freed" Ghetto. He demanded the immediate withdrawal of the Red Cross. On his part, the Swiss doctor demanded assurance of safe conduct through Russian occupied territories before lowering the flag and departing.

About twenty-four hours after Russian troops arrived at the walls of the Ghetto, the Swiss doctor was seen departing, flying the Swiss flag. The Russian troops then entered. No formal handover took place.

Even after the Red Cross had departed, misunderstandings persisted. Perhaps the Russian commander had been unprepared for what he found, although this is rather difficult to believe. Russian forces had liberated Auschwitz and many other camps and should have known what to expect.

At first it looked as if the Russians would take quick action. A day after the departure of the Swiss administrator a column of trucks arrived. Parked along the Ghetto's main avenue, they stood guarded by Russian soldiers. Like others I kept walking past the American made trucks, US Army markings crudely painted over with markings of the Soviet Army, wondering what they carried. The Russians made no move to unload.

"We liberated you and brought you supplies; now it's up to you," a Russian officer told the Red Cross appointed Judenrat. At least that's what a widely believed story asserted.

Tereczin's inmates did not feel liberated. The Germans were gone, but where was "liberation?" This was not what we had expected or dreamed about. We were still starving, most of us were sick, and hundreds of people were dying every day.

The next day the Russian commander issued a proclamation: Theresienstadt was under the control of the Red Army; the Ghetto's leadership, the police, all the kitchen staff and even the medical staff were dismissed. Then the Russians went into action, vigorously, efficiently, and effectively.

Cleanup was the first priority. Without repairing the sewage system, getting rid of rats and other infestations, and burying the dead, and without bringing in unpolluted water and cleaning the filthy kitchens, the raging epidemics could not be brought under control.

German prisoners of war and civilian prisoners – local Nazi officials and Sudeten Germans who had not managed to escape – were brought in. Russian soldiers guarded the POW's, Czech gendarmes the civilians. (I thought I had seen a few of the gendarmes before, under the Nazis. I may have been mistaken. The gendarmes wore the same uniforms worn by the former ghetto guards, but with new insignias.)

To distinguish civilian from military prisoners, and of course from inmates, a humiliating broad stripe was shaved across the top of the heads of the civilian prisoners, front to back. I could not but feel sorry for these hapless prisoners.

No, feeling sorry for them was not quite the emotion I felt. As far as I was concerned most, if not all, deserved what they received. It was the humiliation that embarrassed me. I knew far too well the feeling of humiliation. Anyone who humiliates another human being degrades humanity and with that only degrades himself.

With the appearance of the Germans, tensions rose in the Ghetto. Some former concentration camp prisoners, seeking revenge for years of brutal incarceration and for the murder of family, relatives and friends, attacked the Nazis. (Shortly before the entry of the Russian troops, inmates had beaten a German soldier to death. Apparently, noticing the Red Cross over Tereczin, the soldier thought he had found sanctuary.)

The commander issued a stern warning: anyone who harmed a German prisoner, military or civilian, will join the German non-military prisoners. No further incidents occurred.

With cleanup under way, the Russians attacked the two most urgent problems: Controlling the epidemics and feeding the starving inmates. All inmates were inoculated against various communicable diseases. Those suspected of being infected by cholera or typhoid fever were isolated.

Food, the most important and direct manifestation of liberation, turned out to be disappointing. The Russian Army wasn't stingy with food – we had plenty to eat. But the Russian dietitian supervising the inmates' menu prescribed an extremely boring diet of soft foods only: gruel and porridge, pureed vegetables with mashed potatoes, and no meat. We complained about this "hospital" food; we wanted real food, meat and potatoes. I don't know if the diet made sense, but I consoled myself that at least I didn't feel hungry anymore.

Housing turned into a major problem. Russian troops had taken over the Kasernen of the SS and Ghetto guards. But to give medical care to the many sick, several of the larger Kasernen were made into hospitals. The former SS archive had become an isolation hospital staffed by Red Army people while the other hospitals were staffed with medical personnel brought in from Czechoslovakia. The overcrowding of the remaining quarters didn't help to stem the still spreading epidemics.

Our group was forced to give up our quarters and move into one of the crowded Kasernen. We hated the move, but what could we do?

Although the Russians achieved much, and in a very short time, they had to acknowledge that they couldn't do the job on their own, and the daily death rate remained high. To bring epidemics under control and nurse the inmates back to health, outside help was needed. The commander appealed to the international community. The Red Cross responded, and this time the help was accepted.

Soon drugs and other medical supplies arrived from Switzerland together with packages of food. The Russian dietitian relaxed her strict dietary rules and the food packages – condensed milk and cheese – were distributed directly to the inmates. We ate the thick sweet condensed milk with a spoon, right out of the can. Later, the Swiss added fresh eggs to their food packages.

(The funding for the relief had come from the United Nations Relief and Repatriation Agency – UNRRA – though the Swiss made their contribution. We felt grateful toward the Swiss.)

Yet our daily existence had changed little: We still lived in dirty quarters and slept on straw sacks; we were still restricted to inside the ramparts and knew nothing about the world outside; and we were still under the control of armed men. We didn't have to work, but idleness too can be demoralizing.

Slowly conditions began to improve.

A Dose Of Zionism And A Pot Of Russian Tea

Not unexpectedly, liberation loosened the coherence of our gang of six. With survival no longer in question, other concerns moved to the forefront, related to each individual's background and outlook and his thoughts for the future. Still, five of the six did remain together until we were just about home.

Even with the war over and the Nazis defeated, to me Germany was still the enemy. Returning to Frankfurt, to the house on the Weiherstrasse to rejoin my mother and my sister, was only as an interim step. My future was not in Frankfurt, nor anywhere else in Germany or Europe, though at the moment I had no idea where it would be or what my future would be. For my friends, however, Germany was home.

What was this "liberated" world like, the world that I was about to enter? The future, hidden behind a dense fog, was frightening. A shocking thought came into my mind: being a prisoner had advantages: a prisoner did not have to be concerned with the future; all tomorrows, if there were any at all, will be like all todays and all yesterdays. I thought myself rather poorly prepared to cope with the "free" world out there.

I felt curious about the Russian soldiers, these citizens of another dictatorship. What I knew about the Soviet Union was colored by political propaganda: The Soviet Union was a Communist hell or a Communist paradise.

But my wish to learn more about the Soviet enigma had to remain mostly unfulfilled. The Russians made little effort to overcome the language barriers, and I was left with the impression that fraternization between inmates and soldiers was not encouraged. After about a month in Russian liberated Tereczin, I did not know much more about the Russians than I did before they arrived.

With order established and with gains being made in controlling the epidemics the Russian commander appealed to the inmates to get involved in their own and the Ghetto's rehabilitation. Help was needed in cleanup and in the food services, and especially in caring for the sick. The inmates' response to his appeal was strong.

The medical personnel and many of those who had worked in the kitchens were willing, even eager, to go back to their jobs. However, not all of the kitchen personnel were acceptable to the Russians. The officer in charge rejected several of the former cooks and many of the kitchen help: they failed to meet the hygienic standards he demanded.

Our group of six too responded to the appeal. The fellows wanted to help in the hospitals. I suspected what interest them was not so much caring for the sick but the young nurses (who were not Jewish) the Czech government had brought to Tereczin.

Neither the sick nor the nurses were of interest to me, I was looking for an activity that was more "Jewish." I soon found what I was looking for in a group of Zionists led by a young man from Prague.

What he was looking for, he explained, were young people who wanted to prepare themselves for going to Palestine to build a Jewish country. Europe, he told his recruits, was the graveyard of the "old Jew;" the "new Jew" did not belong here, he belonged in Eretz Israel. This new Jew will have the strength to take care of himself; he will not have to depend on other soldiers, Russian or American, to liberate and protect him.

So far, these were but clichés. But this young Zionist was ready to go beyond talk; he had a plan of action: The ghetto had to be made more livable for its inmates, and it was our task to make it so and not the task of German prisoners. What better training was there for building the Land of Israel than rebuilding the decrepit town of Tereczin? When the time finally came to go to Palestine, we would not go there as helpless ex-prisoners but as experienced builders.

I loved these words. When he was ready to translate words into action, I was ready to join in.

The Russians accepted the offered help. With much enthusiasm, though not always which much skill, we set to work. Our first assignment involved rebuilding a rat-infested kitchen and installing a shower for the kitchen personnel. The major in charge of the kitchens insisted that all personnel handling food had to shower before doing their work.

The job of removing the broken and filthy floor and the cleaning of the drains and sewer connections, and chasing the rats, was given to Nazi prisoners. With that completed we set to work installing new concrete flooring. Those with some experience in construction showed the other volunteers how to mix cement, how to lay down a smooth concrete surface and how to prepare mortar and lay bricks. Though the work was hard and most of us tired quickly, not having yet fully recovered, I rather enjoyed what I was doing.

The Russians found useful activities for nearly everyone, and they did not mind using a bit of coercion to do so. The young fellows who had participated in the raid on Leitmeritz and "liberated" bicycles could still be seen riding around on their bikes. Many Russian officers also rode around on bikes, but these Russian Army bikes were beaten up old things. The commander ordered the confiscation of the "liberated" bikes. But he gave the young bikers a way out: They could keep the bikes if they made themselves available as messengers.

Having become "experienced" in putting down concrete floors, our Zionist gang was preparing to put down a cement floor in some decrepit building when the Russian major directing the rehabilitation projects came by on his old beat-up bike. As he was chatting with our foreman one of the messenger boys arrived, riding a gleaming, nearly new, bicycle. He had a message for the major. The officer's eyes lit up:

"Let's see the permit for the bike," he asked. The boy handed it to him. Holding the permit between his two hands he made a motion as if to tear it up. "Paper," he said with a grin, "paper tears so easily."

We had stopped working, watching the major. Shades of the SS? Would he rip up the permit? With a short laugh the Russian returned the permit to the rather shaken young man.

With hardly any information reaching us from the outside world, not even Russian news reports or communist propaganda, I still felt isolated and still felt that I was in a prison.

We had hoped to be able to learn what was going on in Germany and what had happened to our families. To my disappointment, there was nearly a complete lack of communication with the world outside the Ghetto. Hardly any contact had been made with other Allied nations. We had hoped that the Americans, or the British, would show up. America, perceived as rich, powerful, and generous, had been expected to provide much aid, perhaps take us out of the Ghetto and move us into better facilities.

We had believed that Tereczin, the last of the camps to be liberated and holding a large portion of what remained of Europe's Jews, would have drawn at least the interest of Jewish organizations. (Mauthausen, a concentration camp located on the Austrian side of the Czech/Austrian border, was liberated about two weeks before by American troops.) We had thought representatives from various governments would come searching for missing citizens. And we had expected journalists from major news organization would invade the Ghetto to look around; there were so many stories here. But neither governments and nor journalists appeared interested. Only a small number of UNRRA officials came for short visits, conducted a few brief interviews and left.

The Russians had restricted visits from the West. Indeed, Tereczin had been closed to visitors, the commander justifying the closure as a necessary precaution until the deadly epidemics had been brought under control. A small number of visitors besides the few UN people had come to the Ghetto, but these had been mostly officials from Czechoslovakia.

One day exciting news spread through the ex-ghetto: A "Palestinian" had been given permission to visit Tereczin. On the day of the visit I did not report for work. Instead I went to the central square; there the "Palestinian" was expected to greet the liberated inmates. When I got there, a large crowed was already waiting at the square.

It was an emotional scene when the jeep came to a stop and a soldier, wearing the Magen David as a shoulder patch, got out and stood where the SS Adjutant once strutted. The crowd cheered as the rather embarrassed looking young man said a few words in English or Hebrew or some other language, it didn't matter. There were tears in many people's eyes.

I am not a pushy person, but at that moment I pushed, shoved, and elbowed my way through the crowd until I stood right next to the soldier from Eretz Israel. No longer were we just victims, depending on others to fight for us; we too could fight! Until the arrival of this Jewish soldier we had merely been freed prisoners, wards of the victors. Now for the first time, many among us felt truly liberated.

Russian soldiers cleared a path for the jeep. The visit's half-hour time limit had expired.

The government of Czechoslovakia finally broke the isolation of the former ghetto, insisting that its citizens be placed into hospitals and convalescence homes in and around Prague. With the leader of our construction team and several of its Czech members departing, our exercise in Zionism came to an end.

Though fraternization between soldiers and inmates was not encouraged, I did make a friend among the Russian soldiers. I didn't speculate why this soldier befriended me and why he wanted to find some way to be of help; I simply accepted the offered friendship. Perhaps he was Jewish, though he never said so, and wanted to be of some help to a young Jew; or perhaps a change in policy was encouraging soldiers to befriend individual young people – later there was some hint that this may have been so, but I had little direct evidence – or perhaps he was a good person and had picked me at random.

His limited knowledge of German and my complete ignorance of Russian made communication rather difficult. Hence we had no real conversation which may have clarified his motive.

I was standing in line for my portion of gruel and creamed vegetables when this soldier approached me. He asked whether I was getting enough to eat. I gave an affirmative nod, thinking that he was checking up on the kitchen. He pointed at the gruel with an expression that was a mixture of amusement and disgust:

"Not good for young men," he said. "Young men must have meat."

He promised that he would get me something better. Next morning, as I was picking up my breakfast, he was waiting for me. He had made arrangements for me to become a helper in the Army kitchen. Working there I could eat real food, like the Russian soldiers.

His plan, however, failed. The Russian Army cook, a woman of enormous proportions, did not like the arrangement. Her antagonism made it impossible for me to do any work or to help myself to any food, not even to leftovers. She insisted that the army food was no good for me; the doctor had said so. She watched me like a hawk, making it impossible for me to snitch even a little bit of food. For couple of days I hung around her kitchen watching her prepare a stew with lots of meat, red beets, and cabbage, served together with mashed potatoes. (It looked really good.)

My Russian friend, however, had not given up trying to do something for me. He arranged for us to meet early in the morning, even before breakfast; and every morning my Russian friend brought me a pot of strong, black Russian tea.

A few days before I was finally able to depart from Tereczin, my friend failed to show up for our morning rendezvous (I don't know why) and I had to do without my morning pot of tea. But by then it no longer mattered: My roommates and I were counting the hours till we would receive permission to leave.

Marking Time

The people of Europe were on the move.

Laborers brought to Germany to serve the Nazi war machine, freed prisoners of war, and liberated inmates of labor and concentration camps all were trying to find their way home. These people thought of themselves as belonging to the victorious nations, yet victory had brought them only uncertainties.

Then there were the Germans who had fled from the advancing

Russian troops and the Germans who had been expelled from territories Germany was expected to cede to Poland and Czechoslovakia.

Added to these people, and complicating the situation, were the "Displaced Persons." (At the time the term had not yet been coined.) These were mostly people from Eastern Europe, especially from the Soviet Union, who did not want to be repatriated to their homeland. Many feared being accused of treason; others dreamed of finding a better life in the West, especially in America.

Europe's transportation system was in shambles. Rails, highways, bridges, all had suffered heavy damage making it difficult to feed, care, and transport these multitudes now roaming central and Eastern Europe.

So of what importance was Europe's Jewish remnant of a few thousand waiting in Tereczin when tens, or even hundreds of thousands had to be taken care of?

Some European countries tried to find surviving Jewish citizens and bring them home. Especially The Netherlands made efforts at repatriating survivors, while Poland made no efforts at all. A few cities in defeated Germany had attempted to locate "their Jews" and, with permission of the occupying powers, bring them back. But the process was slow and the efforts seldom successful. Had we known about these attempts we may have delayed our departure. In retrospect I'm glad we didn't know.

Nearly four weeks had passed since May eighth, when Russian troops entered the Ghetto. Many in the Ghetto didn't even know whether they had a home to go back to. With communication with the outside world hardly existing, we felt we were in Limbo, suspended in time.

Becoming ever more restless, and being convinced that no one was taking action on our behalf, my friends and I decided to take action on our own.

The delay of repatriation was not solely due to the chaos that prevailed in Europe or to inaction by the authorities, but also to the Russians' efforts, supported by the various authorities in Europe, to prevent deadly epidemics from spreading throughout devastated Europe. Stringent control procedures for the release of inmates had been put in force.

The Ghetto had been divided into "health zones." The health status of each zone was closely monitored and evaluated. Sick residents had to report to the clinics or hospitals. New cases of cholera and typhoid fever were removed to an isolation hospital. Since some inmates tried to hide from the authorities that they were sick by failing to report, health monitors regularly checked for sick people.

As the deadly epidemics came gradually under control, the Russian chief medical officer felt justified to relax the rules for departure. Inmates no longer had to wait for organized repatriation. If within a period of twenty-four hours a zone reported no new cases of cholera or typhoid fever, the residents of that zone could apply for permission to leave Tereczin.

Every morning the number of new cases in each zone was posted, and every morning would find us checking the latest figures.

My friends and I were housed in one of the largest and also most crowded of the Kasernen, which had been designated a health zone. Unfortunately, our Kaserne had one of the largest numbers of new cases of cholera and typhoid fever. Our requests to be moved to other quarters were denied.

Since it was impossible to protect ourselves from being infected by isolating ourselves, we believed our best defense against infection, in addition to the inoculations we had received, was to keep up our strength and to keep ourselves as clean as possible.

After the many weeks of starvation and filth, food no longer was a problem; cleanliness, however, still was. The clean-up program was progressing rapidly, but priority for installing and cleaning showers and sanitary facilities had been given to kitchens and hospitals.

With the crowded living quarters lagging behind in the clean-up, personal hygiene remained a problem: toilets were overflowing and many latrines were contaminated. We didn't have enough soap for washing ourselves, nor sufficient cleaning material to keep our rooms, bathrooms, and even clothing, clean. The smell of disinfectant, however, covered all the other odors.

Taking a bath or shower had become an obsession. With all the fellows in my group, except myself, working in a hospital where bath and shower facilities were most readily available, this was no problem. Now I too wanted a hospital job. Other places where showers were available were the kitchens, but I didn't want kitchen work. Luck was with me. After our Zionist group had broken up, one of the young Zionists had landed a job in one of the smaller hospitals. Ready to go home (he was from Bratislava), he turned the job over to me.

It was not a pleasant hospital, serving primarily old people whose chance of recovery was slim. My friend had assured me I would have nothing to do with the sick. The job, as he had described it, was simple: The nurses at the hospital had to take a bath before going off duty. The job was to see to it that there was adequate hot water available in the bathhouse. As reward for keeping the hot water boiler going from mid-morning to late evening, I too could have a bath before quitting for the night. He warned me that the nurses would complain bitterly if the water was not sufficiently hot.

I gladly took the offered job. The work wasn't hard. (Cleaning the bathtub was not part of my job) Most of the day, I sat comfortably outside the bathhouse, only occasionally interrupting my daydreaming or snoozing to check on the fire. A few times a day I had to fetch firewood and coal.

Unfortunately another task was associated with the job, a task my friend had failed to mention: When one of the patients died, my duty was to help take the body, wrapped in a white sheet, down several flights of stairs into the basement morgue. The bodies weren't handled very gently.

With the epidemics coming under control, our Kaserne too finally reported a drop in new cases. The six of us decided that the time had come to prepare for our departure. With the Russians and the Red Cross overly generous with food, we began gathering travel provisions and food we could take home with us. But that was about the only preparations we could make. We tried to gather information about traveling, about railroads, buses, and accommodations; but we were not very successful. The little information we managed to gather was all rather discouraging, so we ignored it.

In anticipation of our departure we quit our jobs. We decided to rest up for what we expected to be a difficult journey. But first we had to have a farewell party.

One of the fellows had "liberated" three bottles of French Cognac (he refused to tell from where and how), and a farewell party seemed to be a good excuse for disposing of them. Two of my roommates, who worked in one of the hospitals, invited a couple of nurses to join us in our barracks room for the party. One of the nurses brought a large cake. With three bottles of cognac, a cake and two attractive young women, we had what was needed for a party.

What we talked about as we partied in our corner of the crammed barracks room I can't recall. We attacked the three bottles and the cake with gusto and as the clock moved toward midnight, there were three empty bottles, a bare cake plate, and very sleepy and somewhat drunk party makers.

Time had come for the two nurses to return to their quarters at the hospital. They had to be on duty in the morning. But there was a problem: only one of the nurses, a pretty dark haired woman, and I were still able to stand on our feet.

More interested in cake than in cognac, I had drunk sparingly. The other nurse had passed out and the other fellows were beginning to snore.

The pretty nurse and I half dragged, half carried her colleague, who refused to wake up, through the dark streets of Tereczin. By the time we had put her in her room at the hospital the two of us had sobered up.

Ready to return to my quarters, I bade her good night.

"You really don't have to walk back in the dark," the pretty young woman suggested, "you can stay in my room and return to your place in the morning."

I declined the invitation.

A few days later our block's posted number showed just one new case of cholera. Hardly daring to breathe the contaminated air, we anxiously awaited the next posting. Would it be zero?

It took another day or two before the coveted "zero" showed up. When we first saw the zero, we were doubtful. It must have been a mistake. We walked through our Kaserne trying to find out if anyone knew of anybody who had to be moved to the hospital. No one did. The zero was not a mistake. Then it hit us: Within twenty-four hours we would be able to apply for permission to leave, and another twenty-four hours after that we would be out of this place. We weren't sure where we were going, but this did not matter; finally we could turn our backs on this horrible place.

Next morning a quick check: still zero. We rushed to the administrative headquarters to apply for permission to leave. A couple of officers, one Russian, one from the Czechoslovakian Army, questioned us briefly. Then together with other young men applying for permission to leave, a Russian officer addressed us. He spoke about the disadvantages of returning to Germany or to any other country in the Capitalist West and of the advantages for going to the Soviet Union.

Unfortunately, the officer said, the Soviet Union had lost many young people fighting the fascists, but for us this meant that there were many opportunities. The Soviet Union needed young people to help in rebuilding their war-devastated country. He promised free education, a chance to learn a trade or a profession; some would be able go to a university with the Soviet government paying all costs.

Despite his glowing words, he did not pressure us and I came away with the impression that the officer hadn't really expected much success from his talk. As we were leaving each of us was handed a slip of paper, signed by the officer, certifying that we were eligible to leave Tereczin. We were told to return next day to pick up our travel passes.

With this slip of paper we went to the warehouse to pick up backpacks. (Our luggage had been confiscated upon our arrival at Theresienstadt.) There was of course little chance I would find the pack I had brought with me. Then back to our room to pack our few belongings. I had saved three loaves of bread, four eggs, two cans of Swiss condensed milk and a package of cheese, also from Switzerland. The food nearly filled my backpack, but I had little else to pack. My dirty clothing I threw away, leaving me with just one shirt, some underwear and a couple of socks.

I did not sleep much that night.

Next morning we rose early. After breakfast we rushed to the office at the headquarters building to pick up our passes. Of course they weren't ready; the twenty-four hour waiting period was not yet over.

We returned to our "room." I looked around: three double bunks with thin straw mattresses, a small table, four chairs, that's the memory I'll be taking back with me.

Later in the afternoon we returned to the headquarters building. There our passes were waiting for us.

Those who left Tereczin on their own, that is, who were not part of organized repatriation, were given travel passes signed by a high-ranking Russian officer. The "salmon colored" pass requested, in Russian, English, French, and German, that Allied personnel in liberated Europe should provide all possible assistance to the bearer of the pass. Without the pass we would, most likely, have become stranded in one of several refugee camps set up by the Allied Forces in Germany. Instead we made our way home in a relatively short time.

The passes issued to us by the Russians played an important role in our travel home and even later. This pass was indeed a magic wand, opening many doors for us. Only a small number of these salmon colored passes had been given out. Why we received them, and why more of them were not issued, will remain, at least for me, an unsolved mystery.

(The last time I made use of this pass from the Russians was when my mother, Claire and I applied for visas to the United States. It served as proof that I had been in a concentration camp. I had other evidence to present to the American consular official, but the salmon colored pass seemed to impress him the most. To my regret he did not return it to me but placed it in our file, or so he said. I suspect that he had kept it as a souvenir.)

At six o'clock in the evening of June ninth, 1945, six young men walked out of the gate of the old fortress and recent ghetto/concentration camp of Tereczin and walked into a devastated Europe.

CHAPTER 19

THE RETURN

Starting Out

On a bright cool evening at about six o'clock, six of us, five of my friends and I, walked through the Ghetto's main gate, leaving Tereczin. The day was the ninth of June 1945, one month and one day after the fighting in Europe had officially ended. I was free; a chapter of my life was behind me. An odd feeling indeed being outside the confining walls without guards, German, Czech, or Russian,

Only after we had waved our good-bye to the Czech gendarmes and were walking along the deserted highway, did it come to us how little we knew of the conditions in liberated and now Russian occupied Czechoslovakia. We knew even less about conditions prevailing in Germany, our goal at the moment, occupied and ruled by Russian, American, British, and French forces.

We assumed the air attacks and the fighting during the Allies' push into Germany had increased the destruction beyond what we remembered. We had no information about what had happened to the Jews that were still in Germany after we were deported to the Ghetto. What might the Nazis have done to the tiny remnant in a last orgy of destruction as the evil empire reached its doom? We were going home not knowing whether "home" still existed, or if anyone was waiting for our return. We had survived, but had our folks survived the double danger of Nazi madness and the last few weeks of fighting? We didn't talk about this, we didn't want even to think about it; we went ahead as if "home" were still there.

Before leaving the "safety" of Tereczin we had been warned of sporadic fighting in the area and that our inability to speak any language but German could prove troublesome; Germans were treated with hostility by both Russian troops and local population. Full of youthful confidence, we paid little attention to these warnings. We believed, naively, that with the Nazis gone, there was no further danger. With our salmon-colored passes and our armbands showing our concentration camp number, authenticated by an official stamp of the Russian authorities, we felt we should be able to handle any problem that could arise.

Our first day's goal was Litomerice, about twelve kilometers from Tereczin. We hoped to reach the town before darkness. There we would spend our first night as free men, most likely in the railroad station. In the morning, we hoped to take a train to Prague. Once in the capital of the reborn Republic of Czechoslovakia, it should be possible for us to arrange a trip home.

It didn't take long before our naive assumptions were put to the test. We hadn't walked very far when we ran stopped at a roadblock manned by a group of men who looked as motley as the "uniforms" they were wearing. Their "uniforms" were a mixture of German, Czech police and what we assumed were pre-war Czechoslovakian army uniform pieces.

Pointing their weapons at us they demanded, in a rather unfriendly way, to see identifications and asked where we were going. Although they wore armbands of the colors of the Czechoslovak Republic, we could not be sure whether they were legitimate militia or a band of marauders. But they had the guns, so we did as we were told.

After examining our Russian issued passes, they turned a bit friendlier. A couple of the guys were locals and knew of Tereczin. They asked a few questions concerning the present conditions there.

"Be sure to be off the road before darkness falls," one of the militiamen warned. "After dark only one rule prevails: 'Shoot first then ask'. Especially be wary of the Russians, they are trigger-happy, hunting for SS men still on the loose."

But they weren't the only ones on the loose, we were warned; also still roaming around in the dense forests of the area were bands made up of Nazi collaborators, German soldiers, and all kinds of other riff-raff. These bands came out at night, raiding villages for food or attacking militia bases for arms and ammunition. Wishing us good luck they let us go on.

After passing through a few more militia controlled roadblocks and once being stopped by a Russian patrol, we finally reached the Litomeric train station. Without our special passes we felt sure we would never have made it this far. Silently we thanked the Russian commander.

It was nearly dark. The station was closed, but we found an unlocked side door leading into the dimly lit waiting room. No one was there. We decided that the waiting room was a good place for us to spend the night. After a few bites from our provisions, we stretched out on the benches. I had no problem falling asleep.

I was rudely awakened by someone poking my rips with something I soon recognized as the barrel of a rifle. Somewhat groggy from sleep, I got up from my bench to see what was going on. My fellow travelers were already up, facing a group of armed men pointing their weapons at them. I glanced at the station clock, which, surprisingly, was running. It showed a few minutes after midnight. I joined the group.

The leader of the gang looked us over.

"Who are you?" he demanded, speaking German. He ignored our armbands.

We explained that we were from the Tereczin concentration camp trying to find our way home. Carefully taking our salmon-colored passes out of our pockets, we presented them to the leader. He took one and looked at it briefly. He appeared unimpressed.

"Where did you steal this?" he asked, handing the pass back. "You are German soldiers, probably SS."

More angry than afraid, we repeated our story.

Now he examined each pass more carefully, then handed each to his companions.

"I'll believe you," he said after a moment's hesitation, still sounding uncertain.

He looked at his companions, who stood there impassively, shrugging their shoulders. A new idea seemed to have entered his mind.

"I believe you," he repeated this time with a firmer voice, handing back our passes, except one. "I believe that you are who you say you are, but," he added with concern in his voice, "you are in bad company. This guy," he pointed at the tall blond fellow among us, "this guy is SS."

We again protested; we had been together in Tereczin for many months and knew each other well. The Czech militia leader remained adamant in his belief.

"SS men have their blood type tattooed under their arms," he informed us. "Take off your shirt!" This was an order. "I'll show you that I'm right."

Our friend complied.

Of course there was no SS tattoo to be found. After a brief discussion with his fellow militiamen, the leader offered an apology, handing the pass back to the suspect. Several SS bands were operating in the area, he explained, one had been spotted near Litomerice. He warned us to be careful. Turning even friendlier he asked how he could be of help.

We inquired about trains to Prague. One of the militiamen told us that though at the present there were no regular scheduled trains, early in the morning a train would be leaving toward Prague. However, he doubted the train would go that far. We thanked him and after a few more words of warning to watch out for marauding Germans, the militiamen left. We went back to sleep.

We had no definite plan for getting us home but had agreed on a simple strategy: keep moving, don't become stranded in a refugee camp. No more camps! Not for us, not even refugee or repatriation camps set up by the United Nations or even the Americans. The UN camps' reputations were not encouraging. Already back in Tereczin we had heard stories of the poor conditions that prevailed in the camps and we doubted that the American camps were any better.

Masses of people, refugees, repatriates, former camp inmates and a multitude of others, were on the move, mostly from east to west. We were but a tiny drop in a large stream. Many of these wanderers had to spend considerable time in these camps, several weeks, or even months, before being able to continue on their way.

We felt that we had to get out of the Russian zone of occupation and into the American zone as quickly as possible. Once there, we believed, help to get us home would be more readily available. Nearly everyone, friend and ex-foe, had great faith in America.

About five o'clock in the morning we were awakened again, this time by a railroad clerk opening the station: A train to Prague was being readied. We did not need tickets to board the train; our salmon pink passes were sufficient.

Within a short time, with the steam engine's whistle blowing reassuringly, we pulled out of Litomerice, putting more distance between Tereczin and us. The first night in freedom was behind us. We were embarked on the second leg of our journey, although we did not know how far it would take us.

A Red Friend

Like the first moments after awakening from a nightmare, my first days out of the Ghetto were confusing. What was real and what was part of the nightmare?

I had always taken pride in my knowledge of geography, and I had studied maps of the area through which we were now traveling many times: During the Munich crisis, at the outbreak of the war, and at many other occasions. Yet during the first few days out of Tereczin, the first few days of our Odyssey, I became confused: where was north, where south, east or west; in which direction should we be traveling; what were the nearby towns; how far was Prague? I had only vague ideas about the towns through which we passed as we made our way out of the Russian occupied territory.

After having traveled for about two hours, the train out of Litomerice came to a final stop. "Traveled" is somewhat of an exaggeration. The train had stood still more often than it had moved. I doubted that we had come very far. The final stop was a rail yard on the outskirts of a rather large town. (The town may have been Klatno, but I'm not sure.) We hadn't understood the announcement, but when we found ourselves alone in the coach and heard the engine being uncoupled from the train we too got off.

Speaking German was not very popular at the moment, so we made our inquiries rather cautiously, hoping that our Tereczin armbands gave us protection against the hostility toward Germans. But trying to obtain information proved to be rather frustrating, and not because of the language barrier, or hostility, but few people seemed to know what was going on. All knew where they wanted to go; few knew how to get there.

Little war damage was visible, but we learned that not far beyond the yard a damaged bridge had collapsed, or had been blown up, or it had become too risky, for a train to pass over it. Harassed railroad employees tried to answer the many questions, but the officials seemed nearly as confused as the passengers.

The problem, explained a rather annoyed and frustrated railroad man, one of the few willing to talk to us, was the Russians. Sure, there was lots of damage to the railroad, but this was not the real reason for the uncertainty. Repairs were making rapid progress and many tracks were usable. The real problem was the lack of engines. The Red Army had first call on the few engines available.

"The 'liberated' Czech people" he complained, "had exchanged one occupier for another."

Hanging around the station was of no use. Reminding ourselves of our pledge to keep moving, we were about to turn our back to the railroad and instead look for the highway going west, when we ran into a group of former Tereczin inmates. Waiting for the promised train they had allowed themselves to become stranded. Now after several days, they were ready to move on to try their luck elsewhere. We suggested that we join forces; they readily accepted. Without further delay, the group, now grown to eleven, marched off in the direction that we believed would take us to a road leading to the Americans.

Our impatience nearly made us miss an opportunity. We had taken only a few steps toward the station exit, when the railroad official with whom we had spoken earlier called us back. He had good news: a train would be leaving shortly for Kardovy Vary (Karlsbad). There, he was quite sure, we could get a train into the American zone. Since going to Kardovy Vary meant traveling west, we boarded the train. Again no one asked us for tickets.

The train was crowded, overcrowded would be the better word. With all seats taken, people sat on their luggage, or on the floor, stood or sat in passageways, on the entrance platform, or wherever else they could find a bit of space. We squeezed into a corner that appeared to be not yet fully occupied.

At first we were ignored, though passengers stared at our Tereczin armbands. Finally a man broke the ice by asking questions about them. Now recognizing us as "anti-Nazis," the passengers turned friendlier. From many of the comments I gathered that most were not too delighted with their Russian liberators. Soon we found out why.

Settled on the floor in our corner, we waited and hoped, like everyone else, that the train would soon get under way. One passenger told that only the day before he had sat on a train for over an hour before having to get off again.

A group of Russian soldiers climbed on board, a good sign that the train would depart soon. One soldier carried a beer barrel, another an accordion. Before they settled down the soldiers went through the carriage relieving the passengers of watches and fountain pens. They seemed not at all embarrassed by their actions. One showed me the three watches he was wearing on his arm, and laughingly assured me that these were not all that he had; he had several more in his pocket. Indeed, the soldiers acted in a rather friendly manner while robbing the liberated Czechs. The passengers complied with the soldier's demands in silence.

Having collected all they could get, the Russians now demanded that the passengers make room for them. If they couldn't squeeze further together, some passenger would just have to get off. Again the passengers obliged, squeezing more tightly together.

Settled comfortably, the soldiers formed a circle around the one with the accordion. After a few chords, the accordionist played a few brief melodies. In the meantime, the soldiers had tapped the barrel of beer and were wetting their throats. A few moments of humming, and the soldiers began to sing to the accompaniment of the accordion. They had good voices and apparently were used to singing together. I assumed what they were singing were Russian folksongs. It was pleasant to listen to them. The atmosphere in the carriage became relaxed. The train began to move.

Early in the afternoon, not quite twenty-four hours since we had walked out of the gate of Tereczin, the train came to its final stop. It had halted not in a station, but in a rail yard. A railroad official announced that this was the end of the line. Our carriage was nearly empty. Many of the passengers, including the Russian soldiers, had gotten off at intermediate points. I don't remember how long this train ride had lasted.

We too climbed down from our coach. Avoiding bomb and shell craters and maneuvering around damaged and burned out rolling stock and other debris of war, we made our way through the yard, emerging into a small and surprisingly pleasant and peaceful looking park; there we paused.

We weren't sure what to do next. We weren't even sure that we had arrived in Kardovy Vary or at some intermediate point. No signs could be seen anywhere.

As we stood somewhat irresolutely, a split developed among us. The five who had left Tereczin together argued in favor of moving on, even if we had to walk all the way to the American sector. It was mid-June, the days were long, and hence there was plenty of daylight left for us to cover more distance. Perhaps we could find shelter for the night in a town or village a bit closer to the Americans.

Others, perhaps less adventurous, or more sensible, proposed to go to the nearby town, inquire about transportation, perhaps get a hot meal, and find a comfortable place for the night. In the morning, refreshed, we would be back on the road.

We were about to decide to go separate ways when a short balding man hailed us. He wore an armband showing the colors of the Czechoslovakian Republic. We were not the only ones wearing armbands for identification. Thousands upon thousands of people were on the road trying to find their way home or trying to avoid being forced to go home. All wanted to make sure that they would not be taken for Germans. Hence the armbands, or some other sign showing that the wearer was not German; or, if German, a victim of Nazism.

The man introduced himself as a Sudeten German. Prior to Germany's annexation of the Republic, he had been in the Communist Party. Arrested by the Nazis, he had spent the war in jail. Once again an active Party member, he had not been expelled from the liberated Republic like other Germans. Recognizing how difficult it was for former inmates of labor and concentration camps to find their way in chaotic Europe, the Party had assigned him to help repatriates aimlessly wandering around the country. When a train arrived at these tracks, he went looking for ex-prisoners of the Nazis.

After listening to our story and arguments, he offered information and advice. The local authorities had taken over a hotel in town, which now served itinerant ex-prisoners. He would escort those who wished to stay to make sure that they got accommodations for the night and that they would have something to eat. For those insisting on keeping on the move, he would obtain food-ration coupons.

Our Communist friend then left, shepherding those who preferred to stay in town for the night. The remaining six, five from our group out of Tereczin plus one man we had picked up on the way, settled down on the grass in the park enjoying the warm spring sun.

The new member in our group of six was a rather quiet middle-aged man. He appeared somewhat confused. Prior to coming to Tereczin, he told us, he had been in various labor camps, being rather vague about that. He had left Tereczin a couple of weeks ago, not sure where he wanted to go. It was enough just to be out of the ghetto. (We fully understood that.) Since then he had been wandering around, living mostly on bread from Tereczin, occasionally eating a meal at an emergency soup kitchen. Now he was ready to go to Mannheim in Germany, the city from where he had come. He wasn't quite sure why he wanted to go there; no one from his family was still alive. He was sure of that.

After about two hours of waiting and no sign of our friendly Communist, we were ready to find our own way out of town. From the beginning, I had had my doubts about his story. A communist the Nazis had put in jail and not in a concentration camp didn't quite ring true.

As we were debating which the best way out of town was, he showed up. Good to his word, he returned bringing food ration coupons for each of us. He pointed us in the direction of a grocery store where we could redeem the coupons. Then he explained to us how best to reach the main highway going west. Wishing us good luck he left.

At the grocery store we traded some of our coupons for bread and honey. Since we had no money we offered the grocer additional coupons. He took them gladly assuring us that they were worth more to him than money.

With evening rapidly approaching we set off for Meyershofen, a small town on the way to the American zone of occupation. There we hoped to find shelter for the night.

Farewell To The Russians

The six of us appeared to be the only people on the road, perhaps the only people in the whole area. Yet as we reached the outskirts of the city we saw a few signs that a war had passed through here only about a month ago. The houses we passed showed no sign of war damage, yet they looked deserted; their doors were closed, their windows shuttered. Except for the evening chatter of a few birds we seemed to be walking on a silent empty planet.

At a larger building at the edge of town three large flags were displayed: the flag of Czechoslovakia, the flag of the Soviet Union and, to our delight, the flag of the United States. The building, we learned, marked the farthest advance of US troops. Here the fast moving Americans had halted, waiting to link up with the slower advancing Russians. After the link-up the Americans withdrew a few miles to the west.

Today it is tempting to see the events of those days in the light of the Cold War between the Western Democracies and the Soviet Russia dominated Eastern Block. I must be careful not to exaggerate the vague sense of tension that I felt as we crossed the demarcation line from the Russian side to the American. Yet tension there was. Perhaps tension always exists when two armies face each other, even if they were allied in a common enterprise.

The wary Russians believed, or pretended to believe, that secret deals had been made between American field commanders and their German counterparts. These deals would permit German forces to surrender to the Americans rather than to the Russian forces they faced in battle. The Germans, having ceased resisting US troops, continue to fight the advancing Russians. They had hoped to gain additional days for German soldiers to escape to the West. To assuage Soviet suspicions, General Eisenhower had ordered his divisions to slow their advances and not accept the surrender of German units facing toward the Russians.

As we neared the town of Meyershofen, we finally met up with some people. A man was sitting at the side of the road holding a Swiss flag. With him were a woman and a large German shepherd. The dog was harnessed to a small cart that carried the pair's luggage. After a rather formal introduction, which included the dog, he told us that he and his wife were on his way to the town of Meyershofen. There, he hoped, it should be possible to spend the night before proceeding to the town of Falkenau, which he knew was in American hands. We would have to get there quickly, he said, as the town would soon be turned over to the Communists.

(He was correct. US forces pulled out of all of Czechoslovakia, leaving the Red Army as the sole occupier.)

Once in Falkenau, he would be able to make arrangements for his return to Switzerland. He felt sure that we too could find assistance. Rather impressed with his apparent understanding of the situation, we happily agreed to his suggestion to travel together to Falkenau. Together with the man, his wife, and his dog we resumed our trek to Meyershofen.

On the way the Swiss tried to explain why he had been in Bohemia and Moravia during the war. He had been there on business when fighting prevented him from going home. His use of the German designation for the area "Bohemia and Moravia" rather than "Czechoslovakia" made me rather suspicious of him. He surely must have seen our armbands, yet he never asked questions.

Apparently he had seen nothing wrong with doing business with the murderous Nazis. Despite his defensiveness on that issue, he seemed rather self-assured. He kept telling us what we should be doing to get home, yet apparently he was the one who had been stranded; he seemed relieved to have met up with us. Perhaps we provided some protection against communists who probably had given him a hard time. I thought he had run out of provisions and hoped we would share with him what we had.

As the sun sank behind the horizon, we reached the small railroad station of Meyershofen. The stationmaster, a tall sad looking man, must have seen us coming. He came out of his house next to the station to greet us and to introduce himself. Though a Sudeten German, he and his wife had been permitted to remain in their home, while all his friends and neighbors had been driven out. Being familiar with the operation of the local signals, switches, and turnouts, his service was needed. With much of the railroad infrastructure east of the station severely damaged, the small, undamaged station had taken on increased importance. As soon as a Czech replacement had been found, he lamented, he too would be forced to give up his home.

He warned us that it would be dangerous to be out in the open at night. Russian patrols were shooting at anything that moved. (We had heard this comment many times. I'm not sure the Russians were quite that trigger happy.) We could sleep in the station house, but first we would eat a bowl of vegetable soup his wife was preparing. All the vegetables for the soup, he stated with pride, came from his garden, grown by himself with his wife's help. His garden was alongside the railroad tracks; he offered to show it to us in the morning.

We accepted his offer. In return for his hospitality we gave him some ration coupons, a loaf of bread and a jar of honey.

Over dinner, as his mood became a bit happier, the stationmaster became talkative. Mostly he talked about his garden and the importance of his small station to the railroad system in the area, although at the moment no trains were operating. (I suspected that during the last few weeks he had no one to talk to but his wife.) While he thus talked, his wife never said a word except repeatedly asking us whether we liked her soup.

All the while our friend from Switzerland ate heartily, including taking big slices of the bread we had placed on the table. He made no contributions to the meal nor did offer to pay the stationmaster for the soup. He tried to tell his story, but no one paid any attention to him.

Before retiring for the night, the stationmaster informed us that every morning a truck loaded with coal passed by on its way from Falkenau to the nearby city. Late in the afternoon the truck would return empty. Until a few days ago, a short daily train had passed through the station rather than a truck. However, disputes between the occupying powers had halted the train. Now the once-a-day coal truck constituted the whole traffic between the two zones. Perhaps, the stationmaster suggested, the truck driver could take us to Falkenau on his return trip.

(I wondered about the recipient of this daily truckload of coal. It certainly was far from enough for a whole city.)

Early next morning, just as the stationmaster had said, a truck showed up loaded with coal. The driver agreed to take us to Falkenau on his return trip.

Late in the afternoon, after a brief good-bye to the stationmaster and his wife and thanking them for their hospitality, we climbed into the coal truck to continue on our way out of the Russian zone of occupation. We gave the truck driver what was left of our ration coupons. The coupons would be of no use to us on the other side of the demarcation line. Our Swiss friend again failed to make a contribution.

We had been traveling steadily and mostly in silence, when the truck slowed down. In front of us was a barrier manned by Russian soldiers. Apparently the truck and its driver were quite familiar to the guards, for a soldier lifted the barrier at once, letting us pass, the driver and the soldiers exchanging a few friendly words as we drove by. Well, I thought, getting out of the Russian zone had certainly been easy and unexciting.

Continuing toward Falkenau, our progress slowed as the truck lumbered up the steep road curving its way through increasingly rugged looking hills. As the truck rounded another curve, it slowed down even further, finally coming to a stop. Heavily armed Russian soldiers were blocking our way. These were not friendly ones like the men at the barrier we had passed way back. These guards surrounded our truck, pointing their guns at us, fingers at the trigger. On both sides of the road we could see dug-in machine guns, protected by sandbags, their muzzles pointing in the direction of the Americans.

I wondered if anything had happened to cause this display of force. To my disappointment that we were not yet in the American zone was added fear that our journey would be forcibly interrupted. Perhaps the Russians would make us get off the truck and detain us for questioning. However, our driver sat calmly in his cab waiting; perhaps he was used to this Russian behavior.

Finally an officer stepped out of the woods. He walked over to our truck and looked briefly into the cab, ignoring us. He shouted something to his soldiers, who stepped back to allow us to proceed. As we passed the Russian soldiers I felt like waving to them, but thought better of it. They still didn't look friendly.

Winning A Bet

The late afternoon sun, its light filtering through the dense forest, was moving rapidly toward the west, the direction in which we too wanted to travel. The pine scented air smelled fresh and clean. As the truck passed through the zone separating American and Russian forces, we encountered no other truck or car, no horse drawn cart, or even anyone on foot.

The truck slowed down. Leaning over the side, I spotted two soldiers, and to my relief, they did not look like Russians. The soldiers, apparently Americans, sat in a vehicle (a jeep) parked under a tree near the road. No barriers blocked the road and no machine guns were visible, just two fellows and their transportation. The line that separated the neutral zone from the American zone was unmarked. I didn't even see a US flag.

The truck stopped. One of the soldiers stepped out of the vehicle and slowly came over to us. He exchanged a few words with the driver then leisurely walked to the back of the truck to look us over. We were ready to show him our Russian issued passes, but he showed no interest. He made a quick count and apparently satisfied, he waved to the driver to proceed. He returned to his jeep as leisurely as he had come.

Our driver put his truck into gear and we rambled off. Our first encounter with the mighty American Army had not been very dramatic.

Darkness began to descend as we entered the town of Falkenau. The driver dropped us off near the freight yard. There we said good-bye to the Swiss couple and their dog.

Falkenau, a mining and factory town a short distance from the German border, was the easternmost terminal of the United States Army's European railroad system. Here we would be able to find opportunities for hopping on a train going west. We decided to check out the railroad freight yard before looking for a place for the night. To our chagrin, we learned that a train of empty freight cars had left only a short while ago and that no other train was expected to leave for at least another day. Disappointed, we looked for a place for the night.

We wandered through the rapidly emptying streets. With curfew approaching a local police officer stopped us. After some questioning and looking at our salmon-colored passes, he directed us to a refugee center near the edge of town.

The refugee center, a hotel taken over by the Allied military, was a way station for Eastern Europeans who had worked for, or who had been forced to work for, the Nazis, and who refused to be repatriated to their now communist dominated homelands.

We of course did not see ourselves as refugees, nor did we think we had anything in common with the "Fremdarbeiter" who refused to be returned to their homeland. Many, I thought, had surely been sympathetic to the Nazis. Nevertheless we decided to stay there for just one night. Next morning we would move on, even if there were no trains.

As soon as we had entered the hotel lobby and before we could ask any questions, a person of apparent authority stopped us. To our surprise, she was not an American officer, but a major in the French Army. With visible impatience the major listened to our request for shelter for the night. In a rather curt tone she told us that this was no place for us. Even our salmon-colored passes failed to do the trick this time. After pleading with her, assuring her repeatedly that we only wanted shelter for one night and were demanding neither food nor transport, she grudgingly relented.

She would put us up for one night, but we were to understand that she was not responsible for any meals or any other services. Still not quite trusting us, she repeated emphatically that the kitchen was closed for the night. She gave us a room number and left.

We went up the few flights of stairs to the room the major had assigned us. One look into the room and we decided that this room was not for us. There were no bunks, just a few mattresses on the floor. Neither the mattresses nor the floor looked very inviting. The room, which apparently had been occupied by overnight "guests," had not been cleaned for some time; it was filthy.

We checked the toilets; the conditions we found there only reinforced our decision: the lodging was not acceptable. We returned to the downstairs lobby to tell the major of our dissatisfaction, but she had left for the day.

On the ground floor, just off the entrance lobby, was a large day room, at present deserted. Furnished with a few couches, some armchairs, and a couple of tables with chairs, the room looked rather comfortable and fairly clean. After inspecting the ground floor toilet, although finding it to be not much better than those upstairs, we agreed that the day room would do for one night. We figured we would be up long before anyone wanted to make use of the room.

Before we could get too comfortable, a man came into the room. This was not an ordinary man; this man was huge in all dimensions. He looked down on us for a moment and then addressed us in a strange, somewhat German sounding language. (He was from the Alsace, he explained. There the local language is a mixture of French and a southwest German dialect.) He introduced himself as the cook.

Waving our Russian delousing certificates at him, we told him that we could not accept the room the major had assigned to us. We tried to explain to him the elaborate delousing procedures to which the Russians had subjected us before we had been permitted to leave the concentration camp, exaggerating a bit. We declared that we were not about to sleep in the assigned room in order to acquire another variety of lice.

With a sweeping gesture of his huge hands, the cook commanded silence.

"Never mind her," he boomed, his voice matching his physical size. "You make yourselves comfortable here."

Then: "Are you hungry?"

We told him the major had said the kitchen was closed.

"Never mind her," the cook repeated with another sweeping gesture of his hands. With that he disappeared, apparently going to kitchen. We sat down at one of the tables and waited. Within a few minutes he returned with a few loaves of bread and large soup bowls and spoons, which he placed in front of us. We were indeed hungry. Not waiting for anything else we dug into the bread.

A short while later the cook reappeared carrying a large steaming pot of stew.

"Courtesy of Hitler's Wehrmacht" he boomed. "They left us a large supply of canned beef stew. You might as well enjoy it."

We ate, and ate, and ate, but the pot of stew seemed to be inexhaustible. We gave up, finally.

"Eat up!" the cook urged, or rather demanded. "You cannot leave anything over." He had watched us eat, a satisfied smile on his face. For a moment I hesitated, then I took another serving of stew. The cook looked once more into the pot.

"I bet you a loaf of bread that even you cannot finish this."

I added another loaf of bread to my backpack and as a "bonus" the cook gave me a can of the "Wehrmacht" beef stew to add to my provisions.

We slept well that night, curled up in armchairs or stretched out on the two couches. We planned to be up early next morning, to be out of the hotel well before anyone wanted to use this room. We hoped to be on our way to the freight yard before the major showed up.

An American Soldier

We rose early after a good night's sleep. The day was breaking and although the sun was not yet fully above the horizon the clear sky promised a nice day. We hurriedly washed up and had just put our few things together when we heard the unmistakable voice of the French major. She stood in the lobby, a clipboard in hand, looking very busy and issuing orders in her loud and impatient voice. If she had noticed us, she gave no sign of it. Most likely she didn't remember us from the night before. We were being ignored, which we thought was just fine. Not finding the friendly cook from the night before to thank him once more and to say good-bye, we grabbed our backpacks and walked out of the hotel to find our way to the rail yard.

The activities we encountered outside made us change our plan. A line of American Army trucks was parked in front of the hotel. The hotel's "guests" were milling about, while French officers tried to create some order. The commands were shouted in French, and some other language that we assumed was Russian. At first we failed understand what was going on.

Asking around, we learned that a convoy was being organized to take a group of Eastern Europeans to refugee camps in the American zone of Germany. These people, we were told, refused to return to their Soviet homeland.

We decided to give up our attempt to find a train, at least for the moment, and try instead to hitch a ride into Germany. We didn't know where in Germany the convoy was going, but this did not deter us. Once in Germany, we felt, we would have no difficulty continuing on our own.

With order slowly being established, the refugees lined up to board the trucks. A French soldier handed out cigarettes. With no one yet challenging our presence, we joined the line and received a carton of French cigarettes, courtesy of the French Government. Not one of us smoked, and certainly not these black French cigarettes, but in this post-war chaos, cigarettes were as good as money, or even better.

We joined a line ready to board a truck. However, a French officer stopped us from boarding. The refugees we had joined, he explained, were Ukrainian women and we certainly did not look like Ukrainian women.

Forced to step aside, we watched the loading procedure. Now determined to join the convoy, we had to find a stratagem for doing so. With loading nearly completed, we noticed that the truck at the convoy's tail had plenty of space.

No one was paying attention to us. The drivers were already in their cabs starting their engines.

We signaled to the women on board that we wished to join them, offering our French cigarettes as a bribe. Delighted with the cigarettes, or with having us on board, they helped us to get over the already closed tailgate, accompanied by much laughter. They quickly pulled the tarpaulin shut to hide us from the French officer making a final inspection. Within minutes we were rolling.

The convoy, the women told us, was going to the Bavarian city of Bamberg. Going to Bamberg seemed all right with us. From there we surely could get a train home. We were in high spirits; it should not take the convoy very long to get to Bamberg. Perhaps in a day we would be home.

The truck convoy moved considerably slower than we had expected, and the distance from Falkenau to Bamberg was far greater than we had thought. As the highway made its way toward the mountains along the border between Czechoslovakia and Germany, it passed through the area where the last remnants of the defeated Wehrmacht had been trapped. The fields on both sides of the road were strewn with abandoned materials of war: Trucks, tanks, artillery pieces, even some airplanes. Much of the equipment was damaged, but much looked still use-able. In one area we could see evidence of the fury with which the Allied fighter planes had attacked the trapped Germans: The field was covered with twisted metal barely recognizable what it once had been.

Gradually we left this macabre picture behind us. The road had begun to climb, snaking its way through the Bohemian Forest. Summer had not yet come to this region, but spring was at its best. The day, though sunny, was cool; the air was filled with the spicy scent of the trees, mostly fir and pine that covered the rising slopes. Their scent was mixed with the fresh smells of soil and emerging grass, watered by the heavy morning dew. Wild flowers, just opening their blooms, decorated the edges of the highway. Ghetto Theresienstadt with its filth, its hunger, its diseases, its thousands of dead bodies, I felt sure, would soon be forgotten.

The convoy had been moving in a steady pace, without any stops. I hadn't noticed when or where we crossed the border into Germany. Only when we passed through the city of Richard Wagner, Beyreuth, did I realize how far we had come.

Finally there was a long needed stop. We fully expected to be chased away. We planned to find our way back to Beyreuth where we would look for new transportation.

To our surprise the driver of our truck, an American soldier, had been aware of our presence. Handing out a box lunch to his passengers as they jumped down from the vehicle, he apologized for having nothing for us. After he had marched off with his charges to the nearby inn, we found ourselves a pleasant spot under the trees for "picnic" lunch of our own.

Early in the evening the convoy reached Bamberg, its final destination, coming to a halt in the center of town. Here the Ukrainians were turned over to UNRRA personnel, the US Army's involvement completed. We were ready to say good-bye to our friendly American driver and move on.

Instead of saying good-bye he asked us to wait whether we had a place for the night; he would take us there. We told him we would go to the railroad station for the night. In the morning we would take a train, probably to Frankfurt Am Main. He wouldn't hear of it.

"Go to the station in the morning. You will have plenty of time for your train. Now I'll find you a place for the night." With that he "ordered" us back on the truck.

"If you wouldn't mind staying with a Negro unit," he said, hesitating for a moment. "They always have extra space in their barracks. If you really don't mind, I'll take you there."

We couldn't understand why we should object staying with American soldiers. Off we went to the "Negro" barracks outside of town.

A sergeant greeted us as we pulled up at the gate. He said we were welcome to stay with his unit for the night. But even before we could climb down from the truck an officer (white) appeared demanding to know what was going on. Told, he said one word: "No!"

Shrugging his shoulders our driver took us back to the city. There, in front of City Hall, we got down from the truck. We urged the American not to worry about us any further. But he was determined to find us a place for the night.

"I've brought you here, now you are my responsibility. I will not let you sleep on benches in a railroad station waiting room!"

"Actually," he continued, after a moment's thought, "you are the responsibility of the 'Krauts'." (This was the first time I heard this expression used. It was the American soldiers' word for the Germans.)

The time was after the hour of curfew and the city, including its Medieval City Hall, appeared shut down. But our driver was not to be deterred. Banging on a side door of the City Hall building, and shouting loud enough to wake up the neighborhood, he attracted the attention of a night watchman. He ordered the watchman to fetch somebody with authority, and do it "pronto."

"These are survivors of a Nazi concentration camp," he told the flustered watchman, "the city must take care of them."

The German assured the American he would find an official who would be able to do something. We entered the building, crowding into a narrow, dimly lit corridor. The watchman disappeared.

Within a few minutes a man nearly as flustered as the night watchman showed up. He introduced himself to the American, not to us, as the official in charge of providing aid to refugees and returning German soldiers. Freed concentration camp prisoners would surely fall within his jurisdiction. He assured the soldier that he would take good care of us.

Finally we could thank our American friend. He left, apparently satisfied. We followed the official to his office.

Once seated behind his desk, the official's nervousness disappeared; now his manner became "official." Rummaging in a desk-drawer for a while, he finally came up with several sheets of ration-stamps, spreading them on his desk. He counted us, than counted the stamps. Satisfied that he had an adequate number of stamps, he carefully divided them into six equal sets, one set for each of us. Then he handed the stamps to us.

"Now you can have breakfast in the morning," he said, adding with a chuckle "now you won't have to starve." I didn't think that was funny.

Politely we thanked him for the food coupons. Before saying good-bye, we asked for direction to the railroad station. There we would wait for the morning train. The city official sat up straight behind his desk:

"It is after curfew time and you cannot be out in the street. The Americans are very strict in enforcing the curfew."

Having taken responsibility for us it was now his duty to find us a place for the night. Next door to the city hall is a Catholic convent, he informed us. The good sisters there ran a hostel for German soldiers returning home from prisoner of war camps. Since, in a sense, we too had been prisoners of war, he felt sure the sisters would put us up for the night. If we did not mind staying in a convent with former German soldiers (now he sounded a bit less sure of himself), he would take us there. To his relief we accepted the offer, assuring him we would stay just one night. Early in the morning we would be on our way.

When we arrived at the convent, the sisters were serving dinner, fried potatoes and a green salad, to a group of German ex-soldiers. One of the sisters made the introduction, telling the former Nazi soldiers that we came from a concentration camp. They made room for us at the table. We unpacked a loaf of bread, making it available to everyone.

As we entered the room the table conversation came to an abrupt halt. It did not pick up again. Awkwardness was in the air. These former soldiers, not yet civilians, were still wearing their uniforms, though stripped of all insignias, medals, etc. However, it was still possible to see where the swastikas had been. Most of the soldiers appeared to be in their mid to late twenties. Not one of them looked as haggard as I remembered the prisoners of war had looked that the Russians had brought to Tereczin for the cleanup. Had any of these men ever taken part in "actions" against Jews in Poland and Russia?

We had not removed our armbands with our prisoner number on it. I watched the faces of the Germans to see if I could detect any reaction, but I could not discern any. No comments were made, no questions asked. To me these defeated defenders of the Nazi Reich were still the enemy, and I wondered whether they still considered us their enemy. We all concentrated on our food.

Before climbing into our bunks, one of the sisters told us that very early in the morning, soon after curfew was lifted, a convoy of trucks would leave for the freight yards at Furth, there to pick up fruit and vegetables for the city's market.

Perhaps one of the trucks could give us a ride to the Furth station. While there was no rail traffic in and out of Bamberg, the situation in Furth, a main railroad hub, was different.

I had the impression that the sister was specifically addressing us and did not include the former German soldiers. Did the sisters wish to be rid of us as quickly as possible?

In appreciation for the dinner, we gave the sisters the ration coupons from City Hall together with some of the food we had in our satchels. I contributed my can of Wehrmacht stew. Then we retired to our bunks for a night's rest.

Nuremberg

Sometimes an experience seemed pregnant with symbolism. What was I doing in the city of Nuremberg, the city of the annual triumphal Nazi Party celebrations, the city whose name is synonymous with the Nazi's racial laws? We, my five travel companions and I, had certainly not planned to come to this city.

Was it fate that had brought me here? On my return from hell had I to see first the ruins of the place where hell had been conceived? That only then could I feel free?

Getting up early in the morning, we said a brief farewell to the sisters, thanking them for the night's shelter. Then we hurried out into Bamberg's market square, anxious not to miss the trucks to the Furth rail yards. But there was no sign of trucks, nor did we see any people waiting for them. Our anxiety seemed to have betrayed us; apparently we were much too early.

After standing around for what seemed to us a long time, doubts began to set in. Perhaps the good sisters had misled us, wanting to get rid of the Jews. We were ready to leave to try our luck elsewhere, when people, carrying empty shopping bags, showed up. Not long thereafter a number of trucks arrived.

We climbed into one of the rather battered looking vehicles, of which none looked any better, ready to tell the driver to where we wanted to go. But the driver didn't seem interested, nor did he ask for money.

So far on our travels the weather had been favoring us. That morning was no different: cool but pleasant, promising a bright and warm early summer day. Though we had to stand in this badly bouncing vehicle, the fresh air, the green fields, the wild flowers along the edge of the road, and the prospect of being home soon, put us into high spirits.

The column of trucks had been on the way for some time, traveling on an otherwise empty highway, when it came to a stop at a roadblock. American soldiers ordered everyone off the trucks to check for identification papers and travel permits. Everyone's IDs were in order, but no one, except the drivers of course, had permits.

We showed our Russian salmon colored passes, and once again they did their job: We were permitted back on the trucks to continue with our journey; all others had to stay behind.

Now the driver of our truck asked where we wanted to go. He could drop us off at Furth as we requested, but he guessed correctly that we wanted to catch a train going west. Furth, he said, was not the right place for us. But, as he was going on to Nuremberg, he would take us there. He could drop us off at the main railroad station. There we would have no problem getting a train to Frankfurt. This sounded even better than what we had hoped for.

As the truck pulled away, I looked back at the hapless former fellow travelers standing forlorn on the deserted highway. For them it was a long way home. Thus humiliated, did they feel hatred for us, the Jews, who had been given preferred treatment by the occupier of their country? Or were they angry with themselves for having supported a criminal regime whose war was responsible for their present predicament? My guess was that their sentiment was more the former. I was aware that I did not feel sorry for them.

As soon as we climbed down from the truck in front of the Nuremberg railroad station we realized that we had made a big mistake. No train would depart from this station, not now, not for a long time to come. The station was a blackened burned out shell. The rubble strewn station plaza was deserted, not one soul was in sight. I couldn't believe that the driver of the truck had been unaware of the conditions we would find here. Had this been his revenge? We, the hated Jews, had been permitted to continue with our travel while his good German compatriots had been forced off the trucks.

We stood in front of the wreck of a station, undecided what to do. Debris of war was all around us. Two dented and scratched up German army helmets lay on the ground near us, their swastikas clearly visible. A machine gun mount (the machine gun was gone) stood behind sandbags, an empty cartridge belt hanging over the bags. Spent cartridges were strewn over the ground as if they had rained from the sky. In whatever direction we looked, we could only see destruction. Bullet holes pockmarked the walls of the ruined and burned out houses, many of them scarred by shrapnel; here and there holes had been blown into their walls.

The advancing American troops had offered to bypass the city to prevent damage to the many historic sites and public buildings dating from the Middle Ages. The Germans, however, had refused to declare Nuremberg an open city, vowing to defend it street by street. Now the medieval inner city, the city of the Meistersinger long preserved as a historic treasure, was no longer a monument to past glories; now it was a monument to a nation's insanity.

During more peaceful days this city had been known for its children's toys and Christmas gingerbread. This city of past peaceful endeavors, the city in which more recently hatred had been glorified, this city was dead. It gave me an eerie feeling, standing there.

A US Army truck pulled up and stopped. The two African American soldiers sitting in the truck's cab looked relaxed. They peeled a couple of oranges, tossing the peels into the street where they fell among the debris of war. Then the soldiers drove off.

We had to do something. Just standing there cursing the truck driver, or our own naivety, was of no help. We reasoned that if a truck could come into this ruin of a city, then a truck must also be able to leave. Our problem was to find it.

The best place to look was at city hall. Even in this destroyed city somebody must be in charge. True to our pledge never to stand still we set off to find city hall, or a building, or part of a building being used for that function.

It stood to reason, that City Hall was somewhere in the old, medieval, part of the city. With no direction signs anywhere in sight, we had to guess where to go. We could see the medieval city wall (also marred by bullets and exploding shells), which still enclosed the inner city. This gave us the general direction in which to go. Somewhere not far from where we stood there hadto be a city gate.

But before moving on, we decided to briefly explore the area around the station. We wanted to be sure that we could find our way back. If we couldn't find City Hall or didn't find any help, we were prepared to walk to Furth. From the station, we felt sure we would be able to find the highway to Furth.

Luck was with us. The very first street we came to after crossing the station square revealed signs of life: people. We spotted a couple of men at the far end of the street some distance away. As we walked toward them, we noticed a boarded up store in an only partially destroyed building. A crudely fixed door stood open.

The store had been turned into a soup kitchen. A man giving the appearance of a police officer or a guard, who wore a gun, asked for identification. Our salmon colored passes gained us entrance. Inside the poorly lit room a few people stood at tables eating; there were no chairs. A woman behind a counter dished out what looked like a thick soup. Asked, she explained to us that very few people were left in the city: some city workers, a few city officials, a small police force. No businesses or stores of any kind were open. The soup kitchen provided lunches for those who had to come into the city during the day; no one stayed in the city over night.

For the ration coupons we had received at the Bamberg city hall, the woman set out six bowls of soup, six slices of bread and something to drink. We had no money, so we couldn't pay; but this didn't bother anybody; money, it seemed, did not mean much here.

Luck continued to be with us. Our armbands had aroused the curiosity of a truck driver having his noon meal. He broke the silence prevailing in the room, asking questions. After listening to our story, he offered to take us to Furth, late in the afternoon or early in the evening, when he would be returning there. He promised to meet us in front of the central railroad station. We believed him.

After finishing our lunch we returned to the station. Not one of us wanted to explore the ruins around us. The place was depressing and I felt depression was taking over the mood of our small group. We spoke little. So the remainder of the afternoon we sat on a low wall among the debris of war.

As the sun slowly sank below the horizon, and the fading light and deepening shadows making the city's ruins ever more eerie, the truck pulled up.

The driver stopped alongside a freight train just beginning to move. We jumped off the truck waving a quick good-bye and thank you to the driver.

"Where to?" we shouted to people standing or sitting in a freight car slowly moving past us.

The answer that came back was what we had hoped for: "Frankfurt."

We climbed up into the car as the train began to gather speed.

The Bread Of Affliction

I slept on and off as the train traveled through the night. Progress was slow; the train made a great number of stops. Each time the train interrupted its progress I woke up with a start; and each time I had to reassure myself that I was traveling toward Frankfurt and not in the opposite direction. As in the cattle car about four long months ago, I wondered what awaited me at the end of this journey. Now as then, every time the train halted, I tried to get an idea where we were and how far we had come. Yet even with the large door of the freight car open I had no more success than during the last journey; this train too stopped only on sidings marked with to me incomprehensible railroad signs. I worried, were we going in the right direction?

Even the arrival of daylight failed to help. I was becoming rather frustrated with my inability to determine how far we had come and how far we had yet to go. My friends, and others on board, took this all much more calmly.

"Stop fretting and go to sleep. We'll know when we get to Frankfurt," was their comment.

Mid-afternoon the train rolled into a large switchyard and stopped. Finally, and to my relief, I recognized a familiar name: Hanau.

Hanau, an industrial city east of Frankfurt, has extensive rail facilities. The facilities had been heavily bombed during the war and much damage could still be seen, but substantial repairs had already been made. Apparently the US Army was using this rail center as a hub for its rail operations. A large amount of rolling stock, much made in America, occupied the yard's tracks. With much of Europe's transportation systems destroyed, the US Army had to bring their own engines and rolling stock from the States.

We had been standing in the yard for some time when a railroad worker called out that the train would proceed no further. No engines were available. Answering the many questions, he added that trains had to wait their turn for engines. He had no idea when the turn came for our train. Not today any more, he was sure, more likely sometime tomorrow or even perhaps in the morning.

So close to my goal I had no patience for sitting idly in a switchyard, and surely I didn't want to spend another night in a cattle car. Besides, I didn't quite believe that the train would get an engine tomorrow; perhaps there would be one the day after. However, I reasoned, with all the activities here I should be able to hitch a ride on another train, one that was ready to leave.

I urged my friends to get off this train to look for another. But being that close to home, perhaps two or three hours and even less for me, they preferred to wait. What's another night? they reasoned. I reminded them of the pledge we made to ourselves to always keep moving; it failed to make them change their minds. Saying a final good-bye, I grabbed my backpack and jumped to the ground.

For a while I wandered around the yard watching the activities. No one bothered me. I noticed that several trains appeared about ready to be on their way; one had an engine already under steam.

The train was packed with French soldiers. A railroad worker said it was headed for France. I figured that the train must be passing through Frankfurt and it surely would have to stop there, or at least slow down enough for me to jump off. I decided to climb aboard. The French soldiers were ready to pull me up, when an officer stopped them. "No civilians!" was his curt command. Not even my salmon colored pass made him yield.

Evening was approaching fast. It did not look as if any of the other trains would be moving soon. I did not want to return to the train on which I had come and I didn't want to spend the night wandering around in the rail yard. I decided to find my way to the passenger terminal. There, in the waiting room, if there still was one, I could wait till morning when I could try my luck again.

The passenger terminal couldn't be too far away. Following along one of the tracks, I soon saw some lights that, I argued, must be coming from the terminal. Continuing in the direction of the light I eventually reached some steps leading up to a platform. Climbing up the steps, I found that the platform extended into the severely bomb-scarred passenger terminal.

A passenger train stood at the platform that had been cleared of debris. The locomotive, at the front of the train, belched smoke and steam. People were on board. A railroad man was busy shutting the doors of the passenger coaches. I asked where the train was headed.

"Frankfurt," was the reply. "If that's where you are going," he added, "better hurry up. The train is about to leave. We are late already."

He did not ask me for a ticket (I did not even have to show him my salmon colored pass); he just told me to get on board. The compartment was nearly empty, which suited me just fine; I was in no mood to talk to anyone, and most of all I did not want to answer questions. Taking the window seat, I made myself comfortable just as the train began to move. I felt strange being by myself on this last leg of the journey home. It was the first time since walking out of the gate of Tereczin that I was not with my friends.

The train pulled into the Frankfurt Ostbahnhof, the very station from which a few months ago I had departed for Ghetto Theresienstadt. I looked out of my coach window for my first glimpse of the station. It had not changed much from that day; some more destruction and perhaps here and there some repairs.

I got off the train. The German railroad personnel looked the same as before, only the swastika had disappeared from their uniform. A couple of German policemen stood at the exit. Their uniforms were brand new and more civilian in appearance than the Prussian military type worn by the police in the past. Except for a couple of bored looking American military policemen standing near the station entrance, the American occupation was not in evidence.

The German policemen were urging the arriving passengers to hurry; curfew time was quickly approaching. Now the night curfew applies to everyone, I thought, not only to the Jews. I made my way out of the station.

I had no trouble finding my way from the railroad station to the house on Weiherstrasse; it wasn't a very long walk, perhaps half an hour. The few people who had gotten off the train were hurrying home. I was not in a hurry. Walking rather slowly, I soon found myself in a deserted street. The curfew did not bother me. I had full confidence in my Russian issued pass.

The day was June fourteenth 1945, five days since I had walked out of the gate of Theresienstadt, only four months since I had said good-bye to my mother and Claire. Only? How could I think "only"?

These past four months could not be measured by clocks and calendars, the ordinary scales of time; these past four months were black holes, dimensionless yet large. I didn't want to think about these four months, not now, and perhaps I never will want to think about them, remember them. It would be better to forget; life was in front of me, not in the past.

Was the memory of these four months already fading? I tried to picture our room, the last one, the one from which my friends and I had departed to freedom; I tried to recall the names of my travel companions, I could not do this either. The harder I tried the paler my memory became. The ghetto and even the adventures of the way home seemed to lose their reality, dissolving into disconnected, shadowy happenings.

Only a few days ago I had been walking with my friends along a road, similarly empty as the one on which I now walked, similarly surrounded by destruction. Where had that been? I searched my memory but could not place it. Yet I still could see the man who was walking toward us. His German soldier's uniform was tattered, his head bandaged, the once white bandage dirty, stained with blood; one arm was held in a sling; he was limping, his haggard face unshaven. As he came face to face with us he stopped. We too stopped walking.

I don't know if he had seen our armbands identifying us as ex-inmates of a concentration camp. After a brief moment of silence he stretched out his good hand in an imploring gesture:

"Comrades," he addressed us, "do you have some bread to spare? I haven't eaten for days."

We stood in silence, staring at him. A German soldier, the enemy who only a short time ago had wanted to kill us; the enemy who had murdered the women and children of my people, and now he stood in front of me begging for bread.

No one moved. Unstrapping my backpack, I took out a loaf of bread from Ghetto Tereczin, one of the loaves I had saved for home, cut it in half and handed one half to him. I did not say anything to him, not one word, and if he said thank you, I didn't hear it. I returned my half of the loaf to my pack, closed it, and returned it to my back. Then my friends and I continued on our way.

I walked slowly, almost reluctantly, toward home. At times I paused to look at the destruction on this now desolate, once so busy street. Nary a house was undamaged, whole blocks were completely destroyed. I had to walk in the middle of the road; the sidewalks were covered with the debris of collapsed buildings; here and there a bomb crater had been roughly filled in with dirt, often inadequately.

A bicycle was coming up fast behind me. As the bike drew level with me, the rider slowed down. He looked at me briefly.

"The dirty Jew is back," he said in a loud voice and repeating it. He wanted to be sure I heard what he said. Then he sped away.

I won't be back for long, I said to myself, be assured I will not remain in your cursed country, not for long. Now I began to walk faster.

As I neared the intersection from where I would be able see the house on Weiherstrasse, for the first time I wondered whether it was still there. I rounded the corner and to my relief there the house stood, just as I had left it. Someone was looking out of a second floor window. I recognized Otti, Mrs. F's daughter. She saw me and let out a piercing scream. I hadn't known, of course, that only a few days before a man, returning from Tereczin, had reported that I was dead.

(My mother told me this many years later, on her deathbed. Had she believed him? She didn't say, I didn't ask.)

My mother met me downstairs at the entrance door to the house. There wasn't much to say. We went upstairs into the apartment where I greeted my sister.

My mother made a pot of coffee. I unpacked my backpack, placing the can of milk, the cheese, and the eggs from Switzerland and a loaf of bread from the bakery of Tereczin on the table.

Then we sat down to eat.

Printed in the United States
By Bookmasters